ASIAN MEDIA PRODUCTIONS

ConsumAsiaN Book Series
edited by
Brian Moeran and Lise Skov

The ConsumAsiaN book series examines the way in which things and ideas about things are consumed in Asia, the role of consumption in the formation of attitudes, experiences, lifestyles and social relations, and the way in which consumption relates to the broader cultures and societies of which it is a part. The series consists of both single-authored monographs and edited selections of essays, and is interdisciplinary in approach. While seeking to map current and recent consumer trends in various aspects of Asian cultures, the series pays special attention to the interactions and influences among the countries concerned, as well as to the region as a whole in a global context. The volumes in the series apply up-to-date theoretical arguments frequently developed in Europe and America to non-western societies – both in order to analyse how consumption practices in Asia compare to those found elsewhere, and to develop new theories that match a specific Asian context.

ASIAN MEDIA PRODUCTIONS

Edited by

Brian Moeran

CURZON

First Published in 2001
by Curzon Press
Richmond, Surrey

Editorial Matter © 2001 Brian Moeran

Typeset in Times by LaserScript Ltd, Mitcham, Surrey
Printed and bound in Great Britain by
Biddles Ltd, Guildford and King's Lynn

British Library Cataloguing in Publication Data
A catalogue record of this book is available from the British Library

ISBN 0–7007–1334–4

CONTENTS

CONTENTS

Part III Advertising

Part IV Producing Consumption

ACKNOWLEDGEMENTS

This volume is a result of the fourth *ConsumAsiaN* workshop, 'Asian Advertising and Media', held at the University of Hong Kong, April 22–25, 1998, under the aegis of the Department of Japanese Studies and financed by the Louis Cha Foundation. I would like to thank the following for their assistance in making the workshop possible in the first place and then so successful: Chan Lai Pek, Lily Choi, Lai Mei Fong, Lee Chi Keung, Rebecca Leung, Michael Martin, Kavita Mathai, Kirsten Refsing, Wong Heung Wah, Wong Mei Ling, and Mai-San Young.

All the papers in this book were first aired at the workshop, with the exception of those by James Lull and Ulf Hannerz who were present and contributed to the discussions. Also participating in the workshop and presenting papers were: Lagrimas Cunanan, Todd Holden, Perry Johansson, Alan Knight, Laura Miller, Yoshiko Nakano, Masahi Ogawa, Salil Tripathi, Wang Jian, Christine Yano, and Katja Valaskivi. There were also three 'Industry Speaks' lectures – by Clara Wong, CEO, Saatchi & Saatchi, Hong Kong; Frank Brown, President, MTV Networks Asia; and Jonathan Hulburt, Regional Account Managing Director, Dentsu Young Rubicam, HK. As organizer of the workshop and editor of this book, I would like to thank them all for their various kinds of input. The talks by Frank Brown and Rima Cunanan were particularly memorable and I am only sorry that they could not be included here.

My gratitude goes, too, to all my contributors – not only for travelling all the way to Hong Kong and participating so vociferously, but also for being so patient with their editor who has taken longer than any of us would have wished to put this manuscript together in book form. Moving from one job in the Asian sub-tropical region to another in what occasionally seems like the Arctic, rather than just a part of Scandinavia, has been rather more time and energy consuming than anticipated. Perhaps I am getting old!

Oh, and Dada, thanks for the pics.

Brian Moeran
Copenhagen

LIST OF ILLUSTRATIONS

Introduction

THE FIELD OF ASIAN MEDIA PRODUCTIONS

Brian Moeran

Asian Media Productions is about the production, marketing, reception and contents of Asian advertising and media, as well as about how these processes both distinguish Asia as a region and tie it to the rest of the world.

What is the significance of the three words: Asian, media and productions? When we talk of *Asian* media productions, people in the region's advertising and media industries readily envisage almost three billion potential customers for their work. In this respect, the sheer size, potential and unpredictability of the region are bewildering, and yet still under-explored – both by those working in the industries concerned and by those who, like academics, seek to understand, analyze and explain it to the rest of the world (in whose common economy or system Asian media are structured and interact). But what is 'Asia'? Clearly, given its sheer variety of peoples, languages, beliefs and customs, Asia does not constitute a cultural whole. Is it then, as has been claimed (Nandy 1998), a geographical entity? One immediate problem here is that the geographical region of Asia is not necessarily seen as encompassing the same 'Asia' by those living in different parts thereof. In other words, there are different 'Asias' for different 'Asians' so that, although the maps tell us that the larger part of Turkey and the Russian Republic are in the same Asian land mass as Tibet, New Guinea and Japan, the respective inhabitants of these countries have difficulty in finding much in common with one another (even those who, like Turks and Japanese, are said to be part of a common Altaic language group). Most people in east Asia tend to draw their continental boundary line along the south-east Asian coasts of Burma, Thailand, Malaysia and Singapore (a regional division echoed in ASEAN and other political alliances, as well as hinting at the legacy of Japan's former aspirations to a 'Greater East Asian Co-Prosperity Sphere'), relegating the south Asian sub-continent to the status of an 'other Asia' (Jain 2000:208). Those living in south east Asia itself, however, especially in countries facing onto the Andaman Sea, are more inclusive of Bangladesh, Tibet, Bhutan, Nepal, India and Pakistan within their vision of 'Asia'. For many 'Asians', the 'middle east' is precisely not Asian, although it is more physically proximate to the people of Pakistan and India, spiritually proximate to parts of Malaysia,

Indonesia and Brunei, and economically proximate to Filipinos working overseas in Saudi Arabia and Dubai. If anything, therefore, Asia is as much a mental as a geographical construct.

And then there are Asian *media* productions. Where once each country in Asia tended to keep its media industry and its contents more or less to itself (with the usual reliance on media inputs from the United States), recent developments in technology and the accompanying moves to globalization have led both to the emergence of pan-Asian media (like CNN, Channel [V] and MTV) and to the intra-Asian flows of Asian media contents. We thus find, on the one hand, organizational networks of capital and influence that seek to exploit the power of their audiences as 'consumers' and, on the other, specifically Asian narratives to attract those audiences' identification of themselves as 'Asians' (or, at least, as 'not American' or 'not western'). It is this combination of money, power, alliances and fantasies that forms the theoretical undercurrent of this book.

Consider the following media bites:

- Cantopop star Jackie Cheung belts out a Mandarin theme tune for Coca Cola's 'inspiration' ad campaign for *Tian Yu Di (Heaven and Earth)* ready-to-drink teas, launched in Shanghai and Huangzhou in the autumn of 1998. Another Cantopop favourite, Kelly Chan, endorses Shiseido's new cosmetics line, *Pies Nus*, as well as Epson's Photo 700 colour printer, whose colour quality is reflected – we are told – in the Hong Kong Chinese singer's make-up and hairstyle. The television commercial in which she appears coincides with the release of a music video and her new album. Hewlett Packard selects MTV veejay, Nadya Hutagalung, for its Desktop 695C printer ad campaign in the Asia Pacific region, while, for its campaign for greater China, Sprite has Taiwanese pop diva, Zhang Hui Mei, dancing among a group of masked young people in a busy Shanghai street. World table tennis champion, Jiang Jialiang, appears in a Maxam skincare product ad called 'Tea'; Japanese pop star, Kaneshiro Takeshi, stars in an imitation soap opera campaign for Hong Kong Telecom's mobile phone network, *One2Free*; and even the former colony's first chief executive, Tung Chee-hwa, appears to be endorsing a Procter and Gamble soap product, *Zest*, in a satirical commercial put out in Hong Kong in mid 1998.

- 86 per cent of all households in Hong Kong and Singapore own VCRs; 80 per cent in South Korea; 76 per cent in urban Vietnam; 61 per cent in Guanzhou; 58.7 per cent in Malaysia and 57.1 per cent in Taiwan. 69 per cent of the population of Japan and 31 per cent of that in Hong Kong own mobile phones.

    100 per cent of all households in Hong Kong and Guanzhou have colour television, as do 99.5 per cent Taiwanese and 96.5 per cent South Korean households. 93 per cent of urban dwellers in Vietnam and 54.5 per cent in India own black and white television sets.

Average weekday television viewing hours in the late 1990s were: Japan, 4.1 hours; Taiwan, 4.0 hours; and Indonesia, 3.2 hours. In Guanzhou and Hong Kong, people watched TV for 2.8 hours daily; in Shanghai, Singapore and the Philippines, 2.4 hours; in Malaysia, 2.3 hours; South Korea, 2.1 hours; Thailand, 2.0 hours; and India (seven cities), 1.85 hours.

The top three newspapers in Singapore sell 2.3 million copies daily; in Indonesia, 7.6 million; South Korea, 11 million; India, 23.9 million; and Japan, 33 million (including the world's largest newspaper, the *Yomiuri Shimbun*).

The top three categories for advertising expenditure in 1998 were: India – toilet soap, toothpaste and soft drinks; Thailand – housing projects, cosmetics and hair care; China – haircare, video machines and tonics/vitamins; Hong Kong – communications, real estate and publishing; and Taiwan – real estate, passenger cars and mobile phones. (Source: AC Nielsen samples in *Adweek Asia*, May 1998 to March 1999)

- Two satellite music stations – MTV and Channel [V] – are fighting for market share in the potentially lucrative Asian youth market. Across Asia MTV reaches nineteen million homes every day, while its main rival, Channel [V] – set up by Star TV in 1994 – claims to reach 40 million (*Adweek Asia,* 26 March 1999). Of these, 21 million are in mainland China, three and a half million in Korea, 4.3 million in Taiwan, and ten million in India, with the remaining homes scattered throughout east and south east Asia. By the last year of the millenium, after being off air for a year as it ditched its 'classic Coke' approach and re-tailored its programmes for local tastes and advertisers' needs, MTV reached 4.4 million in Taiwan, two and a half million in Indonesia, and ten million in India. Neither station was said to be profitable at the time (*Adweek Asia,* 4 December 1998).

- The Japanese high-tech robot cat, Doraemon, made its first print appearance at the beginning of 1970 and was later broadcast as an animation series on television screens all over the country. It soon became an all-time hit. Sales of Doraemon books of all kinds have come to about 110 million; of videos of its filmed versions two and a half million, with more than 60 million people going to cinemas to see the 17 films that had been put out by the mid-90s. The series is still running in Japan, nearly thirty years later, and can also be found on television screens in many other Asian countries. Merchandizing connected with Doraemon can be found on the clothes, stationery, and household goods – even on a school bus (Shiraishi 1997:268) – used by young people all over Asia. Royalties connected with Doraemon merchandizing between 1979 and 1994 came to US$153 million (Schodt 1996:217).

The arrival of Japanese animation has helped local comic industries thrive in almost all Asian countries (particularly Taiwan and Hong Kong). These themselves are beginning to go global. Malaysian cartoonist 'Lat', or Mohamad Nor Khalid, for example, recently found himself dictating his stories about Malaysian village life (*Kampung Boy*) to a Hollywood scriptwriter as part of a move to turn his cartoons into an animated series for television (*Far Eastern Economic Review*, 22 July 1999).

- The hard-hitting daily, *Manila Times*, found itself losing a US$2.6 million libel case to the President of the Philippines, Joseph Estrada, after calling him an 'unwilling godfather' for what the newspaper called 'a rigged contract' for a hydro-electric power deal involving an Argentinian firm. While the New York-based Committee to Protect Journalists and the World Association of Newspapers in Paris gave their support to the *Manila Times*, others argued that the paper, which had to close temporarily, had abused its freedom by publishing unsubstantiated allegations. Estrada later used his state-of-the-nation speech to address criticism that he was trying to muzzle the media (*Far Eastern Economic Review*, 13 May 1999).

  Meanwhile, Thailand's deputy prime minister, Trairong Suwannakhiri, sent his private secretary and 'six gun-toting deputies' to raid the *Thai Post* following its publication of a story describing how he had fled from protesting fishermen during a visit to southern Thailand (*Far Eastern Economic Review*, 5 August 1999).

- The authors of a *Newsweek* story found themselves in hot water when they quoted a diplomat as saying that Thailand's economic advantages were 'sex and golf' (*Far Eastern Economic Review*, 5 August 1999) – two hobbies much enjoyed by the Japanese, who now employ Thai and Filipina girls as 'hostesses' in their clubs and bars.

  In Shishi, a small town in the southern part of the Chinese province of Fujian, 10,000 illegal copies of films – 1,000 of them pornographic – are turned out every day by video pirating shops. Known as an 'adventurer's paradise', Shishi attracts thousands of tourists and porn peddlers from all over China, and postal and railway workers assist in the dissemination of porn products by wholesale mail order.

  One television station employee was so absorbed in watching a porn video that he absent-mindedly flicked the wrong button and succeeded in airing its contents on one Chinese city's prime time news programme (Zha 1995:142–3).

- At seven o'clock every evening, 300 million people in the PRC sit down to watch the news on China Central Television (CCTV) – not so much for the news itself, as for the fifteen minutes of commercials that follow the news. Of the 30 or so companies that advertised during this quarter of an hour in 1998, nine were manufacturers of VCD players – one of whom, Idall, paid approximately US$14.5 million (Rmb 210 million), for the premier fifteen-second slot following the news in 1997. The other advertisers were promoting telephones, cosmetics, personal computers, air conditioners, snacks and drinks (HK Trade Development Council 1998a; 1998b).

  CCTV's turnover is said to have approached half a billion American dollars (Rmb four billion) in 1998. Not surprisingly, most satellite, cable and terrestrial television stations in mainland China now ignore sponsorship and subscription fees and rely almost entirely on advertising to cover running and programme production costs. According to Gallup, almost 50 per cent of all people nationwide and 68 per cent of urban residents, are influenced by TV commercials in making their purchases (Hong Kong Trade Development Council 1998b:37). The People's Republic is destined to become the world's fourth largest advertising market by the year 2003 – after the US, Japan and Germany. By the year 2015 it will be the largest in the world.

So many 'newsy' facts; so many soon-to-be-outdated statistics; so little analysis. What these media bites show, on the one hand, is the way in which Asian entertainment industries – from pop music to children's publishing – now intermesh, so that a Hong Kong beauty queen can become a celebrity in Japan and a Japanese cartoon character become a hit in almost every country in east and south east Asia. This mixing of genres goes on, of course, in all media and entertainment industries, but here its content is often specifically 'Asian'. At the same time, we see that the talk about the 'potential' of Asian media is part factual, part hype, part evasive. The claimed reach of 40 million by Channel [V] may seem like a large audience in the context of Europe or the United States, but it amounts to only just over one per cent of the total population of Asia. There may be millions of Asians, too, who read numerous daily newspapers (that are potentially so powerful that they are liable to government interferences of one sort or another), and there may be millions more who own television sets in urban areas of mainland China and Vietnam. But what of the millions in rural areas – and, as William Mazzarella points out for India in this book, it is the rural populations of most Asian countries that are still comparatively large and underdeveloped – who do not have access to the wonders of television and satellite dishes? As Mark Hobart notes, media statistics do not tell us what *they* think and talk about among themselves, nor what *they* (want to) eat and drink, or use to brush their teeth and wash their hair. And, although so much advertising money is spent on promoting real estate in Taiwan and Hong Kong, it does not tell us anything about the grossly inflated prices of land and accommodation in many Asian cities and the sacrifices that people have to make in order to be able to provide a roof over their and their families' heads. We may justifiably ask ourselves, therefore, what are the social and cultural forces connected with media organizations, their productions and audiences around the Asian region, from mainland China to Bali, from India to Japan.

Finally, the focus of this volume is on Asian media *productions*, rather than on Asian media 'worlds' or Asian media 'cultures', because media products are *intentional*. They are consciously shaped by different people during the course of their movement through the various stages of re/production, distribution or circulation, representation, and reception or consumption. In other words, at each linked point in the chain of media communication and exchange, a determinate moment of 'encoding' and 'decoding' meanings takes place (Hall

1980) when not just media producers, but sponsors, marketers, advertisers, critics, and targeted and untargeted audiences make their sometimes complementary, but usually diverse contributions to the production of media. Each of those participating in a media 'world' (Becker 1982) or 'field' (Bourdieu 1993a), therefore, is an active agent in the construction and maintenance of that 'circuit of culture' (du Gay et al. 1997) or cultures that constitutes Asia today. Taiwanese viewers of Japanese television dramas, account executives working on a condom advertising campaign in Bombay, a Japanese corporation manufacturing comedians, journalists in a south China newspaper balancing what should or should not be put out as 'news', Balinese villagers discussing the seduction of television commercials, a Tokyo advertising agency arranging a series of performances by an Italian opera company – all these are actively engaged in the production of media and meanings that have often already been produced by others and are reproduced for others to create their own media productions.

Media Cultural Studies

The study of media is a 'blurred genre' (Geertz 1983). In the western academic world it was initiated for the most part by sociologists, before being taken up by those working in communications, cultural studies, literary criticism, political science, sociology and, more recently, anthropology. Most of these disciplines have developed rather differently in the UK, continental Europe, the USA, Canada, Australia and Latin America, giving rise to different and fragmented approaches to media. Thus, while British cultural studies in Birmingham was firmly grounded in sociology, for example, American cultural studies has been seen as little more than 'a kind of textualism' and contemporary American sociology as 'often both ahistorical and unsociological' in its study of media and the culture industries (Wolff 1999:503, 501).

Since one of the aims of *ConsumAsiaN* (the Consumption in Asia Network), and the book series associated with it, has been to bring together scholars from different disciplinary backgrounds in an attempt to enter into sustained dialogue with one another and – who knows? – break new theoretical ground, I do not here wish to enter into lengthy discussion of the merits and demerits of each of the disciplines represented in this edited book. After all, its contributors come from a range of disciplines, including anthropology, communications, cultural and media studies, and their reading, writing and research are clearly not exclusive to any one discipline. So, since all culture these days *is* media culture in the sense that the media have become the dominant means by which culture is produced, disseminated, received, talked about and consumed, and since all of us are concerned with analyzing 'the complex relations between texts, audiences, media industries, politics, and the socio-historical context in specific conjunctures', I propose to follow Douglas Kellner (1995:37) and use the term 'media cultural studies' to describe our field of multidisciplinary study.

I recognize, however, that each of the approaches to the study of media mentioned above has its critics, both from within and without. Cultural studies in particular, perhaps, is going through a turbulent period (Ferguson and Golding 1997), spurred on as much by clashes of personality, it seems, as by arguments about theoretical and methodological issues (although these are by no means absent). It may be that the field of cultural studies is the victim of its own success and that the metatheoretical trend, or 'virtualism' (Miller 1998), fashionable among some scholars is related to its institutionalization as an academic discipline competing for attention with literary studies and English in the humanities and with sociology and anthropology in the social sciences. But 'cultural studies' itself has always been an ambiguous term in the context of contemporary theory (Grossberg 1993:21) and is still very much a contested terrain (Grossberg et al. 1992:22), so that those who wish to enter the cultural studies fray need to ensure that they clarify *who* precisely is doing *what*. To do otherwise would lead them to overlook, or at least play down, the considerable importance of the work of a number of scholars who, in Britain and Australia in particular, have devoted their attention to the study of the production, distribution and reception of different media forms (for example, Ang 1991; McRobbie 1998). *Asian Media Productions*, then, seeks to build on the insights of those working in cultural studies, as well as in sociology, and so contribute to the growing body of knowledge on contemporary media.

Many of the contributors to this volume are anthropologists. In the past, anthropologists doing research on media tended to find themselves shunted unceremoniously to the edge of their discipline since what they had to say resonated little with 'core' disciplinary issues. Yet, as Ulf Hannerz (1992:26) observed some years ago:

> By now it ought to be impossible for anthropologists to pretend that media do not exist. As a sizable portion of the flow of meaning in societies passes through media, it must take a willful disregard, or the most unthinking commitment to the ethnographic routines of the past, to leave them out of what is claimed to be a general study of culture.
>
> Yet, the growth and spread of media have had curiously little impact on the mainstream of anthropological as well as sociological thought.

Although it sometimes seems as if anthropology has turned a blind eye to media, there has in fact been quite a lot of work done here and there (see the early work by Powdermaker [1950]), particularly in visual anthropology where the work of ethnographic film makers tends to be marked (for example, Ginsburg 1992). In many ways, though, anthropologists have allowed those working in literary and cultural studies to seize the high ground of a field that they might usefully have cultivated and harvested to benefit their discipline as a whole (cf. Appadurai 1991:195–6; 1996:51). This failure is disheartening because, by studying media cultures in societies that were not part of the 'first world' of the west studied by sociologists, literary critics and cultural studies scholars, anthropologists might have brought more influence to bear on theoretical developments in their fellow disciplines. Now, it seems, a change is in the air. Belatedly, and possibly in reaction to a swing in theoretical fashion that jumps on the bandwagon of 'all that is solid melts into cultural studies', one or two anthropologists have called on their discipline to remake itself (Rosaldo 1994) and media have begun to grace academic publications in anthropology (see, among others, Spitulnik 1993; Calderola 1994; Das and Abu-Lughod in Miller 1995).

The refashioning of media anthropology, sociology and cultural studies – hopefully as part of a more united discipline of media cultural studies – will in large part, I think, depend upon how they develop their ethnographic practices. Although anthropologists may occasionally be accused of fetishizing 'fieldwork' – a word with which James Clifford (1992:99–100), for example, has problems – we should realize that they are not sole proprietors of a methodology which has also been taken up by sociologists and those working in cultural studies (see, for example, Blumer 1969; Grimshaw et al. 1980), even though they may be puzzled by the variety of practices that the latter, for example, label 'ethnographic' (Ang 1996:187). Thus, when it comes to the interdisciplinary practice of fieldwork, we find ourselves facing a complex situation in which ethnography is 'rediscovered' (Spitulnik 1993:299). As Barnard (1990:69–70) notes:

> Ethnography, in fact, entered Cultural Studies through responses to already existing 'ethnographic' studies of British sub-cultures. These, in turn, had been the result of the application to the British scene of naturalistic methods derived from the Chicago School ... [which] – through the influence of Radcliffe-Brown's period in Chicago – had already been exposed to and influenced by this British tradition!

It is, I think, accepted these days that the groups traditionally studied by anthropologists are not necessarily or any longer 'tightly territorialized, spatially bounded, historically unselfconscious, or culturally homogeneous' (Appadurai 1996:48), and that, since the media form one set of institutions that 'contribute greatly to making the boundaries of societies and cultures fuzzy' (Hannerz 1992:30), we might begin to develop a new kind of ethnography to deal with the ways in which media assist in 'the loosening of the holds between people, wealth and territories' (Appadurai 1996:49, 53–5; see also Hannerz 1996:102–111) and open up deterritorialized spaces, or non-places (Augé 1995), for people to live and imagine their lives in new ways (see also Clifford 1992). A number of different chapters in *Asian Media Productions* begin to explore this issue. Ulf Hannerz, for example, has been 'parachuting' in among foreign correspondents all over the world to discuss their work. For her part, Liz MacLachlan did fieldwork with a television team assigned to cover the aftermath of the Kobe Earthquake among inhabitants of a city who suddenly found themselves uprooted and homeless. In his pursuit of how an advertising campaign for KamaSutra condoms was made, William Mazzarella found himself following a chain of contacts that linked Bombay's advertising and entertainment worlds with the advertiser, on the one hand, and the Government of India, on the other. Mark Hobart nicely illustrates the mix of traditional community and 'deterritorialization' through media by relating how Balinese villagers talk about the words and images used in television commercials now coming to their remote rural homes via the wonders of technology and an academic research programme.[1]

This shift in the object(s) of ethnographic focus, however, should not preclude the continued necessity for *grounded* – and also, as Hobart argues, interventionist – ethnography (which can still usefully take place in organizations, as seen in the chapters by Joel Stocker and myself). Clearly, and in spite of a suggested need for change (Fox 1991), one of the strengths of anthropology has been its attention to and practice of participant-observation and long-term fieldwork. Although such attention and practice have shifted since the mid-late 1980s from fieldwork itself to the writing up of fieldwork (Clifford and Marcus 1986; Geertz 1988), ethnographic writing itself cannot exist in a vacuum (the postmodern trend notwithstanding). As John Van Maanen (1988:xiii) says:

> We need now, more than ever, concrete, sharp, complex, empathetic, and politically sensitive portraits of what others might really be like if we are to learn, tolerate, balk, help, confront, instruct, or otherwise adjust to the uncountable ways of living and being that surround us.

Such portraits are absolutely essential in media and entertainment industries: partly because we still know so little about them; partly because their practitioners tend triumphantly to assert, and so merely rely on, the 'accuracy' of their market statistics and target audience figures to 'prove' their success; partly because of the criticism – itself homogenizing – that the media and the 'culture industry' help produce consensus and manufacture consent (Adorno and Horkheimer 1979:120–67). As many of the chapters in this book reveal, media organizations differ considerably from one another and thus can hardly be lumped into the single category, 'culture industry'. Moreover, they have too much trouble producing consensus internally, as well as between themselves and their sponsors (cf. Moeran 1996a), to be able to manufacture among their audiences the kind of consent suggested by Adorno and Horkheimer. And anyway, as we are learning from a number of important studies (for example, Ang 1996; Morley 1992), and as we see in Hobart's chapter on Balinese villagers' reactions to television commercials, audiences have a habit of 'decoding' in diverse ways the meanings 'encoded' in media productions (Hall 1980). It is participation in and observation of the linked but distinctive moments of media production, circulation, representation and reception that lead to unanticipated insights into the broader social worlds of which they are a part, as well as into various kinds of overt and covert, consensual and resistant, empowered and disempowered strategies employed by those involved.

It is true that ethnography 'holds no exclusive claim to methodological adequacy' (Morley 1997:128) and that such factors as planning, foresight, connections, language ability, personality, impulse, accident, flexibility, endurance and sheer luck play an enormous part in the end product of research. But ethnography – in the sense of living where people live, doing what people do, and going where people go (Watson 1997:viii) – is what will make or break media cultural studies. It is what holds this book together – as we can see in Koichi Iwabuchi's detailed interviews and correspondence with young Taiwanese viewers of Japanese dramas, John McCreery's hands-on experience of how Japanese advertising campaigns are made, and Kevin Latham's preparation of documentary programmes for a south Chinese television station. In brief, *Asian Media Productions* makes a substantial contribution to the study of media in three important ways. Firstly, a large number of chapters are based on intensive participant-observation of media over a long period of time, in what has become time-honoured methodological practice. Secondly, they focus on a wide variety of media practices, ranging from production to reception, by way of marketing, representation and content analysis. Thirdly, they take as their object of study media forms in Asia, outside the comparatively exclusive Euro-American sphere hitherto discussed by those in sociology and cultural studies.

Asian Media Cultural Studies

By focusing on Asian media's structured interaction in a global economy, *Asian Media Productions* poses two related questions. Firstly, what implications does the ethnographic evidence presented here have for an alternative, more realistic social theorizing of the media? Secondly, what analytical categories should we use to describe and understand the region as a whole?

One set of answers to these questions stems from *how* we go about studying Asian media. Although at the turn of the millenium cultural studies seems to be *the* buzzword among academics in Japan, and although it has clearly also taken off in Taiwan, media cultural studies are only just beginning to become an intellectual force in Asia. The question then is: what will be the intellectual influences on such studies? If such issues as resistance, class and sub-cultures have pervaded British media cultural studies; and if, in the USA, problems of gender, race, ethnicity and multi-culturalism have been the emphases, what are we to expect of an Asian media cultural studies? Is there, indeed, going to be a specifically 'Asian' media cultural studies?

One recent volume, published as a result of two international cultural studies conferences held at National Tsing Hua University, Taiwan, in 1992 and 1995 (Chen 1998), addresses the kinds of issues current in European and American media cultural studies – (post)colonialism, nationalism, multi-racialism, identity, media and democracy – but with the difference that approximately two thirds of the contributors are themselves Asian (a welcome difference which I wish I had been able to emulate in *Asian Media Productions*). But, in that volume at least, the ethnic shift from Anglo-American to Asian scholars is not in itself sufficient to achieve the stated aims of the *Trajectories* project: a critical reflection upon the appropriateness or otherwise of received theories and methodologies in western media and communication studies; a countering of those essentializing processes of colonialization, marginalization and erasure that have often taken place as a result of the unreflecting imposition of western theory upon the societies, cultures and practices of the Asian region; and an opening up and diversification of existing theoretical positions and discourses (Chen 1998:xi–xii).

How and where, then, are we to start? Given my earlier argument that Asia is as much a mental construct as a geographical region, we might begin with one appeal to that construct within east and south east Asia – the 'Asian way' – that has been actively cultivated by Asian politicians such as Malaysian prime minister, Mahathir Mohamad, and Singapore's elder statesman, Lee Kwan Yew. Keen to challenge claimed attempts by western powers to assert their global intellectual and cultural hegemony, on the one hand, and keener still to explain, even boast about, their success when their economies were on the upsurge (and duly mocked by western commentators when their economies 'crashed'), various politicians, businessmen and intellectuals have argued that Asians have culturally distinct attitudes towards rights, duties and responsibilities. Although there is no coherence in the doctrine of Asian values, it is primarily concerned with the organization of society as a means towards differentiating (a superior) Asia from (an inferior) west and strengthening Asian solidarity by positing (a false, or – in my term – mental) unity (Ghai 1998). Thus, they argue, although such 'universal' values as democracy, human rights, and freedom (of speech and of the individual) may be 'right' in the historical and geographical context of Europe and the United States, they become rather more problematic in similar Asian contexts where, at best, they are assigned different nuances and, at worst, dismissed as 'imperialist interventions'. Since British cultural studies, in particular, has long engaged critically with political issues – trying to understand hegemony, attacking oppression, domination and their supporting ideologies, and siding with the forces of resistance and struggle, as well as with marginal and oppositional cultures – an Asian media cultural studies, while mindful of Meaghan Morris's comment (1990) about the machine-like banality of some of the critiques in question, will almost certainly need to renegotiate these theoretical positions in the light of Asia's different historical conditions.

One area of concern is the relationship between media, democracy and the market – as intimated in the vignettes on Asian media earlier on in this Introduction and discussed in detail by Latham in his contribution on news production in south China (see also Zhao 1998 and Li 1998). After all, in Hong Kong, the owner of the *Hong Kong Standard* newspaper – a firm supporter of Beijing – managed to evade criminal proceedings in spite of the part that she was believed by many to have played in fabricating circulation figures for prospective advertisers. Magazines like the *Far Eastern Economic Review* regularly report incidents in which the media run foul of Asian governments, whose interpretations of 'freedom of speech' (or more often, freedom of images), as hinted above, are not necessarily those to which western authorities are accustomed. This links up with other concerns such as global markets and the public sphere, free trade, dependence theory, a new world information and communication order, and so on. Can it be said that external (mainly western) media influences constrain local developments, on the one hand, and/or, on the other, contribute to rising tensions and conflicts over political sovereignty, national policies and plans, as well as socio-cultural issues in Asian societies (Anderson 1984; French and Richards 1996; Frith 1996; and as illustrated by James Lull in the following chapter)? After all, as Richard Wilk (1994) shows for Belize, the advent of satellite television takes people from colonial into real time, as they experience simultaneously events going on elsewhere in the world. 'TV time' thus threatens the power bases of political and cultural elites who strive to control its uncontrollable nature. One of the more interesting general focuses for discussion here is the not-necessarily-compatible interests of governments, media organizations, corporate advertisers and audiences, and who gets left out of what, where, when and why in Asian media productions. After all, media do not *have* to give in to political pressures. They can even stimulate political reflection and encourage their audiences to imagine possibilities for social change – as James Lull (1990:96–145) shows in his discussion of Chinese people's reactions to the political drama *New Star* (*Xin Xing*).

In general, media participate more in an organization of diversity than in a replication of uniformity (Hannerz 1992) in their globalizing processes. In spite of the seeming standardization of media productions and their reception (people in Indonesia, India and Taiwan can listen to the same music and watch the same videos at the same time; almost anyone in possession of a satellite dish in Asia can keep up with CNN's hourly 'news' programmes), therefore, media generally expand and contribute to cultural diversity. In this respect, globalization is 'a complex set of interacting and countervailing human, material, and symbolic flows that lead to diverse, heterogeneous cultural positioning and practices which persistently and variously modify established vectors of social, political and cultural power' (Lull 1995:150).

Now globalization itself is not new, although the globalization of media is. There has been a single global world economy since 1500, with worldwide division of labour, multilateral trade and financial flows, dominated by Asians for at least three centuries until 1800 (Frank 1998). This point is worth making, if only to remind ourselves that the 'unity in diversity' of which Hannerz speaks is not a recent technological phenomenon, but has itself been generated by the world economy or system in a manner that has been continuous yet cyclical (Frank 1998:352). The fact that the centre of this system temporarily shifted from Asia to Europe and then America in the nineteenth and twentieth centuries has had a number of unfortunate effects for those of us studying Asian media: one of these is the Euro-/Americo-centrism of the 'universalizing' social 'sciences'; the other is the still inherent danger of 'orientalist' assumptions (Frank 1998:14).

Clearly, one related issue here is media dissemination of images of the 'other'. Asian media have tended to appeal to a synthesized mental construct of

Asia, if only because it promises the 'massest' of mass markets. Hong Kong films, Cantopop music and Japanese animated cartoons, for example, have in recent years begun to target and be accepted by different Asian audiences in an active blending of a synthesized 'Asian culture' that is beginning, perhaps, to give rise to a shared feeling, especially among young people, that many Asians do after all share some kind of 'common culture' and that they are participating in a process of 'Asianization' backed by urban middle class lifestyles, (primarily Japanese) commodity culture and image alliances (cf. Moeran 2000a:33–36).

Unlike our experiences of American and other western media, part of this synthesis demands that there be no cultural opposition. Ding-Tzann Lii (1998:132–5), for example, points out that peripheral Asian media tend to both regionalize and localize the expansion of capitalism by making different versions of the same production for different target areas. As a result, many Hong Kong films do not make cultural judgements of the 'other', but render her/ him/it culturally neutral and de-objectified as part of a process of Asianization (that is, a fusion of different Asian cultures into a single Asian Culture). Along similar lines, Koichi Iwabuchi has argued for the 'culturally odourless' nature of Japanese media, Saya Shiraishi for their 'soft power' and I myself for a 'soft corollanization' of Asia that permits and encourages the acceptance of foreign Japanese/Asian commodities and media productions, together with their integration into an emergent 'Asian way' (Iwabuchi 1998, 1999; Shiraishi 1997; Moeran 2000a).

At the same time, however, we cannot ignore the comparative ease with which stereotyping does occur in media productions which have to rely on a visual and verbal shorthand to communicate meanings effectively (see Moeran 1996b). This is an issue raised by Joel Stocker in his discussion of the 'otherness' of Japan's second city, Osaka, and its people. But such otherness can, and often does, extend beyond national boundaries – particularly in the guise of 'orientalism'. 'Asia' and 'the west' have been seen as 'absolutely different' (Said 1978:96) and forming closed systems 'in which objects are what they are *because* they are what they are, for once, for all time' (Said 1978:70). Yet 'oriental' and 'occidental' are neither exclusive nor stable, but practical categories, since different people see things differently, depending on their motives, aims, choices, strategies, social positions and so on (Herzfeld 1995). In other words, 'oriental' and 'occidental' take on meaning only in relation to each other, although this does not mean that orientalism necessarily belongs 'only to those who are white' (Chow 1993:14). The kind of self image held by many Asians – together with all those opposed notions of individual and society, egoism and reciprocity, egalitarianism and hierarchy, modernization and tradition that haunt comparisons between 'the west' and Asia – can be said to have developed in contrast to their stylized images of the west (Carrier 1995:6). This 'internalized west' (Nandy 1998:144) takes the form of what Mazzarella in his original *ConsumAsiaN* workshop paper called 'auto-Orientalism'. It is this sense of alienated self that people in different Asian cultures often use to talk, not just to Europeans and Americans, but to those living in other Asian cultures (Nandy 1998), so that orientalism can be seen as the obverse side of the same coin on whose face is stamped the image of nationalism (Chow 1993:5–7). One area that needs further investigation, therefore, consists of the selective visions of Asia and the west that both Asian and western media encourage and sustain in their productions.

Another obvious area of interest – and one explicitly touched upon in this book by Hannerz, Mazzarella, Carolyn Stevens and Shuhei Hosokawa – is that of gender and sexuality. Although there is now a considerable body of work emerging on the representation of women in media,[2] we need to find out the extent to which women are involved more generally in Asian media productions. For example, has the successful combination of NHK's first female chief producer, Okamoto Yukiko, and one of the most successful of all Japanese TV drama script writers, Hashida Sugako, in bringing *Oshin* to television screens all over the world (Harvey 1995) encouraged greater employment of women in television industries elsewhere in Asia? Why are account executives in Singapore advertising agencies predominantly women, while in Japan they are almost invariably men? Are there media other than (televised) pop music where young women are both major stars and consumers? How come women are regularly appointed chief editors of international fashion magazines in Hong Kong and Shanghai, but not in Japan? How much do such appointments affect the contents of media productions, and with what short- and long-term effects? As Hannerz suggests, when women become foreign correspondents, the contents of journalistic reporting on Japan for western media take on a markedly different tone.

Just what it is about their societies that concerns people living in different parts of Asia, and how their media organizations reflect such concerns, is, of course, a major issue. For Bourdieu (1986:139), the structural homology between producers and consumers in the field of cultural production is linked to the role of the dominant class and its fractions. But in some parts of Asia – Japan is an obvious example – it might be argued that class systems of the kind that evolved in France and other parts of Europe do not exist, and that it may be more appropriate to talk of status groups, defined in particular by access to and success in education. Also, in many Asian societies, different forms of social organization tend to be preferred and thus dominate – networks, for example, or quasi-groups – and these militate against longer-term, diachronic, fixed entities such as class. Regional variations are also given great importance: Tokyo *vis-à-vis* Osaka (as we see in Stocker's discussion of Japanese *manzai* humour); Beijing *vis-à-vis* Shanghai; Delhi *vis-à-vis* Bombay. As a result, as Bourdieu himself says (1986:148), we need to take account of the fact 'the objective structures of the field of production give rise to categories of perception which structure the perception and appreciation of its products'.

So far, the issues discussed with regard to Asian media tend toward the anticipated. Perhaps, though, there will be a shift in emphases – as in media cultural studies in Latin America – and scholars will trace how different countries' popular culture and media forms have adopted, adapted to, and been transformed by imported cultural products: either from the USA or, as is increasingly likely to be the case, from other countries, especially Japan, within the region. It is the *intra*-Asian cultural flows, of the kind discussed here by Iwabuchi, that are likely to be important in future discussions of Asian media forms (see also Iwabuchi 1999). Here we might find useful concepts like syncretism and hybridization proposed by Latin-American scholars like Martín-Barbero and García Canclini (1995). We might also need to start looking for a structural equivalent to *mestizaje*, the mixing of Indian and Spanish heritages, in our discussions of Asia where China, Japan and the USA have all been culturally dominant and interacted with other countries in the region to produce what may now be in the process of becoming a creolized but common Asian cultural form.

If nothing else, we need more research.

Asian Media Productions

As mentioned at the beginning of this Introduction, *Asian Media Productions* looks at the various ways in which advertising and media are conceived, produced, received and talked about in different parts of Asia. The book consists of twelve chapters – many of them written by academics who have themselves had considerable exposure to the workings of media organizations. Apart from those already mentioned, James Lull has worked extensively in radio, Koichi Iwabuchi in television, and John McCreery in advertising. Carolyn Stevens has spent some years working closely with a Japanese pop group. As a child, Ulf Hannerz appeared on Swedish television in a quiz show, while I myself was paired with a famous *manzai* comedian and appeared regularly on Japanese television for a couple of years back at the very beginning of the 70s.

The first part of this book, Asian media flows, consists of three rather different takes on what is generally discussed under the heading of globalization: one by James Lull who examines Asian media in the context of a dynamic and indeterminate 'system' of global communications; a second by Koichi Iwabuchi, whose concern is with how Asian media forms are received in other parts of Asia (particularly, in this instance, with Japanese television dramas broadcast in Taiwan); and the third by Kathy Frith who looks at how cultural regulation is used in advertising as a means of counteracting the perceived threat of global material culture emanating from 'the west'.

Lull is particularly concerned with two arguments made by Samuel Huntington in his book *The Clash of Civilizations and the Remaking of the World Order*: firstly, that the west no longer dominates the world in politics, economics and culture in the way that it once did; and secondly, that the world can be divided into nine 'civilizations', of which at least six – Sinic, Buddhist, Islam, Hindu, Japanese and western – co-exist in Asia. Lull asks what the roles of media and symbolic forms are in the maintenance of civilizations under conditions of global reterritorialization at present taking place, and suggests that we look at 'highly-personalized clusters, grids and networks of relevance', rather than at 'cultures' or even civilizations *per se*. After all, however much particular governments may wish to preserve and conserve cultural identities – as Frith shows us in her discussion of advertising regulation in Vietnam and Singapore, and as Lull himself nicely illustrates with his example of how urban Chinese (mis)interpreted the Japanese soap drama *Oshin* – culture can no longer be fully 'protected' or faithfully reproduced in a world where material and symbolic goods are causing all kinds of structural and stylistic disruption and change. At the same time as contributing to changes in the local environments, however, we need to recognize that global products also have their forms changed by local appropriations and indigenization processes, so that – wherever we live – we find ourselves more and more involved in what Hannerz (1992) has referred to as the 'creolization' of cultures. It is in the way individuals appropriate and customize their own versions of such creole cultures for their own self-understanding, well-being, social influence, growth and pleasure that, Lull says, we find at work a 'superculture'.

In such discussions of the globalization of media and popular culture, as Iwabuchi points out, there is often an in-built assumption of western (American) domination, so that arguments – like those put forward by Huntington and addressed by Lull – tend to focus on the inter-relations *between* the west and the rest. By contrast, Iwabuchi turns his attention to the flow of media products *within* Asia and to interaction between two *non*-western countries – Taiwan and Japan. Although he has, elsewhere (Iwabuchi 1998; 1999), argued that some Japanese popular culture or media exports are 'culturally odourless', his argument in his chapter in this book is that it is a peculiarly Japanese 'smell' to television idol dramas that sells them to other Asians. People living in Hong Kong, Taiwan and Korea in particular nowadays feel a sense of living in and sharing a (post)modernity that is not just American and that cannot as a result be represented well by American popular culture.

Iwabuchi's emphasis, then, is not on the spread of global western media and Asian responses thereto, but on the regionalization of media forms within a particular cultural-geographical area of east Asia (and so neatly problematizes Huntington's distinction between 'Japanese' and 'Sinic' civilizations). His particular theoretical concern is with the articulation of cultural proximity, as he seeks to understand why particular programmes become popular with different audiences and what sort of pleasure these audiences find in them. By outlining certain historical factors, such as the liberalization of Taiwan itself since the late 1980s, as well as structural factors affecting the development of media industries – particularly cable TV – in Taiwan, *and* text analysis, *plus* detailed research on audience reception, Iwabuchi is able to show how the concept of 'cultural proximity' is both spatial and temporal. There is a consciousness among many east Asians, at least, that they are living in the same time, thanks to a narrowing economic gap and the simultaneous circulation of information and commodities.

Figure 1 Statue of Mao Zedong and other advertisements, Chengdu.
(Photo courtesy of Dermot Tatlow)

Thus – and this doubtless would add to Huntington's pessimistic view of the decline of the west, though lending support to Lull's focus on networks of relevance – Asian, and perhaps other non-western, modern countries can now by-pass the west and enter into direct bilateral flows with one another.

It is this possibility that is clearly perceived by those politicians who, as we have seen, have argued forcefully and frequently in terms of uniquely Asian values underpinning the success of their 'different' market economies. In two states with such different political systems as Vietnam and Singapore, as Frith points out, the common factor linking them is the belief that local cultural values can bind a people together. But while the Vietnamese government is concerned with the perceived social evils of capitalism (prostitution, gambling, drugs and advertising), the stated aims of media industries in Singapore are to support nation-building, mould national identity, promote social harmony and exercise self-restraint in such a manner as not to cause racial or religious tensions. Thus both nations have developed two very different sets of advertising regulations to support their different ideological positions, although both are equally concerned to offset the potential damage caused by global advertising campaigns that play down cultural differences and treat the world as a single homogeneous global market.

The delicate balancing act between national political interests and market capitalism is the subject of Kevin Latham's essay on journalists and the rhetorics of transition in south China. This second part of the book is concerned with the production of news and Latham details how media producers have found themselves embroiled in China's transition to a socialist market economy which obliges them to confront the vagaries of market competition while remaining strictly under the control of party and state. As in Vietnam, in mainland China the masses are seen to be vulnerable to 'incorrect thinking' and thus in need of appropriate education and guidance, so that, as in Singapore, the role of the Chinese media is to support party policy and help the government build (this time a socialist) society.

In certain ironical respects, the ideological stance adopted by the communist party that media should make up a system which is ideally uniform as a whole, as well as in all its parts, supports the arguments put forward by Adorno and Horkheimer (1979:120–67) that the culture industry is 'enlightenment as mass deception' in mainland China (although it might also be described in practice as 'deception as mass enlightenment'). But, as Latham shows, newspaper journalists and other media producers know that their readerships and audiences are far from gullible or malleable, and that they constitute highly selective people with particular tastes that need to be catered to. This in turn means that they cannot merely publish party-line news and reports of party-dominated meetings, but have to provide their audiences with materials that stimulate their interest.

They also have to attract the advertising now crucial to media organizations' commercial viability since it is their key source of revenue. This is intriguing because in Europe, as well as in Japan (Yamamoto 1984), newspapers started out by being the mouthpieces of political parties and were only able to escape the latter's domination by accepting advertising. As a result, newspapers all over the world have come to depend on advertising revenue for financial stability – a fact which has obliged them to adapt their contents to the needs of commerce (Williams 1976:18–21, 25). But, while newspapers everywhere seem merely to have changed masters – from politicians to businessmen – advertising is in mainland China still a state monopoly. This paradox in the perpetuation of hegemony is echoed in journalists' fear of the consequences of political chaos and the perceived requirement of national unity during the transitional period in which Chinese now find themselves.

Liz MacLachlan, in her chapter on television news coverage of the Kobe earthquake in January 1995, also explores the emergence of journalists as political subjects. She, too, is more directly concerned with the relation between news credibility and economic resources – something that she points out is generally overlooked by those who have studied news from the angles of production, text analysis or reception – and argues that 'the greater the economic resources available for news production, the more likely a news organization will be able to produce news its audience finds credible and trustworthy'. Focussing on three different news organizations and their coverage of the Kobe earthquake, she shows how a Tokyo-based commercial programme with limited resources was obliged to be sensationalist in its reporting (and thus accused of being both non-factual and insensitive to the plight of the earthquake's victims), whereas the national broadcasting corporation, NHK, with its local networks and comparatively unlimited resources, was able to provide comprehensive coverage that was seen to be authoritative and journalistically responsible.

One interesting pattern emerging out of MacLachlan's fieldwork research is that, in their search for an 'angle', the smaller, outside news organization picked up on foreign journalists' comments on the Japanese government's lacklustre handling of disaster relief and thereby obliged the larger, more credible and more conservative NHK to follow up the criticisms and bring them to the public domain in a *credible* light. Thus, in Japan, smaller news organizations cannot effectively or directly challenge the *status quo* or powers that be, but force or help others to do so.

Mention of the role played by foreign news organizations brings us to Ulf Hannerz's paper on foreign correspondents in Japan. Here we are not concerned with media productions *by* Asians; nor is the work of foreign correspondents produced *for* Asian audiences. Rather, in that the news that they relay comes *from* Asia, Hannerz notes, we are dealing with productions *of* Asia intended for non-Asian audiences.

Hannerz is not concerned with the 'parachutist' type of journalist who goes somewhere at a moment's notice to cover a major news event (such as the Kobe earthquake). Rather, his interest is in the everyday activities, relationships and careers of correspondents who are stationed abroad for greater or lesser periods of time. The immediate problem here concerns the conflict between one of the principle aims of media (to report 'news') and the need to assimilate the language and culture of the place being visited. The ideal foreign correspondent must have a fresh eye for the peculiarities of the place to which s/he is posted; if s/he stays too long, s/he will tend to take things for granted, to 'go stale'. And yet, to understand what is going on, s/he needs – in the case of China or Japan – fairly long-term immersion in language learning in order to appreciate local issues.

This conflict tends to be resolved in favour of 'news' which, as Hannerz points out, is an ambiguous term that refers not only to something that has just happened, but also to something that we have not heard about before and so find interesting, even surprising. It is this latter aspect of 'news' that tends to be emphasized in correspondents' reporting on Japan, which thus becomes the focus of 'dramatized difference' (with regard to its people, its customs, its political system, its business and industrial organization, and so on). Such feature stories on difference Hannerz sees as being part of the longer time span of Japan's relations with the west, although he also notes that some correspondents – faced with a breakdown of the interpretive framework until recently provided by the cold war[3] – have been experimenting with news of gradual, medium-term change in their reporting on Japan.

Another, more general, point made by Hannerz concerns the similarity in concerns between a news media foreign correspondent and an anthropologist.

Both are sent out 'to the field'; both report over great cultural distances and so both act, in the felicitous phrase of Clifford Geertz, as 'merchants of astonishment'. Both somehow need to engage with 'the native's point of view' while remaining sufficiently detached to be able to address and appeal to their audiences back home. Both tend to adopt an 'ethnographic present' as part of their long time span perspective of cultural difference. They thus wrestle with similar problems: what to focus on; and how to mediate to their audiences the foreignness of what they learn.

An anthropologist by training who then worked as a copywriter in Japan's second largest advertising agency, Hakuhodo, for thirteen years starts off the third part of the book. Here the focus is on advertising. John McCreery's position is that we should never be fooled by the smooth accounts of how ad campaigns are conceived and executed, since these are basically little more than PR exercises by those concerned (for example, Ogilvy 1985; Ivy 1995). As William Mazzarella also shows in his discussion of the launch of the KamaSutra premium brand of condom in Bombay in the autumn of 1991, ad campaigns do not develop with the sort of polished smoothness suggested by the likes of David Ogilvy and Fujioka Wakao (Ivy's informant). Rather, advertising is what McCreery aptly calls 'a messy muddle' of industrial, artistic and business processes, which include corporate politics and frequently tense interpersonal relations (see also Moeran 1996a:133–168). It is these *processes* that influence the final form of the advertising *product*.

One criticism arising from this shift in emphasis is that, too often, those writing about advertisements establish what Mazzarella calls a '*cordon sanitaire*' between the ad world and its products. In this respect, semiotic analysis is insufficient in itself unless it becomes part of the social world in which advertising is dreamed up, created, produced, sold (firstly to the client), distributed, and publicized. At the same time, the kind of fine-grained attention to advertising practice espoused by McCreery and Mazzarella militates, as the latter points out, against our continuing to see the advertising industry or those who work therein as merely reflecting 'underlying ideological interests'. On the one hand, as McCreery makes clear, advertising is a culture industry in which no single person can ever know all that goes into producing a single campaign – especially when the client itself is a large organization and fields a number of different people from different divisions, with different organizational interests, agenda, and personalities all brought to bear on each step in the production of an ad campaign. On the other, as Mark Hobart shows in his analysis of Balinese villagers reacting to advertising on television, different people have different acquired skills and competences that each employs variously in the process of reception of particular media productions.

The kind of anthropological fieldwork carried out by these authors and others (see, for example, Moeran 1996a; Miller 1997; and, from a slightly different perspective, Lien 1997), then, indirectly addresses a major issue of power relations both within and between media and their clients. Informants' practices and motivations may be shown to be complex, but – as Mazzarella points out and as is also clear in my own chapter on how an advertising agency gets involved in cultural promotions – this does not alter the fact that they also 'tend to reproduce certain troubling relations of power' which need to be teased out and analysed. This is one of the points made by Hobart who looks at how audiences are affected by media and argues that their intellectual practices reveal 'subtle ways of understanding how advertising works and how people are implicated in contemporary mass media'. His analysis reinforces the point that the reception of media productions is a skilled accomplishment that 'depends on a range of acquired skills and competences which individuals employ in the process of reception' (Thompson 1995:40). He thus stresses the importance of seeing audiences as agents who use media to reflect upon and change their lives. It is in this sense that media reception itself becomes a production.

There are several nice touches in this chapter that should make the alert reader pause to reflect. The fact that Balinese villagers argue forcefully, and with great coherence, that images are not as important as words in television commercials because 'words ... tell you the significance of what you have seen', runs contrary to almost anything written or said these days about visual images by those in the media and academic industries. At the same time, though, we should recognize that two of the more articulate informants are themselves media performers (actors) for whom language is vital. Maybe this is why their sophisticated disquisition on advertising's seduction – the requirement that viewers collaborate in such seduction which, with desire, is 'a product of a relationship between image, object, occasion, inclination, means and decision, the willing of an act' – places them in a position broadly similar to Baudrillard's analysis of consumption, as well as within a broader, complex dialogue that brings in notions of excess, intoxication and disappointment.

The final part of the book is concerned with the collapsing of distinction between producers and consumers in Asian – specifically Japanese – media productions. Carolyn Stevens and Shuhei Hosokawa examine the content of Japanese music variety programmes over a 40 year period between 1958 and 1998 and show how there have been various shifts in production processes that themselves symbolize broader social changes in the consumption of music in that country. From comparative freedom in programming in the 1960s, television stations soon developed marked territorial lines between professional entertainers, amateurs, and audiences. These were, however, gradually broken down in the 80s and 90s, partly as a result of a shift in television's power structure effected by artists who were able to produce their own music and control their business activities without station interference.

The rise in the power of the performer was marked by a decline in the popularity of music shows which also had to cope with the fact that, on the one hand, its music stars were no longer supported by the visual effect of seven-inch record covers after the introduction of three inch compact discs, while, on the other, its audiences were more inclined themselves to sing, rather than merely listen to, pop songs thanks to the boom in *karaoke*. The new strategy developed in music variety shows was the introduction of the MC, a non-musical participant who made use of personality, banter, surprise and informality to unnerve celebrity guests and control the progamme's discourse. As a result, pop musicians found themselves not just singing, but participating in (frequently unnerving) talk shows where their private lives would often be held up for all to see. This programming strategy has effectively broken down the distance between stars and audiences, as the former are 'humanized' and the latter permitted glimpses into the 'backstage' of 'unrehearsed reality', thereby learning to domesticate celebrity identity and to discriminate between artists through their talk, rather than just their songs.

In a parallel piece on the production and consumption of *manzai* stand-up comedy in Japan, Joel Stocker outlines the strategies by which a production company, Yoshimoto Kōgyō, seeks to maintain control over its productions in the face of competition from media conglomerates. Stocker argues that production and consumption are mutually determined and shows how, as part of its activities, Yoshimoto has developed an extremely popular manzai comedy school, together with supporting theatres and performance venues, where people from all over the Kansai region can come to learn how to be comedians and, just possibly, themselves become famous. Just as young women have been involved both as music stars and as consumers of popular music through television programming (which is itself intricately linked to the pop music industry), so is manzai comedy produced and listened to by young people (mainly coming from the Osaka-Kansai region). Both groups (the latter containing a high percentage, but not majority, of women) refuse to be manipulated by the media, but instead actively participate in constructing the 'game' that is being played. Indeed, some of the most popular manzai comedians direct their cynicism at the very entertainment industry in which they work, while, for their part, manzai fans practise a perceived street-smart, fast-talking comedian lifestyle in the streets of downtown Osaka.

Nevertheless, performers still act as mediators between corporate sponsors (who pay for the programmes in which they appear and achieve their fame) and consumers, presenting the 'human face' of corporate Japan – a position also adopted by advertising agencies involved in promoting cultural activities and events on behalf of sponsors and media organizations. Here we find a layered 'intertext of promotion' (Wernick 1991:95) in which one media message gets fused with another, and there is continual cross-referencing among different media as a result of an agency's or production company's interventions. Thus, a comedy duo that makes its name as a manzai team becomes the star MC on a television variety music show. Both television and Yoshimoto programmes are examples of total entertainment and commercial packaging, in which – ideally – there should be a blurring of media genres, so that commercials become fragmented music videos, videos commercials, programme contents linked to sponsors' products, and every star appearance an opportunity to promote a carefully constructed image. Media productions are packages which both control and meet audience expectations.

The underlying purpose of such promotional activities, I argue in the final chapter of this book, is strategic. Advertising agencies put on Italian opera, create animated cartoons, or help run the Paris-Dhakar rally in order to create and cement business ties with their client and media organizations. On the one hand, there are the obvious marketing benefits that accrue from successful promotions – merchandizing rights, for example, or new information on consumer tastes that can be used for other accounts or promotional ideas. On the other, there is the careful cultivation of client contacts in the hope that these will lead to new and bigger accounts, which will allow an agency to cement its contacts with media organizations that may themselves, as a result, put it in touch with new clients. Promotional activities thus afford participants the possibility of an endless cycle of profitable business partnerships and the building of cultural, and thus economic, capital.

The Field of Media Productions

At the beginning of this Introduction, I explained how and why 'productions' was a key word in the book's title. My aim is not to privilege production in the sense in which it has been used by Adorno, Horkheimer and early British Cultural Studies (Williams 1977:136), but to show that different stages in the circuit of culture comprising production, circulation, representation and consumption are all 'equally important and *related* through the ways in which products are circulated and given particular meanings via the range of production-consumption relationships' (Negus 1997:69–70). This stance is still, perhaps, a little unusual. In discussing cultural studies, Keith Negus (1997:69) has argued that there has been 'a broad theoretical shift from approaching the production of culture through a *macro* perspective which stresses social and organizational *structures* and *economic* relationships, towards a more *micro* approach which focuses on everyday human *agency* and the making of *cultural* meanings'. This shift has been important because it has helped scholars question economic determinism, although it has tended to leave out an approach to media production which looks at everyday human agency and the creation of cultural meanings in media forms. Ironically, the fact that many of those working on media recently have tended to focus on the (micro-)reception rather than the production of symbolic forms neatly dovetails with the structured break that is seen to exist (Thompson 1995:29) between the separate contexts of production and reception in mass communication generally. Yet it is in the staging of choices and selections for consumption that the power of media exists, so that it is in this area of what Hobart's Balinese informants would call 'refined coercion' that we need in-depth ethnographies of culture industries.

In the rest of this Introduction, therefore, I want to try to bring these separate contexts back together, by looking at the ways in which media organizations function within their own particular industry structure, as well as at the part they play in other industries' structures, since the operations of 'media worlds' directly and indirectly affect their productions. That is to say, like the society of which it forms a part, the media industry establishes structural possibilities for action within the bounds of such paired concepts as freedom and constraint, and innovation and procedure. By examining media organizations as part of an overall structure or series of structures in one or more 'fields', we can move beyond economic determinism to grasp the full extent of their structural power. According to Lull (1995:174), there are three fundamental axioms to be accounted for in studies of the media: structure, which he sees as unfixed and non-determining (a point to which I shall return); social actors, who interpret and use the symbolic environment to their own ends; and the symbolic and polysemic messages themselves. He argues, further, that 'any creditable theory of the media' must somehow account for two contradictory forces: one, the way in which a society's political-economic-cultural elite articulates ideological and cultural structures; the other, how individual persons and subgroups construct meanings, identities and ways of living from what they read, see and hear in media forms (Lull 1995:165).

Although Lull suggests that the most helpful approach in addressing this dilemma is that of Anthony Giddens's structuration theory,[4] I myself believe that we might usefully adapt Pierre Bourdieu's theory of cultural production to the field of media since Bourdieu's ideas are, in the long run I think, more flexible and illuminating than those of Giddens (who does not appear interested in either media or cultural production).[5]

As I see it, a multidisciplinary media cultural studies should establish the external conditions for a system of social relations of production, distribution, representation and consumption. It should also find out what functional rules characterize the field of social relations (the importance attributed in many Asian media industries, for example, to the cultivation of contacts), while accounting for the structure of corresponding media productions and its transformations (which then depend more on those interpersonal relations among contacts than on 'professional' criteria of objectivity, quality, and so on). Nevertheless, different groups of media producers competing for cultural legitimacy make use of certain 'objectively' defined principles of 'selection' (hard work, trust, goodwill, and so on) that are in fact always defined within a system of social relations obeying a certain logic.

In short, as with cultural production more generally, media productions constitute a field that consists both of positions and position-takings, which are closely related to corporate, as well as individual, actors' habitus and dispositions. Positions offered to and adopted by participants in media productions include choices between commercial and highbrow, documentary and infotainment, the market and creativity, consecrated and untried, and so on. Advertising agencies, for example, approach particular sponsors and media organizations who are known to be disposed towards one kind of television programme or another kind of cultural event, and so encourage institutional

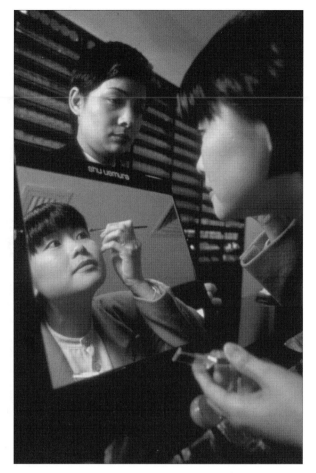

Figure 2 Japanese cosmetic shop in Hong Kong.
(Photo courtesy of Dermot Tatlow)

homology around certain cultural forms. A brewery by its very position in the field is unlikely to support an animated cartoon film for children; a toy manufacturer is hardly going to be persuaded to finance a performance of Italian opera. At the same time, an agency, as well as bringing different fields together, operates within its own field, offering a package that it knows will not or cannot be offered by rival intermediaries, to an advertiser who, by accepting that it is 'right' for the package, consolidates the position that it has already taken in the field of media production. An oil company will thus sponsor a series of documentaries on the environment (and not on the history of the Pacific War) that is televised by a station or network known to be 'serious', and offered to it by an agency commonly admired for being 'intellectual'.

In other words, within this system of social relations of production, distribution, circulation, representation and consumption as a whole, there are the positions that are *actually* taken at a given moment of production – very often as a result of the power relations that exist among those involved – and those that *could possibly* be taken within the field. As I have tried to show above, positions are not taken haphazardly. Rather, people and organizations take their positions intentionally and strategically according to a structure of differentiation that operates both within and across multiple fields. Interaction among those occupying particular positions – as among those participating in a French post-election television debate analysed by Bourdieu (Bourdieu and Wacquant 1992:255–60) – is affected by the intersection of the hierarchized fields of which they may also be members.

Every new position actually adopted in some way displaces the structure as a whole and so leads to concomitant changes in the positions taken by others in the field – a point exemplified by Stevens's and Hosokawa's discussion of changes in the production of Japanese music variety shows over the past 40 years. As I have shown in my discussion of advertising in Japan (see Moeran 1996a:285–6), position-takings arise quasi-mechanically, but they are nonetheless – or, as a result – defined and determined relationally and negatively by what the others are (*the* most basic principle of structural linguistics and marketing). In advertising, for example, products are given qualities that other similar products do *not* have, in order to differentiate them from their 'rivals'. Similarly, different newspapers present a different 'face' and different television stations produce different programmes (although inevitably worked out along the same structured formulae: soaps, quiz shows, talk shows, cops and robbers, and so on) in order to mark them out as 'different' from their competitors.[6] As Kellner (1995:40) says, 'difference sells'.

Let me illustrate this general theoretical point with an example from Japan. The field of media productions that I will outline here is that of advertising although, as will soon become clear, this is closely tied to related media fields of television, magazine and book publishing, as well as to other industry fields such as toy manufacturing. The advertising agency in which I conducted my own research was founded in March 1956, four years after the first independent television license was issued by the Japanese government, and three years before Japan's first television network (JNN) was set up. Precisely because the new agency was a comparative late-comer to the advertising scene, it was unable to gain ready access to the then lucrative newspaper advertising space that was more or less monopolized by older, established agencies like Hakuhodo and Dentsu. As a result, it had to look elsewhere for business in order to succeed and, since its senior founding member had previously worked in a large publishing house, he made use of connections established in the publishing industry to help his Agency buy advertising space in weekly and monthly magazines.

Magazine advertising as such, however, did not occupy a particularly large slice of the national advertising cake; nor was it particularly profitable. This meant that, in order to survive, the Agency needed to find a way of getting round the stranglehold exerted by the large, firmly entrenched agencies that had been in business since around the turn of the century and had, as a result, built up seemingly impregnable networks of personal communication with those selling advertising in the main medium of newspapers. The increasing popularity and obvious potential of the new medium of television provided the upstart agency with the opportunity it sought, since commercial television stations were desperate for programme ideas that would attract both sponsors and audiences and established agencies were for the most part reluctant to invest in a new medium when they were living comfortably off the old ones.

The Agency's present success (it is now among the top ten largest agencies in Japan) hinged on its seeing a link between the new medium of television and the old one of magazines which were beginning to be its strength at the time. In 1964, it dreamed up the idea of transforming printed comics into animation films and televised the manga series, *Eightman*, which immediately drew more than 30 per cent audience ratings. In 1966, it televised *Super Jetter*, simultaneously arranging for serial rights in a children's comic magazine (it had previously been in book form only), and for merchandising rights. Three years later, it transformed a drama about baseball, *Kyojin no Hoshi*, into an animation series that drew the highest annual ratings of all television programmes for the next three years. By 1973 it was creating its own animation series – for example, *Majinger Z*, which fuelled a long-term 'robot boom' among young children in Japan – and these it was then able to sell to publishing houses to be printed in magazines. *Doraemon*, mentioned at the beginning of this Introduction, was first televised in 1980 and is one of the Agency's major success stories.

In establishing a niche market for itself in television and magazine publishing, the Agency was able to enter into business relationships both with major manufacturers anxious to sponsor its animation series and with television stations keen to put on popular new programmes. It soon found that it was able to diversify in its television programming, and that television stations, through their own networks, would then introduce the agency to sponsors that it might not otherwise have been able to reach. Moreover, the fact that the television stations were closely linked to newspapers in terms of investment capital, personnel and news supply (see Westney 1996:60) allowed the Agency to make contacts with personnel in such major publications as the Yomiuri, Asahi and Mainichi newspapers (all of which have their television networks) and so to break the monopoly on space buying hitherto held by Dentsu, Hakuhodo and other large and well-established agencies. Yet, like all other organizations in Japan's advertising industry, and in spite of its growth and diversification, the Agency continues to bear as its distinguishing mark the historical point at which it entered the field. Just as the British fashion industry cannot escape the tag of 'swinging London', so is the Agency, whose activities are now spread far and wide within all aspects of Japan's domestic economy, dubbed the 'cartoon agency'.

As can be seen from this illustration from Japan – and as is clear in a number of papers in this book – a field of media productions is thus a field of strategic possibilities, which contains within it, but goes beyond, the 'population' of organizations and individual people linked therein by their interaction.[7] It is the field as a whole and how it is constituted that together condition the ways in which media forms and messages are produced.

At the same time, as Stevens, Hosokawa and Stocker show in their discussions of music variety shows and a *manzai* comedy production company, there is often a 'structural homology' between the spaces of production and the field of consumers:

> The internal divisions of the field of production are reproduced in an automatically (and to some extent consciously) differentiated supply which meets the automatically (and also consciously) differentiated demands of the various categories of consumers. Thus, ... each class of clients can find products for its taste and each class of producers has some chance of finding consumers for its products, at least in the long run.
>
> (Bourdieu 1993b:143–4)

Thus we can say that there are genres of newspapers, films,[8] television programmes, magazines, pop music 'voices', each of which can be replicated and replaced to enable the cycle of fashion to continue[9] as consumers shift from one media production to another (in Japan, for example, from TV 'noodle western' *Mito Kōmon* to *Abarembō Shōgun*; from young women's fashion magazine *With* to *More*; from *The Seven Samurai* to *The Magnificent Seven*); and from one genre and 'star' to another, whose 'difference' is minimal, but who simultaneously exhibits enough personal difference or 'style' (in clothes, speech, lovelife, and so on) to make him or her stand out in the overall structure of the genre concerned (which itself exists in relation to other genres to form systems of genres [Negus 1998:365]). We need, then, to consider how media productions become manifestations of the field as a whole by taking into account both the producers of the material work and those involved in the production of that work's symbolic meaning (media critics, journalists, academics, and so on).

In other words, for our theory of media production to be 'creditable', we need to develop a multi-layered analysis of its field of strategic possibilities. On the one hand, we must analyse the *values* that media producers (as well as media audiences and critics) bring to bear on a work – values which evolve out of use, technical, social and appreciative constraints, thereby contributing towards the total symbolic and commodity exchange value of a media product, and which are intimately entwined in the social interaction that goes on among those concerned (Moeran 1996a:290–97). For example, as McCreery and Mazzarella show in their analyses of different advertising campaigns, it is the ways in which different personnel – account executive, market analyst, copywriter, art director, product manager, celebrity, photographer, stylist – interact in the creation of a campaign that together permit the final advertising image to become what it becomes and to be received as it is.

At the same time, however, these individuals interact as members of a set of institutions (advertising agency, manufacturer, media organization, marketing consultancy, production company, model agency, fashion house, style shop) which are constantly (re)positioning themselves strategically *vis-à-vis* one another *and vis-à-vis* other similar institutions in the field – as the Agency illustration above reveals, and as I show in my own chapter on how a Tokyo advertising agency promotes cultural events in concert with its clients and in competition with other agencies. We thus find three superimposed layers of production that involve: firstly, the media work itself; secondly, the individual players or actors involved in the production of the media work; and thirdly, the institutions that constitute the structured field of media production. Together these create, fashion, manipulate and maintain an intricate web of symbolic, cultural, social, educational and economic capital discussed by Bourdieu.

So media productions are the culmination of transactions, negotiations, hard bargaining and compromises between those who control the means of production (advertisers, TV stations, publishers), and media producers (ad agencies, production companies, newspapers) who themselves negotiate, bargain and compromise among themselves (account executive, marketer, art director, copywriter) as they go about creating media representation and reception. In all of this there is an in-built element of self-censorship that arises from the knowledge that their products *must* meet the perceived (tried and tested) tastes of their average reader, viewer, or spectator, although at the same time they develop an ideal among themselves that really 'good' works 'create' their own public. Here they find themselves tempted to define the cultural value of their media productions in relation to legitimate 'high' culture, so that media actors often end up borrowing and adapting elements from the latter in their continuous effort for 'effect' (both in the production's form and on its intended audience). We thus find on Japanese, Taiwanese, Hong Kong, Korean and other Asian countries' television, 'period' dramas that re-enact in simplified, readily understood, structured forms the great epics of Asian civilizations which are thereby transformed and baudlerized into 'mass entertainment' – as Lull hints at in his discussion of Disney's *Mulan* in the opening chapter of this book.

Media, Economy and Culture

The field of media production as outlined so far has focussed more on the way in which media organizations operate as economic profit-making businesses than on their ability to accumulate 'cultural capital'.[10] And yet, as in cultural production in general, the accumulation of cultural capital is a crucial element in the field of media production. Large corporations, for example, are eager to convert their economic capital into cultural capital by sponsoring special media events – car rallies, pop concerts, sports of all kinds, art exhibitions – which then

Figure 3 Chingmy Yau in Qing dynasty costume drama, *Royal Tramp*, Part II.
(Photo courtesy of Dermot Tatlow)

enable them to reconvert that capital into further profits. Media organizations, especially newspapers and television stations, themselves participate in and report favourably on such events, thereby accumulating cultural capital for themselves by association both with the events themselves and their participants (stars, athletes, artists), and with the sponsoring organizations (together with other relevant factors like timing, venue, audience attraction, and so on). Advertising agencies and other intermediaries (stadiums, managers, museums, even department stores) also gather cultural capital through their participation in successful events (where success is defined through the mutual interplay between economic and cultural capital). Finally, the system of stardom contributing to and sustaining the events functions, like the system of cultural production, primarily by disavowing the commercial and expressing 'disinterest' in economic capital. There is thus a systematic interplay in the field of media productions between economic and cultural capital (also supplemented, of course, by social capital), so that the field of media – like the field of cultural production in general – creates its own cultural logic and currency which can be converted by recognized rates of exchange into economic capital. In short, 'the characteristics of the commercial enterprise and the characteristics of the cultural exercise, understood as a more or less disavowed relation to the commercial enterprise, are inseparable' (Bourdieu 1986:138).

Now, if the 'economic' and the 'cultural' are hybrid categories, and if it is impossible to divide them absolutely in what amounts to a 'cultural economy' (du Gay 1997:3), then we need to beware of simply *reducing* media productions to an economy of media. As Ang (1996:32) has argued: 'the conflation of commercialism as an economic principle of production, which is utterly capitalistic, with commercialism as a cultural system of producing goods for consumption, which certainly has connections with the popular', has tended to obscure debates about media (in her example, commercial television). The advantage of Bourdieu's approach, therefore, is that it allows us to recognize the autonomy of particular practices, operating in a way that is *like* an economy, within a particular field which contains its own 'internal dynamic, structuring principle and processes' (Featherstone 1991:87). Moreover, although each social field constitutes a system in which each particular element takes on values (in the Saussurean sense) from its position *vis-à-vis* other elements, Bourdieu moves beyond structure as such to examine the *processes* by which elements change both their meanings and positions over time (Featherstone 1991:88).

In media as in art, the interplay between the 'commercial' and the 'non-commercial' reappears in many places. For example, a Hong Kong magazine's editorial department may believe that it should be 'free' to publish 'what the public wants', but often finds itself at loggerheads with staff of its advertising department which is attuned more to the needs of the publisher's corporate clients than to the magazine's readers. This interplay is a principle which helps generate many of the judgements that we make about media productions. It is also, as Bourdieu points out, an opposition between small- and large-scale production: between where emphasis is placed on qualitative aspects of production itself (for example, the 'creative shops' in the advertising industry) and where it is placed on marketing, audiences, sales and other quantitatively measurable gauges of success (the J. Walter Thompson approach to advertising in days gone by).

The commercial/non-commercial principle is most obvious in television industries which, as in Japan, are structured according to the British model, with government license and commercial channels – each of which, as MacLachlan shows, has a different approach to programming and news content. But it is also sustained in the way in which people talk about media organizations. In Japan, for example, the first ranking advertising agency, Dentsu, is known as 'power relations' (*chikara no aru jinmyaku*); while its immediate rivals, Hakuhodo and Asatsu-Daiko are called the 'intelligent' and 'human' agencies by those working in the advertising and media industries. Similarly, the largest selling newspaper in the world, the *Yomiuri Shinbun*, is seen to be a commercial giant while its main competitor, the *Asahi Shinbun*, is looked upon as a highbrow, intellectual, slightly left-of-centre publication.[11]

Media organizations, then, struggle with one another to dominate the field of production and the market by means of the successful accumulation of economic and cultural capital. This is the whole point of the promotional strategies devised by the advertising agency in which I conducted my own research, as it seeks to

31

alter power relations between itself and its clients, on the one hand, and between itself and other agencies, on the other. Its strategies can be seen to be aggressive since it wishes to upset the rankings of an industry dominated by the world's largest advertising agency, Dentsu, and supported by the 'intelligent' agency, Hakuhodo (where McCreery used to work). The latter's tactics can be seen to be defensive in that they wish to maintain their dominant positions. For its part, 'my' Agency is concerned only to overturn the hierarchy, not to disturb the principles upon which the field of advertising itself rests (cf. Bourdieu 1993a:83).

As Mazzarella shows in his discussion of the creation of the KamaSutra condom advertising campaign in India, media are concerned with the production of 'universes of belief'. For this 'a vast operation of social alchemy' (Bourdieu 1993a:81) is required among all those involved: ad agency personnel, model, photographer and management of the client organization. This social alchemy functions at both individual and institutional levels which simultaneously produce media products and the need for such productions. Those involved do not necessarily deny the ordinary practices of the economy – as in Bourdieu's description of art production – but they may well try to lessen the force of such practices by means of various PR practices. Thus, as mentioned above and as I show in my own chapter on promotional culture in Japan, a brewery may sponsor a cultural event (opera, football game, art exhibition) to 'celebrate' its centenery (half century, seventieth year from founding, or whatever), while simultaneously hoping that the money spent will in fact boost product sales. Here the sponsor relies on the public's inability to perceive – or its willingness to ignore, accept and affirm – the 'non-commercial' activities in which it is involved and so permit the culture-image-profit-culture cycle to continue.

In some respects, media can also be said to act as cultural businesses and to consecrate their productions (in much the same way that an art dealer 'discovers' a painter, or a publisher an author). This is particularly the case, perhaps, with their use of celebrities, for whom media act as 'symbolic bankers' and so enter into what Bourdieu (1986:133) calls a 'cycle of consecration'. Here, we need to consider those educational institutions that produce agents – singers, comedians, talk show hosts – capable of renewing the field, as well as those that ensure the production of competent consumers (a major role of media organizations themselves). Occasionally, as with the comedian production company discussed by Stocker, a single institution enables such cultural consecration by providing people with the 'proper' cultivated disposition to produce *and* consume a particular media form in the field.

Such institutions of consecration, however, are often themselves consecrated by the media – either in a general way, by means of documentaries and discussions of the institutions concerned, or in particular consecration events (such as the success of mainland Chinese artists at a Venice Biennale, the Asian Youth Orchestra's concert season, or the announcement of entrance examination results at Tokyo University). But, importantly, the media also consecrate their

32

Figure 4 Miss Chinese International Beauty Pageant.
(Photo courtesy of Dermot Tatlow)

own fields of cultural production (the Oscars, the Grammy awards, the Hong Kong Young Designers' Contest, the Miss Chinese International Beauty Pageant, the Golden Horse Film Festival in Taipei, and so on), and thereby bring a relatively limited field of production (film, popular music, fashion) to the attention of a large number of people not normally or consciously involved in the producers' world. In this way, media consecration rites establish the symbolic power of the field as a whole in cultural production, and create a potentially larger market for the particular field concerned, thereby shifting it from (relative) restriction to large-scale production.

At the same time, such rites have a temporal function (which emphasizes their symbolic power) since media are able to record and instantaneously diffuse images of the *instant* of consecration. For this they generally need to provide – in the role of 'your host for tonight' – the equivalent of the education system's lector teacher (Bourdieu 1993a:134): people who 'explain' the events, the people involved, their backgrounds, details of past events, or even – as Stevens and Hosokawa relate – take centre stage and mercilessly make fun of their guests. It is they who are physically present at the customary opening of the Oscar envelope, followed by the joyful 'And the winner is . . .'; they who calculate the points required by the last finalist if she is to be crowned 'Miss Asia'; they who intone a description of the lowering of the British and raising of the Chinese flags to mark the ceremonial handover of Hong Kong on July 1, 1997. Because they become themselves celebrities by assimilation, consecrated by their roles in each climactic rite of consecration, such media people need to be carefully selected and vetted for their positions.

In some respects, then, the media perform for the field of (large-scale) cultural production as a whole the same consecrating role that the education system performs for the field of limited production (Bourdieu 1993a:123). The difference between them lies in the virtual *simultaneity* of production and consecration. Whereas training and education systems create a time-lag between cultural production and (scholastic) consecration – Shakespeare was, after all, one of the great unknowns for more than 200 years after his death – media offer almost simultaneous recognition of productions since their consecratory events occur regularly at fixed times every year. Moreover, they are staggered during a 'season' to ensure that there is virtually no overlap among different cultural fields, while re-enforcing the overall symbolic power of media production itself: Grammy and Academy Awards; Miss Universe, Miss Asia, even, once, a Miss Tibet; Cannes, Tokyo, Manila, Taipei Film Festivals; Paris, Tokyo, Seoul, Hong Kong Fashion Shows.

Coda

In this Introduction, I have tried to outline what I see as some of the more salient issues and difficulties faced by all of us who are interested in doing research on Asian media, as well as to hint at problems and possibilities underlying a media cultural studies made up primarily of the disciplines of sociology, anthropology and cultural studies. Some of the problems are terminological. What do we mean when we use words like 'Asia' or 'productions'? Others are more methodological. How best, for example, can we encapsulate and theorize Asian media productions?

In answer, I have suggested that we need to recognize the plurality of Asia, as well as of its media productions and of the disciplinary theories that we bring to bear on their study. I have argued, moreover, that precisely because of the plurality of media productions we need to do our research by means of grounded ethnography, which itself should be the fundamental feature common to all of us working in our different disciplines. Although I have suggested that American, Australian, Canadian and European research on Asian media productions, together with a crucial input from Asian scholars, may well together encourage us to rethink what has hitherto been primarily western-oriented theorizing about media, I have in fact made use of Pierre Bourdieu's insights into cultural production and applied some of these – albeit inadequately – to the field of Asian media productions by providing an illustration of the field of Japanese advertising and one agency's position and strategy therein. At the same time, I have highlighted the interplay between economic and cultural processes in the field of media productions, as well as the rites of consecration that characterize it. I realize that I have only just begun to scratch at the surface of what is an extremely complex set of issues surrounding the production, marketing, reception and contents of Asian advertising and media, but hope that others will find the ideas expressed here interesting enough to develop further. The show, as they say, must go on.

Notes

1 This kind of approach has been variously labelled: Appadurai (1996) talks about 'ethnographic cosmopolitanism', 'cosmopolitan ethnography' and 'macro-ethnography'; Augé (1995:75ff.), who provides a useful background discussion of the distinctions between place and non-place, place and space, landscape and gaze, word and world made so much of by Appadurai, prefers an 'anthropology of super-modernity'.

2 In Japan, for example, see Inoue et al. (1989); Ōtsuka (1991); and Skov and Moeran (1995).

3 Ghai (1998:20–1) argues, incidentally, that it was the end of the cold war that prompted the rise of 'Asian values' as a political doctrine.

4 Although Lull (1995:169) believes that structuration theory is well suited to his ideas about media, communication and culture, he cites examples that are all 'agency' oriented (how audiences react to and cope with ideology and hegemony) and does not, in my opinion, demonstrate the workings of the media industry's 'structure' (in terms of interlocking media organizations and their everyday operating methods) other than in a discussion of ideology, consciousness and hegemony.

5 In the following paragraphs, I have relied on Bourdieu (1986; 1993a) for my arguments. In some cases I have quoted directly from his work, but substituted the words 'media' for 'cultural' and 'media productions' for 'art works', 'cultural productions' and so on.

6 It is for this reason that those analyzing media products for their symbolic and ideological content should ensure that they do not see them as isolated works but contextualize them within the particular genre in which they are produced and distributed.

7 This is where Bourdieu (1993a:35) differs from Howard Becker (1982) who proposed the idea of 'artworld' in his discussion of cultural production. I myself have tried to develop Becker's ideas in my discussion of the production, appreciation, marketing and consumption of Japanese folk art and suggested that we apply them – together with a 'political economy of values' (see also Moeran 1996a:290–97) – to any aspect of culture that we link with notions of beauty or taste (Moeran 1997:217).

8 As shown by Kellner (1995:101–122), for example, in his discussion of a range of (anti)war and (anti)feminist Hollywood films.

9 The temptation here is to refer to Lipovetsky's (1994) – itself fashionable – argument that fashion has taken over the economy of consumer society by reorganizing mass production and consumption according to the laws of obsolescence, seduction and diversification. There are, however, so many flaws and contradictions in his argument, as well as a blithe ignorance of any history outside Europe and America, that I prefer to relegate this particular Frenchman to a footnote.

10 In this respect, I have hopefully bucked the anthropological trend 'to develop cultural points of view toward the economy, but hardly economic points of view toward cultural processes' (Hannerz 1992:101).

11 Similarly, Japan's largest department store, Mitsukoshi, represents 'money and tradition', and its competitors, Takashimaya and Seibu, 'tradition and culture' and 'youth and culture' respectively.

Part I

Asian Media Flows

Figure 5 Hong Kong film superstar, Chow Yun-Fat, in
another gangster shoot-out
(Photo courtesy of Dermot Tatlow)

1

GLOBAL CULTURAL POLITICS AND ASIAN CIVILIZATIONS

James Lull

The storyline of one of the most important films in the history of Chinese cinema, Chen Kaige's *Yellow Earth*, features a young soldier from the People's Liberation Army trekking through the hinterlands of the northern provinces in the late 1930s in search of folk songs from various rural regions. His job was to bring the traditional melodies and lyrics back to his commanding officers so that the peasants' songs could be transformed into popular tunes praising the communist revolution. The songs were then used as a vital part of the revolutionary force's national propaganda campaign. Set in a desolate mountain village, the movie also revealed the miserable conditions in which Chinese peasants lived at the time, and still do in some areas today. This masterpiece of China's fifth generation of filmmakers, and the first of the Chinese 'new wave' films, was extremely controversial when it was released in 1985. Abstract, open-ended, and deeply metaphorical, *Yellow Earth* did not follow the didactic format typical of Chinese cinema after 1949. Chinese cultural authorities thus wondered about director Chen's intentions and about the audience's response. Is *Yellow Earth* a heroic or tragic story? A tale of progress or backwardness? Whose purposes are served by the film, the Communist Party or the Party's critics?

Complex symbolic forms such as *Yellow Earth* together with a host of mass media and personal communication technologies exploded onto the world stage in the second half of the twentieth century in ways that have captured the attention of cultural observers everywhere. Film, television, popular music, satellite broadcasting, fax machines, e-mail, cellular phones, and the internet have changed social and cultural realities on a global scale. The rapid proliferation of mediated symbolic displays makes cultural options far more diverse, multiple, and contradictory than ever before. Unprecedented access to mass and micro communication technologies and the robust symbolic spheres those technologies embrace and promote encourage the social construction of new and modified cultural visions, lifestyles, and identities. And as the Chinese cultural authorities have discovered trying to manage their film and television industries since the modernization plan began in 1979, social communication today is not easily supervised or contained. It is within this context of dynamic and indeterminate global communications activity and cultural flexing that Asian media and advertising now develop and interact.

Analyses of communications technology and the symbolic forms they produce and circulate of course must be situated in broader discussions of ideology, economics, politics, and culture. With respect to Asia or any other part of the world, we must look at current cultural developments simultaneously from multiple vantage points. There are national considerations to be sure, but the nature of contemporary cultural activity requires that global, civilizational, regional, and personal spheres be considered as well. The discourses of postmodernity and globalization can help stimulate this multidimensional reflection. We do indeed witness the breaking apart of signs from their original locations and meanings, an increasing capacity to instantly transmit messages globally, and a tendency for certain cultural themes to appear everywhere. At the same time the lived realities of cultural life are becoming more diverse, fragmented, private, and hedonistic, in relative ways, across the social classes. In key respects, culture has been transformed as a social construct away from relatively general and received 'ways of life' to more diverse and constructed designer cultures and 'lifestyles' (Chaney 1996). At the same time, however, the discursive and lived dimensions of culture as a unifying force also serve the intensified needs of some social collectivities. Both these tendencies – toward cultural privatization and collectivization – are enhanced by the ever-widening circulation that communication technologies give symbolic forms. In this chapter, I will address key elements of this contemporary cultural complexity, using developments from Asia to exemplify how some of these processes unfold.

Global Cultural Politics

> Somewhere in the Middle East a half dozen young men could well be dressed in jeans, drinking Coke, listening to rap, and, between their bows to Mecca, be putting together a bomb to blow up an American airliner.
>
> Huntington (1996:58)

Clearly one of the most influential recent theories of how the world's populations are organized and interact is offered by Samuel Huntington in his book, *The Clash of Civilizations and the Remaking of World Order* (1996). Huntington makes two particular arguments that pertain to any analysis of Asian media and advertising. The first of these is that the west no longer dominates the world in politics, economics, and culture the way it once did. The west will watch its influence over world resources continue to drop, a development that began in the 1930s. By 2020, western nations will represent or manage only ten per cent of the world's population (down from 48 per cent a hundred years before), control but 30 per cent of global economic production (down from 70 per cent), 25 per cent of manufacturing output (down from 84 per cent), and less than ten per cent of world military manpower (down from 45 per cent), according to Huntington

(1996:90–1). The continued rise of China, India and the Muslim world as global powers will largely define culture and politics in the twenty-first century.

Huntington's other claim of interest to us here is that the world can be divided into nine 'civilizations', which he argues forms the ultimate cultural classification system. At least six civilizations – Sinic, Buddhist, Islam, Hindu, Japanese, and Western – exist in Asia. He believes that civilizational liasons and differences will determine the future of global human relations: 'We are witnessing "the end of the progressive era" dominated by western ideologies and are moving into an era in which multiple and diverse civilizations will interact, compete, coexist, and accommodate each other' (Huntington 1996:95). I will use Huntington's provocative theses to frame this brief commentary on global developments in Asian communication and culture.

Let's first take up the claim that the west no longer dominates world politics, economics, and culture the way it once did. It certainly makes good sense to reject any view that implies global communication can be reduced to some giant stimulus-response relationship wherein the west inevitably dominates and transforms the rest in all manner of social and cultural life. This is not to say that western nations have not benefited from their exploits over the past 500 years. Clearly they have. But the terms of social and cultural power have become less clear or determined in today's 'communication age' so rich in technology and symbolism. The main reason for this is that two fundamental characteristics of culture – its constant evolution, and its synthetic nature – are fed nutritiously like never before by current practices in global communication. Political, economic, and coercive power no longer dominate as social forces the same way they did years ago. Traditional forms of influence have been joined by 'symbolic power' – the use of symbolic forms to shape actions and events – and situated uses of symbolic forms and discourses for personal and social purposes in specific historiocultural contexts (Lull 2000).

Global popular cultures strikingly reflect the cultural metamorphoses and transformations of social influence that are now underway. Perhaps the most visible and criticized symbol of global popular culture is the McDonald's restaurant chain. One scholar even uses McDonald's as the paradigmatic instance to argue that a western concept – fast food – and an ensemble of specific culinary products can combine to *cause* significant negative cultural changes. The author refers to this alleged cultural subversion as *The McDonaldization of Society* (Ritzer 1993). Such an argument may appeal at surface level, not least because some intellectuals like to use McDonald's to represent what their personal taste (and class) is *not*. A more careful analysis, however, reveals that no hamburger hegemony exists (and that the children of these scholars, if not many of the scholars themselves, actually love Big Macs and those skinny, salty french fries). No doubt eating at McDonald's is a western-style cultural experience, but that does not make it exploitative, corrupting, or unhealthy. To reduce the discussion of global cultural influence by simply attacking a popular restaurant chain does little to explain what's going on. Even worse, the simplistic argument misleads.

41

A more insightful look at global McDonald's is the edited text of James L. Watson, *Golden Arches East: McDonald's in East Asia* (1997). Contributors to this book analyze the techniques of McDonald's commercial food production, the expansion of the franchise into Japan, Taiwan, Hong Kong, South Korea, and the People's Republic of China, and most important, the reception of McDonald's by consumers in those cultures. Watson concludes that East Asian cultures have not been victimized by this culinary nuance, but instead have accommodated, indigenized, and generally enjoyed it. The way this has happened reflects a much larger issue than 'fast food coming from America'. It gives empirical evidence for understanding the complexity of contemporary cultural activity in the 'global ecumene' (Hannerz 1992, 1996). Why wouldn't McDonald's be successful in Asia? Are the world's peoples bound to eat the same food, and take it in the same way as their parents and grandparents? Should we expect cultures to be so static?

Watson thinks not: 'Culture is not something that people inherit as an undifferentiated bloc of knowledge from their ancestors. Culture is a set of ideas, reactions, and expectations that is constantly changing as people and groups themselves change' (Watson 1997:8). Culture has always been organic and dynamic, but today's global flow of people and artifacts of all kinds demands that the organic quality of life become more differentiated, and that the changes will come and go more quickly than ever before. The McDonald's phenomenon should thus be viewed as part of a relatively fast-paced 'revolution in family values that has transformed east Asia' (Watson 1997:8), a profound change that has been complemented, but not caused by western popular culture. McDonald's therefore may indeed be a paradigmatic case, but it is one of global cultural change, not subversion. The phenomenal success of the hamburger franchise speaks loudly and clearly of its far-ranging appeal and acceptance.

Let's broaden our discussion of the cultural consequences of postmodernity and globalization. Along with McDonald's, we'll bring into consideration another common target of critical inquiry – the Disney Corporation. In the summer of 1998, one of McDonald's biggest promotions in the United States and around the world was a marketing tie-in between its 'Happy Meals' and the Disney animated film, *Mulan.* We can use this combination of popular culture elements to describe key aspects of how various forms of influence are constructed in the global play of economic and cultural forces.

Hollywood films, television programs, computer software, popular music and nearly every type of popular culture originating from the United States or any developed nation operates with the assumptions of a global market. This practice understandably has alarmed some observers – scholars, journalists, and tourists among them – who have noted the increasing presence of western, especially American, pop culture iconography in foreign countries (often in expensive hotels, restaurants, and shopping areas) and quickly draw negative conclusions about the influence they believe such materials have. Like McDonald's, Disney has been an easy, frequent target of critics. A classic example of the typical criticism is a book by Ariel Dorfman and Armand Mattelart (1972), a commentary on the supposed devastating effects that Disney comic books and other media forms have wrought in South America. Many other books which promote this 'cultural imperialism' view of the global political economy could be cited here. A poignant and necessary critique of the cultural imperialism perspective is John Tomlinson's work (1991, 1999).

But let's return to Disney and the film *Mulan*. Based on a centuries-old Chinese fable, overall *Mulan* promotes Chinese culture positively to a global audience. At the same time, however, the production is extremely critical of some Chinese traditions. The heroic lead character, Mulan, is a young woman who disgraces her family because she inspires little hope for marriage. When China is threatened by a Han invasion, Mulan disguises herself as a man in order to join the Imperial Army and defend her people. After many exciting battles of wits and weapons, Mulan heroically defeats the enemy nearly single-handedly and wins great respect and admiration from her fellow soldiers and countrymen and women, who in the end discover she is a female. Ultimately, Mulan brings great honor to her family, all the while deflecting attention away from her personal achievements.

Chinese paternalism takes a serious hit in the process. But not only that. Mulan's constant companion in the action-filled, animated drama is a small and mischievous red dragon who, the story goes, had been deemed incompetent by Mulan's family ancestors to be their guardian. To the certain surprise of Chinese historians and folklorists, and probably to the dismay of many ethnic Chinese parents all over the world who brought their children to see the film, the voice and personality of the little red dragon is played by Eddie Murphy, a black American comedian-actor still best-known for obscenity-laced, racially-explosive humor and a stereotyped in-your-face urban black 'attitude'. The little anti-hero dragon doesn't utter expletives in *Mulan,* but he does chatter incessantly in exaggerated street slang with a distinct black accent. He is rewarded for his loyalty and daring at the end of the movie when Mulan kisses him while ignoring the handsome Chinese lead male character.

This Disney production makes strong statements that problematize gender, culture, race, and family. Some of the statements reinforce traditional Chinese culture, others contradict and ridicule it. Lots of anti-social cinematic clichés are used too, presumably to keep the attention of the young audience. Children in attendance on the day I saw the film – about half of them apparently of Asian descent – laughed heartily at the many pratfalls and visual depictions of action-packed violence. Stereotypes are everywhere in *Mulan*. The feared invading enemy, for instance, is shown in the form of dark-skinned predators. Physical exaggerations such as excessively slanting eyes and slumping shoulders permeate the animation. In the end, Mulan's cross-dressing guise and male affectations are removed in order to normalize her sexually.

This complex and contradictory film stimulated extreme reactions of all kinds. One viewer cried as he told a local newspaper reporter in an area populated by many Americans of Chinese background, the Silicon Valley of California, that watching *Mulan* made him feel more proud than ever to be Chinese. Other Asian Americans said they were simply happy to be represented, and so positively at that, in any Disney production. *Mulan* exemplifies an intricate interlacing of cultural representation and interpretation. Though some objections to the film's portrayal of Chinese and to the violence have been raised, there should be no doubt that overall *Mulan has* had an extremely positive effect as a cultural message. Moreover, the film has taught people everywhere, including young Chinese, about Chinese culture. Japanese, Koreans, Filipinos, Vietnamese and all other Asian peoples are introduced to this Chinese cultural legend in their own countries not by film producers from China, Taiwan, Hong Kong, or Singapore, but by an American multinational corporation based in southern California, mightily reinforced globally by the McDonald's promotion. Disney is one of the few corporations in the world capable of creating this inspiring folkloric spectacle of animation and distributing it successfully to a global audience. Even the way the film has been produced demonstrates an unprecedented global interconnectedness made possible by modern communications technology, as Disney assembled the visual and audio elements of *Mulan* without having to bring all the creative talent together physically in space and time.

The film entered a global media mix of discourses about China. During the same period when *Mulan* was playing in movie houses worldwide, China was the subject of intense scrutiny and criticism on other fronts. News media were reporting details of the communist country's sale of nuclear missile technology to Iran; Chinese men were accused of illegally trying to sway American foreign policy through fundraising bribes given to the Democratic Party; Bill Clinton was lecturing the Chinese on human rights during his visit to the People's Republic; the films *Kundun* and *Seven Years in Tibet* continued to call attention to the delicate political and cultural situation in the estranged western region. Even the *yuan* began to shake in the persistent tremors of the Asian economic crisis.

A '*Mulan* Parade', with the jive-talking voice of Eddie Murphy as the little dragon introducing the event, was a featured spectacle at the Disneyland theme park in 1998 and 1999, a marketing strategy that promoted the film and the (contested) culture. The money, creative talent, technical expertise, and business management skills invested in *Mulan* by Disney turned a tremendous profit for the entertainment enterprise. McDonald's sold tons of Happy Meals, and the other sponsors benefited financially from the film tie-in too. It's an old and true story: the Hollywood film and television industries make a lot of money by producing films and TV shows that appeal greatly to world audiences.

It can happen fast. The most popular television program on the air in China during the first decade of modernization, the 1980s, was a compilation of Disney animated programming, *Mickey Mouse and Donald Duck*, that appeared Sunday nights on Central China Television (CCTV), the satellite-linked national broadcasting system. The program quickly outdrew domestic productions, which tend to be very didactic and dull. *Mickey Mouse and Donald Duck* inspired not only fanatical viewing, but rampant illegal production in China of Disney-based dolls, toys, and other domestic artifacts and promotional items that caused Disney to pull the plug temporarily on new episodes. Finally, an American-Chinese joint venture was put together – including formation of a Chinese Mickey Mouse 'club' – to capitalize on the enthusiastic response to Disney memorabilia by Chinese children. Indeed, one striking and undeniable contemporary Chinese stereotype worldwide is the presence of Disney characters on the clothing of Chinese girls and young women. Mickey Mouse, one might say, seems to be really very Chinese!

The *Mulan* film, *Mickey Mouse and Donald Duck*, and other popular culture products are successful in large measure because they provoke emotional reactions across a range of cultural groups. This effect was implied in the writing of Marshall McLuhan years ago (1964) when he claimed that the purveyors of popular culture, the electronic media, retrieve orality (and the emotional attachments oral communication implies) from the discipline, privacy, and rationality of print media and literacy. Today's mix of electronic mass media and cyber-communications in fact enhances both mediated emotionality and rationality. We may not live in McLuhan's global village, but we do inhabit an increasingly globalized, symbolized, and digitalized environment which emphatically stimulates the entire range of human senses, especially the emotional dimensions.

Communication and Global Power

Technological advances in electronic and digital mass and micro media have come primarily from the west and Japan. But if the United States, Europe, Australia, and Japan intend to maintain their technological and economic superiority, then, according to Samuel Huntington, they must prevent others from having access to modern communications hardware and software in order to keep a competitive advantage. But, of course, that is precisely the opposite of what is happening in global trade. Communications technology itself has been used to make any pretenses of cultural exclusion practically impossible: 'Thanks to the interconnected world which the west has created, slowing the diffusion of technology to other civilizations is increasingly difficult' (Huntington 1996:93).

Such conditions reveal the fundamental fallacy of theories of imperialism, especially since the personal computer was invented. Microsoft, for example, was embroiled in heavy legal proceedings in the United States from 1998 to 2000. As we all recall, the company was accused of monopolizing the software industry through release of its Windows 95 and Windows 98 operating systems because it linked its internet browser, the internet Explorer, to sale of those systems. Bill Gates consistently defended Microsoft's marketing practices and phenomenal success by claiming that the company had simply been giving people exactly the products they wanted, and for a reasonable price. Lack of effective international regulation makes the Microsoft monopoly even less strong at the global level. The profit margin for Microsoft's products drops precipitously outside the United States because the vast majority of software used outside North America and Europe is copied illegally. I will never myself forget an experience I had in Taipei in the middle 1980s. Computer supply stores of Taiwan at the time provided a free pirated copy of any American software program, valued at hundreds of dollars in some cases, as an incentive to customers to buy a cheap box of ten floppy disks. Pirated manuals in English and Chinese to accompany the software were also available for a price. Similar practices still can be found today from India to North Korea and everywhere in between.

Without engaging in any 'more developed country/less developed country' relativizing or moralizing, we can say confidently that global practices in communication and culture reflect the dynamics of market forces in countries everywhere, and reveal the ultimate inability of the producers of original products in communications and popular culture to maintain control over the disposition of their wares, soft or hard. Software pirating and hardware cloning are simply among the most recent forms of cultural borrowing. Cassette dubbing of popular music, and videotape copying of movies have long been part of the cultural landscape all over the world, particularly in Asia, where well over half the music products sold have been copied illegally (Frith 1992).

When we view these tendencies as a whole, we see that the rapid spread of both mass media and micromedia communications technology in many respects does *not* lead to a clear-cut advantage for any nationalistic ambitions of the United States or other relatively developed countries, or even necessarily for the marketplace objectives of multinational corporations. The circulation of symbolic forms and the transfer of communications technology from the 'center to the periphery' end up supporting Huntington's argument about 'the fading of the west' in terms of political, economic, ideological, and cultural power. In many ways globalization actually breaks down power differences and hierarchies. The roots of this tendency are not new. The late twentieth century spread of communications hardware and software coincides with Thomas Sowell's well-documented claim that 'throughout history, one of the great sources of cultural achievement, both for groups and for nations and even civilizations, has been a borrowing of cultural features from others who happened to be more advanced in given fields at a given time' (Sowell 1994:30).

Such technological and cultural appropriations, at least in the past century, are frequently regarded as typical of the Asian region. The classic example of course is the Japanese ability to import and improve western technology, especially in transportation and electronics, which became a fundamental characteristic of that nation's economic success since World War Two. Of course, much of the Japanese success has also stemmed from the country's ability to export effectively to the world market, particularly in the 1960s and 1970s, while greatly restricting imports. But Asian appropriation of western ideas and products is not limited to capitalist-driven imitation and export. The notion of 'socialism with Chinese characteristics', for instance, has been a philosophical underpinning of political structuring in the People's Republic of China, especially after the falling out with Moscow in 1960. Since then China has welcomed western technology, particularly big-ticket items that can be used for development of its defense and communications systems. Without doubt Asia has looked to the west in order to develop – much more so than the west has looked to the east. Still, overall, as Huntington notes, 'East Asians attribute their dramatic economic development not to their import of western culture, but rather to their adherence to their own culture. They are succeeding, they argue, *because they are different from the west*' (Huntington 1996:93; emphasis mine).

Japan, China, and many other countries have been careful – at official levels anyway – not to 'lose control' of their cultural order, tradition, and authority in the midst of the industrializing and modernizing. The most extreme measures in this regard were taken in the summer of 1998 when Afghanistan's Taliban government – which two years earlier had shut down the country's only TV station – outlawed television, videocassette recorders, videotapes, and satellite dishes outright as part of a religiously-mandated cultural crackdown. But even far different cultural environments – the Nordic countries, for instance, which have always limited electronic media and supervised programming in the name of cultural protection – also wrestle today with the fundamentally borderless influences of satellite telecommunications.

Several intriguing themes emerge in the process of all this global mixing and matching of cultural representation, interpretation, and use. Precisely because culture is such a dynamic realm – both pragmatically and discursively – the importation or exchange of material and symbolic goods necessarily disrupts and changes structures and styles that are already in place. The 'protection' of culture, thus, can never be well accomplished so long as human beings think, create, travel, and interact with media and internet content. Outside influences inevitably become indigenized in various ways into local scenes and scenarios, a process which alters the local material and symbolic environment while it changes the imported forms.

Let's return to our discussion of McDonald's restaurants in East Asia for some examples from the lively realm of global popular culture to help demonstrate how the indigenization process works. Virtually all the contributors to James Watson's (1997) edited book mentioned earlier report that McDonald's did, of course, clash at first with established culinary and social territory in the Asian countries. But over time McDonald's has become just as familiar in the Asian urban landscape as noodle houses and *bentō* boxes. For more than twenty years now in Japan and Hong Kong, 'an entire generation of children has grown up with McDonald's; to these people the Big Mac, fries, and Coke do not represent something foreign. McDonald's is, quite simply, "local" cuisine' (Watson 1997:2). And while McDonald's introduced certain nuances of public dining to Asia – like encouraging Japanese customers to eat with their fingers – the Asian accommodation of McDonald's has taken place as much on eastern terms as western. The McDonald's menu, for instance, is localized (mutton-based Maharaja Macs in India; *teriyaki* burgers in Japan, Taiwan, and Hong Kong; McSpagetti in the Philippines, and so on). In the face of McDonald's worldwide policy to move customers in and out of the restaurants as fast as possible, young people in Hong Kong have instead turned McDonald's into after-school hangouts. They spend hours there 'studying, gossiping, picking over snacks; for them, the restaurants are the equivalent of youth clubs' (Watson 1997:7). Sometimes McDonald's can even perform culturally as a socially liberating medium. Watson (1997) cites the case of Taiwan where McDonald's serves as a public space that is not traditionally associated with, and dominated by, the patriarchal authority of men. McDonald's can function this way precisely because it is not derived from traditional cultural structures and assumptions.

Clearly the impact of 'outside influences', a term which is itself outdated and misleading given the diminished fixity of geography in contemporary cultural analysis, is thus not determined and not necessarily negative. All forms of popular culture and all communication devices must turn a profit for their industrial producers or they will disappear. But film, TV, McDonald's, the internet, and other profitable modes and codes of popular culture are put to work in a wide range of ways by their interpreter/users. Such materials stimulate reflection and change, disruptions which are often interpreted by critics as damaging and exploitative. But cultural artifacts including movies, TV shows, pop songs, and hamburgers cannot succeed in any market unless they respond to local needs, desires, orientations, preferences, and curiosities which, of course, are themselves sometimes stimulated or accelerated by the presence of the new material or symbolic resources. For example, several key television programs in China have resonated with the deep yearnings and frustrations of urban dwellers during various periods since the modernization was initiated, despite the government's efforts to supervise all media experiences. The imported Japanese soap opera *Oshin* was one particularly striking example of how this can work. Chinese media authorities said they put *Oshin* on the national television system during the early years of modernization to encourage people to work hard in order to succeed as Oshin herself did. The disciplined Oshin was supposed to be a role model for Chinese women. One common interpretation of the program by Chinese viewers, however, was that Oshin was able to accomplish so much in her life not just because of dedication and hard work, but because she was able to start a business freely and compete in a market economy – not exactly the message the communists had in mind (Lull 1991). *Oshin* resonated with a range of political and cultural circumstances in various other countries where it was broadcast too. It inspired a heated debate in Iran about the role and rights and women in society, for instance.

We've seen many examples now of how the now-familiar 'new' media and information technologies also disrupt cultural and political traditions and authority in the Asian region. Students' use of fax machines and photocopiers during the 1989 uprising in China challenged government control, and more recently e-mail and the internet further threaten political and cultural stability. While the government oversees internet web site development and maintenance in China today, the authorities cannot keep up with the creative sidesteps and initiatives of the rapidly-increasing number of users, as the policy-making chaos of early 2000 made clear. Chinese people can quite easily access sensitive sites including Human Rights Watch, *Playboy*, the *New York Times*, Human Rights in China, and China News Digest. Web surfers inside China avoid censorship by linking their machines to computers outside the country. 'Tunnel' is an online journal of dissent originating in China. Each issue is delivered secretly to the United States, then distributed widely in China from an anonymous email address. Confidentiality and security for the Chinese originators of the journal is maintained by using false names and hiding in the vast galaxies of cyberspace. Moreover, just like their attempts to regulate radio, television, and film, China's ideological and cultural censors make inconsistent decisions about internet-based communication – despite public appearances to the contrary.

Mass media, popular culture, the internet, and personal communications devices are also often put to work in ways that strengthen, not weaken, traditional customs, languages, and social relationships. For example, hundreds of Mexicans were arrested for celebrating too enthusiastically after watching televised coverage of their national team advance to the second round of 1998 World Cup football action. Not so unusual, perhaps, except that the arrests took place in Los Angeles, not Mexico City. The *two* top-rated radio stations in Los Angeles (KLVE-FM, KCSA-FM) broadcast in Spanish, not English, and play *banda* and ballads, not rock, not rap – unless it's *rock en espanol* or *rap en espanol*. In total, eight radio stations in the Los Angeles area broadcast in Spanish, and several English-language stations target the huge Hispanic audience there. The beloved composer and singer of Mexican popular music, Juan Gabriel, recently performed for 20,000 fans in San Jose, California, helping immigrants in the heart of Silicon Valley connect symbolically with romanticized memories of the country they left behind. These are among countless instances where media and popular culture interact to reinforce cultural values for persons and groups who live or work outside the places of their ethnic and cultural origins – sometimes in ways that do not advance the interests of the host country's dominant ideology and culture.

The Asian Civilizations

Two tendencies – the grouping together of people who are connected through cultural commonalities, and the fear and hatred that can characterize relations between groups from different cultures – are what Samuel Huntington believes will determine future alliances and conflicts. His outlook is gloomy: 'The end of the Cold War has not ended conflict but has rather given rise to new identities rooted in culture and to new patterns of conflict among groups from different cultures which at the broadest level are civilizations' (Huntington 1996:130). He goes on to further define what he means by civilizations and what that implies: 'Civilizations are the ultimate human tribes, and the clash of civilizations is tribal conflict on a global scale. Cold peace, cold war, trade war, quasi-war, uneasy peace, troubled relations, intense rivalry, competitive coexistence, arms races: these phrases are the most probable descriptions of relations between entitites from different civilizations. Trust and friendship will be rare' (Huntington 1996:207).

This focus on cultures as civilizations is the second of Huntington's arguments that pertain to our discussion of Asian media and advertising. I wrote the first draft of this chapter during the period when American President Bill Clinton and his family were touring Xian, Shanghai, Beijing, Guilin, and Hong Kong on an official state visit. My hometown newspaper, the *San Jose Mercury News*, carried two major stories about Clinton's China trip on the day I began to write that first draft (Sunday, June 21, 1998). The headlines for these stories reflect what Huntington is saying: 'China, U.S. in Awkward New Dance' and 'U.S. Businesses hit Great Walls in China Deals'. Indeed, it is amusing to watch Clinton lecture the Chinese about individual human rights, freedom of speech, democracy, and the immorality of the Tiananmen Square crackdown with Jiang Zemin smiling confidently at his side. One constantly gets the impression that underneath the formal politeness, and the genuine friendship the two world leaders may have for each other personally, civilizational differences nonetheless remain fundamentally unchanged and suggestive of future actions between the superpowers.

Civilizational discord will develop noticeably *within* Asian civilizations early in the new millenium too, according to Huntington. In his charting of civilizations by geographic areas, Huntington identifies China, Taiwan, Korea, and Vietnam as the Sinic civilization; much of the remainder of Southeast Asia as Buddhist; Indonesia and Malaysia as Islamic; and Japan as Japanese. India is a perilous 'cleft' nation composed of Hindu and Islamic civilizations, which Huntington claims is precisely why the country is ridden with conflict. Pockets where western culture is dominant – Hong Kong and parts of the Philippines, for instance – also exist in Asia.

It is not my intention to interrogate Huntington's thesis about civilizational groupings, clefts, and divides. There is a discomforting and misleading ease with which he mainstreams and stereotypes cultural groups. This bias is reflected in certain facile passages from his book: 'Asians tend to think of the evolution of their societies in terms of centuries and millennia and to give priority to maximizing long-term gains. These attitudes contrast with the primacy in American beliefs of liberty, equality, democracy, and individualism, and the American propensity to distrust government, oppose authority, promote checks and balances, encourage competition, sanctify human rights, and to forget the past, ignore the future, and focus on maximizing immediate gains. The sources of conflict are in fundamental differences in society and culture' (Huntington 1996:225).

Such thinking easily can be criticized for its essentializing of enormous groups of people who may share history, customs, territory, and language, but can by no means be so neatly explained or predicted. Nonetheless, Huntington's account of world political, economic, and cultural developments is impressive in its scope and historical detailing. I take Huntington's argument, then, less as a rigid scientific analysis wherein cultural activity can somehow be predicted with precision, and more as a subjective yet very sophisticated and reasonable overall interpretation of some, but not all, cultural patterns at the global level. Of special interest is how popular culture representations, mass media, and micro communication technologies fit into this picture of a world divided according to civilizational differences. What are the roles of media and symbolic forms – the discursive dimensions of culture – in the maintenance of group identities and the construction of more and more personalized, customized lifestyles under conditions of global reterritorialization?

Diasporic cultures such as Indian communities in London (Gillespie 1995) and in the United States (Appadurai 1996), Iranians in Los Angeles (Naficy 1993), or Vietnamese in Silicon Valley, California (Lull and Wallis 1992), demonstrate just how strong the symbolic cultural connections can be. Relations of every type – economic, political, linguistic, musical, religious, criminal, sporting, familial, and so on – are maintained, reinforced, and developed across wide geographic divides. For Huntington, the presence of these patterns of cultural continuity spanning vast expanses of time and space reveals one important strain of civilizational coherence. For instance, he suggests that Chinese 'co-prosperity', the economic success of Chinese people at home and in overseas communities, can be traced to a 'bamboo network' of family and personal relationships in a common culture. As the People's Republic of China gains momentum in the global economic system, business contacts among the world's ethnic Chinese will produce even greater amounts of money and influence. This trend is fueled by the vague and unsteady regulation of international commerce, and by the lack of laws and other legal documents *inside* China which has led to a system based primarily on interpersonal dependence and trust (Huntington 1996:170; see also my discussion of *guanxi wang*, 'relationship networks' in China: Lull 1991:95–126, 211, 222).

Often deterritorialized versions of distant cultures – the diasporic communities – benefit in certain ways from their dislocation because they can conveniently call on cultural memories for nostalgia, history, comfort, and confidence without having to be troubled, even terrorized, by the problems they left 'back home'. As media technology develops and symbolic representations of popular culture proliferate, it becomes easier for diasporic communities to accomplish many cultural feats. Connections to the homeland are not always productive or positive, however. Hostilities between immigrant groups from the same homeland also travel to new common geographic territories, where they are not just reproduced, but modified and often intensified. In California, for instance, gang warfare between Mexican youth from families who originate in the northern versus the southern states of Mexico is a site for the common marking of cultural difference – even among young USA-born, Spanish-speaking combatants who have never been to Mexico. These gangs and the nature of their confrontations are glorified by Hollywood movies which further stir hostilities not only in California and the rest of the United States, but in Mexico too because the films also play there.

Culture in the Communication Age

Diasporic cultures often exhibit striking stresses and styles that develop between tradition (assuming that 'tradition' can be more or less commonly agreed upon) and 'local' influences, typically of another civilization. Both sides of these stresses and styles are served by the symbolic content and connectivity of mass media and personal communications technologies. At issue in any such manner of cultural adaptation, according to many scholars, is a core concept in cultural analysis – collective identity. But now more than ever the very notion of collective identity is in question. The world population – especially the international middle class, but not only them – swims in a sea of multicultural symbolic forms, instant communications and interactions, a dynamic rush of global popular culture, and vital regional cultural flows such as those discussed in the following chapter by Koichi Iwabuchi. The hyper-presence of contemporary symbolic resources has fundamentally altered basic dimensions of cultural activity and collective identity in Asia and everywhere else. In this chapter I have pointed to certain key developments and issues in global cultural production relevant to Asia that have helped create the contemporary conditions, with an aim to update and broaden somewhat the scope of conventional (usually quite programmatically pessimistic) discussions of the consequences of globalization.

Culture continues to serve as a useful concept for those who live it, and for those who analyze it, because humans will always be 'sense-making' beings who seek some degree of coherence and sociality. For cultural theorists, however, making sense of how sense is made in globalization – not to mention understanding to some degree the emotional and sensory features of life – requires approaches that match up well with the symbolic, synthetic, and mobile nature of contemporary cultural forms and processes. In addition to the more general definitions and discussions of culture which continue to highlight the coherent, the collective, and the communal, culture should therefore now also be understood as *highly-personalized clusters, grids, and networks of relevance* that serve as individual-based, customized instruments of self-understanding, well-being, social influence, growth, and pleasure – what I like to call the 'superculture' (Lull 2000, 2001). The very essence of cultural construction today reflects diversified and accelerated synthesis – drawing from mediated representations of universal values, global media images, civilizational archetypes, and national ideologies to regional influences, subcultural styles, and everyday (more 'local') situations and routines. Consequently, patterns of thought and behavior are becoming more and more fragmented and generative than they are unified and limiting, and the role of individual persons in shaping cultural experience more central, original, and creative than ever before. Global consumerism – despite its obvious excesses and inequities – is basic to the cultural realigning. To one extent or another, we are all becoming more individualized spectators in the global cultural galleries, and solo window shoppers in the global cultural malls. It must be stressed in this context, however, that while culture has become more a personal construct in key respects, it continues to help demarcate friend from foe, the familiar from the foreign, in a world of expanded social contact and competition between groups. How Asian nations and peoples (and everyone else) sort out and manage these co-acting and precarious cultural navigations is a challenge about which at this juncture we are left to only speculate.

2

BECOMING 'CULTURALLY PROXIMATE'

The A/Scent of Japanese Idol Dramas in Taiwan

Koichi Iwabuchi

In recent years, the theories of modernity and modernisation have been criticised for their Eurocentric perspective. It is often argued that they give a priority to time rather than space. Spatial differences are subsumed under a singular developmental time of western modernity. Now that many non-western countries have achieved a certain degree of modernisation, the emphasis is being put more on space and academics are becoming engaged in discussing modernities 'plural' (for example, Featherstone et al. 1995). The same trend can be discerned in the discussion of 'globalisation'. Few would still argue that globalisation just facilitates homogenisation of the world based on western modernity. What is becoming commonly held among scholars is, as William Mazzarella shows in his chapter on an Indian KamaSutra condom campaign, an idea that two contradictory forces such as global-local, homogenisation-heterogenisation and sameness-diversity, operate simultaneously and interpenetrate one another (cf. Appadurai 1990; Featherstone et al. 1995; Robertson 1995; Hannerz 1996).

Although a straightforward homogenisation thesis has been criticised, arguments about heterogenisation, hybridisation and creolisation often do not transcend the west-the rest paradigm. We still tend to think of global-local interactions in terms of how the non-west responds to the west and to neglect how the non-western countries 'rework modernities' (Ong 1996:64). This tendency is most clearly elucidated in the study of what Appadurai calls 'mediascapes'. Globalisation of media and popular culture is still based upon an assumption of unbeatable western (American) domination and arguments are focused on how the rest resist, imitate or appropriate the west. There have been fascinating analyses of the (non-western) local consumption of western media texts (Miller 1992, 1995) which transcend a dichotomised perspective of global-local. However 'global' still tends to be exclusively associated with the west. A dynamic interaction among countries in the non-west has been seriously under-explored.

In this chapter, I will explore such an interaction through the recent popularity of Japanese TV dramas in Taiwan.[1] In the 1990s, particularly in the last few years, Japanese popular culture such as TV programmes, pop music and animation has without doubt become increasingly popular in east Asia more than before. This is not to say that this is a new trend in east Asia. On the contrary, as Ching (1994) argues, Japanese popular culture has been influential in the region at least since the late 1970s or early 1980s. Comics and animation aside, Japanese popular music has also been widely covered in Hong Kong and Taiwan and there have been crazes for several Japanese TV dramas and idols. Japanese TV programme formats have been exported and massively copied (pirated). In Taiwan, it is not too much to say that most variety shows are at least partly copied from popular Japanese programmes. However, the nature of the recent popularity of Japanese TV dramas in east Asia is different in that they are consumed by wider audiences. In the 1980s when Japanese idols were popular in east Asia, the audience was limited to a certain group of Japanophiles. A female in her mid-20s told me in Taiwan that those who liked Japanese idols were somewhat marginal then, but now, in the late 1990s, it has become a part of everyday life for many young people to chat with friends about their preferences for Japanese idols or TV programmes.

It can also be argued that the popularity of Japanese TV programmes has much to do with the historical fact of Japanese colonial rule over Taiwan. From food and housing to language, we can easily find many examples of Japanese cultural influence on Taiwan. Older people who were educated under Japanese colonial rule speak fluent Japanese and still enjoy Japanese language books, songs and TV programmes. What is significant in Taiwanese situations is that many hold a relatively positive feeling toward their former colonial ruler. The bitter memory of Japanese colonial rule has diminished by contrast with the repressive and authoritarian rule of the KMT government which moved from mainland China after the second world war (see, for example, Liao 1996). This surely makes Japanese TV programmes much more accessible than in other parts of Asia, particularly South Korea. However, the main audience for Japanese TV dramas consists of younger people, most of whom do not understand the Japanese language and thus enjoy the dramas through dubbing or subtitles.

Elsewhere I have argued that Japanese cultural exports have been mainly 'culturally odourless' products whose attractiveness for the consumer has little to do with images associated with the country of origin. Examples of this are consumer technologies, animation programmes and know-how about producing pop stars. The fact that Japanese cultural exports have been limited to such culturally odourless products has much to do with the question of the universal appeal of Japanese culture, but Japanese cultural industries have also consciously promoted odourless products (Iwabuchi 1995, 1998). As Featherstone (1996:9) puts it, unlike American commodities, 'Japanese consumer goods do not seek to sell on the back of a Japanese way of life'. However, the recent popularity of Japanese TV dramas in Taiwan suggests that 'Japanese odour' does have the potential to sell. The textual appeal of the dramas is closely associated with lifestyles and social relationships of present-day Japan – embodied in living Japanese actors, not in animated or digitalised characters.

This 'Japaneseness' is quite different from Japanese traditional culture, the beauty of which was discovered by 'the west'. 'Japaneseness' with which modernised 'Asia' (Taiwan in this chapter) finds resonance in Japanese TV dramas has more to do with a Japanese modernity which is not just a response to western modernity. Unlike traditional culture, by which the irreducible difference of one culture from others tends to be emphasised, popular culture, though highly commercialised, reminds Japan and 'Asia' alike of cultural similarities, a sense of living in the shared time and common experience of a certain (post)modernity which cannot be represented well by American popular culture. The ascent of Japanese dramas is closely associated with the scent of a modernity in Asia that Japanese dramas embody.

The Question of 'Cultural Proximity'

The appeal of Japanese TV dramas in Taiwan tends to be explained in terms of the intimacy and closeness associated with salient cultural and racial similarities (for example, Ishii and Watanabe 1996). In my field research in Taipei, I also discovered that Taiwanese viewers tend to account for the appeal of Japanese TV dramas, though not completely, in terms of their assumed cultural proximity. In media studies the notion of 'cultural discount' (Hoskins and Mirus 1988) and 'cultural proximity' (Straubhaar 1991) have been used to explain this kind of appeal. Against the view of globalisation as the spread of and response to western (American) popular culture, the emphasis here is on the regionalisation of media and the dynamics of media export within particular cultural-geographical regions (cf. Straubhaar 1991; Sinclair et al. 1996). Straubhaar (1991) has argued that there has been development of national and regional markets in the periphery despite the dominance of the United States in the world TV programme trade. By indigenising American influences, some non-western countries such as Brazil and Mexico have developed a local industry that can produce programmes by itself and export them to their regional markets. The development of 'local' TV markets has been brought about both by audience preference and the maturity of local cultural industries. In his research in Latin American countries, Straubhaar found that the audience's search for 'cultural proximity' in television programmes revealed:

> A preference first for national material, and, when that cannot be filled in certain genres, a tendency to look next to regional Latin American productions, which are relatively more culturally proximate or similar than those of the United States.
>
> (Straubhaar 1991:56)

Language is the most important factor in cultural proximity, but there are other cultural elements such as religion, dress, music, nonverbal codes, humor, story pacing and ethnic types, which all play their parts in making programmes acceptable.

No one would deny the empirical validity of the 'cultural proximity' thesis. The existence of geolinguistic and geo-cultural regional TV markets has been empirically proven and local TV programmes seem to be the most popular in any country. However, precisely because of its apparent empirical validity, the notion of cultural proximity resists further theorising. Cultural proximity seems too obvious to be explored further, but it is this self-evidence that we should question. What seems most problematic with the study of cultural proximity is an ahistorical and totalising way of conceiving culture. Cultural proximity explains the general tendency of audience preference for local programmes and programmes imported from countries of similar cultural make-up, and the significance of cultural-linguistic regional centres such as Brazil, Mexico, Hong Kong, India and Egypt in terms of film/television export. Such a grouping of cultural-linguistic regional markets, perhaps not surprisingly, tends to correspond to that of Samuel Huntington's clash-of-civilisation thesis discussed by James Lull in the previous chapter, although Japan, Africa and Slavic-Orthodox countries are in most cases omitted (cf. Sinclair et al. 1996). And the study of cultural proximity, I would argue, risks sharing with Huntington the problem of seeing culture/civilisation as a static and essentialised attribute, since its analysis tends to be based upon the assumption that the existence of some essential cultural similarities automatically urges the audience to be attracted to media texts of culturally proximate regions without considering historical contexts or internal differences within cultural formations. Primordial cultural similarities are always sought after to prove a general tendency, but the analysis of cultural proximity hitherto tells us little about why certain programmes become popular and others do not, and about what sort of pleasure, if any, audiences find in identifying cultural proximity in a particular programme. It is this void that I will try to tackle in this chapter.

To avoid clinging to a highly generalised idea of cultural proximity, at the same time as making sense of Taiwanese audiences' perception of cultural proximity in watching Japanese TV dramas, we may apply Stuart Hall's concept of 'articulation'. The cultural proximity of a particular programme is articulated when people watch it and find pleasure in it under a specific historical and social conjuncture. As developed by Ernesto Laclau, the concept was originally intended to explain how particular ideological elements become dominant in a specific historical and social conjuncture. The concept is based upon the dual meanings of the term 'articulate'. To articulate is both to 'utter clearly' and to 'form a joint', and it is the latter which Hall emphasises as significant:

> An articulation is thus the form of the connection that can make a unity of two different elements, under certain conditions. It is a linkage which is not necessary, determined, absolute and essential for all time. You have to ask, under what circumstances can a connection be forged or made?
>
> (Hall 1996:141)

It is the sense of arbitrariness and contingency that the notion of cultural proximity, as used in empirical analysis, tends to suppress. We have to ask under which historical conjuncture cultural similarity becomes associated with attractiveness or the pleasure of a text. In the Taiwanese situation, it is the development of media industries, particularly of cable TV, under globalising forces that enables Japanese dramas constantly to be shown in Taiwan. We also need to put these structural factors in a wider context of the democratisation and liberalisation movements in Taiwan since the late 1980s; of the emergence of a pro-Japan leader in 1988; and of the material affluence brought about by the rapid economic growth of the 1980s. It is such social and historical contexts that we have to take into consideration to make sense of how audiences' experience of cultural similarity perceived as such is articulated.

We should also look at a text carefully. Taiwanese viewers might not necessarily watch certain Japanese dramas because they happen to be from a supposedly culturally proximate country, but rather because they present something attractive and pleasurable that Taiwanese viewers do not find in local or American products. A familiar cultural value does not necessarily offer pleasure to those watching programmes. In some cases, audiences may reject a programme precisely because of the negative appeal of the cultural values of their own society. The question is whether and how the attractiveness of Japanese dramas is associated with cultural proximity. The popularity of Japanese dramas in Taiwan cannot be explained solely and automatically in terms of a pre-existing cultural similarity between Taiwan and Japan, but we should also pay attention to how certain cultural similarities are reworked to become attractive in a particular text.

What is also lacking in the study of cultural proximity as usually used is a sense of the active agency of the audience, as highlighted by Mark Hobart in his chapter on Balinese TV reception later on in this book. Cultural proximity should not be defined as a pre-determined attribute of the text that reduces the viewer's active input in constructing the pleasure of the text. Rather, following Miller's discussion of '*a posteriori* authenticity' (1992), I would argue that cultural proximity does not exist *a priori* but occurs *a posteriori*. That is, it is not something 'out there', but needs to be subjectively identified and experienced by the audience. Thus cultural proximity is articulated when audiences identify cultural similarities in a specific programme and context, although one of the problems in studying the regional flow of TV programmes here is the absence of audience research (which has concentrated on the reception of American programmes). Sinclair and his co-authors argue that:

> Far more than for the USA, the success or otherwise of peripheral nation's export is contingent on factors other than those captured by established modes of audience study. This explains why so little audience reception research has been able to be conducted on their products in international markets, and why we need instead middle range analysis to do so.
>
> (Sinclair et al. 1996:19)

While I agree with the authors that middle range analysis – which concerns issues of acquisition, time-scheduling and publicity of programmes – is important in understanding the global and intra-regional flow of TV programmes, it is audience reception research, I would argue, that is imperative in the study of how and why programmes become popular in a cultural sense. In order not to use the notion of cultural proximity in a determinist way, we should explore how cultural similarity is articulated in the reception of particular programmes by audiences. Thus to understand why Japanese TV dramas are popular in Taiwan and what sort of pleasure Taiwanese audiences find in them at a particular historical time in a particular locale, both analyses are indispensable.

The Development of Cable TV in Taiwan

However, before proceeding to an analysis of Japanese drama texts and of how they are received by audiences, we should first look at the context in which Japanese dramas have become routinely consumed in Taiwan. One of the most important factors in the increasing presence of Japanese popular culture in Taiwan – as evidenced by the recent rise of Japanese television programmes there – is the fact that Japanese cultural industries have not actively promoted them. Rather, there has been a strong local initiative as local companies have grabbed business opportunities to sell Japanese TV programmes during the process of media globalisation in Taiwan. In sharp contrast to American or Hong Kong media industries which tried to exploit a good business chance to sell their programmes, the Japanese TV industry has not until recently been very interested in promoting its programmes in Asia. As I have argued elsewhere, Japanese cultural industries are more inclined to strategies of 'global localisation' which attempt to suppress 'Japaneseness' and to find local ingredients (see Iwabuchi 1998).

There is no doubt that the pioneer in diffusing Japanese TV dramas throughout Asia has been Star TV, which started broadcasting in August 1991. Although it has since attracted much academic attention in terms of its pan-Asian satellite broadcast and its possible penetration into China, it should be remembered that the Taiwanese market has also from the outset been a prime target. This is particularly true with the Star Chinese Channel and Music Channel [V], which replaced MTV in 1994. As well as this, in the mid-90s Star TV launched a new Chinese channel, Phoenix, for a mainland Chinese market so that the other Star Chinese Channel is now broadcast exclusively in Taiwan where Japanese programmes, particularly dramas, have been occupying its prime time slots in an attempt to attract a large Taiwanese audience. According to a manager of the Star TV Chinese Channel, Japanese programmes are indispensable for Star TV's strategy of localisation in Taiwan. (It should be noted that this strategy was deployed by Star TV from 1992, well before Murdoch's take-over and the beginning of his localising strategy).

However, it is Taiwanese cable TV that has taken the strongest initiative in promoting Japanese TV programmes, as Star TV is also watched on cable TV. Cable TV started in Taiwan in the 1960s to rebroadcast the three channels to areas which could not receive air broadcast, but it was the illegal cable channels, most of whose programmes consisted of foreign entertainment – Hollywood films, Hong Kong dramas and Japanese programmes – that became popular with audiences. Cable TV in Taiwan – called the Fourth Channel – has developed since the late 1970s to satisfy audience hunger for entertainment programmes which the three free-to-air stations could not offer. The government attempted to exercise a strict control over the illegal cable channels by cutting their cables, but operators quickly reconnected them and the popularity of the Fourth Channel never died.[2] The diffusion rate of the cable channels constantly and rapidly increased because of political liberalisation, democratisation and the Taiwanese government's emphasis upon the need to become an open and cosmopolitan country not to be forgotten by the world.

In this situation, the government changed its policy from banning to regulating the Fourth Channel and in 1993 the new Cable TV Law was finally passed. It should be noted that globalising forces from the United States were significant in this legislation since in the preceding year the new copyright law had been passed and the United States put strong pressure on Taiwan to legalise the cable channels in order to protect American media industries from piracy and to enable them to run their business legally in Taiwan (Lewis et al. 1994). As a result, the new law made it possible for foreign channels and programme suppliers such as CNN, HBO and Star TV to broadcast their programmes via cable (Hara and Hattori 1997). Although, before legislation, about half of Taiwan's households watched the cable channel, the number increased more after the legislation, so that by 1998 more than three quarters of all households were enjoying cable television and Taiwan had one of the most developed cable television systems in the world.

Japanese Cable Channels in Taiwan

The Cable Law requires that at least twenty per cent of the programmes on a cable channel be locally produced, but many cable channels obviously do not abide by this condition. Most channels buy their entire programming from overseas, mainly from the United States, Hong Kong and Japan. This has led to Lewis et al. (1994) arguing that the development of cable TV has facilitated re-Americanisation after a period when people's preference for local programmes decreased the number of American programmes.[3] However, the drastic increase in Japanese TV programmes in Taiwan has also been a significant trend in the last few years of the millennium.

After the Japanese government officially reestablished diplomatic relations with China in 1972, the Taiwanese government banned the broadcasting of Japanese language programmes. However, Japanese programmes were widely watched through pirate videos and illegal cable channels in Taiwan before becoming much more accessible to audiences when the government removed its ban on broadcasting Japanese language TV programmes and songs around the end of 1993. Now, while it might be said that the banning of Japanese language programmes in Taiwan was a result of Japanese colonial history in Taiwan, the colonial connection might actually be more apparent in business links between the two countries. Typically it has been those who experienced Japanese colonial rule and who thus speak fluent Japanese who have been mainly engaged in running Japanese cable channels in Taiwan, using old connections with Japanese business circles. For example, the launch of Po-shin Channel Japanese in Taiwan was brought about through an old close connection between the former managing director of the latter and the president of Tōei Movie Japan. In this sense, then, the Japanese cultural presence in Taiwan is overshadowed by a Japanese colonial presence.

In 1997 there were five Japanese cable channels in Taiwan. Apart from NHK Asia, which simultaneously broadcasts most programmes from Japan by satellite, four other channels – Video Land Japanese, Gold Sun, Po-shin Japanese and JET (Japan Entertainment Network) – buy whole programmes from Japanese commercial television stations which they broadcast exclusively 24 hours a day (repeating a basic programming of six to ten hours a day). In addition, other cable and free-to-air channels also regularly broadcast Japanese programmes.

As a result, the number of Japanese TV programmes imported to Taiwan has drastically increased since 1994. In 1992 the total amount exported from Japan to Taiwan was about 600 hours (Kawatake and Hara 1994). Although no exact figures for Japanese programmes exported to Taiwan are available after 1993, by 1996 one Japanese commercial TV station (TBS) alone exported 1000 hours of programmes to Taiwan. This does not mean that Japanese popular television has become mainstream in Taiwan, since the most popular TV programmes and popular music are almost certainly local products, just as they used to be in the 1970s (Lee 1980). However Japanese TV programmes are 'popular' with a certain audience in Taiwan and the diversification of media has enabled local industries to create a niche market for them. This means that we should therefore look at specific genres and audiences of Japanese TV programmes rather than at Japanese TV programmes in general.

By early 1997 there were around 100 channel suppliers. According to a survey by a research company in Taiwan, local general channels such as Super TV, TVBS and Sanli–2, as well as global/transnational channels such as HBO, ESPN and Star TV Chinese, have the highest penetration. Japanese channels amounted to one quarter of all major 81 channels Gold Sun 19, NHK-Asia 21, Videoland Japan 26 – and had greater penetration than CNN, MTV, TNT Cartoon and Discovery (Red Wood Research Service 1996). This penetration rate, of course, does not necessarily indicate the popularity of the channel, but Ishii and colleagues' research (1996) also tells us that Japanese channels are well watched. Asked which channels they usually watch, people answered that, apart from the three free-to-air TV stations, Video Land Japanese was the sixth most commonly watched channel and Gold Sun the fifteenth.

When we look at cumulative reach, western (mainly American) channels are the most popular cable TV stations in Taiwan, but if we look more closely at particular genres and audiences, we find that this is not always the case. As far as TV dramas are concerned, Japanese programmes attract Taiwanese audiences more than do western/American ones and are even more popular than Hong Kong or local Taiwanese dramas (Hattori and Hara 1997; Ishii et al. 1996). This is particularly true with audiences who are young and female. As Hattori and Hara (1997) suggest, the younger female audience in general likes TV dramas, but do not like American dramas very much, and young males (13–25 years) rate only Japanese dramas highly. In the course of their research, they asked people in Taiwan to give a score of one to ten for each genre. The result was that Japanese dramas rated highest (6.8) in overall score, followed by Taiwan (6.7), western (American) (6.6), and Hong Kong (6.2), and scored significantly higher for both male and female audience in the age groups 13–15 and 16–25. The young audiences' preference for dramas showed an interesting contrast between Japanese and American programmes in that Japanese dramas were the strongest genre among Japanese TV programmes as a whole while TV dramas were the least popular American genre.

Japanese Idol Dramas: Something to Talk About

The development of cable TV has thus been crucial for the constant circulation of Japanese programmes in Taiwan, as Japanese programmes are generally not popular enough for the free-to-air channels. The emergence of cable channels whose target audiences are more narrowly focused has brought about a new pattern of TV popularity. Japanese dramas may not be as dominant as local or American programmes, but they are nevertheless considerably enjoyed by young audiences in Taiwan. This popularity cannot be discerned by ratings, which means that we should look at popularity in qualitative as well as quantitative terms. For example, Japanese programmes have become an indispensable subject in the everyday gossip of the younger generation and, given the scarcity of publicity about them in the Taiwanese media, this popularity of Japanese dramas owes much to oral communication among young people. According to one newspaper reporter:

> Most high school and university students who watch Japanese dramas discuss the storyline with their friends. It is the most common topic for them just as Taiwan prime time dramas (8 p.m. in the evening) used to be.

This reporter works for the most popular daily newspaper, *The China Times*, which started an interactive column on Japanese dramas in February 1996.[4] She told me that *The China Times* had looked for a subject for a special column for teenager readers for the Saturday edition, and that Japanese dramas had seemed the most appropriate.

There are many things that the audience wants to talk about from watching Japanese dramas – one of them being Japanese idols of the kind discussed by Stevens and Hosokawa later on in this book. In Taiwan, Japanese dramas are recognised as an established genre called Japanese Idol Drama, which was coined by Star TV when it started 'Japanese Idol Drama Hour' in June 1992. The title clearly shows that Star TV thought Japanese young idols were the main attraction of Japanese dramas for a Taiwanese audience – a conjecture supported by many in Taiwan to whom I talked. One of the reasons why such people watch Japanese dramas is that they feature good looking Japanese idols. Food, fashion, consumer goods and music are also good topics and things that an audience enjoys watching.

These commodities – now indispensable to the pleasure of Japanese drama watching – did not enter Taiwan suddenly, but gained a certain popularity there before the advent of TV dramas. For example, one very popular fashion magazine for teenage females is *non*・*no*, a Japanese magazine published twice a month and enjoyed just for its pictures, even though most Taiwan readers do not understand Japanese. *non*・*no* was first imported in the late 1970s and became popular during the 1980s. No exact figures are available, but it is estimated that about 100,000 copies of two issues are imported from Japan every month. In 1993, *non*・*no* was by far the most popular foreign magazine in major book stores in Taiwan (*Advertising Age*, January 1994) and, according to Nippan IPC, the Japanese distributing agent, the number exported increased in the 1990s, particularly around 1993–4 – a date which corresponds to the period when Japanese dramas became popular in Taiwan. Like *non*・*no*, Japanese dramas tell their audience how to consume goods for better life-styles, that is, not just *what* but also *how* to wear clothes or to place furniture to look like a person with a stunning life-style.

However, there is more to watching Japanese dramas than just enjoying Japanese commodities. As mentioned above, there is no doubt that their audiences talk most eagerly about the story and the characters of each drama, since they present attractive and pleasurable meanings that Taiwanese do not otherwise experience or feel in watching local or American shows. Japanese dramas are diverse in terms of story lines, setting and topics, ranging from urban love stories to family dramas by way of detective series, but those that become popular in Taiwan are stories about younger people's loves and lives in an urban setting. In most cases, the dramas are filmed in Tokyo and thus show modern urban life in Japan, unlike Taiwanese TV dramas which have rarely been local dramas of this kind, but are more family-oriented or historical with housewives as their main target audiences. It seems to be this void that has turned Japanese dramas into popular texts to be talked about in people's everyday lives.

Watching *Tokyo Love Story*

It was the broadcasting of *Tokyo Love Story* for the first time by Star Chinese Channel in 1992 which sparked off the popularity and recognition of the quality of Japanese dramas in Taiwan (and elsewhere in east Asia). Since then, Star TV has broadcast it four times and TTV, the most popular free-to-air channel also broadcast it twice in 1995. *Tokyo Love Story* has eleven one-hour long episodes and was originally broadcast in Japan between January and March 1991. The drama is a love story of five young men and women in their early 20s. The heroine, Akana Rika, who spent some years in the United States, is an unusually expressive and active Japanese woman. She falls in love with Nagao Kanji (Rika calls him Kanchi), a gentle but rather wavering guy who loves Sekiguchi Satomi, a former high-school classmate, who has an affair with another classmate, Mikami Ken'ichi. Kanji is often perplexed by Rika's straight action in expressing her love towards him, but becomes attracted to her. A famous phrase which characterises Rika symbolically is 'Kanchi, let's have a sex!' Sometimes at a loss over how to deal with Rika's love, Kanji gradually becomes exhausted by their relationship and again becomes inclined to Satomi who has broken up with Mikami. Kanji is indecisive about his relationship with Rika, who finally leaves him and goes to America for work. Kanji and Satomi marry and the drama ends with scenes several years later when Kanji, Satomi and Rika happen to meet in Tokyo. Rika is still an expressive and active woman who never looks back on the past.

The popularity of the programme urged a group of university undergraduate students to conduct research on why *Tokyo Love Story* was popular in Taiwan (Li et al. 1995).[5] They found in their survey of 61 university students that about 83 per cent of them enjoyed watching the drama and about 65 per cent watched it more than twice. A crucial question which was not asked by this quantitative survey and which we should explore further is what kinds of pleasure the audience experienced in watching *Tokyo Love Story*. As Ien Ang (1985:20) argues, 'popular pleasure is first and foremost a pleasure of recognition'. What matters is how audiences can identify themselves with the drama and what sorts of realism the drama can offer people.

The popularity of *Tokyo Love Story* has much to do with a (female) audience's identification with the heroine, Rika. Rika is obviously an attractive personality – particularly for female audiences for whom Rika's active and pure pursuit of love, together with her straightforward expression of feelings, is the object of admiration and emulation. Her confidence in herself and her independent attitude also represent a desirable image of 'modern' or 'new age' woman. However, in my research in Taipei in 1997, I often heard respondents express two somewhat contradictory statements: 'I have a strong feeling that she is exactly what I want to be', and 'I would not be able to become as brave and open as Rika'. It is on Rika's appeal as an ideal role model that the emotional realism (Ang 1985) of *Tokyo Love Story* is based: she is what one wants to be but can never quite become. It may be the case that audiences in Taiwan find Satomi more empirically realistic, since she represents a traditional image of a woman who is dependent, submissive, domestic and passive. But, though she may be more empirically realistic, she is still an object of aversion to many (who told me that they hated Satomi). The juxtaposition of Rika and Satomi brings Rika's attractiveness into sharp relief.

This sort of identification with the desirable is similar to what Richard Dyer (1992:18) calls utopianism when he suggests that:

> Entertainment offers the image of 'something better' to escape into, or something we want deeply that our day-to-day lives don't provide. Alternatives, hopes, wishes – these are the stuff of utopia, the sense that things could be better, that something other than what is can be imagined and maybe realised.

Dyer argues that entertainment does not offer 'models of utopian world', but provides its consumers with the possibility of experiencing 'what utopia would feel like rather than how it would be organised' (Dyer 1992:18). Referring in particular to the musical, he points out the importance of non-representational forms like music and colour, and the simplification and intensification of people's relationships in entertainment's articulation of utopianism. Though Dyer's argument is about musicals, these points fit well the structure of Japanese dramas which, apart from the comparatively large budget and the sophistication of production techniques, are made an attractive new genre for the Taiwanese audience by two structural and technical factors. Firstly, they are not soap operas and always finish in 11–13 episodes (each episode is one-hour long), whereas Taiwanese and American dramas are never-ending tales, so long as ratings remain high. Most people in Taiwan whom I interviewed in Taipei told me that this no-ending style seems unnecessarily prolonged. As Japanese dramas finish in a comparatively short time, making the story line less complicated than in soap operas, they can concentrate on dramatic elements and thus let people enjoy the progress of the narrative. Secondly, Japanese dramas, like movies, use both orchestral music and a theme song quite effectively and repeatedly. Particularly important here is the use of a theme song which is used week after week in the climax scene, not just as background music but as a constitutive part of the scene. Moreover, the song is often produced specifically for the drama so that the lyrics have much to do with the story, thereby encouraging the emotional involvement of the audience which is thus able to enjoy a 'romantic, beautiful love story', as one of my interviewees expressed it.

However there is a crucial difference between Dyer's utopianism and the realism of Japanese dramas that do offer concrete models that look empirically realistic or at least accessible. The attractiveness of *Tokyo Love Story*, for example, does not just lie in giving the audience the sense that 'something other than what is can be imagined and maybe realised'. Emotional involvement in the drama is facilitated by its depiction of something that the audience thinks and feels is at once somewhat desirable and not unrealistic. It is not just a dream of tomorrow but a (possible) picture of today. Things happening in *Tokyo Love Story* also seem to be empirically realistic to most of its young audiences. The same thing could and does happen in their everyday lives. As a young man from Hong Kong explains why he likes the drama in his home page:

> The twenty-something urban professionals of the series face a tightrope of coping that young people in many Asian cities have faced, but rarely more sympathetically. The major attraction of *Tokyo Love Story* to me is that it is not a story about somebody else. It is a story about our generation, about us, about myself. I can easily identify shadows of Rika or Kanchi among my peer group, even in myself.
>
> (KEVIN'S HOME, http://home.ust.hk/~kwtse)

This sense of a 'story about us' was shared by the Taiwanese fans. More than 60 per cent of those who were surveyed by Li et al. (1995), and 75 per cent of the female respondents, also answered that love affairs such as those depicted in *Tokyo Love Story* could happen around them. Li and his co-authors argue that one of the attractions of *Tokyo Love Story* for university students in Taiwan is its new style of portraying love, work and women's position in society. These are all issues that young people are actually facing in urban areas in Taiwan, but with which Taiwanese TV dramas have never sympathetically dealt.

Audience Preference and Cultural Similarity

The question is whether and how Japanese drama's 'realism', the sense of 'our' story, is encouraged by a perceived cultural similarity between Japan and Taiwan. This point can be elucidated when we compare *Tokyo Love Story* with an American drama like *Beverley Hills 90210*. A common comment I heard during my interviews in Taipei was that viewers did not feel the same kind of emotional involvement with either western/American dramas or Taiwanese dramas that they experienced in Japanese dramas. A woman in her early 20s who had just started working for a Japanese cable TV channel and was a fan of Japanese dramas told me that she did enjoy watching the lifestyle and love affairs in *Beverley Hills 90210*, but that she found Japanese love stories more realistic and easier to relate to. Furthermore, some interviewees told me that they could not imagine experiencing the world of *Beverley Hills 90210*, despite its undeniable entertainment value. As a 17-year-old high school student put it:

> Japanese dramas better reflect our reality. Yeah, *Beverley Hills 90210* is too exciting (to be realistic). Boy always meets girl. But it is neither our reality nor dream.

When I suggested that some Japanese dramas are not empirically realistic either, she replied: 'Well, maybe not, but it may happen. Or at least I want to have it'. Thus, while the attractiveness of *Tokyo Love Story* seems to be based upon an ambivalent mixture of empiricist and emotional realism, love affairs in *Beverley Hills 90210* are not 'realistic' either in terms of emotional realism or of empiricist realism.

Whether young American audiences think *Beverley Hills 90210* is a story about themselves or not is a moot point, but Taiwanese audiences seem to think that the attractiveness of Japanese dramas has something to do with 'cultural proximity' between Japan and Taiwan. Given that most Japanese dramas are not dubbed into Chinese but broadcast in the original Japanese language with Chinese subtitles, Japanese dramas are consciously watched as foreign, though not in the same sense as are American programmes. Japanese culture is closer to Taiwan and people's physical appearance and skin colour are quite similar. 'Japan is not quite, but much like us', as another woman in her early 20s said.

> Yeah, Japan is a foreign county and this (foreignness) makes Japanese programmes look gorgeous and appealing. But the distance we feel between us and Japan is comfortable. Americans are complete strangers.

Another female Japanese drama fan in her mid 20s also mentions the cultural distance between Taiwan, Japan and the west:

> I do not think that Japanese dramas are a totally new genre, something I've never seen before, but rather I've never seen such dramas which perfectly express my feeling . . . The west is so far away from us, so I cannot relate to American dramas.

She also said that human relations between family and lovers also look more culturally similar to those in Taiwan, and this made it easier for her to relate to Japanese dramas.

These comments suggest that Taiwanese audiences' emotional involvement in Japanese dramas is fostered by a perceived cultural proximity between Japan and Taiwan. However, it is too simplistic to explain audience preference solely in terms of cultural proximity. It is important to notice, for example, that cultural proximity works together with an emphasis on intimacy and ordinariness which are intrinsic to Japanese drama texts. Most Japanese dramas depict ordinary people's everyday lives, rather than the kind of rich people's glamorous dreamworld often represented in American soap operas so that the difference between *Tokyo Love Story* and *Beverley Hills 90210* in terms of audience identification lies not only in cultural proximity/distance, but also in their degree of textual intimacy. As a female university student said, *Beverley Hills 90210* is not a story about ordinary people and thus has little to do with her everyday life. She said: 'It looks too glamorous'.[6] The newspaper reporter mentioned above also told me that the American medical drama, *ER*, was of high quality and well received in Taiwan, but that it did not get people emotionally involved with the medical world. In contrast, she continued, a Japanese drama about medical students did make many people in Taiwan feel like working as medical professionals. Thus, it was not only the cultural similarity between Japan and Taiwan, but also the focus on medical students rather than on professional practitioners that made this Japanese drama look more intimate and ordinary than *ER*.

Another comment which I often heard from Taiwanese viewers is that the ways of expressing love in Japanese dramas are 'delicate' and 'elegant', and therefore much more acceptable than those of American dramas in which emotion tends to be presented in an exaggerated manner. Japanese dramas are more romantic and subtler in expressing emotion than are American and Taiwanese dramas. This subtlety is associated with ways of directing as well as with story lines. A woman in her late 20s gave me an example of such non-verbal subtlety in a Japanese drama:

> I think Japanese dramas are very subtle in showing delicate feeling. They value the description of feeling deep inside. When a woman cries, her emotion is skillfully expressed by the movement of the fingers. A parting scene is also well directed by the subtle movement of the fingers between lovers.

Another woman in her mid 20s told me:

> I clearly remember one scene in *Tokyo Love Story* that very subtly used the actors' backs to show the delicate sentiment of lovers' parting. Such delicateness cannot be found in other [American and Taiwanese] dramas. I like Japanese dramas because I can feel and experience such delicate feelings.

The newspaper reporter gave me another example, saying that she personally liked the romantic scene in *Tokyo Love Story* where Rika narrated Kanji's life history while putting candles on a birthday cake one by one. She said that she had never seen such an elegant way of celebrating a lover's birthday.

In view of the fact that Japanese idol dramas are popular only in east Asia, we may conclude that the 'elegance' of Japanese dramas may have an appeal especially to audiences of culturally proximate regions. However, the subtlety of Japanese culture in terms of non-verbal communication and the presentation of things and social relationships by 'wrapping' is also appreciated in the west as well (cf. Hendry 1993). Moreover, Taiwanese viewers seemed to regard Japanese subtlety as very different from Taiwanese ways of cultural presentation and most lamented the poor quality of Taiwanese dramas. One interviewee told me:

> Taiwanese dramas unnecessarily exaggerate their stories. In Taiwanese dramas, females always cry, cry, cry. There is no subtlety at all in expressing emotion, as there is in Japanese dramas.

When I asked her whether Taiwanese TV could produce dramas in the same way, she replied:

> No, I do not think Taiwan can produce (romantic) love dramas similar to the Japanese ones. Taiwan dramas cannot present delicate emotions in the Japanese way. I think it is not a matter of learning how to produce TV dramas, but one of cultural difference between two countries.

This suggests that the Taiwanese audience's preference for 'delicateness' or 'elegance' represented in Japanese dramas is not necessarily associated with cultural similarity between Japan and Taiwan.

Li and his co-authors (Li et al. 1995) argue that Rika's attitude to love in *Tokyo Love Story* is different both from that of the characters in American dramas like *Beverley Hills 90210,* which is seen as too open and not single-minded enough, and that found in Taiwanese dramas where it is generally very passive and submissive. A postgraduate student in Taiwan wrote to me in reply to my question about the difference between Rika, who spent some time in the United States and could therefore seem to be 'Americanised', and the image of American women in American dramas:

> About Rika, I think it is true that people in Taiwan identify themselves with her more than with American women. My opinion is, this is because Rika is an Asian woman. She has yellow skin, black hair and speaks Japanese (or Chinese) on TV... I think not many people would relate Rika to America. Her education in the USA was not often mentioned in *Tokyo Love Story.* And I think Rika is not totally Americanized. She kept the American style of femininity only in her pursuing something directly. But she still has some traditional Asian femininity in her personality. For example, she loves a man faithfully. And that is why Asian women identify themselves with her. She is a mixture of American and Asian femininity – she represents the image of a 'New Age woman' to the audience.

As the comment shows, Japan is obviously felt to be culturally proximate because of its 'Asianness': that is, the similar appearance and single-mindedness of Rika in the case of *Tokyo Love Story.* However, cultural proximity should not be essentialised or over-generalised to explain the popularity of *Tokyo Love Story* in Taiwan. Viewers might find some similar cultural values concerning family and individualism in Japanese dramas, but the attractiveness of such values is articulated only when the audience consumes a specific programme. A cultural value is not necessarily read positively. For example, Taiwanese dramas often emphasise traditional values, such as the 'fidelity' of women (Chan 1996:142). At the same time, although most young audiences do not relate to it, Rika's active and 'modern' single-mindedness is favourably responded to by them. Rika's style may be too open to emulate, but her single-mindedness still represents 'our' reality in Taiwan and is therefore something to which the audience there can emotionally relate. What is at stake here is not fidelity or single-mindedness in general, but Rika's single-mindedness represented in *Tokyo Love Story.* In other words, a cultural value – fidelity – is reconstructed in *Tokyo Love Story*, but it is a different kind of fidelity that has been articulated in the process of a Japanese reworking of cultural modernity.

Becoming 'Culturally Proximate'

Some viewers' preference for Japanese to American TV dramas in Taiwan seems suggestive of the shifting nature of the symbolic power of American pop icons. In non-western countries, America has long been closely associated with images of being modern. Whenever American popular culture is consumed, people enjoy a yearning for the American way of life. As Mike Featherstone (1996:8) argues regarding the symbolic power of McDonald's:

> It is a product from a superior global centre, which has long represented itself as the centre. For those on the periphery it offers the possibility of the psychological benefits of identifying with the powerful. Along with the Marlboro Man, Coca-Cola, Hollywood, Sesame Street, rock music and American football insignia, MacDonald's [*sic*] is one of a series of icons of the American way of life. They have become associated with transposable themes that are central to consumer culture, such as youth, fitness, beauty, luxury, romance, freedom.

Indeed, I myself clearly remember eating Kentucky Fried Chicken in the late 1970s in Tokyo and feeling that I was becoming an American. But that stage is now over. In Japan in 1995 I saw a seven-year-old boy express his amazement at seeing Kentucky Fried Chicken in the United States on TV: 'Wow, there is Kentucky in America as well!' In other words, 'American dreams' have been indigenised in some modernised non-western countries so that it seems that some popular American icons have also become 'culturally odourless', in the sense that they may no longer be recognised as essentially 'American'.

Tomlinson argues that terms such as cultural domination or imposition are no longer appropriate to describe a current situation that is not necessarily coercive. He distinguishes globalisation from cultural imperialism in terms of the will to dominate:

> Globalisation may be distinguished from imperialism in that it is a far less coherent or culturally directed process. For all that it is ambiguous between economic and political senses, the idea of imperialism contains, at least, the notion of a purposeful project: the intended spread of a social system from one centre of power across the globe. The idea of 'globalisation' suggests interconnection and interdependency of all global areas which happens in a far less purposeful way. It happens as the result of economic and cultural practices which do not, of themselves, aim at global integration, but which nonetheless produce it.
>
> Tomlinson (1991:175)

Although Chen (1996:56) rightly criticises this kind of discourse of globalisation because it 'neutralises power relations' in the world, we cannot deny that it is becoming increasingly difficult to identify 'the west' ('America') as the only supplier of images of modernity for people of modernised non-western nations which have already achieved a certain level of 'modern' affluence. 'Americanisation' seems to have reached another level of signification. It has become a form; abstract concepts such as freedom, luxury and romance have diffused so widely that there is no longer an unambiguous correlation between the concepts and American symbols. 'Americanisation' has become overdetermined by local practices and contingencies. Unlike the era of high Americanisation when the form of capitalist consumer culture was closely associated with the content of American dreams (Frith 1982:46), the content and the image associated with it now tend to be detached from the form. To appropriate Beilharz's (1991:15) argument about how Althusser's concept of 'overdetermination' points to the limitation of a Marxist concept of economic 'base', 'Americanisation', like the economic base, could be 'a kind of bluff, a slumbering last instance never to be called upon'. The process of reworking modernity by the non-west could be relatively autonomous from the base, 'Americanisation'.

If the conception of 'time' in the modern, secular age became characterised by homogeneity and emptiness (Benjamin 1973), what is now becoming homogeneous and empty in the process of globalisation is the conceptual form of various images associated with cultural modernity. While the former provided the basis of the construction of 'imagined communities' of the nation (Anderson 1991), the latter is not producing a global community but heterogenisation in the world. A globalising hegemony, as Richard Wilk (1995:118) argues, involves 'structures of common difference':

> The new global cultural system promotes difference instead of suppressing it, but difference of a particular kind. Its hegemony is not of content, but of form. Global structures organize diversity, rather than replicating uniformity.

What the recent popularity of Japanese dramas in Taiwan suggests, however, is that the global diffusion of empty 'forms' not only structures diversity, but also (re)activates intra-regional cultural flow and (a sense of) cultural proximity through the consumption of popular/consumer culture. 'Content' and 'image' are at once de-territorialised and re-territorialised at an intra-regional level. As García Canclini (1995:229) argues, these are the two interrelated processes of:

> The loss of the 'natural' relation of culture to geographical and social territories and, at the same time, certain relative, partial territorial relocalisations of old and new symbolic productions.

The re-territorialisation of images is not brought about by the emergence of a new symbolic power. When I asked whether Japanese dramas had had any influence on her, a female interviewee in her mid 20s, who used to love

American programmes but now watches many Japanese dramas made the thoughtful comment that:

> Japanese dramas are more delicate than western ones and I can relate easily to Japanese ones. They are more similar to our feeling ... But not much influence ... Maybe Japan is a sort of mirror, but it is perhaps America that we always follow and try to catch up with.

Even to those who love watching Japanese TV dramas, Japan does not attain the same status as object of yearning that America once had. As the above-mentioned reporter told me, 'Japan is too close to yearn after'. The key expression rather is 'easy to relate to': American celebrities are mainly movie stars while Japanese are intimate TV idols similar in appearance to Taiwanese viewers; American movies are entertaining and glamorous, while Japanese dramas are something to talk about and operate as vehicles for vicarious experience; and things 'American' are dreams to be yearned for and conceptual forms to be pursued, but things 'Japanese' are examples to be emulated and commodities to be acquired.

The popularity of Japanese television dramas in Taiwan does not just suggest that the relationship between Japan and Taiwan is one of centre-periphery. It is true that the flow of audiovisual products is definitely one-way from Japan, but it is a sense of coevalness, of sharing time (Fabian 1983) that also sustains a Japanese cultural presence in Taiwan. A female interviewee in her early twenties who has long been a fan of Japanese popular culture told me that:

> Taiwan used to follow Japan, always being a 'Japan' of ten years ago. But now we are living in the same age. There is no time lag between Taiwan and Japan. I think this sense of living in the same age emerged three or four years ago. Since then more people have become interested in things Japanese.

To some audiences of modernised Taiwan, Japanese popular culture offers operational images; American dreams are concretised into something ready for use and within reach. Mark Liechty (1995:194) elucidated the Nepali experience of modernity as 'the ever growing gap between imagination and reality, becoming and being'. This is no longer the case with Taiwan. A manager of a Japanese cable channel explains this astutely:

> When Taiwan was still a poor country, we had just a dream of a modern life style. It was an American dream. But now that we have become rich, we no longer have a dream for it is time to put the dream into practice. Not an American dream but Japanese reality is a good object to emulate for this practical purpose.

Modernity for people in Taiwan, especially the younger generation, no longer consists just of dreams, images and yearnings of affluence, but of lived reality – that is, of the material conditions in which people live. As Taiwan has achieved a certain degree of economic development, the reference of becoming for some Taiwanese young people has also changed from abstract to practical. Japanese TV dramas offer their fans a concrete model of what it is to be modern in east Asia, something which American popular cultures can never do.

Seen this way, 'cultural proximity', if we can still use this notion, should not be conceived of in terms of a static attribute of 'being' but as a dynamic process of 'becoming'. The emerging dialectic of comfortable distance and cultural proximity between Japan and Taiwan seems to be based upon a consciousness that Taiwan and Japan live in the same time, thanks to the narrowing economic gap and the simultaneous circulation of information and commodities between the two countries. There may be some similar cultural values and background concerning family and individualism, but such similarities should not be essentialised to explain the popularity of Japanese dramas in Taiwan. The experience of cultural similarity perceived as such is a matter of time as well as of space: overdetermined by Japanese colonial rule, an ever-narrowing gap between Japan and Taiwan in terms of material conditions, the urban consumerism of an expanding middle class, the changing role of women in society, the development of communication technologies and media industries, the reworking of local cultural values and the re-territorialisation of images diffused by American popular culture. Articulated under at once the legacy of Japanese colonialism, homogenising and heterogenising forces of 'modernisa-tion', 'Americanisation' and 'globalisation', all elements make Japanese dramas culturally resonant with some Taiwanese viewers' present experience of modernity in the mid 1990s.

Non-western countries have tended to face the west to interpret their position and understand the distance from modernity. The encounter has always been based upon the expectation of difference and time lag. Now, however, some non-western 'modern' countries are bypassing the west and facing one another to find similarity and coevalness. This tendency can be seen in east Asia, among whose countries – in particular Japan, Taiwan and Hong Kong – flows are gradually becoming bilateral. Recently more Japanese young people have also been enjoying popular culture from other parts of Asia: Hong Kong films, Cantonese pop music, or Taiwan idols (*Aera* January 20, 1997). This is not to say that they are becoming the same, but that they are feeling 'real time' resonance in other non-western modernities while simultaneously recognising difference. This should not be interpreted as something like an exclusive Asian value discourse, for the emerging resonance is not based upon exclusive views of primordial cultural traditions, but derived from the discovery of neighbours experiencing and feeling similar things.

My argument here should not be generalised or over-emphasised. Needless to say, the perception of cultural proximity can only explain one aspect of complex processes of audience consumption of Japanese TV dramas. Moreover, western popular culture is still widely consumed in east Asia and there are many young people in Taiwan who do not like Japanese TV dramas. Many economically deprived people are still excluded from the shared experience of modernity in the region. Neither should we deal uncritically with the transnational regional flow of a highly commercialised materialistic consumer culture. Thus the sense of coevalness might not be derived from objective reality, but from an imagination which is fabricated by the instantaneous circulation of information and commodities in the region. It also hides Japan's colonial legacy in the region, which will lend itself to the voices of many Japanese Asianists who are desperately seeking a commonality between Japan and Asia. To be critically engaged with those issues that are not adequately dealt with in this paper, however, we should take intra-regional dynamics within the non-west seriously. This seems to me imperative in the studies of the globalisation of culture which have been highly biased towards the ubiquity of western media and popular culture and have tended to neglect intra-regional interactions.

Notes

1 My research in Taiwan was conducted between December 1996 and January 1997 and again in May 1997 with the support of a Toyota Foundation Research Grant.
2 When the democratisation and liberalisation movement gained currency after the end of martial law in 1987, the opposition party, the Democratic Progressive Party (DPP), also used the Fourth Channel for political broadcasts.
3 ESPN, HBO, Discovery and CNNI are representative of the re-Americanisation of Taiwan.
4 The collection of letters and columns was published in book form in 1997.
5 I thank Su Herng for giving me a copy of this research paper.
6 McKinley (1997:92) finds that young American audiences sense *Beverley Hills 90210* as a story about themselves, even though they clearly recognise the gap between them and the extravagant life style represented in the drama series. What disturbs American audiences emotional identification with *Beverley Hills 90210* is, as McKinley (1997:92) suggests, not the unrealistic materialistic affluence but the lack of realism in the representation of characters and the symbolic meaning associated with general life experiences.

3

CULTURAL REGULATION AND ADVERTISING IN ASEAN

An Analysis of Singapore and Vietnam

Katherine T. Frith

Southeast Asia, is particularly interesting when viewed through the lens of globalization theory. While many theorists in the west see the distance between cultures shrinking (Giddens 1990; Tomlinson 1997) the sheer magnitude of the cultural diversity in southeast Asia sets it apart from other regions of the world. Certainly the diversity is greater than that of Europe, Latin America or the Middle East and thus this region offers an interesting contrast to some of the basic tenets of globalization theory.

European globalization theorists (Hall 1991; Hannerz 1991; Robertson 1991) while recognizing the persistent diversity of global cultures, note that globalization seems to be bringing a certain homogeneity across the globe. American globalization theorists (Drucker 1993; Kotkin 1993; Naisbitt 1996; Huntington 1996) have taken the homogeneity argument even further. Kotkin, for example, contends that the space between cultures is shrinking at such a rate that in the twenty first century the conventional barriers between nation-states will become less meaningful under the increasing weight of global economic formations. He suggests that in the next century affiliations based on nationalism and regionalism will disappear and that affiliations based on race, religion, and ethnic identity will determine the new global order. As we have seen in James Lull's paper, Huntington (1996) supports this thesis by describing the nine 'civilizations' that will operate in the future.

These theorists, all from the developed nations, suggest that in the future, we will see the evolution of business and cultural networks that will increasingly shape our global economic destiny. These supranational cultural-ethnic entities or 'global tribes' will share a strong ethnic identity and sense of mutual dependence that will help the group adjust to changes in the global economic and political order without losing its essential unity (Kotkin 1993:5).

While there is evidence that nations that are proximate in terms of geography, language or culture, share certain interests, as Iwabuchi notes in the previous chapter, there are still areas of the world where the globalization scenario is viewed with a certain degree of ambivalence. As George Yeo, Minister of

Information and the Arts in Singapore stated at the third conference of ASEAN Ministers in 1993:

> A technological revolution is sweeping the world ... We should see this technological challenge as both a threat and opportunity. It is a threat because, as entire communities, we may lose the means to preserve and promote the values important to us.
>
> (Yeo 1993)

Globalization and the ASEAN Nations

ASEAN, the Association of Southeast Asian Nations, is a loosely knit organization that was established in 1967 as a joint effort to promote economic cooperation and the welfare of the people in the region. The five original member countries – namely Indonesia, Malaysia, Philippines, Singapore and Thailand – were joined by Brunei in 1984, Vietnam in 1995, and Laos and Myanmar in 1997.

While globalization theorists might see the world shrinking and moving toward the emergence of supranational entities, this is not the current vision in ASEAN. Rudolfo Severino, Secretary-General of ASEAN noted:

> ASEAN's founders in 1967 intended ASEAN to be an association of all the states of Southeast Asia cooperating voluntarily for the common good, with peace and economic, social and cultural development its primary purposes. It is not and was not meant to be a supranational entity acting independently of its members.
>
> (Severino 1998)

In fact, ASEAN is a grouping of quite disparate nations including one Islamic State (Malaysia), one Buddhist kingdom (Thailand), one Communist state (Vietnam), one Confucian-based state (Singapore), and so on. The only common denominator in ASEAN might be diversity – diversity in size, level of development, and natural and human resources. These countries share differing histories, cultures, languages, religions, races, economic and social institutions, political systems, as well as differing values and traditions.

While Tomlinson (1991:175) and other globalization theorists assert that 'globalization suggests interconnection and interdependecy of all global areas', the Secretary-General of ASEAN has noted that this organization of nation-states has:

> ... No regional parliament or council of ministers with law-making powers, no power of enforcement, no judicial system. Much less is it like NATO, with armed forces at its command, or the UN Security Council, which can authorize military action by its members under one flag.
>
> (Severino 1998)

Each of the states within ASEAN seems to have its own ideological, political, economic and multi-cultural separateness. This is not to say that the region is not a participant in what Ulf Hannerz (1991:108) has dubbed 'the global homogenization scenario', but rather that at this point in time the nations of ASEAN are still actively engaged in the process of 'nation-building'.

Cultural Regulation and the Globalization of Advertising

In ASEAN, the mechanism most commonly used to preserve cultural identity and cultural conservation is cultural regulation. This has been defined by Thompson (1997:818) as:

> Regulatory policies in various fields of culture and leisure activities, whether conceived by public or private agencies (which) aim to foster or control practices in these fields and so have an important influence on the behavior of members of society.

The purpose of this paper is to examine the cultural regulation of advertising in two ASEAN nations, Singapore and Vietnam. These nations form an interesting contrast in that while they share a certain geographic proximity, they do not share a common language, culture, religion, economic system or political ideology. Each country has developed a set of advertising regulations that supports its own ideological position. As Henry (1993:196) emphasizes:

> Regulation theory represents an attempt to escape the notion that capitalism has a single inevitable logic of development. Politico-economic systems develop their own trajectories, influenced by the political, economic and ideological actors and historical alliances within those systems ...

Advertising regulation is worth investigating because the idea of globalization has long been the thrust of multi-national corporations and their advertising agencies. For multinational advertisers the prospect of running a single global advertising campaign, translated into many languages, offers great appeal. Globalized advertising campaigns offer the advertiser greater control over content, reduced costs, unified brand image, and simplified strategy planning (Tansey et al 1990; Mueller 1996). Proponents of globalized campaigns, like Levitt (1983) and Fatt (1967) have recommended that multinational advertisers down-play cultural differences and treat the world as if it were one homogeneous market.

For their part, critics of globalized campaigns (Mattelhart and Schmucler 1985; Janus 1986; Frith and Frith 1990) have argued that advertising must be tailored to particular cultures. These proponents of 'localization' have pointed out that most global campaigns are actually based on 'an unexamined complex of western values and practices and ignorance of the host culture' (Frith and Frith 1990:181). While multinational corporations and their agencies find it far more expedient to think in terms of global or regional strategies than of country-by-country strategies, the governments within ASEAN have historically used advertising regulations to protect local cultures and as a method of slowing down the homogenization scenario.

Advertising Regulation in Singapore and Vietnam

In many ways, Singapore and Vietnam are at opposite ends of the ideological and economic spectrum. Singapore prides itself on being a free-market capitalist society, while Vietnam is a socialist state. The advertising industry is thriving in Singapore, but at this point in time, only a few multinational agencies are allowed to practice in Vietnam. While the rationale for regulating advertising is quite different in each of these countries, the underlying issues that drive these regulations are similar in some respects. As Vincent Lowe has noted regarding media regulations in ASEAN: 'Cultural policies seem the only domain left where individual countries have options with which to reduce dependence' (Lowe 1987:vii).

Vietnam

In a free market society, such as the United States, advertising is assumed to be necessary to a healthy economy. By functioning as a distributive mechanism, matching buyers and sellers, advertising helps to achieve economic coordination (Jeffreys 1997). While many in the US would argue that advertising has its adverse effects (Schudson 1984; Frith and Frith 1989; Pollay 1989; Frith 1996), it is generally seen as being essential to the economy.

However, the history and political ideology in Vietnam have shaped a quite different perspective on advertising. After Vietnam's reunification in 1975–76, the Vietnamese Communist Party (VCP) attempted to follow the Soviet model of centrally-planned economic development. Their economic policies, coupled with the loss of foreign aid and the military conflicts with Cambodia and China, resulted in a stagnant economy and high inflation (which, in 1988, was running at 800 per cent). The collapse of the Soviet Union in 1989 and the end of its financial support to Vietnam helped to accelerate the need for reforms. At the Sixth Party Congress in 1986 the policy of *doi moi* (or economic 'renovation') was introduced.

After an initially difficult period of adjustment to *doi moi*, the country began to enjoy rapid, export-led growth with low inflation during the 1990s. While many in the west assumed that Vietnam would go the way of Russia and Eastern Europe, and that *doi moi* would lead to political as well as economic reform, this has not been the case. The Eighth Congress of the Communist Party of Vietnam was held in June, 1996. The purpose of the meeting, released as a 54 page political report, was stated in the following terms:

> To build a socialist state of the people, by the people and for the people, with the alliance of the working class, the peasantry, and the intelligentsia as the foundation and the Communist Party as the leadership. To fully observe the right of the people to be the master, strictly maintain social discipline, exercise dictatorship toward all infringements upon the interest of the Homeland and the people.
>
> (Parry 1996:22)

At the 1996 Congress, 'Speaker after speaker ... warned against the capitalistic "social evils" threatening Vietnamese society, and the need to stamp out all manifestations of "fanatic democratism" and multi-party politics' (Parry 1996). Among the so-called 'social evils' identified by the government were: prostitution, gambling, illicit drugs and the western-based practice of advertising (Mydans 1996).

Government policies toward advertising in Vietnam

Advertising officially falls under the jurisdiction of the Ministry of Culture and Information. Today, there are approximately eighteen foreign advertising companies with representative offices in the country and 84 Vietnamese companies – including 36 in Ho Chi Minh City and 41 in Hanoi, with a few others operating in the smaller cities (*Saigon Times* 1997). Multinational firms have only been allowed to do business if they have formed an alliance with a Vietnamese firm. Under Vietnamese law, a foreign advertising agency may set up a representative office in Vietnam 'to conduct research' but is only allowed to employ three foreigners in the office.

> The activities of international agencies remain restricted. Representative offices – the only type of venture so far approved for ad agencies by the government – are allowed only to monitor commercial business handled in other countries and conduct research and other information gathering activities. They cannot have Vietnamese companies as clients.
>
> (*Business Times,* 24 February 1995)

The government bureaucracy makes its presence felt in all aspects of the advertising industry. In terms of media buying Vietnam has a policy similar to China: that is, foreign companies are charged more than locals for media time and space. In addition, no foreign agency can actually buy media directly but must do so through a local agency (*Business Times,* 24 February 1995).

International advertising agencies have petitioned the Vietnamese government to be allowed to set up joint ventures or branch offices to legitimize their business operations, but so far only a handful have been successful. In a move to help their case, foreign agencies have banded together to try and form an independent advertising standards authority. Industry sources said the initial reaction of the Vietnamese authorities was positive (*Vietnam Business News,*

Figure 6 Motorola ad by a railway track in Vietnam.
(Photo courtesy of Dermot Tatlow)

April/May 1996). However, the local press is not supportive of the growing presence of multinational advertising firms.

The official *Vietnam News* has charged that Vietnamese advertising companies are being pressured into playing second fiddle to foreign companies: 'Foreign advertisements are inappropriate in Vietnam as they eclipse advertisements regarding social and cultural policies' (Schwartz 1996). In 1996, a campaign by the government to remove foreign signs from shops and office fronts was put into effect in the major cities. The *New York Times* reported that 'on store fronts and billboards all over the country neat swatches of paint have recently been applied, under government orders, to blot out the brand name of foreign consumer products' (Mydans 1996).

Currently, there are twenty Vietnamese advertising agencies that have been officially licensed by the government (*Saigon Times* 1997). Vinexad (Vietnam National Trade Fair & Advertising Company) is the oldest and largest agency in Vietnam. Headquartered in Hanoi, this agency was originally part of the Ministry of Trade. Other large local agencies include: Saigon Advertising Company (SAC), Youth Advertising House (YAH), Vietnam Marketing Center (VMC), and Vietnam Advertising Company (VAC) (Marshall 1994).

Based on Decree 194/CP which regulates the advertising business in Vietnam, multinational agencies can establish business cooperation contracts (BBC) with local agencies. Most foreign agencies find this arrangement unreasonable since it is a form of investment which gives them no legal status in

Vietnam. The BBCs are normally only given for a short period of time and as David Bell of Bates has noted: 'There is a restriction on time and we give away too much technology for no security and no equity, so we build a business and in five years they say goodbye' (*Asia Times,* 20 June 1996).

The foreign agencies now operating in Vietnam are barred from carrying out direct revenue-generating activities in the country. The result is that the agencies must bill offshore for any services they perform for their multinational clients. The Vietnamese press has attacked the foreign agencies for this practice, claiming that they are operating illegally and are avoiding taxes. According to the government sponsored *Saigon Times* (1997:15), 'about two-thirds of the total revenue of the advertising sector in Vietnam belongs to foreign companies'. The agencies have responded by explaining that they would be happy to pay taxes if they were allowed to officially do business in the country (*Asia Times,* 20 June 1996).

According to the government, the original plan was to have foreign advertising agencies find a local partner through which to do business. Through this type of cooperation, the Vietnamese advertising businesses supposedly could gain valuable experience and skills. Since all media buying has to be handled by local agencies, the local companies would share the profits. However, after opening their representative offices, the foreign agencies began to organize their personnel and work independently. According to the *Saigon Times:*

> To date, many foreign advertising companies are running representative offices which can provide full services ... Some even have 40 strong personnel and all the departments necessary for an independent advertising company.
>
> (*Saigon Times* 1997:13)

Both foreign and local agencies realize that Decree 194 has become obsolete and are lobbying the government for new policies to push forward the development of the advertising industry.

The cultural regulation of advertising in Vietnam

Advertising in the mass media was banned in Vietnam before *doi moi* (*Business Times* 1995). When advertisements first began to appear around 1990, the government initially took a liberal attitude toward them. In December 1994, however, it published the first set of directives for the advertising industry. These regulations were essentially designed to protect the national language and culture. While some areas of advertising regulation remain vague and hard to enforce, others – like the use of Vietnamese language – are strictly enforced. The government expects all advertisers to conform to the following advertising code:

- Advertising must reflect truth;
- Advertising must not be contrary to public morals or dignity or customs of Vietnamese;

- The use of the Vietnamese flag, anthem, emblem or leader's picture, Communist Party flag, or any international anthem, is forbidden;
- Advertising is banned on all the front pages of newspapers (foreign language publications are exempt);
- Advertisements must not last longer than five days in print and radio (and cannot be broadcast more than ten times a day) or for eight consecutive days on television (and are restricted to five times per day on TV);
- Advertising must not exceed ten per cent of local newspaper content or 30 per cent of foreign language publications and ad time on TV must be limited to five per cent of total air time;
- Billboards are prohibited in public spaces and in a public streets;
- Advertising is not allowed in the vicinity of about twenty types of structures – for example, government or military buildings, parks, squares or temples – and the spaces near them must all remain advertising free;
- All advertisements must be in the Vietnamese language;
- If an ad needs to use some English, then it must also show the Vietnamese words at the top and the English at the bottom (or risk having the English words painted over by government employees);
- Any ad with a European or American lifestyle is prohibited. All ads must show the Vietnamese lifestyle;
- The following are prohibited in all advertising:
  leotards
  bikinis
  kissing between adults
  kissing between children
  encouraging gambling
  alcohol and tobacco (except beer)

In addition, in 1995 Vietnam saw the banning of *all* tobacco and alcohol ads. The ad ban was only strictly enforced in mid-1995 and did not include ads for beer (Marshall 1995). Recently, the government has begun to tighten controls on tobacco and alcohol promotions and sports sponsorships which has further hurt the foreign agencies.

Advertising executives complain that there is no centralized censorship body to approve advertising concepts and that they have to spend the money to produce ads first and only later find out if they can be used. The Ministry of Trade, the Ministry of Culture and Information, the Customs Department, and every single TV station and newspaper – all can, and do, censor advertising in Vietnam. Television stations and print media are all government sanctioned and censor the ads they carry, seeking advice from the Ministry of Culture and Information when they are 'unsure of an ad's suitability' (*Business Times* 1995).

Vietnam's policy toward the advertising industry is interesting to study. Like China, its communist neighbor to the north, Vietnam is in the process of

Figure 7 Advertising in a Hanoi street.
(Photo courtesy of Dermot Tatlow)

experimenting with advertising and, like China, is wary of allowing this 'capitalist tool' to grow too rapidly. The population of Vietnam is one of the fastest growing in the world and, when coupled with China, amounts to one and a half billion people. This is a massive emerging market, and these two governments' determination to regulate the cultural content and expression of capitalism by regulating advertising could create a major block to the growth of capitalism in the region and the inevitable homogenization of cultures that capitalism generally brings with it.

Singapore

Singapore is in a unique position in southeast Asia. Originally a part of the British colony of Malaya, Singapore left the Federation of Malaysia to become an independent nation in 1965. Today, it is an island republic with a population of approximately three million. The government is a parliamentary system based on the British model.

The Singapore economy is small by international standards with a gross domestic product of US$94 billion in 1996, with a relatively rich economy whose per-capita GNP in 1995 of $24,700 ranked fifteenth in the world (Ministry of Trade and Industry 1998). Nonetheless, while Singapore's trade policy emphasizes strengthening global multilateral free trade and positions the city state as a major regional business hub, its government views certain aspects of globalization with suspicion.

The stated functions of the Singapore media industries are to support efforts at nation-building, to help mould national identity, to promote social harmony and to exercise self-restraint and good sense so as not to cause misunderstanding or tension between different ethnic, racial and religious groups (Mehra 1989:105). So, while the government does not actively censor advertising, the official (though non-legislated) values of the government have been effectively enshrined in society and thus in the workings of its media practitioners.

Like other countries in the region, the population of Singapore is multi-racial, multi-ethnic and multi-lingual. Of the approximately three million people who live on this small island, the predominant ethnic group consists of the Chinese who make up over 75 per cent of the total population. They are followed by the Malays at about fourteen per cent, and Indians who comprise approximately seven per cent. The remaining four per cent is made up of 'other' assorted Asian and expatriate groups (Stravens 1996).

According to Senior Minister Lee Kuan Yew, each of the four major segments of the country – English, Chinese, Malay and Tamil – has different key values and world views. In an effort to build 'one nation' from these diverse groups, the government of Singapore has rejected the 'melting pot' concept.

> Parents are determined to remain the different kinds of Asians they are and to keep their children that way. We cannot obliterate the cultural and religious distinctions between their racial groups. We can't even try to remove the language differences, yet we have to create enough shared values and a single national identity.
>
> (Lee Kuan Yew 1989:19)

The creation of 'shared values' and a single national identity was first conceived in 1988 by the then First Deputy Prime Minister, Goh Chok Tong. A set of the Shared Values – incorporating elements of Singapore's cultural heritage, attitudes and values – was first promulgated in 1988 as a blueprint for the development of a national ideology that all Singaporeans could abide by. The following are the Five Shared Values:

1. Nation before community and society before self;
2. Family as the basic unit of society;
3. Community support and respect for the individual;
4. Consensus, not conflict;
5. Racial harmony and religious harmony.

Thus, any advertising that runs in Singapore must not only be 'honest, truthful and decent' (the Code of Advertising Practice), but it must also abide by Singapore's Shared Values.

In addition, Clause 16.1 of the Code of Advertising practice states: 'No advertisement should, by claim or implication, unfairly discriminate against, cast in a poor light or denigrate any race, religion or sex'. One example of how this affects advertising practice is in the area of public service advertising campaigns, which are plentiful in this nation state. Rather than type-cast a specific 'racial target audience' for say, an anti-smoking campaign, three separate versions of each commercial are produced – one for each of the three main ethnic groups. Each of these versions feature distinct ethnic talent, and are translated into one of the three main languages – Chinese, Malay and Tamil. This is done so that a message aimed at reducing the incidence of AIDS, for example, does not spread the perception that AIDS is a problem for only one ethnic segment. So, the context within which advertising operates is one where the protection of cultural identity and the reinforcement of government ideological messages on cultural values and cultural harmony is of foremost importance.

The Code also states that: 'Advertisements should not portray or condone undesirable or immoral values'. While this is not specifically aimed at eliminating undesirable 'foreign' values, there are a number of cases where advertisements were pulled from the media because they contained visuals or headlines that were 'alien' to the culture. When Hutchison Paging, a Hong Kong telecommunications corporation entered the Singapore market, it ran full page ads in the *Straits Times* featuring a Caucasian male model with a nose ring and a chain connecting his nose ring to his pager. The ad caused a great deal of controversy with letters to the paper complaining about the negative influence that this type of advertising had on Singaporean youth. In response, Hutchison voluntarily withdrew the ad from the media.

Unlike many other ASEAN nations that routinely practise formal censorship of advertising, Singapore uses a system of self-regulation. This is conducted by a self-regulatory board, the Advertising Standards Authority of Singapore (ASAS). The board follows the guidelines on ethical advertising that are embodied in the Code of Advertising Practice (1976) and is set up as a watchdog body to ensure that advertisers adhere to the Code. It includes representatives from the local media industries, the Consumer Association of Singapore, the Singapore Advertisers Association (SAA), the Association of Accredited Advertising Agencies (4As), the Singapore Joint Chamber of Commerce, the Singapore Manufacturers Association, the Singapore Medical and Pharmaceutical Associations, as well as representatives from the Ministries of Health, Trade and Industry, the Environment, and the Singapore Broadcasting Authority (SBA).

ASAS has its own staff who review the ads that appear in all major print media and sample television commercials each day. They also deal with complaints from the public and have the power to act against offensive ads by instructing the advertiser to amend the advertising or withdraw it from the media. While ASAS is not a government body, it does receive some funding support from the government. It can react to complaints lodged by the public or by members of the government, and it has the power to require that any offending ads be withdrawn. Local advertising practitioners generally follow the Code of Advertising and ASAS receives few complaints each year.

In terms of the advertising industry, Singapore has tried to position itself as a regional advertising center for the southeast Asian and Asia-Pacific regions. The good communication facilities, the English-speaking environment and the presence of most of the top international advertising agencies reinforce this position. Nonetheless, the government has made it very clear to those in the culture industries, like advertising, that the practice of advertising must be guided by the principles of nation-building and respect for the cultural diversity of the society.

Discussion

Although the ways in which advertising is regulated in Vietnam and Singapore differ, the underlying issue that guides each of these governments is the belief that there is a set of local cultural values that can be expressed as a rhetoric of public culture, and as such, can act to bind a nation. While the expression of these values might differ from nation to nation in ASEAN, there seems to be consensus that the underlying values that connect these disparate nations are uniquely Asian or, as David Birch (1995) puts it: 'the writing of a public culture of what it means to be 'Asian' and what the values of Asia might uniquely look like'.

While theoreticians in Europe and the US are enmeshed in debates about globalization and modernity, the politicians and cultural managers in southeast Asia are caught up in the on-going discourse on the consequences of modernity and modernization (Birch 1995). They are aware that the consequences of globalization may not differ significantly from those of the colonialism of the past.

For the most part, globalization theories flow from the developed nations, and the fear in southeast Asia has been that the process of globalization best serves the developed world. The critique of western *vis-à-vis* Asian values (Stravens 1996) has dominated the public discourse in this region for over a decade. Led primarily by Lee Kuan Yew (1989) of Singapore and Mahatir Mohamad (1989) of Malaysia, the discourse on Asian values and Asianization manages comfortably to fit the ideologies of most ASEAN governments.

At its core, the Asianization debate – as it has been manifesting itself in places like Malaysia, Singapore, Vietnam and Indonesia – has been a response to the belief that civilization can only be measured by material achievement (Adas 1989). As the major force that propels a society toward consumer culture and material achievement, advertising has long been viewed with concern in ASEAN (Frith and Frith 1989). Advertising valorizes individual material success over the collective well-being of a people and, in ASEAN whether those people be Singaporean or Vietnamese – *collective* success is considered a core cultural value. As such, the practice of advertising continues to be suspect in many parts of southeast Asia, and continues to be regulated – dramatically in Vietnam, and softly but forcefully in Singapore.

Part II

News

Figure 8 Journalists in Hong Kong
(Photo courtesy of Dermot Tatlow)

4

BETWEEN MARKETS AND MANDARINS

Journalists and the Rhetorics of
Transition in Southern China

Kevin Latham

In the last twenty years of reform under Deng Xiaoping, and now continuing under his successor Jiang Zemin, Chinese people have been party to the implementation of far-reaching economic reform policies which have dramatically affected their lives in diverse and often contradictory ways (Davis and Vogel 1990; Davis and Harrell 1993; Davis et al. 1995; Feuchtwang et al. 1988).[1] Central to these reforms has been the introduction of market competition to many areas of economic activity and the new rhetoric of the market has been accompanied by the rhetoric of transition: transition from a state-controlled, planned economy aimed at the elimination of class struggle to the establishment of a socialist market economy implemented in accordance with the rhetoric of Deng Xiaoping's 'socialism with Chinese characteristics'. This transition has been marked by the juxtaposition of continued state planning and control alongside, or in conjunction with, the development of capitalist market competition; a juxtaposition which has come to dominate the running of state and collective enterprises and manifested itself in numerous and diverse contradictions and conflicts of interests (Smith 1993).

Media production in China has not been exempt from the effects of these dramatic changes. In fact, in many ways the media epitomize the contradictions inherent in this economic and social transformation. Throughout the reform period, the Party and the government have adhered closely to the principle of the media being the 'mouthpiece of the party' (Li 1991; Zhao 1998; Latham 2000). Yet, through the 1980s there was a massive increase in media production with the establishment of thousands of new television and radio stations as well as newspaper titles throughout the country. The old system of state subsidy that had financed all media production through the Mao period, became less and less tenable and media organizations were increasingly forced to fund themselves through advertising, subscriptions and sales (Zhao 1998; Huang 1994; Hussain 1990; Latham 2000 and forthcoming).

Whereas other forms of production have been encouraged to move towards the private sector, the media have remained closely bound to state control.

Media producers[2] have not, on the whole, been offered the opportunity to take their trade out of the state sector (though it may be in prospect for some on the entertainment side of media production [cf. Fang 1997]) even though they have found themselves embroiled in this economic 'transition'. The difference between their situation and workers in other state enterprises is that the nature of their products has continued to be seen by the government as crucial to the appropriate ideological understandings of the transition. Thus, their programmes and newspapers remain subject to Party control in a manner unlike the products of many other state enterprises. Media production – more specifically news media production (see below) – takes a unique place within this transition and as a result, journalists are placed in crucial locutionary or 'inter-locutionary' positions. It is their practices which constitute and perpetuate hegemonic Party discourses but which also divert and question the boundaries of party control and domination.

This paper explores the ambiguous, but crucial, positions in which journalists and other media producers find themselves in the reform period – caught as they are between the conflicting pressures of state control, with associated expectations of their ideological role in society, and highly competitive markets, which demand audience-centred popular media production. I investigate the emergence of journalists as political subjects in China, starting with a closer look at the contradictory pressures acting upon journalists in China before moving on to consider three broad areas of their everyday practices. First, I look at how journalists conceptualize the media market and how such conceptualizations impinge upon their everyday production of news. Second, I consider editorial practices as the locus of the conflicting pressures to conform with state and Party expectations while also producing popular audience-friendly news. It is important to consider the situated practices of journalists, often working under considerable time-pressure, for instance, without the luxury of considering, in the immediate context, the significance of these practices in relation to broader political issues. Third, I investigate how journalists conceptualized audiences and readerships in ways that reproduce the contradictions of Chinese media production in the reform era. On the one hand, old ideas remain of the audience as child-like, uneducated and in need of careful nurturing, protection and guidance. On the other hand, audiences are viewed as customers and consumers whose tastes and demands dictate media production and take priority in the competitive market atmosphere of contemporary China. I conclude with a discussion of how these various journalistic practices reveal the crucial position of journalists within a shifting hegemony of Party control in China. The various rhetorics of transition, with all their contradictions and tensions, still perpetuate this Party hegemony through these everyday practices of journalists, but, at the same time, they reveal cracks and weaknesses in this hegemony that can only become more apparent as economic reform continues apace.

Between Markets and Mandarins: news production in south China

Guangdong province, neighbouring Hong Kong, has been at the forefront of economic reform and the development of private sector capitalism in China (Vogel 1989; Smith 1993; Ikels 1996; Fang 1997) and journalists in the province have found themselves at the heart of recent economic and social transition. Television, radio and print journalists increasingly compete for audiences or readerships and advertisers (Latham 2000). Yet, at the same time they continue to have fundamental responsibilities for the production of propaganda – the ideological education of the populace in line with the Party's ideas of the development of a socialist market economy. In this way, they are subject to strict Party and government control of the nature and distribution of their products, as well as government extraction of a proportion of advertising revenue. Media institutions are riven with the contradictions between hierarchical centralised planning and control, on the one hand, and the pressures of production for an increasingly competitive market, on the other.

The situation facing media producers in Guangdong in the late 1990s is given by Fang Kang writing in the *South China Television Journal*, a professional publication for and by television producers and journalism theorists co-produced by Guangdong, Hainan and Shenzhen Television Stations. In a forward-looking piece entitled 'Television Development Strategies for the 21st Century', Fang outlines television's situation within changing economic circumstances:

> A market economy makes a greater number of informational demands of television. On the one hand, the market economy demands that Guangdong television be in its service and, on the other hand, Guangdong television must itself comply with the market economy.
>
> Television's management and administration will become more industrialized. While maintaining its political attributes and operations, its industrial attributes and operations will be greatly strengthened and it will move towards 'collectivization'.[3]
>
> As television moves towards the market, apart from news programmes and news documentaries, other programming will see a greater degree of socialization.[4] Programme production companies in society will become ever more numerous.

> (Fang 1997:4)

Journalists in Guangzhou find themselves increasingly working in a competitive market where good quality programming is demanded to attract audiences and advertisers, their key source of revenue. At the same time, media production is a state monopoly. Private television stations, radio stations, newspapers and magazines are illegal and all media production must be under state ownership and control.[5] As Fang suggests, in the near future it is likely that entertainment programming will become increasingly liberated from strict state control and move into the hands of producers with a greater degree of independence. News programming, however, whose integral relation to the government, Party and the ideological promotion of policy[6] is considered too valuable, and perhaps vulnerable, is not to be released from the Party fold at this stage. More than other media producers, journalists therefore find themselves between markets and mandarins, working simultaneously with two parallel but conflicting, notions of news production (Latham 2000).

This situation is exemplified in some comments made by the editor-in-chief of a local (town level) newspaper in the Pearl River Delta with whom I spoke in the summer of 1997. One of the difficulties he faced in daily editorial decision-making related to the reporting of local news. He was under instructions to include and in the main keep to the reporting of immediately local news – from the town or its immediate vicinity. When in the past he had tried to include broader news coverage, he had been told by his party and government superiors that the balance was wrong: he had too much news from outside and not enough immediately local news. However, he pointed out that people in the town, less than an hour from Guangzhou and of considerable commercial and economic importance in the Pearl River Delta, were interested in news not just from the immediate vicinity but from Guangzhou, the Pearl River Delta and indeed beyond from Hong Kong, Macao and overseas. At the same time, Guangzhou papers were increasingly easily available in the town, papers which with a broader news remit[7] therefore offered considerable competition to his own papers. Competition between papers was intense and for this editor such competition was keenly felt, not least because his entire revenue came from sales and advertising.[8] For him, giving the readers what they wanted to read was therefore of fundamental importance as the most basic of marketing strategies.

The editor concerned, therefore, found himself subject to contradictory pressures: on the one hand, to comply with Party expectations and on the other, to sell as many papers as possible meeting the demands of his readers. He made these contradictory pressures clear when he explained the first two things he would do each day when the first draft of the paper arrived on his desk. First, he would check the front page for any 'mistakes' in order to avoid chastisement from his superiors. Second, he would go through the paper and check that all the advertising space was filled.

The local radio station in the same town was also run almost entirely on the basis of advertising revenue, a matter clearly reflected in the primary concerns of its managers and journalists. The main aim of the station was the maximization of audiences which were assessed in quarterly surveys. The timing of programmes was seen as crucial to this aim and arranged in accordance with the conceptualised audience at any particular time. For example, they broadcast a programme particularly aimed at taxi-drivers whom surveys had revealed were among their largest group of listeners at certain times of day. The station also ran special programmes aimed at families for the evening dinner-time slot prior to national television news and also broadcast a late night show for migrant workers who often worked late shifts, did not have access to television and tended to listen to the radio before going to bed. At the same time, news had been made more chatty and less formal to appeal to listeners. Journalists at the station considered speed and immediacy as two of the most important advantages that radio journalism should exploit to attract audiences. Acknowledging the geographical limitations of these advantages, however, they explained how they considered local news to be their prime concern, and attached great importance to on-the-spot reporting from events as they happened, whenever possible. This was practicable for radio journalists using mobile phones, but not for newspaper and even television journalists who therefore found it hard to compete in this particular niche of journalism.

At the same time one editor at the station emphasised the need to keep 'propaganda'[9] to a minimum and as far as possible replace it with cultural or entertainment news. Listeners on the whole found propaganda boring. In this respect reporting of meetings posed a particular problem which again highlights the kind of conflict of interests that journalists faced. 'Meetings news' was the least popular kind of news with listeners who were not interested and did not want to hear it. Journalists therefore tried to find ways of keeping it to a minimum whilst fulfilling their unavoidable political obligations. Not reporting them was not an option.

Television producers have been facing the same problem. Pointing out how similar reductions have been attempted at Guangdong Television, Xie, also writing in the *South China Television Journal*, nonetheless points out that:

> Conventional, routine meetings reports are still to be found on our station and some city level stations. Meetings news receives a lot of airtime and long shots of leaders attending meetings are still to be seen. This does not fit with the demands of our news reforms and at the same time it weakens our competitiveness with other news media. It is also a waste of limited channel resources because it inevitably reduces the airtime available for broadcasting other information. Of course, the reform of meetings news has only just started and the emptiness of meetings reports persists. There are even some meetings reports that do have content, but still bore people because of the many shots of the meeting. The chairpeople of our meetings have still not got used to giving relaxed, natural interviews outside the conference hall. This state of affairs will probably persist for some time to come, but it is our responsibility through our work, slowly to take steps towards improving meeting reporting.
>
> (Xie 1997:13)

Journalists thought in terms of attracting and keeping audiences. Their work was not simply the provision of a public service, though it was certainly that; it was also the creation of products which would be in competition for the attention of audiences against other media products:

At present, because the quantity of all kinds of media is unceasingly increasing, competition is intense. Moreover, growth in audience information demands and the related market size have stagnated. This has caused the competition between similar media (terrestrial television and cable television) and different media (like television and radio, television and newspapers) to grow ever more intense by the day. In particular in our area of television, because external[10] programmes have penetrated the cable television network, this has completely opened up this most important of informational media so that programme management has faced serious challenges from all sides, with television news programmes being the first to be affected.

(Xie 1997:13)

Competition for Guangzhou-based television stations came in many forms. Besides the two local stations – Guangdong and Guangzhou Television (each with numerous both terrestrial and satellite channels) – viewers in Guangzhou in the late 1990s could receive numerous other provincial channels[11] and many or all of the eight Central Television channels. However, whereas the largest competition for many local stations in other provinces is likely to be from the central television (CCTV) channels, in much of Guangdong, especially the Pearl River Delta, the main competition, as Xie suggests, is from Hong Kong television (see also GDDSZJT Reform Group 1997). Hong Kong television has been watched in Guangzhou and other parts of Guangdong since the early 1980s with varying degrees of control and restriction, but with rapidly expanding cable networks in the 1990s, Hong Kong television viewing has become virtually ubiquitous.

With this 'external' programming, television audiences and producers alike[12] in Guangzhou have been exposed to different genres of television: Hong Kong soap operas, 'infotainment'[13] programmes, as well as foreign films and dramas. However, one of the most distinctive differences between Hong Kong and mainland television is to be found in news production. Hong Kong news, produced along the lines of European and North American television news, makes a stark contrast to the mainland news produced within the tight epistemological framework of party propaganda and the promotion of state socialism (Latham 2000; see also Lull 1991; Li 1991; Cheng and Tong 1993). It is, therefore, important to note that this exposure has made Guangzhou audiences increasingly aware of, and familiar with, alternative genres of news production.

There are three interrelated areas of news production practice that may be fruitfully considered in more detail: first, the conceptions of the market in which these producers see themselves competing; second, the kinds of editorial practices adopted by producers; and, finally, the conceptualizations of audiences that producers work with in the production of news. Through a consideration of these issues, which I undertake in the following sections of this chapter, I suggest that it is possible to come to a fuller understanding of the political engagement of journalists in Guangzhou.

Conceptualizing Markets

One day in the summer of 1997, I was talking to a television journalist about news production in Guangzhou and China more generally. One of the first things she pointed out was that competition was intense. However, we had been discussing the role of news media as the mouthpiece of the Party in China and how that was fundamental to understanding news production. Journalists could not just report anything they liked, however they liked. The extent of market competition clearly had its limits.

In the course of the discussion I asked how competition actually affected her. Her reply made it clear how closely felt this competition was to journalists' immediate concerns. Their wages, she pointed out, were bound up with bonus payments that were dependent on the profitability of the work unit. Furthermore, welfare provision, such as housing, health care and pensions, came through the work unit which meant that the greater the profitability of the work unit, the greater the welfare provision. The market and competition affected journalists in the most fundamental of places: in the pocket and in other important aspects of their everyday lives.

State enterprises, particularly in the 1980s, did not allow the forces of market capitalism to reach full fruition because of their continuing bureaucratic collectivist surplus extraction and welfare responsibilities (Smith 1993). Institutionally, media work units in the 1990s still did not function as fully capitalist enterprises and continued to have these social and welfare obligations. However, at the level of workers' understandings of their general situation, the market and competition figured widely. These very welfare benefits were one of the key things that were at stake in this competitive market. For many of them the market was not purely economic rhetoric from which state employees were distanced or separated by a protective work unit. Rather, it was a principle of media production and the mechanism by which welfare and bonus payments were calculated.

Furthermore, the market was not simply an abstract principle in accordance with which one conceived the competitive status of the programmes or articles that people produced. Principles of open competition have also been introduced to the internal practices of media institutions. For example, in 1997, Zhujiang (Pearl River) Television Station – the flagship Cantonese language station of Guangdong Television that was set up in 1983 specifically to compete with Hong Kong television – gave the station a complete face-lift and programming re-organisation to try to win back some of its greatly diminished share of the Guangdong (especially Pearl River Delta) audience (GDDSZJT Reform Group 1997).[14] At the same time, the station started experimenting with internal competition, introducing an open tendering system for programme ideas in an effort to overcome previous institutional restrictions on programme development. The rhetoric of the new system was that of pure 'competition: the only way to stimulate vitality' (Fan and Chen 1997). The stimulus for the change is the perception of intense competition for audiences, which requires better programmes, which are best brought about in another internal environment of open competition in which producers face the dangers of failure (Fan and Chen 1997:19–21). The competition of the marketplace has started to become everyday media production practice.

Competition between media producers, however, is not always seen as totally fair. The economic transition – with its associated juxtaposition of both market competition and state subsidy and control – was seen by many journalists as creating unequal market conditions. The competition for advertisers, and hence audiences, for television producers in Guangzhou was bound up with the continued state control of media units. In Guangzhou, for instance, this has produced the bizarre situation in which local television stations compete for advertisers with their own bosses in the Department of Broadcasting and Television (housed in the same building as Guangdong Television) who resell advertising time on cable-provided Hong Kong television. Furthermore, with news production, as outlined above, journalists must still work within limits laid down by government and Party officials. As Fang explains, this produces a 'special market' in television production:

> When it comes to economics, under the precondition of preserving the guidance of public opinion and the function of [the Party's] mouthpiece, it is necessary to comply with the requirements of the development of the market economy, to perfect and develop the television market system. This is a special market. Although it has the same characteristics as normal markets, it also has its own special nature. Its special nature is as follows: television has a strong political and propagandist nature. Its principal function and deployment of resources, like its allocation of financial investments and frequencies etc., is not totally suited to the principles of market economics; but in many aspects there exists a market system.
>
> (Fang 1997:12)

Rhetorically, the Party is able to maintain a clear demarcation of domains. The market is to provide new sources of income for investment in programme production, new technology and the entry into a globalizing media world. That is the 'modernization' of television production in China. Television and other media are also to meet the greater informational demands of a populace increasingly embroiled in a market economy (Fang 1997). At the same time, however, free, open competition is not appropriate when it comes to the political, ideological guidance of public opinion. It is in these circumstances that we find journalists, at times, suturing what are on the face of it contradictory positions. For instance, contributors to the *South China Television Journal*, even when not explicitly laying down the party line, are nonetheless all careful, when writing about the market and competition, to include reference to the maintenance of political control of the media. Although the topic of discussion is the development of market-driven media production, they nonetheless feel obliged to reiterate the longstanding and increasingly anachronistic dogma outlining the function of the media in socialist China. Hence, though the Party may rhetorically demarcate the areas appropriate to market competition and those to be protected from it, in the daily practices of media production, these domains cannot be clearly differentiated at all.

Newspaper editors, television journalists and radio producers made it clear that the everyday practices of running a newspaper, a television station or a radio station were always situated somewhere between these conflicting demands and in a realm totally immersed in both the dogma of Party ideology and commercial competitive interests. The perceived demands of market competition inevitably lead journalists and editors to push the limits of political control – whether it be in minimizing the reporting of meetings, attempting to include greater regional or extra-regional news coverage, or resorting to populism and sensationalism (Latham forthcoming). The once largely unchallenged political domination of media production by the Party has now become infused with the tension created by the conflicting pressures of market competition – a tension which is played out daily in the practices of editors, journalists and other media producers.

However, in conceptualizing media production as such a tension, it is important to avoid the potentially simplistic reduction of this tension to a clumsy opposition between domination and resistance. The notions of market competition and the leadership of the Party give us some of the important vocabulary with which media producers talk about their work, but they do not in themselves make clear the agentive aspects of people's practices. Journalists, in their everyday practices, are at times perpetuating Party ideologies and at others attempting to circumscribe them, but neither case is usefully formulated as either simply submission or resistance. To consider the political subjectivity of journalists and the vital position they play in China's party-dominated hegemony, it is necessary to look more closely at, first, editorial practice and then conceptualizations of audiences.

Editorial Practice

In the summer of 1997, I helped in the production of a number of English language documentary programmes for a television station in Guangzhou. One of my tasks was to write and present introductions to the films. Ideally I would meet the producer about half an hour before recording. She would tell me the content of the films, which I had not seen, and indicate particular aspects that she wanted emphasised. This could be propaganda: the positive contribution of the work unit featured in the film to the modernization of China, the selfless human concern of hospital workers for the people in their care or sacrifices made or innovative action taken in the service of the people. She might also want to emphasise areas of novelty or points of unusual interest: the development of a particular medical or agricultural technique for instance. On the other hand, she might stress a particular perspective from which she wished to shine a favourable light on the work unit featured in the film whose managers quite possibly saw this as free advertisement.[15] Neither commercial interests nor politics were ever far away. I was left to write the introductions and possibly correct the voice-over script. On occasions this all happened in five minutes as we got into the recording studio, while the producer and technicians waited for me to write and memorize the introductions.

Time was of the essence. Everyone had a job to do. The studio was booked for a specific time. We all had other things to be getting on with. The tape had to be finished within a couple of hours, including subsequent editing, for the tapes to be dispatched to the broadcasting section ready for the next day. This was no time to be questioning the particular ideological slant of an item or thinking about how one conceptualised television production. This was work. I wrote what I thought the producer wanted me to say and in a way that I assumed would be acceptable within the conventions of Chinese news and documentary production as I understood them, though this is something I became aware of after the fact rather than consciously in the course of doing it. So, for instance, I might write or phrase pieces in accordance with the notion of holding up model workers as an example to be followed or the promotion of public-spirited service. These pieces were written with a quite different notion of news production in mind to those I would have employed in a non-Chinese context. If what I said lacked particular points or emphasis the producer would put me straight. I would write and memorize again. Meanwhile everyone waited.[16]

We have seen how ideologies of the market came into play in editorial decision making and production practice with efforts to maximize popularity with audiences or attempts to produce better programming in line with audience demand conceived in terms of market forces. In this instance, however, it is also clear how the everyday practices of journalists simultaneously reproduced Party and government ideologies. Journalists in situations like the ones in which I was involved became the instruments of the complex agency of Party-state hierarchy (cf. Inden 1990, Hobart 1990). Through the adoption of conventional, accepted forms of representation, the producers in effect shifted responsibility for their actions onto the Party structure and, through such conventional instrumental practices, the ideology of state socialism was perpetuated and reproduced, as was the notion of media production as the mouthpiece of the Party.[17]

Such perpetuation or reproduction of Party ideological forms, however, does not necessarily entail belief or faith in that ideology. In fact, most producers would at times, among themselves or to me, express some degree of scepticism towards Party control and the notion of the media that went with it. This could take many forms, some relating to the rising importance of market competition, some more general – complaints about unfair competition, frustration at the limitations of truly investigative reporting or comparison with foreign media, for instance, which they saw as free to say whatever they liked in a manner that they were not. Such alternative understandings could be manifested in editorial practice in numerous ways, such as the attempts to minimize meetings news discussed above (see also Latham forthcoming). One newspaper editor told me how he was pleased to be able not to include propaganda on a recent Guangzhou clean-up campaign (see Latham 2000) despite Party directives to editors generally to do so, because of the specialist economic nature of his newspaper. Being well educated in both Chinese and foreign journalistic theory, he also explained how he would in different ways try to push the limits of Party control, to try to produce a more innovative and interesting quality newspaper.[18] Yet despite such protestations and practices of news production, in the pressured and habitual circumstances of everyday media production, these same journalists would routinely formulate news stories in compliance with their ideas of Party expectations of the media.

In these ways journalistic practices dealt with conflicting and contradictory notions of what was news, what was newsworthy and how news production fitted into society. Journalists were, therefore, the locus of shifting and contending practices of discursive social reproduction. These practices, furthermore, were crucially placed within a shifting hegemonic formation in China in which the party clearly held the dominant position. To understand the nature of this hegemony, how it is changing and the crucial role of journalists within it, it is helpful to consider how journalists conceptualized their audiences, the subject of the next section.

Conceptualizing Audiences

Ien Ang (1990) has noted the unknowability of audiences and the practical necessity of imagining television audiences for media producers (see also Hartley 1992:101–146). In the European and American cases that she deals with, she notes the ways in which media producers have conceptualised or constructed images of audiences through surveys and analysis of programme ratings. In contemporary media production in Guangzhou there are different conceptualizations of the audience that come into play, relating once again to the ambiguous position of media production between state ideology and control and the developing rhetoric of market forces.

The Party conceptualisation of media audiences, the general populace, is made clear in Fang's discussion of the need for the establishment of a 'Public Opinion Centre' within Guangdong Television in order to:

> All the better, create a good public opinion environment for national reform, the 'open door' policy and the modernization of socialism and to constitute the good psychological preparation of the masses.

> (Fang 1997:8)

The role of the media, constituted as the mouthpiece of the Party, is to support party policy and help the government build a socialist society (Li 1991:347–8). The presupposition of this understanding is that the masses are vulnerable to incorrect thinking and in need of the appropriate education and guidance in order to properly understand government and Party policy. Fang's public opinion centre would aid this:

> ... In the situation of facing the various misleading opinions of foreign and external television, [the establishment of the centre] would preserve the strong correct guidance of public opinon.

> (Fang 1997:8)

This is a paternalistic and 'paedocratic' (Hartley 1992) conceptualization of audiences adopted in line with Chinese communist understandings of human nature as infinitely malleable in social practice (Munro 1977, especially pp.15–25).[19] Xie states this explicitly when discussing 'spiritual civilisation' reporting in Guangdong television:

> ... The final objective of the establishment of spiritual civilization is to transform people, to change the norms of people's thought, outlook and actions, to raise people's cultural qualities and spiritual tastes.[20]

> (Xie 1997:12)

At the same time, as journalists have increasingly been drawn into thinking of their work in relation to market competition, they have come to conceptualize audiences in new ways. Recent writing by Chinese media producers and journalism theorists is strewn with references to attracting and keeping audiences and to increasing their share of the television audience (for example, Fang 1997; Xie 1997; GDDSZJT Reform Group 1997; Fan and Chen 1997). Fan and Chen (1997:20), for instance, explain the need for internal competition within Zhujiang Television Station:

> We face the intense competition of television and media production just as commodity production faces the market ... If you have commodity production you have market exchange and all products are differentiated in the marketplace into high and low (quality), good and bad.

The driving concern arising from such competition is to attract audiences:

> What does a television station rely on to attract audiences? What does it rely upon to improve audience ratings? It has to rely on good television programmes.

> (Fan and Chen 1997:19)

The conception of audiences in this way is quite different from that revealed in Party understandings of the media outlined above. Here audiences are a diverse set of highly selective people with particular tastes that must be catered to (Fang 1997). Audiences are constituted as consumers not as vulnerable, malleable objects, even if Party rhetoric does sometimes attempt an articulation of the two (for example, Fang 1997, Xie 1997). There is a common argument in writing about media and journalism, for instance, that drawing closer to audiences by catering to their tastes will better enable the ideological transformation of public opinion.[21]

This conceptualization of audiences has been reflected in various practices of journalists. The ways, for instance, in which the local radio station centred its production around audience surveys and adapting programming to maximise audience share. As Tim Wilson (1997) has noted, papers like the *Nanfang Weekend* have increasingly turned to sensationalist reporting in a bid to expand readerships in an increasingly competitive market place (see also Latham forthcoming).

Here we have two different frameworks in relation to which audiences were conceptualised in media production. These contradictory conceptualisations of audiences may be voiced in certain rhetorical writings, as we have seen, as well as in the production of particular programmes or the writing of particular newspaper articles. However, there is another way in which these conceptualisations come into conflict with each other: in media producers themselves.

One television journalist explained to me how she found the censorship of Hong Kong television frustrating. Like others, she found it aggravating when watching Hong Kong television to realize that news stories, for example, were cut. She thought it a little anachronistic at a time when news was becoming available to many people, particularly those of a higher educational level like herself, from so many external sources, such as the internet, Hong Kong newspapers, foreign travel and visitors or international telecommunications to name but a few. However, she explained why she understood the necessity of the practice nonetheless, an explanation that she also gave as the justification for continued Party control of the media more generally.

Many people in Guangdong, she explained, despite the extent of recent development in the province, were still of a relatively low educational level. Such people could be easily 'confused' and may not fully understand Hong Kong television and the kind of reporting that it carried. One had to take the overall national picture into consideration, she explained, and especially people's greatest fear: chaos. Hence, this journalist referred to quite different notions of audiences. She had one notion of the majority of the people as vulnerable and in need of protection and appropriate education. And another notion of more educated people, like herself, capable of critical understanding. At the same time when discussing competition, she had explained the need to make attractive programming to meet audience demands in a highly competitive world.

Other journalists made similar points saying that most people, in Guangzhou at least, were sceptical of the political content of media production (cf. Latham 2000), again referring to their own experiences as television viewers and newspaper readers themselves. One, for instance, explained various reasons why he and others preferred Hong Kong television – mainly because of the soaps, but also because of faster news reporting. He further explained how he would bring to bear such notions of the audience drawing upon his own experiences, in his own programme production, to try to make programmes more popular.

Though both of these journalists, and others, were involved in the production of programmes aimed at the paedocratised audience of Party dictat, they nonetheless at times also rejected that notion of the audience as one that could adequately summarise the specific viewing tastes and practices of people in Guangzhou. This was a rejection informed by their own tastes, practices and knowledge of others as media consumers. Such a paedocratic notion was not their own and they clearly thought it inappropriate for large sections of the population and both inaccurate and inadequate as a general formulation. Yet, as we have seen in the previous section, in the situated, practical circumstances of news production, they perpetuated at times the practices of conceptualizing audiences in that way.

In their duality as both producers and themselves consumers of news, journalists were the locus of various antagonistic conceptualisations of audiences that have arisen with the increasing impingement of competitive market practices on the realm of media production in Guangzhou. Furthermore, the increasing importance of alternative conceptualisations of media production in terms of markets and consuming audiences – along with the sometimes personal scepticism of producers (and audiences) increasingly familiar with and drawn to alternative notions of media production (as seen on Hong Kong television for instance) – reveals some fragility to the Party-dominated hegemony in China. It remains, in conclusion, to consider how this is the case.

Conclusion

The fear of chaos (Latham 2000) can be seen to be crucial to the perpetuation of the current hegemonic formation in China in which the Party maintains its dominant position. Most journalists, as well as many non-media people, would offer similar justifications to that given by the journalist above for the maintenance of Party control of media in China. The fear of chaos resonates, for many, with the events of 1989, but equally significantly with those of the Cultural Revolution, the warring chaos of twentieth century China and even further back into imperial history. The destructive and highly negative consequences of such chaoses, for many within living memory, should be avoided at all costs.

The fear of chaos, however, was crucially voiced in relation to other rhetorics. For instance, the Party promotes a strong rhetoric of national unity accompanied by acknowledgement of the problems of modernization that China faces due to the size of the country and its population (cf. Anagnost 1997:12–13, 117–137). Such rhetoric was reproduced by many people in Guangzhou who explained the need to consider the national picture as a whole. Though Guangdong may represent a special case, they would say, one had to take into account the national situation marked by a massive population of relatively uneducated people. Once one did this, the maintenance of strong ideological leadership and control by the Party, even in Guangdong, had to be sanctioned. The perceived alternative for many would be chaos.[22]

Alongside this there was a general appreciation by many in Guangzhou, whatever particular personal complaints they may have had of their immediate economic difficulties, that under reform they had become significantly better off than before. Were the country to fall into chaos, the economic and other freedoms that people had gained would be jeopardized (cf. Tang 1996). For most people, this would not be a price worth paying – whatever advantages might be associated with an immediate liberalization of the media. As one newspaper editor put it, step-by-step change is always preferable to sudden change, as the latter inevitably runs a high risk of bringing chaos. This, for him, reflected some conflict of interest. He was a strong advocate of media liberalization and saw his own work as constantly pressing the limits of media control. Yet, at the same time, though in principle he favoured liberalization, he understood the need for any change to be gradual, even if at times that meant frustration, possibly subdued, in his own work.

This editor's comments also highlight another important aspect of Party rhetoric – the rhetoric of transition itself. The transition in question is from one economic system to another, but associated with that, for many people, were assumptions that greater economic freedom under a market economy would continue to bring with it, as it has over the past two decades, ever more social and, perhaps, political freedoms. For journalists this was usually seen as increasing freedom in media production. The combination of an assumed carrot of gradual liberalization dangled before them, along with the perceived potentially dire consequences of too sudden a change, was for most journalists sufficient reason to tolerate whatever frustrations they had with the present. At the same time, the immediate personal awareness of the consequences of transgression clearly played a part in the routine maintenance of conventional production practice.

However, the rhetoric of transition has a double edge to it. On the one hand, it is precisely the rhetoric of the Party – and, articulated with fears of chaos, part of the justification for continued one-party rule – to keep chaos at bay: a strong, central, omnipotent government is a prerequisite. On the other hand, transition is articulated with notions of liberalisation – making it the rhetoric of a future in which tight, one-party rule may be a thing of the past. This double edge, this tension within the rhetoric of transition, also holds the key to understanding the vulnerabilities of the Party's hegemony in China. Ci Jiwei (1994) has characterized the shift from Maoism into the reform period as one from utopianism, which has at its core a deferred hedonism, to undeferred hedonism in the practices of China's emerging consumer society. For Tang (1996) such consumerism is, likewise, the contemporary idiom for dealing with the 'anxieties of everyday life'. Hence, rhetorics of the future are clearly having to face up to their limitations in contemporary China. Journalists voice their visions of future media liberalization as the self-justification for their participation in perpetuating the Party's dominant position in China's hegemony with which they feel somewhat uncomfortable. Yet, clearly this self-justification is one that will sooner or later require a pay-off.

Hence, the rhetoric of transition, the fear of the consequences of chaos and the requirements of national unity figured crucially in the perpetuation of the hegemonic formation that I have been outlining here. However, it is also clear that this hegemony is constantly shifting and contested in relation to the complex manner of its perpetuation. Though this hegemony may be dominated by the Party and ultimately be supported by the threat of state violence, this domination is dependent upon the acceptance of these rhetorics by those, such as journalists, in crucial positions, who perpetuate it. The media now are seen by the Party to be just as necessary to the ideological support of reform, modernization and the transition to a market economy as they are to the support of Party rule. Just as an analysis of media production reveals the dominance of Party control in the current hegemony, at the same time it reveals the weaknesses, dependencies and fissures of this hegemony. The rhetoric of national unity, for instance, comes to look increasingly anachronistic (Anagnost 1997, Dirlik and Zhang 1998) and sometimes fails to adequately account for people's daily experiences. At the same time, it seems reasonable to assume that the fear of chaos will undoubtedly diminish the further China moves away from the tragic experiences of the Cultural Revolution and through a period of extended social calm.

Most people in Guangzhou – media producers and others alike – are highly aware of the forms of media control. Anyone who watches Hong Kong television news regularly cannot miss them. This awareness necessarily entails the knowledge of alternatives, however they may be conceived or understood, and inevitably entails the potential weakening of the claims to legitimacy of such forms of control. This legitimacy becomes increasingly dependent upon the acceptance of other rhetorics such as those relating to chaos, national unity and economic prosperity rather than carrying a persuasive force of its own. Hence, the political engagement of people in Guangzhou may not exhibit the theatricality of open dissent, but what I hope to have shown in this paper is some of the ways in which the practices of people in their everyday lives are nonetheless highly political. In everyday practice people maintain hegemonic formations, but any hegemony is founded upon its own instability (Laclau and Mouffe 1985).

The Chinese Communist Party has always put the media at the heart of its system of political control and journalists practices are therefore inevitably political. In everyday practice they simultaneously maintain, and yet also circumvent and redirect, the Party's hegemonic strategies. This is not a matter of domination and resistance. In their daily practices, journalists often perpetuated ageing and increasingly anachronistic ideologies, but they were rarely, in fact, dominated by them. There was no small degree of complicity in maintaining this hegemony as we have seen. However, at the same time, they were often trying to overstep or extend the limits and boundaries imposed by these anachronisms, whether primarily for commercial or for political motivations. In this sense they were not 'resisting' the power of the state and the Party – they were not dissidents – but they were certainly playing with and in the interstices opened up between political control and commercial competition. In this way, the political subjectivity of journalists has to be understood in relation to the specific conditions of contemporary China where politics and the constitution of political subjectivities move in rather more mysterious ways than entailed by the straightforward categories of authoritarianism and dissent, which stereotypically characterise accounts of Chinese politics.

Notes

1 This paper is based on fieldwork carried out in the summers of 1996, 1997 and 1999 as well as other interim visits to Guangzhou, Hong Kong and other towns in the Pearl River Delta. I am grateful to the Nuffield Foundation, SOAS Research Committee and the Sino-British Fellowship Trust for their generous funding of this research. I am grateful to participants at the *ConsumAsian* conference in Hong Kong at Easter 1998 and Stephen Hughes at SOAS for their comments on an earlier draft of this paper. I must also thank Silvia Ferrero for her invaluable comments on all versions of this paper. All shortcomings and errors remain, of course, my own.

2 Although I deal primarily with journalists in this paper much of the discussion is relevant to the situation of media producers more generally, by which I mean all those generally working in television, radio and print media production. I use the term 'journalists' as a broad category that includes different ranks of reporters, editors, script-writers, and news programme producers: that is, all those involved in the production of news.

3 Note that collectivisation here refers to decentralisation: that is, to the transfer from state to collective control. 'Industrialization' here implies improvements in productivity and efficiency. Below, for instance, he goes on to relate this to what he calls 'factorification', commoditisation and increasing efficiency in the production of higher quality programmes.

4 Here, again, 'socialization' means movement out of state control: that is, a kind of privatisation.

5 The terminology of state ownership and state control has taken on semantic subtlety in the early 1990s. Ikels (1996:3) explains: '... The party in the winter of 1992–3 reformulated its rationale for the various economic reforms. It stated forthrightly that its objective was to create a "socialist market economy". Theorists carefully explained away the seeming oxymoron of a market economy that is socialist at the same time. The essence of socialist economy, they pointed out, is ownership of the means of production, not management of the means of production. So long as the state remains the owner of the means of production, it does not really matter who is responsible for running the factories, utilities, airlines. To make this point even clearer, state enterprises now are referred to in the media not as *guoying* (state-operated) but as *guoyou* (national [that is, in state ownership]) enterprises'. Note that this refers to financial matters. For media producers, political control is of fundamental importance, of course. Media work units have become more independent in terms of financial control (see below), but much less so in terms of political control.

105

6 See, for instance, Li (1991), Cheng and Tong (1997) and Latham (2000).

7 For example, the *Nanfang Daily* and *Nanfang Weekend* report national and international news, as well as southern news generally. The *Guangzhou Daily* and *Yangcheng Evening News* both also have national and international news as well as local news of Guangzhou. In addition, they both run supplements on the Pearl River Delta.

8 In this regard, he also complained of the unfair market situation in which some local newspapers continued to receive large state subsidies, while others like his were left to the vagaries of market competition.

9 Note that the term *xuanchuan*, usually glossed as propaganda, does not have the strong negative connotations that the English word does. 'Information' might be a closer gloss to the more neutral sense of the Chinese which can equally refer to marketing or advertising as to political persuasion. Here, however, the term was clearly referring to political information, what the party wanted people to know. 'Propaganda' therefore seems like an appropriate term to use.

10 For instance, Hong Kong television.

11 To receive in excess of twenty channels was not unusual. Among others, I myself could receive Xinjiang, Zhejiang, Hunan, Guangxi, Sichuan and Jiangsu channels, in addition to the local and national channels and Hong Kong channels.

12 It is important to remember, as I shall discuss later, that producers themselves also make up audiences.

13 In the late 1990s the two Chinese language Hong Kong television stations gave daily prime time evening slots to *Sihng Si Cheui Gik* and *Gam Yat Taai Jan D*. These were hour-long magazine programmes that reported on social issues in the news which were of immediate interest to viewers in Hong Kong (for example, food scares, school exams and so on), alongside gossipy show-biz news and entertainment guidance. These are often referred to as 'infotainment' programmes, or more derogatorily by 'real' news producers as '*baat gwa san mahn*' – 'divination news' – referring to traditional Chinese forms of divination regarded by many as superstitious. The reference here suggests the unreliability of these programmes and their lack of journalist rigour.

14 Cf. Zhao (1998:95–100) on the setting up, and success, of Pearl River Economic Radio to compete directly with Hong Kong radio stations which had become very popular among Guangdong audiences.

15 A worker at a hotel which was featured in one of these documentaries and who was involved in helping the camera crew, told me how lucky the hotel was to be having a free advertisement made for it. She was not aware of the making of a documentary. With the combination of familiar rhetorics of public service along with the clear exploitation of such commercial motivations for programme making, we can see the kind of complex hybrid programming which the reform period has brought about.

16 Though this represents practices relating to particular programmes in which I was involved, the circumstances under which they were produced were, as far as I am aware, not unlike those under which other documentaries were also made.

17 Note that I am not suggesting that this production entails the perpetuation of ideology among consumers of such media products. That is dependent upon viewing practices in which quite different articulations to those I describe here may be taking place (cf. Hall 1980; Morley 1980, 1989, 1992).

18 This is reminiscent of Pickowicz's (1995) discussion of Chinese film-makers under reform. In many ways, I see his account of the 'velvet prisons' of film production as dealing with similar issues to my concerns in this chapter. However, I suggest that the metaphor over-determines Party control.

19 Elsewhere (Latham forthcoming) I have argued that newspaper journalists have increasingly come to work with the important conception of their readers as consumers. In the current political and economic climate in China this is at least as important as 'paedocracy'.

20 Anagnost (1997) has argued that the rhetorics of 'civilisation' in contemporary China have also played a vital role in the opening up of China and the subjection of the Chinese populace to the forces of global capitalism.

21 It is worth pointing out a certain double-edged quality to the notion of *yu lun* usually glossed as 'public opinion'. It is both the common understanding of the populace and the result of ideological manipulation of that common understanding (see, for example, Fang 1997).

22 I have argued elsewhere (Latham 2000) that these rhetorics function as empty signifiers in perpetuating China's Party-dominated hegemony.

5

TURNING SEEING INTO BELIEVING

Producing Credibility in the Television News Coverage of the Kobe Earthquake

Liz MacLachlan

Ever since the Frankfurt School in the 1920s initiated its critical inquiry into the role of mass media in propagating the logic of fascism and capitalism, anthropologists, sociologists, political economists and other media critics have been asking what it is that makes people believe what they read, hear and see in the media. Research on media credibility over the years has yielded fascinating results, especially with regard to the study of news. In general, these studies fall into one of three theoretical/methodological categories – sociological production studies, critical text analysis and ethnographic reception studies.

Production studies address credibility issues by going directly to the newsroom to see how reporters consciously and unconsciously promote the 'reality' of their news stories through various rhetorical and visual techniques. These techniques include a commitment to objectivity (Schudson 1978; Gans 1980), the use of publicly recognized sources to verify claims (Sigal 1986; Fishman 1980), the 'balance' of opinions to demonstrate non-partisanship and identify conflict (Gitlin 1980), the eschewal of value-laden terminology and overt emotional expressions (Carey 1986), the use of technical terminology and special effects (Cardarola 1992; Burns 1977) and the building of tautological 'webs of facticity' to substantiate claims by third party sources (Tuchman 1978).

Text analyses focus on the news product itself, identifying structural features and patterns of disclosure that persuade readers to accept its claims as true. Screen theorists focus on the notion of 'positioning,' arguing that the unique televisual features of broadcast news – its ability to broadcast live, the delivery of text through speech, the use of images and special effects – create 'truth conditions' which are more compelling and convincing to the audience than written news reports (Stam 1992; Morse 1986). Discourse analysts uncover patterns in reporting and editing – the choice of words and images, the order in which facts are presented, the way in which events are explained – which point to deeper patterns of underlying assumptions and implicit points of view. Taken together, these assumptions make up the dominant discourse, a point of view which the viewer must assume in order to understand the text. Mainstream American news broadcasts, for example, generally represent existing power structures dominated by white males and a capitalist order as natural and inevitable (Gray 1991; Hartman and Husband 1974). Alternative or opposi- tional discourse representing black, female or other perspectives are also possible, but they are less obvious and more contradictory (Fiske 1989, 1996; Gross 1989).

Reception studies center on the interaction between the text and audience to see how the process of interpretation works and to locate junctures between seeing and believing. Most involve ethnographic audience studies identifying not only who watches (Ang and Hermes 1991; Morley 1980), but also where and how they watch (Morley 1986; Lull 1990; Sreberny-Mohammadi 1991). The contribution of these studies is in demonstrating the diversity of text interpretations asserted by the audience at the point of reading while simultaneously acknowledging the limitations on interpretations imposed by the authors at the point of production.

Many of these studies ultimately draw connections between the power to make audiences believe in the news and the power to advance ideologies promoting the interests of the rich and powerful. Yet despite these conclusions, there is little discussion of economic cost inherent in maintaining these rhetorical and visual devices. Production studies explain the importance of certain news practices which demonstrate the credibility of news to its audiences, but more often than not fail to identify the monetary costs involved in performing these practices or to compare these news organizations with others that cannot afford to perform such practices. Text analyses note the suggestive power of live television and special effects, but similarly do not discuss the immense costs involved in achieving such effects or evaluate their effectiveness through comparisons with news that is not produced in such a fashion. Reception studies do address economic influences, but limit distinctions of money to that of audience income and not to production budget. These omissions are especially surprising given the amount of money media organizations put into their news operations in an attempt to produce news that is as 'realistic' and believable as possible, and even more so when considering the great diversity of news organizations – not only in developed countries where large and small news stations operate in a competitive market, but in developing countries where international satellite and cable news programs such as Sky TV and CNN broadcast in competition with local stations.

In this chapter I will address the relationship between economic resources and television news credibility. I will do so by comparing the ways that three differently financed news organizations covered a common news event and by evaluating how coverage of each was received by its audiences. It will be my contention that the greater the economic resources available for news production, the more likely a news organization will be able to produce news its audience finds credible and trustworthy.

The common news event discussed will be the 1995 Kobe Earthquake Disaster. The three news organizations will be the local (Kobe-based) private broadcast station Sun TV, the national public broadcast station NHK and the Tokyo-based production crew for the nationally syndicated commercial television program *The Sunday* (hereafter referred to as '*Sunday*'). My comparison will be based not solely on the end product (in other words, news broadcasts) via content analysis, but rather on the conditions and processes of production at the beginning stage of production, that is, at the point of information gathering. The information I use comes from the following three sources: published accounts of experiences in reporting the earthquake written by journalists themselves; interviews with journalists who covered the Kobe story; and fieldwork observations collected over a three day period I spent in Kobe immediately following the earthquake with several news crews including those from *Sunday*.[1]

Reporting from Kobe: Three Versions

The Great Kansai Earthquake hit Kobe at 6:17 a.m. on January 17, 1995. Registering 7.12 on the Richter Scale, the earthquake toppled buildings, split the earth and initiated a series of fires that would take three days to put out. By the end of the week over 5,000 were reported dead and 300,000 estimated homeless. In terms of property damage and loss of life it was the worst national disaster to hit Japan since the Great Kanto Earthquake in 1923.

Within minutes of its occurrence, journalists the world over were alerted to the disaster through phone calls, pagers and wire dispatches. National network television news producers in Tokyo acted quickly, designating their Osaka affiliates as the earthquake news headquarters and dispatching reporters and equipment to the Kobe area. By the end of the day hundreds of news crews had left for the city; meanwhile thousands of Kobe residents were struggling to get out.

Local news reporters: Sun TV

One group of earthquake survivors who did not attempt to leave Kobe were staff members of Sun TV, a small commercial television station located within the city limits. Although the station itself was badly damaged in the quake, these news men and women were determined to continue broadcasting to the thousands of local audience members who would turn to the station for vital disaster-related information. Monzen Yoshiyasu, a reporter for the station, described the difficulties faced by the Sun TV staff:

> The earthquake hit just as the technicians were setting up for the day. Machinery and research materials flew across the office and the phones stopped working. After a few moments, the generator kicked in bringing a weak electricity current, but the heavy door of the studio had been ripped off its hinges and the cameras had all fallen with a crash ... The weather camera which usually took in the Kobe vista was broken. The fax machine connecting the station to the Kyodo wire service was also broken.

110

As soon as we got the emergency phone line up and running, we received calls from station employees who provided live audio reports from different parts of the city. Since the caption-printing machine was out, we had to write the names of the speakers and areas by hand and hold it up on a piece of paper in front of the camera. As staff members began filtering into the office they reported things they had seen on the way to work and that was also broadcast ...

In this way we began our emergency broadcast which would last for six days, 24 hours a day without commercial interruption. On that first day only one-third of the staff, or about 50 people, were able to make it to the station. Neither the station's management nor the staff had imagined they could fall victim to such a disaster, and consequently, we were left without so much as a 'how to' manual to deal with this disaster ourselves.

(Monzen 1995:16–17)

The news staff at Sun TV were clearly more than detached observers of the earthquake disaster; they were active participants through their own experiences as victims. Despite the limitations they faced as producers of news – the shortage of staff, malfunctioning equipment, lack of transportation and a breakdown of communications with 'official' sources of information (wire services, government press clubs) – they were committed to serving the information needs of the community. In order to do so they were forced to improvise, using whatever means of information gathering they could.

A few reporters traveled to the various 'Centers for Emergency Control' (*saigai taisaku honbu*) located throughout the prefecture to gather official information, but most stayed in the newsroom processing the almost endless source of information provided by audience members who called into the station. They broadcast information on where to find shelter, food, water, blankets and medical care and carried open appeals from families looking for lost members. They advertised hotlines for legal and financial counsel and provided names of shelters where pets could be boarded temporarily. They even included in their broadcasts such 'dirty' news as the location of functioning toilets, bath houses and short-term storage places for ancestral tablets and bones. As routines of confirmation were relaxed and the audience was given a greater role in the news production process, Sun TV was transformed into a virtual televisual bulletin board broadcasting messages to and from its Kobe audience. The reporters produced the news, but as they themselves acknowledged, it was the audience who wrote it.

National public broadcasting: NHK

As a public broadcasting system operating at both the national and local level, NHK had a dual broadcasting commitment – to serve victims in the affected local areas and to serve audiences across the nation at large. As the largest television station in Japan (employing over ten times the number of employees as the next largest commercial station) it was able to honor this commitment to its constituencies by dispatching hundreds of reporters from all over Japan into the disaster zone to assist the local Kobe bureau members in gathering earthquake-related news. Some reporters roamed the streets of Kobe gathering 'tissue paper' news detailing the status of bus routes, the location of medical and food supplies, directions to refugee centers, the names of stores open for business, and other information needed for daily living. Other reporters went to local authorities to gather more general information related to the disaster – official death tolls, Richter scale measurements of the aftershocks, the extent of damage to public transportation systems, the state of 'lifelines' (waterworks, electricity and gas lines), and so on. Still others rode in helicopters and satellite-equipped vans broadcasting live images of collapsed buildings, houses on fire, rescue attempts being made. Meanwhile those in Tokyo gathered information from press clubs and other official channels on the deployment status of the Self Defense Forces, the amount and quality of international aid offers, the estimated cost of damage in economic terms, and other news from the capital.

NHK's ability to cover the earthquake story thoroughly and authoritatively was enhanced also by the quality of reporters it sent to Kobe. These reporters were almost without exception former residents of the Kobe area and consequently equipped with enough local knowledge and social connections to give them an edge over the competition. While other out-of-town reporters were struggling to find places and people to interview, 'local' reporters at NHK were able to quickly reinsert themselves into the local community. One NHK reporter for instance was able to secure an interview with an old friend in Kobe despite the friend's reluctance to appear on camera without any make-up and in her 'messy' home. The reporter remarked: 'It was convenient for NHK [to use me] because I knew the area and could interview my friends. I wanted to go because I am a journalist, but at the same time, I wanted to go because I had friends there that I wanted to contact'.

The existence of such a large pool of 'local' reporters was no coincidence; it was the result of a training system at NHK which assigns rookie reporters to local bureaus for a period of no less than five years before transferring them either to another local bureau or to the Tokyo head office. This pattern, modeled after that of the national dailies and wire services in Japan, is designed to ensure that large news organizations like NHK maintain a uniform standard of news production across local bureaus while at the same time using these smaller news stations as the training ground of future national news reporters. Commercial stations by contrast, operate as independent organizations with network affiliation but entirely separate staff and accounts. Transfers and training programs involve moving employees between departments within the company, but rarely if ever outside the station itself. Thus while commercial news reporters are trained to have a broader range of skills outside of news reporting (for instance in accounting, sales, entertainment programming), NHK reporters will have more experience as news reporters in different fields of specialization and geographical areas. In the case of the earthquake story, these experiences proved invaluable in giving NHK a competitive edge over other news organizations.

Commercial television news magazines: Sunday

Sunday is a ninety-minute infotainment program broadcast once a week live on Nippon Television Corporation (NTV), a national commercial network. Part gossip, part hard news, it consists of a series of news reports introduced and analyzed by a team of regular panelists who range from university professors and journalists to baseball players and TV celebrities (*tarento*). The staff behind the scenes who produce the reports are a mix of freelancers, part-timers and employees of independent production companies who have been contracted by the station to work exclusively on the program. None involved in the production of the show, apart from the head producers and a few trainees, is actually employed by the station itself.

The program is described by its producers as a 'news program' (*nyūsu bangumi*) but it actually falls under the auspices of the 'Social Information Section' rather than the news department. As a result, while content consists almost entirely of news stories, success is measured entirely by audience ratings. Since most staff members are not full-time members of the network station, the pressure to keep up ratings is backed by the very real threat of firing. As a result, program staffers find themselves in a Catch 22: they are obligated as producers of a 'news' program to present material in a factual and journalistically responsible manner; yet at the same time they must make the program as entertaining as possible.[2]

The first *Sunday* reporting team assigned to the earthquake story arrived in Kobe on January 19, two days after the initial quake. The team consisted of five members, a director, a director's assistant, a cameraman, an audio/light technician, and a reporter. None was very familiar with Kobe, and for a few it was their first time to the city. Unlike Sun TV or NHK reporters who had lived in Kobe, this news crew had no friends in the city nor any knowledge of the city's geography to guide them through its ravaged streets. Unlike newsroom reporters from out of town who could rely on press clubs for official statements and briefings, they lacked the credentials that would gain them entrée into meetings. Unlike Tokyo reporters for national commercial stations who were able to share resources, film and staff owned by local affiliate stations, they were considered independents and denied access. What information the news crew of *Sunday* would get in Kobe they would have to find on their own.

With little information to go by, they set off first to a place they had heard about in the news – the city of Nagata. This city had been the scene of the worst fires in Kobe and cleared only twelve hours earlier as safe for entry. They spent the day in Nagata filming the worst scenes of destruction, the long lines for food in refugee centers and the activities of the Self Defense Forces who had just moved into the area. Over the next several days they filled out their film stock with more scenes of damage including collapsed highways, the Kobe railway station and other famous landmarks. By the time they sent their film to Tokyo for editing at the end of the week it contained reels of film footage showing the worst damage done to Kobe, but little official information to put it in context. The resulting report was a rather sensationalist rendering of the earthquake damage, long on impressions and short on hard facts.

By the second week, however the news crew at *Sunday* found ways to compensate for their lack of connection to the area. They began to focus on small manageably sized stories documenting the experiences of individuals, families and small groups of survivors who allowed themselves to be interviewed and filmed. These reports focused on the 'emotional' truth of the earthquake in its aftermath, revealed through stories of valor, hope, and tragedy told by these local heroes. One story followed a single family as it struggled to cope with life in a refugee center, while another covered the efforts of a group of apartment owners to collect enough money to pay for the demolition of their own building which had been irreparably damaged in the earthquake.

The *Sunday* reporters also kept close tabs on articles that came out in the foreign press which covered themes largely overlooked by other Japanese reporters. Such reports included information on the fate of non-Japanese victims and reactions to the earthquake by the international community; many were openly critical of the Japanese government which was judged too slow in responding to the needs of the victims. In particular these reports asked why it had taken so long to mobilize the Self Defense Forces for rescue operations, and why it took so long for official information pertaining to the damage sustained to be released. Most found the answer in the notoriously dense Japanese government bureaucracy. The American wire service AP, for example, broke a story of a group of French doctors who had flown into Kobe to treat victims but instead were put to work in kitchens. Other foreign papers followed with stories describing how a team of rescue dogs sent from Switzerland had been held up in quarantine kennels and how offers of aid from international relief agencies were being refused by the government. T. R. Reid, in an article in the *Washington Post* summed up the critical attitude of the foreign reporters:

> Western reporters tended to accentuate the negative, focusing on the worst scenes of destruction and the most crushing moments of personal loss. American journalists in particular seemed to be on the prowl for confrontation, prodding cold, hungry victims with questions like, 'Do you think the government has done enough to help?'
>
> (Reid 1995:17)

These foreign news stories, initially avoided by the Japanese national news press, represented an untapped wealth of cheap and reliable 'scoops' to the *Sunday* reporters. Since they were already prohibited from gathering new information from the official government sources, they had nothing to lose by broadcasting information that might anger these sources, especially if all they were doing was quoting the criticisms made by foreign reporters. Moreover, the assignment of blame was not considered unfair even by the major newspapers and television stations. In fact, as soon as programs like *Sunday* broadcast reports criticizing the government, most of the other major news organizations followed with similar attacks.

Criticism of Media Coverage

The intense media coverage of the earthquake disaster was a double-edged sword to the residents of Kobe. On the one hand, national and international coverage focused public attention on the plight of the Kobe people, inspiring charity drives, generating international offers of aid and stirring up public support for future government subsidies to the area. Yet in the immediate short-term, the news coverage often worked against the efforts of survivors to recover from the disaster and to come to terms with an uncertain future. Most Kobe residents responded by quietly enduring overzealous reporters and insensitive news reports, but some confronted the media through calls and letters of protest to news editors. Some even stepped into the media ring themselves, offering quotable critiques of certain media organizations to their competitors. Soon Kobe reporters were openly accusing national reporters of putting the needs of Tokyo viewers over the needs of local survivors, while NHK and print journalists were going on the record condemning commercial stations for blatant sensationalism, and minority rights activists and local leaders privately rebuking those media organizations they felt were referring to minority groups in inappropriate ways. In this way, the nationwide debate over how the earthquake should have been covered began its short but influential life.

Victims' rights

One of the most prominent debates over media coverage concerned where the proper balance lay between respecting the rights of the victims and responding to the information needs of the nation. Many victims complained that the media were violating their rights to privacy by filming refugee centers, hospitals, rescue missions, and other places where those who did not want to be caught on film could not easily slip out of the viewfinder. The problem was especially acute in refugee centers where a lack of walls or other physical barriers left victims completely exposed to the camera's prying lens. Many victims were still in shock or denial. Many had not bathed since the quake and felt self-conscious. For these earthquake survivors, the questions posed by the reporting outsiders who simply wandered in and out of these centers was too much to bear. When one TV news magazine reporter was shown on television asking a refugee the simple question, 'Don't you feel cold?', viewers bombarded the network complaining that the victim's rights to privacy had been violated (Reid 1995).

An even more serious accusation made against the media was that, in the race to get the best film footage, reporters and camera crews added to the confusion and impeded rescue efforts by creating traffic jams on the ground and noise pollution overhead. One victim complained:

> The helicopters were just interested in outdoing each other and didn't care about the people. They didn't help. The helicopters added unwanted noise and took pictures of burning from above rather than landing and getting into the area. People kept saying 'why don't they come?' It gave more pain and instilled more distrust to the injured people.
>
> (Horikoshi 1995:12)

Given the emotional grounding of these criticisms, national reporters did not address these allegations in public. In private however, they were more candid. With regard to charges of impeding rescue efforts through the use of helicopters, many reporters admitted to bad judgment. One Tokyo-based reporter told me:

> I think in an accident, we should exchange information with other companies like they do in foreign countries. Here in Japan we can quote from *The New York Times* and other foreign papers, but we don't with Japanese newspapers or TV stations. Of course it's a question of exclusivity, but sometimes I feel we should cooperate. Each station sent helicopters that were on the spot and took pictures. In an emergency such as this, we should have cooperated with each other.

On the subject of violations of rights to privacy, journalists had mixed reactions. On the one hand, many justified their interactions with the victims as not only necessary for the public interest, but in many cases as helpful to the victims themselves. An American reporter who covered the story for one of the larger news agencies related her experiences in interviewing one victim who welcomed the chance to speak before the camera: 'There seemed to be a need to express feeling to the media. There was a woman I interviewed who clearly wanted to tell her story to the camera. It made her feel better to be able to share her tragedy with the public'.

In my own experiences accompanying the *Sunday* crew in Kobe, I witnessed countless interviews with victims, and did not once see them ask for an interview from a person who did not seem willing, if not eager, to tell his or her story. In fact, over the two days I spent in Kobe with reporters, only once was a reporter refused an interview, and only then because the respondent's wife cut the interview short. If anything, I also felt many of the victims saw the cameras as a chance to document their experiences and share them with others. While it was also true that many did not want to be interviewed, those who did made their willingness clear through hand gestures, eye contact, smiles and other non-verbal forms of beckoning, and it was these people whom reporters chose to approach.

This concern for the feelings of the victims was evident in gestures off the camera as well. On the morning before we left for Kobe the field producer reminded us that sewage systems had been ruptured and functioning toilets were few and far between. Out of consideration for the victims, he told us, we should make sure to use the toilet beforehand, and to refrain from drinking more than the minimum amount of water necessary so as not to inconvenience the victims by using their facilities. Later on that day, after having worked several hours filming in and around Kobe, we decided to take a quick lunch break and went back to the van to fetch the lunch boxes (*bentō*) we had bought from an Osaka convenience store that morning. Having just filmed the long lines for *onigiri* (rice balls) and water in a Kobe schoolyard, we discussed whether or not to donate our lunches to some of the refugees we had interviewed. In the end we decided it would be too difficult to choose among the needy and instead threw our jackets over the windows and ate in a guilt-filled silence. Back in Tokyo I brought some of the pictures I had taken of the crew in Kobe into the station. In one of the pictures the crew had stopped and faced the camera. The photo showed five tired looking film crew with only one of them, an assistant, smiling. When the others saw the picture they scolded the assistant, telling him he had been selfish and stupid to smile at a time like that. For them, lack of a properly somber expression was tantamount to showing happiness at the victims' tragedy.

Sensationalism

A second debate revolved around the degree to which reporters should emphasize the actual damage done to Kobe. At one extreme were commercial television reporters like those at *Sunday* who went to great lengths to film the most dramatic signs of damage and, if possible, get themselves reporting in the foreground. Fires, collapsed buildings, overturned highways, derailed trains, crushed landmarks – all of these made frequent appearances on commercial news programs. When those stories had run their course, *Sunday* producers recycled the film by producing critiques of the government's handling of the situation and a 'what if' scenario of an earthquake in Tokyo, anticipating the damage and informing viewers of the best ways to prepare for the 'big one'.

Reports like this, however, were the exception rather than the rule – at least according to *Washington Post* reporter T. R. Reid. He found Japanese reporters on the whole to be more positive than foreign reporters with regard to the damage sustained by the earthquake:

> The Japanese media seemed more inclined to view the disaster through a broad lens that included buildings still standing as well as those smashed to the ground. And Japanese reports focused far more on harmony than discord among the hundreds of homeless victims.
>
> (Reid 1995)

He substantiated this claim by relating an interesting anecdote:

Taken as a whole ... the Eastern and Western reporting created distinctly different impressions. This is reflected in the reactions of two people who came to Kobe a few days after the quake:

Shigehiko Tojo, of *The Washington Post*'s Tokyo bureau, had been watching Japanese TV reporters from Kobe almost around the clock. But when he arrived here, he said, 'I was just stunned at the extent of the damage'.

A few days later an American journalists arrived, having watched earthquake news on the major American networks. 'I was amazed how much of Kobe was still there', she said. '... I had no idea that there were houses and tall buildings still standing all over the city'.

(Reid 1995)

Among the Japanese reporters I spoke with, most felt that it was NHK above all other television stations that downplayed the extent of damage done to Kobe. One NHK reporter attributed this to an unintended side effect of the managerial preoccupation with presenting confirmed facts rather than visual images, even if the latter were clearly the more accurate:

I think NHK did not show enough to convey the extent of the damage, and from the morning to the afternoon [of the first day], many people did not realize how big it was because it was our duty not to dramatize the events. In fires and other disasters, we want to give exact figures. For example, we did show pictures of devastated areas, but people who watched would have had to have a good imagination [to comprehend the extent of the damage] ... We could have given several concrete explanations of victims or the damage [but] we couldn't do that because the station likes confirmed numbers. The station wants to be careful with the casualties.

Another NHK reporter attributed this tendency to underreport the negative to a deliberate strategy designed to keep victims from falling into despair:

We were told to encourage the people. This was told to all representatives of the major mass media. Do you know the word '*gambare*' (persevere)? They [the victims] tend to lose hope, patience. Of course we provide facts, but we have to encourage people. The analysis of prevention of the earthquake is the second phase and now it's important to know how to make the buildings stronger. But in the first week the victims were walking on the line between life and death. People were crying and panicking. We had to create balance.

In conveying public criticisms of the government, NHK was equally careful, making sure to clearly distinguish criticisms as the opinion of others from network position or stated fact. One NHK reporter described the procedures taken to ensure objectivity:

118

We [NHK] criticized the government, too. The risk management was not there. And even after a few weeks the food was still bad in the refugee camps and there was not enough water ... We used the voice of the people to criticize the government. We said things like 'the criticism of the government is rising from the people'.

This same reporter then went on to explain that, despite the precautions taken, finding a scapegoat in the government was merely a matter of journalistic routine:

Generally speaking, though, if something very bad happens, we need someone to blame, and the government is convenient. The government knows this and they don't fight back. But I think this is a good way to effect a change in our thinking of the concept of disaster. We can talk about disaster, warn the people about it, but it's not so easy to make the necessary changes to the infrastructure without an example. This [earthquake] was a big lesson for Japanese disaster prevention. We needed to provide specific examples in order to effect change.

The remarks are revealing. What the reporter implies is that, although reporters at NHK will take the necessary precautions to distinguish criticisms from fact, the assignment of blame is ultimately arbitrary and routine. NHK in this sense is no different from the 'sensationalist' commercial television reporters who quote criticisms of government for lack of other news. The difference is that NHK does it in a way that seems more objective and thus more factual.

Minority groups

While news producers and their audiences debated the amount of earthquake damage to show and the appropriateness of criticizing the government relief efforts, they all agreed on a third reporting matter – that minorities should not be referred to at all in news broadcasts. This included two groups who were heavily represented in the Kobe area, ethnic Koreans who reside in Japan as permanent residents, and Burakumin whose ancestral associations with certain 'polluted' industries incur strong social stigmas.

Part of the reason for this media blackout was historical precedent. During the 1923 Great Kanto Earthquake in Tokyo, hundreds of Koreans were lynched by mobs on suspicion of arson and looting. Reporters and minority rights representatives alike feared the same could occur again if the media were not careful in their coverage. One reporter explained,

We had this terrible experience in Kanto regarding Koreans and I had to bear that in mind. [The Koreans] were afraid too. The leader of the Korean group I spoke with said he was afraid that kind of killing would happen again so when I wrote the script about the Koreans, I tried not to over-emphasize the fact that the Korean people were gathering in a certain place.

With regard to Burakumin, the taboos against coverage were even greater. One NHK reporter told me:

> Burakumin were in Nagata-ku, but I didn't report anything about them. No one at NHK did. We did interview victims from Nagata-ku, and many were Burakumin, but the bureau chief also reminded us that such-and-such an area is where Burakumin are living so please consider carefully before you say anything.

Another cameraman for a prominent Japanese wire service told me that reporters at his company had been instructed to avoid mentioning the fact that the fires in Kobe were centered mainly in Nagata because large pockets of the minority population lived in the area who might be stigmatized by the association. Instead they were asked to refer to the location of fires by the non-specific words 'here, there, and over there'.

As a result of such censorship policies, most news organizations managed to avoid public criticism for their coverage of minority groups. Even so, problems did arise. A reporter for *Sunday* told me that she was criticized for using the word '*jikeidan*' to refer to a neighborhood watch group because the same word could be interpreted as meaning 'lynch mob'. Another time, she was accused of indirectly implying that minority groups were involved in the looting that occurred in the aftermath of the earthquake. The controversial comment was made during a live question-and-answer session with the news anchor when to the question 'is there any looting going on in Kobe?', she answered: 'Yes there is, depending on the area . . .' (*hai, basho ni yotte*). Audience members in Kobe called the station's affiliate in Osaka to complain that the remark indirectly implicated Burakumin and Koreans who were known to live in particular areas. It was not the direct references, but oblique and unintended references that created controversy.

Economic Resources and Credibility

Of the three news organizations surveyed – Sun TV, NHK and *Sunday* – it was *Sunday* that received the bulk of public criticism. Grouped with other national commercial news programs, *Sunday* was accused of being sensationalist, insensitive to the victims, muckraking, impressionistic and only loosely committed to keeping to the facts. By comparison, NHK was considered comprehensive, authoritative, and journalistically responsible. Sun TV was widely praised by its viewers for its commitment to the victims, but these viewers were limited to the Kobe area only and not the nation at large.

Many accused the commercial reporters of intentionally exaggerating facts and ignoring victims' needs for privacy purely for the commercial reasons of generating higher audience ratings. Yet, as I have argued, commercial reporters were just as committed as other reporters to the truth and to observing victims' rights to privacy. If commercial reporters did appear to be exaggerating the truth, victimizing the victims and making a scapegoat of the government, it was not because they accepted such acts as the price for higher ratings. It was because they lacked the necessary economic resources to make their stories appear otherwise. Economic resources, and the lack of them, were the main cause of the differences in the reporting between NHK and *Sunday.*

Even by commercial news standards, *Sunday* was small. It sent only five people to Kobe, none of whom had any previous experience in the area or contact with local officials. Most of their information was gathered in the streets through interviews with eyewitnesses and personal observations; little originated from government sources. Their stories reflected the nature of these information sources – small human interest stories, criticisms of the government through quotes of the foreign press, 'what if' scenarios of future disasters and visual damage reports.

NHK, by contrast, was able to mobilize hundreds of news crews to send into the Kobe area, including not only reporters and film crew but video editors and field producers as well. They had the contacts to gather macro-level information through official sources and micro-level information through local friends and acquaintances. They had helicopters to use for filming, satellite trucks to use for broadcasting, and editing equipment to use for processing film and inserting graphics. These resources provided NHK with a fount of news information based on authoritative sources, wide-ranging and in-depth research, a large pool of video images, and candid and comfortable interviews with victims who happened to be friends rather than strangers. Resulting stories may have at times underrepresented the damage done to Kobe, but overall they were detailed, compassionate, authoritative and journalistically responsible.

NHK was widely regarded as the most credible source of earthquake information. This was not simply because it told the truth, but because, having the advantage of greater economic resources at its disposal, it told the truth better than its competitors. News organizations like *Sunday* also told the truth, but lacking such production resources, failed to do it in a way that won the confidence of its audience. Economic resources enabled reporters to package the truth to make it more believable. Economic resources turned seeing into believing.

Implications

If greater economic resources lead to more credible news, what can we conclude about the roles of differently funded television news organizations in maintaining the political, economic and social *status quo*? One hypothesis is that the larger and more economically endowed the news organization, the less likely it will be to use its powers of persuasion to challenge the authority of society's elite since it already benefits from the current system of power relations. By the same token the smaller and poorer the news organizations, the greater the incentive to challenge the *status quo*, but the weaker the ability to do so effectively. Is this true? Has the Japanese media system worked itself into a deadlock which leaves no room to challenge existing power relationships? The answer is no, and yes.

Challenging the powers that be

Small commercial news organizations like *Sunday* were among the few Japanese news organizations to challenge the official version of the earthquake. They did so by resorting to their own observations when official information was late or clearly counter to observable conditions. One NHK reporter described the differences in the attitudes of NHK and commercial reporters with regard to official statistics.

> NHK is perceived to be the most reliable source and there is a simple reason why. Our way of confirming the facts is more rigid. Commercial news reporters tend to write more easily [sic] and I really felt that in Kobe. I had close relations with other reporters and it was astonishing. I would ask them: 'How can you write that kind of report?,' 'How can you be so definite?', and they would say: 'Well, I don't have any confirmation but ...'

Sunday reporters also challenged the government by broadcasting criticisms of the relief efforts made in the foreign press and by showing the long lines at refugee centers, chaos in the hospitals, grass roots relief efforts, and other evidence that the needs of the victims were not being met by the government.

These reporters were met with skepticism and resentment. Part of the problem was that the widely trusted NHK did stick with the confirmed facts and refused to broadcast criticisms of the government for the first several days of earthquake coverage. By challenging the government's version of the earthquake, these reporters were also challenging NHK's version as well. Rather than being seen as legitimate challenges to the government's damage assessment system or relief programs, such reporters were dismissed as sensationalist and muckraking.

Yet ultimately, these smaller programs did make a change. By broadcasting foreign criticisms of the government, they paved the way for NHK to bring that criticism to the public domain in a more credible light. They did so by creating an opportunity, even a need, for NHK to include these criticisms as part of an analysis of the ongoing relief efforts.

This pattern of smaller or outsider news organizations forcing larger more credible news organizations to convey the same information to the public is well known in Japan. It was, for example, the foreign press who broke the deadlock on stories of the crown prince's search for a bride when it announced news of an impending engagement (Bardsley 1997); the weekly magazine *Sunday Mainichi* which brought an end to the unofficial ban on reporting the private life of the prime minister by publishing complaints of unfair treatment made by the mistress of then-prime minister Uno (Farley 1996:142); and the monthly magazine *Bungei Shunju* which paved the way for widespread press coverage of the Lockheed Scandal by first publishing a story alleging then prime minister Tanaka's involvement in a bribery scam.

Smaller less financially endowed news organizations in Japan lack the credibility needed to pose effective direct challenges to the powers that be, but by casting these ideas out into the public domain, they can create obligations or opportunities for the larger media to follow up with their own coverage. Small news organizations do make a difference, only in an indirect rather than direct way.

Keeping the status quo

Underlying the differences between the ways in which these three news organizations covered the earthquake story lay a profound similarity. This similarity had to do with the way they articulated the identities of ethnic and other minority identities.

All of the Japanese news organizations discussed agreed that minority groups in Kobe – Koreans and Burakumin – must not be referred to in broadcasts. The almost taken-for-granted self-censorship of any information that related specifically to minority groups in Kobe was done partly out of self-protection, partly in response to calls from minority rights activists, and partly out of a sincere desire to protect these groups from becoming scapegoats in the confusion and frustration of the disaster. One reporter described the complexity of the problem:

> In this country, the Burakumin and Korean problem is special. You can't solve it, can't see the exit. The roots of this issue are from so long ago, and so integrated for so long, and these two groups have made the issue somewhat political, they organized this group. I think they should do this, and we Japanese should solve the issue, but now it's difficult to talk about it publicly. I am from Tokyo, and you don't get to know about it because there is no area where Burakumin are, and no one tells you. I didn't know about it until I got to Kobe and that goes to show how difficult it is to solve this problem. It's because this prejudice is rooted so deep that their response tends to be so aggressive, extremist, and this makes it harder to talk about it. I don't think I ever heard the word '*dōwa*' [the politically correct word for Burakumin] on television. It is a new word, an invention by political people in this country, and so when we report on issues, we supposedly can use the word '*dowa*.' But many Burakumin don't like this word either.

The decision not to cover the Koreans or Burakumin was made long before the earthquake hit Kobe. It was made out of a sense of an ethical obligation to protect these groups from stigma through association with negative character-istics such as living in poor neighborhoods, or anti-social behavior such as looting. Since these stereotypes were attached to Korean and Burakumin identity, the only way to avoid attaching stigma to individuals, it was reasoned, was to avoid associating them with the minority group to which they belonged.

This point was brought home to me in a discussion with another reporter on the coverage of Ainu in the news. This particular reporter told me that although he used to cover stories on ethnic minorities like the Ainu, he stopped when he learned about the 'silent majority':

> Fifteen years ago I covered Ainu stories. Fifteen years ago, Ainu stories were sort of taboo, but I tried to make them anyway. I focused on cultural stories and avoided political issues. Still, my boss was worried about lawsuits – at that time many news stories were being sued. Now it's better. I used to think like you, but I changed my mind when I learned about the silent majority. *In America, to be represented is to be equal. In Japan, to be equal is to be ignored.* The majority of the Ainu people want to blend in. For them, the reminder of their identity is bad. Only the small outspoken minority tries to bring up the issues. *In Japan, if you want to be equal, you must not stand out. You must be like everyone else. Perhaps if we don't talk about it, we can forget it.*

Ainu are not the only minority group with a 'silent majority' who prefer to be left out of the public domain. According to Suzuki Mieko of the Buraku Liberation League (*Buraku Kaihō Dōmei*), out of the three million estimated Burakumin in Japan, only 200,000 are officially registered with the Buraku Liberation League. The rest 'want to hide it. There is a cultural element of avoiding rather than confronting'.[3] Similarly, of the 700,000 Koreans in Japan, the majority use Japanese names to 'pass' with fewer hassles in daily life.

The avoidance of representing these minority groups in the mass media is done largely with the blessing of those very same minority group members. Yet by refusing outright to cover information relating to these groups, opportunities to bring up other important information, issues and questions are closed off. With regard to the self-censorship involved in covering minority groups in Kobe, important – even potentially life-saving – information about the source and location of fires was expurgated in order to avoid stigmatizing the minority groups living in these areas. The needs of those looking to escape the fires or finding out the fate of loved ones in the area were passed over in favor of the more abstract need to avoid stigmatizing these minority groups.

More importantly, by not connecting the minority groups to the areas on fire, an important association was left out of public purview – that it was the minority groups who were disproportionately represented in poor neighborhoods that were made of wooden (rather than concrete) houses built closely together on narrow roads which prevented the prompt arrival of fire trucks. It also foreclosed the opportunity to ponder the question of why, 72 years after the Great Kanto Earthquake of 1923, Koreans and Burakumin still fear for their lives in times of mass hysteria, confusion and stress.

The policies of the media which deny differences among the Japanese population in the name of human rights disallow opportunities to examine and debate the stigma attached to minority groups in everyday life. Indeed, by negating the existence of these groups through their refusal to acknowledge them in broadcasts, the media may contribute to the continuing stigma against these groups by simultaneously contributing to a stereotype of the Japanese population as an ethnically homogeneous and socially classless one.

Notes

1 In addition to the hundreds of news reporters and crew whom I cannot thank by name, I would like to extend my gratitude to the following news men and women without whose help this project could not have been completed: Shimizu Yutaka at Fuji TV for arranging for me to observe the coverage of the earthquake from their affiliate station in Osaka; Shibata Kaoru at *The Sunday* for allowing me to follow her and her crew in the streets of Kobe as she covered the earthquake story; Igarashi Kimitoshi at NHK for arranging for me to do fieldwork at NHK Tokyo from April to June 1995; and Shiraishi Shigeaki at NTV for giving me my first opportunity to see what Japanese television production was like by hiring me as a summer intern for *The Sunday* in 1990. This project was funded through a Fulbright IIE grant and a Sheldon Shepps Summer Research grant for which I am eternally grateful.
2 Although 'lifetime employment' can no longer be considered a given in most Japanese industries, it was still the predominant pattern in most television stations during the time of research (1994–5). This may have something to do with both the profitability of the television industry in general and the popularity of work in mass communications among top university graduates.
3 Interview with Suzuki Mieko, 12 June, 1995.

6

DATELINE TOKYO
Telling the World about Japan

Ulf Hannerz

Masami Kawashima is having his lunch at a table draped in crisp white linen at the Hourin Country Club outside Tokyo. Coming in from the eighteen-hole golf course which is the club's main attraction, he has passed by the club shop which offers a 14-karat gold cigarette lighter for $4,200, gold-edged Hourin dinner plates for $1,700 each, and a Hourin lamp at $6,600. He sits there, in the dining room, in a marshmallow-soft leather chair, flavouring his meal with a dash of salt from the sterling silver shaker on the sterling silver tray, next to the fresh flowers in cut glass.

And then Mr. Kawashima pulls out a cigarette and his own cheap plastic lighter, grinning 'like an economy-class passenger on a first-class upgrade'. Mr. Kawashima, who in his everyday life 'runs a smoky little beer joint, the kind of place where nobody minds a burp or two among friends after a sloppy bowl of noodles late at night', is on an outing with two friends, his local hairdresser and his neighbourhood liquor store owner. The Hourin, which used to charge a membership fee of $700,000, has sent out 'Dear Golfer' fliers offering a weekday special for $130 – it is 'like the Emperor throwing a Tupperware party'.

This is Kevin Sullivan, *Washington Post* correspondent in Tokyo, offering his readers one striking scene from Japan in recession (Sullivan 1999a). As a part of a wider study of the work of foreign correspondents, I had an opportunity to talk to Sullivan and a number of other Tokyo-based European and American newspeople in early 1999, and in what follows, I will draw on these conversations, and some recent news reporting from Japan, to reflect on the way a country, during one period of time, is portrayed to the outside world; and also on some aspects of foreign newswork more generally.[1] It is perhaps necessary, however, to state first some background understandings of the overall organization of foreign correspondence, and something about my own recent explorations of the craft.

An Anthropologist Among Foreign Correspondents

At the beginning of my project, when I made one of my first contacts with a potential informant, he giggled a little at the idea of being interviewed by an anthropologist – 'So we will be your tribe', he said. But it is, of course, from our anthropological point of view, a very special tribe. I find myself studying not up, or down, but sideways, inquiring into a line of work which is in some ways parallel to my own.[2] Like anthropologists, newsmedia foreign correspondents report from one part of the world to another, and this is certainly one fact underlying my interest in them. How do their practices compare to the field work of anthropologists? What do they report, and how do they mediate to their audiences the foreignness of foreign news?

In general terms, I take the core group of foreign correspondents to consist of those individuals who are stationed in other countries than that of their origin, for the purpose of reporting on events and characteristics of the area of their stationing, through news media based elsewhere (in large part in their countries of origin). In the real world of international news reporting, it is true, the edges of the category get a bit blurred. And it is part of my anthropological angle that I am really more interested in the work of correspondents reporting over greater cultural distances, as it were: from Asia, Africa or the Middle East to Europe or North America, rather than from Washington, DC to Stockholm, or from Brussels to London. This focus actually excludes a large part of the world's foreign correspondents.

But within these limits, I am interested in correspondents reporting to different countries, through different media; again probably in a way characteristic of anthropology, I am concerned with exploring variations rather than with identifying standards and averages. I would admit to some preference for print journalism: partly because it is practically simpler to follow and to scrutinize, and partly no doubt because writing is also what most anthropologists do. In some cases, I should also say, rather than single-mindedly pursuing diversity, I have sought out correspondents of the same organization in different locations, and also their editors at home, to get a view of the same news enterprise from different places and perspectives. In such encounters, too, the fact that the correspondents and I already have some shared background knowledge, and some shared contacts, is good for rapport. Before I met Kevin Sullivan in Tokyo, I had already met *Washington Post* colleagues of his in Jerusalem and in Hong Kong.

Like anthropology, foreign correspondence fits into the world order in a manner which, over the years, we have learned to recognize as problematic. At least since the 1970s debates over the world information order, it has been a quite well-established fact that North American and western European media organizations dominate the flow of pictures, words, and figures between countries and continents. (Characteristically, Japanese media are an exception here; during the years of rapid economic growth, some organizations built up significant correspondent networks, so that now, for example, the *Yomiuri Shimbun*, the large Tokyo daily, has more journalists abroad than the *New York Times*.[3]) Such macrostructural inequalities of international news reporting, I should point out, form a background factor of my project, rather than its main concern. Again, my interests here are more ethnographic, involving the field practitioners of foreign news work, their everyday activities, relationships, and careers. So far a large part of my study has consisted of a series of extended conversations with the foreign correspondents themselves, in four continents. Many of these have been retrospective, encounters with people looking back on their foreign correspondent experiences after having returned to Stockholm, or Frankfurt, or Los Angeles, or New York. Such accounts can give a vivid idea of correspondent personal experiences and allow for reflections on the craft, and beliefs and values that go with it. Yet eloquent as they may be, the off-site commentaries tend not to offer quite as concrete a picture of ongoing newswork as I get when I can meet with the correspondents in their postings. Under such conditions it is easier to talk to them about particular considerations entering into their own dealing with events which may be fresh in their minds; about routines and mundane contextual factors on a reporting scene of which I could also at least catch some glimpses myself. And so I also wanted to find out what a 'dateline Tokyo' might entail.

Tokyo in the Global News-scape

Within the landscape of foreign news, one may draw a basic contrast between two kinds of places. There are the places to which newspeople flock, as 'firemen' or 'parachutists', to cover particular events or sequences of events, for mostly a quite limited time, to deal with 'hard news' – natural disasters, wars or revolutions, or other major political transitions, often more or less unforeseeable. Such sites and events tend to be emphasized in the public imagery of foreign correspondence, and when newspeople write their autobiographies, as a fair number of them do, they are also inclined to devote much space to such excursions: how they rushed to get there, what happened, how they struggled to file their stories. And the notion that foreign correspondents typically spend much of their time in bars, drinking and swapping useful information and tall tales, is also anchored in large part in those situations, in which the correspondents all tend to converge on scarce local facilities.

On the other hand, there are the places where correspondents are stationed more durably. The assumption about these places is that there are continuously a fair number of newsworthy events occurring in the immediate vicinity, and perhaps also that they are at the same time places from which other potential news sites can be reached, more or less quickly and conveniently. Some such places are obviously considered more important than others, and consequently some draw more correspondents than others. Large media organizations, especially the major wire services, are represented in a great many of them; the Associated Press, for example, has some eighty bureaus outside the United States, its home country. But there are also organizations with a mere handful of correspondents of their own, spread out thinly over the global news-scape, and consequently often responsible for very large territories – they are 'Africa correspondents', 'Latin America correspondents', 'Asia correspondents'.

Clearly Tokyo is a place where a sizeable number of correspondents are based for longer periods. Most of them are primarily involved in reporting on Japan, although they also often have a complementary responsibility for Korea (which means that there are not so many correspondents based in Seoul). There are some 'Asia correspondents' among them, although at present it seems more common for people with this kind of reporting territory to be based further west, perhaps in Hong Kong or Bangkok. Generally, if you will have somebody traveling much of the time over a very large continent, you will not put him or her in a notably expensive location at the outer edge of the territory. Nonetheless, some of the Tokyo correspondents will make the occasional excursion elsewhere in Asia. Kevin Sullivan of the *Washington Post*, for example, has recently filed stories from Burma and Bhutan.

How many are there of these people? It would be difficult to establish the number of foreign correspondents, in the world or in Tokyo, since the boundaries of the category are imprecise. Some people do occasional foreign newswork, and there is a considerable turnover. The Foreign Press Center, the Japanese government facility established to serve foreign media, has some 800 correspondents on its list, but of these about half are Japanese nationals working for non-Japanese organizations.[4] Of the approximately 400 expatriates, about half are Americans. The number of Asian correspondents, not least Koreans and Chinese, is now sizeable. The European presence, on the other hand, has recently been shrinking.

The main reason for this is apparently economic. Media organizations just about everywhere have recently been quite cost-conscious. Foreign correspondents tend to be expensive, with uncertain returns in terms of increased readership or advertising, and on the business side in the organization, some people are inclined to think that they are expendable. At least the costs for them should be kept down. And Tokyo, of course, is a place where the price of maintaining a correspondent is high. Consequently some of the larger bureaus of American as well as European media have been downsized, and smaller bureaus have been closed down. Instead of posting a correspondent who is a regular employee of the organization, entitled to a range of benefits, media businesses have also been more inclined to enter into some kind of less inclusive arrangement with a stringer, who sometimes essentially does the same work as a full-time correspondent, but who may also work for several organizations, and who may also not be a full-time newsworker.[5]

Another cost-cutting alternative is to send out someone from headquarters at more or less regular intervals, to stay informed and to do some more concentrated reporting. *La Stampa*, the Italian newspaper, for example, has Fernando Mezzetti stationed at its Turin office, but he makes frequent visits to both China and Japan, and he has previously been based both in Tokyo and Beijing for long periods during his twenty-five years as a foreign correspondent. And then, certainly, he also continuously writes analyses and commentaries on Asian affairs out of Turin. Generally, keeping in touch with distant news sites has become easier with the development of internet, with its global multitude of web sites.

There are critics in Tokyo who feel that the cost-cutting strategies of some foreign media endanger the quality of reporting. Some may go so far as to pick up local stringers who may be from the home country of the news organization, but whose knowledge of Japan is uncertain, and who really have no journalistic expertise either. But then the divide between the stringers and the regular correspondents sent out from headquarters also involves other issues which, in the world of foreign correspondents, tend not to be unique to Tokyo.[6]

Moving Through or Staying On

Many of those more affluent media organizations which do send out their own correspondents – not least American media, but certainly some European ones as well, and also such Japanese papers as the *Yomiuri Shimbun* – believe in rotating these correspondents relatively quickly between assignments. After, say, three to five years on a foreign beat, the correspondent either moves on to another one or returns home.

The assumption beyond such a preference for quicker rotation is that journalists who remain too long in a place risk 'going stale'. They start taking things in their surroundings for granted, instead of seeing stories in them; they find no great pleasure in doing basically the same story the second or third or umpteenth time. The ideal correspondent, according to this view, has a fresh eye for the peculiarities of a beat. Moreover, it helps not to lose touch with the audience at home; to retain a sense of its interests, experiences, and assumptions.

The other side of the coin, naturally enough, may be that the correspondent who moves rapidly between postings may not develop very much, or very deep, local knowledge anywhere. Those correspondents who stay in a place, on the other hand, may become very knowledgeable. They may have a longer-term perspective on stories, remembering what led up to them. They will perhaps have wide and varied local networks which can be important resources in their reporting, and quite possibly they may be considerably more skilled in using a local language.

Tokyo is one of those places in the global news-scape which has a number of committed long-timers – people who want to be in Japan and who do not care to be rotated, who may be intellectually or esthetically engaged in Japanese society and culture, who may have formed family connections there, and who see their involvement in foreign correspondence in considerable part as a way of supporting themselves while remaining in the country where they want to live. They would rather change employers or jobs than move anywhere else. Such people, frequently although not always, become stringers.

The Tokyo correspondents whom I met could often see some of the respective advantages and disadvantages of these two basic types of correspondent careers, but there was also some mutual irritation. One correspondent for a big newspaper, who had been in Japan for a few years but who was probably approaching the end of his posting there, commented that some of the long-timers were really walking advertisements for the value of not staying too long – they were world-weary and jaded in their views, and if they absolutely must stay in Japan, they really ought to turn to some other line of work. Those who had been around longer, and who were likely to stay on, for their part, could be critical of the newcomers' evaluation of news and choice of stories. They suspected that they were more likely to conform in their reporting to the beliefs about Japan held by their editors at home, and to become too dependent, in their search for information, on the '*gaijin* handlers', the experts on handling contacts with Americans and Europeans, which could now be identified in many Japanese organizations.

As far as language is concerned, a long stay is certainly no guarantee of fluency. It is true, however, that many of those who are more briefly posted in. Japan never get around to speaking or reading much Japanese. Some of those more prosperous media organizations who rotate their correspondents do see the value of allowing these to prepare themselves for their new assignments, and may allow them considerable time off for language and area study. But, said one correspondent who had majored in Japanese as an undergraduate and who actually was reasonably fluent in speaking the language, and struggled with some degree of success in reading for example Japanese newspapers, it probably makes more sense allowing a prospective Moscow correspondent to study Russian for a while than to have someone about to be posted to Tokyo study Japanese for the same period – Japanese, for an American or a European, is much more difficult. This correspondent felt the money spent on allowing someone time to acquire quite rudimentary Japanese would have been more wisely allocated to the employment of more local staff in the office, people who could translate and help in newswork.

Yet it is not that there are no such staff, and in some bureaus they are vital to keeping things going. Expatriate correpondents may come and leave, but a local office manager who has been around for decades, who is immersed in the flow of ongoing local everyday life, and who knows who is who and what is what, can be trusted to provide institutional memory, even if he or she is seldom made visible in the public output.

The Foreign Correspondents Club

One of the facts of news life in Japan which, over the years, has led foreign correspondents to feel a bit excluded is the institution of '*kisha* clubs', groupings of reporters durably assigned to cover government ministries and other major organizations.[7] The Japanese members of kisha clubs are treated favourably by the offices to which they are attached, and in turn develop a certain loyalty to them, getting together among themselves to treat news originating on their beat with a certain delicacy. The kisha clubs, in other words, have tended to be a part of what is often seen, not least by outside commentators on Japan, as a great machinery of national consensus. In the past, foreign correspondents have been excluded from the kisha clubs. Now, although this is no longer strictly the case, the foreigners who are not fluent Japanese speakers and cannot in any case devote so much time to any single Japanese news setting anyway, are still handicapped in the places where kisha clubs are active. But in a way, they have something like a kisha club of their own.

The Foreign Correspondents Club of Japan is at present housed on the upper two floors of an office tower in central Tokyo. The organization rather recently celebrated its first half-century; it came into being in the aftermath of World War II, as correspondents began to arrive soon after Japan's surrender.[8] The bar and restaurant on the twentieth floor are popular meeting places also for a number of associate members who are not foreign correspondents; the ambience of this club, like that of its famous Hong Kong counterpart, attracts a wider set of people – in this instance not least from Japanese media and advertising industries, who through their special membership fees help considerably in keeping the establishment viable. But the regular members, the foreign correspondents themselves (at present about 380 of them), keep the organization firmly under their control, and a number of facilities are particularly useful to them.[9] There is a library with books and current newspapers, access to internet and data banks, radio reporting facilities, and a dozen work rooms which some members use on a regular basis. And not least are there frequent luncheon speakers: leading Japanese politicians and bureaucrats, as well as other prominent local people, from business, academia and other circles, and visitors from outside Japan. On these occasions, it is the foreign correspondents who have privileged access to news and commentary, although unlike the members of the Japanese kisha clubs, they are not very likely to huddle together afterwards to agree on a shared story. It was the merciless questioning of prime minister Kakuei Tanaka concerning his finances at an FCCJ luncheon in 1974 that soon after led to his downfall.

The FCCJ takes itself to be the largest organization of its kind anywhere in the world. Tokyo, of course, is a world city, with a great many foreign media representatives, and its facilities are notably well-developed. A veteran member also points out that the relative inaccessibility of Japanese society to foreigners makes an organization of this kind more of a haven than its counterparts in many other places, embedded in more familiar environments, would be. There are said to be members who spend virtually all day at the FCCJ.

Yet at the same time, the club does not count all Tokyo's foreign correspondents as members or active users. Some of those whose postings to Japan are not so long, and who represent large and powerful media corporations, simply have less use for it. The young, busy staffers of the financial wire services – such as Bloomberg, which has expanded quickly in Tokyo in the 1990s – hardly have time for the club, and will not have their membership fees paid by their employers, as the more established general news organizations are likely to do. As far as the stringers are concerned, they would also often have to pay for the FCCJ membership out of their own pockets, and so some number of them stay away.

Three Correspondents

Let us meet a few Tokyo correspondents, to get some sense of particular backgrounds, experiences and situations.[10] The first of them is Kevin Sullivan of the *Washington Post*, a snippet of whose reporting from the Hourin Country Club I began with. When in college in New England, Sullivan took a journalism course with a professor whom a friend of his had been enthusiastic about – and was hooked. Journalism would be his career. He worked for a couple of smallish New England newspapers, but after a youth where his one trip abroad had been to Canada for an ice hockey game, he also wanted to travel. He spent some time in the Gambia in West Africa and did some freelance writing from there, but when he came home he felt it was time to settle down, at least for a while, and after a fashion. He landed a job at the *Washington Post*, covering mostly suburban Maryland affairs, but letting it be known that he would consider a posting abroad at some point. And then, soon after joining the *Post*, he had met his future wife in a softball game at a company picnic. Mary Jordan was the paper's national education correspondent and had been with the *Post* for some time already. It had been suggested to her that she should take a foreign posting, but since she was single and felt it might be a lonely life, she had put it off. Now, however, things turned out differently. Jordan and Sullivan were told a year in advance that they would be going to Tokyo, and were given time off to study Japanese language and history at nearby Georgetown University. Sullivan points out, however, that after several years in Tokyo he may use his Japanese less than when he arrived – he describes his working environment as mostly English-speaking, and intense.

Sullivan and Jordan are in the *Washington Post* bureau in Tokyo together. Their young children's drawings are displayed on their office doors. The stereotype of the foreign correspondent may still be that of the lonely, hardened man, greying and leading a not very wholesome life, perhaps with a string of divorces behind him, but while there may still be some of these around, there are now also many women correspondents, and not so few married couples working as colleagues. In fact, what may be Sullivan's and Jordan's nearest competition in Tokyo is another couple of approximately the same age, Nicholas Kristof and Sheryl WuDunn of the *New York Times*, who arrived in Tokyo at just about the same time. The couples meet occasionally socially, and have their children in the same school. So when one parent from the *Post* team and one from the *Times* team take their children there in the morning and greet each other, there may be some subtle competitive tracking of stories – '... And where is Kevin today?'

To repeat, Kevin Sullivan occasionally travels elsewhere in Asia, but both he and Mary Jordan go to Korea quite regularly, although mostly not together, for the sake of the children. He, like many of the Tokyo correspondents who also include Korea in their beat, finds the difference between that country and Japan striking. Ask a Japanese in the street whether the prime minister is doing a good job, and the answer is likely to be vague, general, non-committal – ask in Korea about President Kim, and you will get a firm, opinionated, elaborate interpretation. If you want to go and look at a Japanese school, apply well in advance through appropriate channels, in a centralized hierarchy, and the people you are to see will spend the time preparing themselves to say as little as possible. In Korea, things can be arranged at short notice or immediately. Sullivan, alluding jokingly to some of his own ancestry, suggests that Korea is to Japan as Ireland to England: the Koreans are informal, outspoken, drink, and write poetry.

Nicholas Valéry, Tokyo bureau chief for *The Economist*, has been in foreign correspondence longer. He was in Moscow and Frankfurt in the 1960s and 1970s, but since then he has mostly gone back and forth between Japanese and American assignments – the former all in Tokyo, the latter in New York, Washington and Los Angeles. His one-room office, where he works with one Japanese assistant, is in a corridor on the eighth floor of the *Yomiuri Shimbun* building, where a number of other foreign news businesses are also based – 'a *gaijin* ghetto', he says.

Despite its name, of course, *The Economist* is not entirely dedicated to economic matters, but is a more general newsweekly with a slant toward economic, political and cultural affairs. And while Tokyo is definitely an important site for economic and business news, Valéry can pursue a variety of interests. His economic knowledge he has actually acquired at work – he came to the *Economist* with a degree in engineering, and finds that many of his colleagues on the magazine staff are of varied occupational backgrounds. There may be doctors and lawyers, but hardly anybody comes fresh out of the university, and perhaps nobody from a school of journalism. Valéry crossed over into investment banking for a while, but came back to *The Economist*. He finds his work continuously intellectually exciting, although writing is sometimes hard, and he is not disturbed by the fact that in line with the long-established tradition of the magazine, his writing appears there unsigned – the people who matter will know who wrote.

His strategy of finding out what he needs or can use, he says, is one of 'vacuum cleaning' – he goes to briefings and to FCCJ luncheon talks, and he obviously has comfortable access to the kind of people he wants to interview, although he notes that over the periods he has spent in Tokyo, there has been a steady increase of 'gaijin handlers' in major organization offices. He speaks Japanese at what he describes as 'survival level' but does not work in it, although he can follow TV or radio newscasts. His Japanese assistant reads dailies and weeklies for him, he checks the Japanese *Nikkei* wire service in English usually several times a day, and his wife is Japanese, so by way of her and an eighteen-month old daughter he is also involved in Japanese life. There is, for example, this children's program in the morning which his daughter watches in her parents' bedroom, about three rice dumplings on a stick. These dumplings are not just any ordinary dumplings; they are alive, anthropomorphized. But they are rather contented with their lot, and convey simple, optimistic, sensible values – a sort of Forrest Gump mood for harder times, it appears to Valéry. And then he realizes that now he hears the signature tune everywhere.

The third correspondent is again a younger man, Påhl Ruin, who has quite recently begun to report from Tokyo to *Dagens Nyheter*, the largest Swedish morning newspaper. He has most of his time in Japan ahead of him, and thinks about what he will want to do with it. He also knows that he will not be there for very many years, but the reasons for this are somewhat special.

While Ruin was going to university in southern Sweden, he began working in the summers for a major regional newspaper, and then he took a position with the journal of Sweden's municipal authorities. Moreover, he married a young woman headed for a career in the Swedish foreign service. Soon after the birth of their first child, she was sent on her first foreign assignment, in Tokyo; and thus, while she went back to work, Ruin spent his first few months in Japan on Swedish parental leave. He had also arranged, however, to work as a stringer for *Dagens Nyheter* during his stay in Japan, which would of course end when his wife was reassigned by her ministry. The paper was pleased by the arrangement. Although by the standards of Scandinavian news media it has a respectable foreign correspondent network, it had not seen it as feasible to station one of its regular staff members in Tokyo, and it had been looking around among Swedish expatriates in Tokyo for a suitable stringer. But given that the income was likely to be a bit unstable, it had been easier for Ruin than for someone else to take this on – there was someone else in the household with a steady income, after all, and the embassy provided him with a roof over his head. So he could do something interesting with his time as a diplomatic spouse, and not be too worried about variations in income between one month and the next.

As far as prospective stories are concerned, coming from the municipal affairs publication, he is interested in developing some understanding of Japanese politics, not least at the local level. He is taking some Japanese language instruction, with the hope of achieving some modest level of fluency toward the end of his stay – his wife's tour of duty in Tokyo is three years. Meanwhile, he works in English, and occasionally with a Japanese interpreter. He reads the five English-language newspapers in Tokyo (published by the major Japanese papers, such as the *Yomiuri Shimbun*), the *Financial Times* which covers Japanese economic news extensively, the *Asian Wall Street Journal*, and the *Far Eastern Economic Review,* and checks the English-language wire service materials of the national Kyodo news agency at the Foreign Press Center. The latter also has a good reference library, and a helpful staff. On the other hand,

Ruin has not joined the Foreign Correspondents Club of Japan, as it would be rather too large an expenditure for his stringer income. As for the connection to the embassy through his wife, he tries to keep a certain distance, not to blur the boundary between her professional life and his.

Instant News, Soft Stories, and the End of the Cold-War Era

Perhaps a chapter on Tokyo foreign correspondents is somewhat marginal to a volume on Asian media productions. It does not involve media productions *by* Asians. Neither is the foreign correspondents' work a matter of productions primarily *for* Asian media audiences. On the other hand, these are productions *from* Asia, at least in a somewhat problematic way; and one may argue that they are productions *of* Asia, intended for non-Asian audiences.

What are, then, the current news stories datelined Tokyo which reach at least American and European publics, and which can be assumed to play a part in shaping their views of present-day Japan? I certainly do not intend to offer any complete inventory here, but I want to try and point to some tendencies, evident not least around the time I was in Tokyo but certainly not only then, and also in the reporting of some of the correspondents already introduced here. Certain of these tendencies are more specific to Japan; but it is also useful to take some more general developments in late twentieth century news media into account.

One of these is the increasingly conscious division of labour which is in large part an outcome of technological change. For those members of the public who follow the news with some regularity, it is pointed out, it is increasingly rare that major 'hard news' stories, about events just occurring, come first through the print media – radio and television are much faster in their reporting. It is even true that the continuous news format of, for example, CNN and BBC World leaves other forms of television and radio programming at a disadvantage. Bruce Dunning, a veteran of some thirty years of Asia reporting and now head of the CBS News Asia Bureau in Tokyo, points out that the old American television networks, such as that for which he works, mostly stick to the format of major morning and evening news programs, and that even this makes them a little less competitive when it comes to breaking news – although they, too, have become a bit more inclined to break into regular programming with such stories. Now he sends his materials either via a Pacific communication satellite to Los Angeles or via an Indian Ocean satellite to London, and then on to New York. It is a very different from the times, early in his career, when film from Vietnam had to be flown out of Saigon by plane.

Already earlier, of course, the major wire services, such as Reuters or the Associated Press, with their very large newsgathering organizations, were mostly faster than the print media's own correspondents in getting to the news, and getting it out, if only to client media organizations rather than straight to the public. Consequently, there was a tendency to let newspaper or the print media correspondents deal more with reporting in which background information, contextualization and analysis would offer 'added value', although for some correspondents even at present rewriting (and, for those not reporting in world languages, translating) agency materials is a recurrent part of the work. But this tendency has now been strengthened in the print media, and Bruce Dunning notes that even on the major news programs of his network, there are now regularly segments of foreign feature stories, relating to the news flow in a slightly different tempo – a visit to a Jakarta trash heap, for example, where people are shown searching for anything that can be useful, illustrates the decline in the Indonesian economy. But even such segments are allowed only two and a half minutes, so there are very narrow limits to background and elaboration.

Then, an increasing emphasis on feature stories – not directly reporting on hard news, although sometimes providing background for it, but frequently not even that either – also has something to do with the state of the world. To a certain extent, the 1990s has been a period when foreign news has been engaged in finding its feet again, after the end of the cold war. The latter had provided an interpretive framework for much international reporting, and some people in the news business have feared that with this ubiquitous shadow over human affairs gone, their audiences would simply turn away from news from distant places. Not least has this been a concern in the United States.

The foreign editor of the *New York Times* in the early 1990s, Bernard Gwertzman, who oversaw the post-cold war transition period in his paper, wrote an important internal memorandum in late 1992 which pointed to new directions for his correspondents (Zipangu 1998:38). In the coming period, he suggested, there would be a broadening of reporting from political news to deal more with environmental issues, histories of ethnic friction, and economic developments which might no longer be confined to the financial section of the paper. Not least, however, 'We are interested in what makes societies different, what is on the minds of people in various regions. Imagine you are being asked to write a letter home every week to describe a different aspect of life in the area you are assigned'.[11] When I talked to Gwertzman's immediate successor at the *New York Times*, Bill Keller, a couple of years ago, he made much the same point slightly differently: foreign correspondents should be interested in 'societies, not only in states'.

In part, then, the response to the end of the cold war, not only in the *New York Times*, has been to try and make foreign reporting, as it is sometimes phrased, 'more seductive'. And here one particular potential of foreign correspondence is worth pointing to. The term 'news' is interestingly ambiguous: it can refer to something that just happened, or something can be news mostly because we simply have not heard of it before, and find it interesting and even surprising. Certainly the news media are primarily oriented to the first of these kinds, to 'hard news', and foreign correspondents tend to take pride in, and be excited by, being present when 'history is made'. But that other kind of news has some particular possibilities for foreign correspondents. A number of things may have a long-term presence in a remote country without our learning of them, until someone tells us. Foreign correspondents can be, as Clifford Geertz (1984:275) once said about anthropologists, 'merchants of astonishment'.

Japanese Stories: Market, War Memories, and Dull Politics

There were two hard news stories from Japan in 1995, two sudden and unforeseen events: the Kobe earthquake (the Japanese television coverage of which is discussed by Liz MacLachlan in the previous chapter) and the poison gas attack in the Tokyo subway by the cult Aum Shinrikyō. Apart from these, however, there may have been few major events seizing headlines around the world in Japan in recent times. What kind of reporting, then, have we been getting out of Tokyo?

One major fact is that if anything has replaced the cold war as a global superstory, it is 'the market'. Tokyo is a major site for economic and business reporting, and financial news services as well as the business press are well represented in the city. Werner Enz, the correspondent of the serious, journalistically conservative *Neue Zürcher Zeitung*, hardly does anything but economic and political reporting – and when the paper adds a second correspondent in Tokyo, the newcomer will do politics and Enz will concentrate on business and economy. In other words, there will still not be much of any other kind of feature stories in their paper, except sometimes by freelancers. Both Sullivan and Jordan, for the *Washington Post*, and Kristof and WuDunn, for the *New York Times*, have a colleague in their respective bureaus (at the time of my Tokyo visit, a woman in both cases) concentrating on economic news, although WuDunn also feels some special affinity for such news, having been in international banking before she went into journalism. And they all point out that even if this is not their specialty, a great many of their stories now relate to the market in some way. Even Kevin Sullivan's story on the outing of Mr. Kawashima and his friends at the Hourin Country Club is, after all, a story about Japan's economic stagnation. In fact, a few months before Sullivan, Påhl Ruin (1999a) also had a story on golf club membership and its relationship to the economy. Both Ruin (1999b) and WuDunn (1999a) reported, too, on the Japanese government attempt to stimulate the economy by issuing free shopping coupons to stimulate the economy – 'With all the strength of her 90 years, Chizuko Miyata clutched her crisp, cream-colored coupons and began dreaming of what she should buy with them', WuDunn opened her story.[12] As far as economic reporting is concerned, one should keep in mind that Japanese business and industrial organization is in part itself a story of dramatized difference, when it is a story of success as well as when it is a story of decline and failure. The *keiretsu*, 'huge corporate alliances welded together by shared values, business ties, and webs of cross-shareholdings' as *Business Week* describes them in a recent cover story on the fall of Mitsubishi, are a case in point (Bremner et al. 1999).

There is also, in reporting from Tokyo, a preoccupation with a certain kind of un-news – the theme of Japanese participation in World War II is recurrent, not least in the media of other countries who were then Japan's adversaries. When the dateline of particular stories is Hiroshima rather than Tokyo, they involve one aspect of this war heritage. Another, coming up again and again in recent times, is that of Japanese war guilt – will the representatives of Japan apologize or won't they? Precisely how strong a vocabulary will they use? Surely there have been vestiges and reminders of past hostility in much western writing on Japan, not least in the United States and Britain. Hammond and Stirner (1997) discuss this, characteristically, under the rubric 'Fear and Loathing in the British Press'. In the period of most conspicuous Japanese economic success in the late twentieth century, older sentiments could mix with new fears in the 'Japan-bashing' of both news commentary and popular culture. And when in the 1990s the issue was increasingly frequently raised of a renewed greater Japanese military responsibility in regional and even global affairs, and the return to greater prominence of the flag, *Hinomaru*, and the anthem, *Kimigayo*, as national symbols, the historical resonances of reporting on the debates were unmistakable. In early 1999, for example, *The Economist* (1999a) ran a cover where three warships in dramatic black and white confront the viewer against a background of the red and white rising sun, over the rubric 'Let Japan sail forth'. In the same period, there are Stephanie Strom (1999), another *New York Times* writer ('There is a new willingness to assume a public role in regional defense that Japan has long shunned because of its military past and the fears of neighbors it once threatened'), Nicholas Kristof (1999a) noting that 'The government is trying to rehabilitate the flag of the rising sun and the national song of praise for the Emperor, giving them legal status despite criticism that in World War II they were emblems of Japanese militarism', and a story by Påhl Ruin (1999b) reporting on a suicide by a school principal, who could not stand the cross-pressure when the school authorities (in Hiroshima) and the parents wanted the national symbols to be used in end-of-term ceremonies, and the left-leaning teachers did not.[13]

Apart from this genre of stories, however, it is true that politics does not figure particularly prominently in reporting from Japan. One reason, evidently, is the relative opacity of Japanese party politics; another is the unwillingness of Japanese politicians to appear flamboyant and make striking statements (except sometimes by mistake) – the same more widespread cautiousness also noted by Kevin Sullivan in his contrasting of the Japanese and the Koreans. Påhl Ruin, coming from a journal of Swedish municipal authorities, may find something of special interest, as he says, in local-level politics, while Werner Enz of the *Neue Zürcher Zeitung*, doing the occasional feature interview with leading politicians, concludes that on the one hand, these never say much of any interest, and on the other hand, they are quite likely to say say different things for international and domestic consumption.[14] One notable exception, and at the same time, confirmation of the theme that Japanese politics makes dull stories, is Kristof's

NEWS

(1996b) story 'Warming to "Cold Pizza": Japan's Leader Repairs His Image Problem' – it turns out that when former Prime Minister Keizō Obuchi took office he was described (by an American publicist) as having 'all the pizzazz of cold pizza', but thereafter, according to Kristof, although 'nobody would describe Mr. Obuchi as charismatic', he turned out to be more effective and more popular than expected, until his untimely death in May 2000. A more real exception, perhaps, is in the continued activities and statements of the controversial, nationalistically inclined politician Shintarō Ishihara, some years ago the co-author of the book *The Japan That Can Say No*, more recently elected governor of Tokyo. (But then Ishihara first earned fame as a novelist.)

News of Difference: *New York Times* versus Zipangu

In any case, the interest in 'what makes societies different' is noticeable in current reporting out of Tokyo. Perhaps some of this, too, has a quality of un-news. Stories which relate, or can somehow be made to relate, to classic, and stereotypical, western notions of what is Japanese, continue to attract foreign correspondents – and probably no less, their editors at home. Geishas, samurais, harakiri and kamikaze seem inevitable, although contexts may be updated and sometimes intriguingly anomalous. Sheryl WuDunn (1999b, 1999c) has done stories both on 'American "Geisha": Culture Shock in Japan' – on the translation of the American author Arthur Golden's bestseller *Memoirs of a Geisha* into Japanese – and on 'A Japanese manager Commits Hara-Kiri Over Company Downsizing'.

Apart from such obvious topics, however, the search for new instances of difference – often entertaining, sometimes titillating – has indeed been prominent in a more general way. Discussing this tendency in the British media, Hammond and Stirner (1997) describe it acerbically as a theme of Japanese 'weirdness', with a multitude of expressions. Certainly, we may remind ourselves here, a preoccupation with Japanese difference is not a monopoly of western journalists. The Japanese themselves have hardly been adverse to dwelling on forms of national uniqueness – the entire intellectual field of *nihonjinron* is evidence of this. Japan has been described, too, as 'God's gift to comparative sociology', in its capacity to offer early and continuous evidence that modernization and modernity can appear in other than occidental forms.[15] No doubt it is precisely the superficially familiar background of generally modern features which often allows the stories of difference to be told to western audiences with particular effect. Yet while we may still appreciate such a source of insights into the possibilities of diversity, we have also recently been made more aware, in academia and not least in anthropology, of the moral and intellectual risks in dwelling on difference: the risks of 'othering' and dehumanizing.

A recent flurry of controversy over the Japan coverage in the *New York Times* may remind us of such issues. What the *New York Times* has to say about events or places tends nowadays to be regarded as especially significant and influential by a great many people in the world, and the reporting of its foreign correspondents is therefore often watched with close attention by representatives of the countries from which they write. When an emphasis on difference becomes a matter of preferred style in its reporting, however, as the Gwertzman memorandum appears to suggest, there may be particular opportunities for the creasing of foreheads and raising of eyebrows, not least in the context of a more broadly ambivalent relationship such as that between Japan and the United States. The reporting of Nicholas Kristof and Sheryl WuDunn – energetic, lively and often, in feature stories, in search of what would strike their readers at home as unusual – provoked an organization of Japanese diaspora journalists and artists in New York, Zipangu, to publish a highly critical bilingual volume, *Japan Made in USA* (1998), discussing a number of the feature stories involved, and containing interviews with some academic specialists and commentaries by others, as well as a response by Kristof. An outsider may feel that some of the Zipangu criticisms were overly defensive, and not always persuasive. Yet the volume drew some supportive comment in Japanese newspapers, and there were other foreign correspondents in Tokyo as well who, while often appreciative of the *New York Times* couple's skills, were less than enthusiastic about some of their stories. An occasional Japanese observer would label them as 'orientalist'.

By the time of my visit in Tokyo, Kristof and WuDunn were approaching the end of their Japanese assignment. To a certain extent, Kristof's interests were perhaps turning in other directions – he had recently done a series of articles titled 'Behind the Global Economy' which were not Japan-related in any very large part, and on an excursion from the Tokyo beat, he had been to Central Africa at the time of the Mobutu-Kabila transition. They were not yet sure where they would be next. There were still articles by both of them on some of the oddities of Japanese culture and society – one by Kristof (1999c), for example, on the now extinct Japanese '*namba*' style of walking, with the right arm moving forward with the right leg, and the left arm moving with the left leg – but by and large, it would seem that more of the controversial stories were from their first year or so in Japan.

It was at the beginning of 1995 Kristof and WuDunn arrived in Tokyo, from a previous posting in Beijing, where their reporting on the Tiananmen Square events had earned them a Pulitzer Prize, the most coveted honor in American journalism.[16] Very soon after they came in to take charge of the Tokyo bureau, there was the Kobe earthquake. While WuDunn managed the news flow through the office, Kristof did a very large part of the reporting out of Kobe. He wrote from there over a period of several weeks, with stories going considerably beyond standard instant disaster coverage.[17] In a background piece (Kristof 1995), he suggested that 'sometimes the way people or nations react to disasters can open a window on their souls', and on this principle, he explored the inequalities of Japanese society, concepts of honor and shame, standards of reciprocity, and some range of other topics. There was an element of somewhat predictable typecasting here as well – how did the earthquake affect the geisha business in neighboring Kyoto? – but one can hardly doubt that this was an exciting moment to report from Japan.[18]

In the period that followed, however, one may suspect that Kristof and WuDunn found Tokyo in some ways a less satisfying journalistic experience than Beijing, with its political and economic upheavals. I met Sheryl WuDunn at the *New York Times* office on the ninth floor of the *Asahi Shimbun* building, home of another major Japanese daily, close to the famous Tsukiji fish market. When I asked her to compare the couple's Chinese and Japanese experiences, she noted that the sensibilities were entirely different. In China, people had been engaged in a struggle to come up from hardly anything, to seize one's chance in life. In Japan, there was none of that sense of drama. There was a sense of agony and drama, perhaps, in a period of economic recession, but this was still an affluent country, and there were things the Japanese already had which would hardly be taken away from them. Apart from that, she felt, in Japan there were always shades of gray. It was difficult to do stories with a point of view. Japanese opinions, again, are not strongly expressed. There is a tendency toward vagueness, no eagerness to be quoted in the press.

WuDunn's remarks here are obviously close to what one would hear from many of her correspondent colleagues in Tokyo. What this definition of the reporting situation had led her and Kristof to do, it seems, was to engage less with a 'native's point of view', which seemed so curiously difficult to extract, than to focus a great deal of attention on what, to the foreign sojourner, was indeed different (although possibly of no great interest to the Japanese, or embarrassing to them). And this had taken them to the stories which had so irritated the Zipangu collective, and not so few others. One had been on the high-pitched voices of Japanese women, as a sign of gender inequality. Another had been on sexual molestation in the Tokyo subway – in fact, one molester had published a book on the topic. Yet another had been on rape fantasies in a women's comic strip magazine.[19] And then, as Kristof had felt that too much Japan-reporting became entirely Tokyo-centered and had taken to visiting a small rural town for stories, he could also report on beliefs in 'fox devils' in the computer age.

It is fair to note that several of WuDunn's and Kristof's colleagues in Tokyo, from the United States or elsewhere, actually at one time or other filed stories on the same topics, or at least made reference to them in some way. Again, probably the international eminence of the *New York Times* has something to do with the special attention given to their writing. Then there might have been something in their reporting style as well – close-up, personalizing (as in WuDunn's opening line about the 90-year old lady with her shopping coupons), and, more often perhaps in Kristof's stories, somewhat ironical, gently mocking. Moreover, questions could sometimes be raised whether what was shown as different about Japan is also typically Japanese. The pornographic comic magazine for women with those rape stories, for example, is hardly in the mainstream of Japanese culture.

Some correspondents, and commentators on correspondence, would argue that a number of those stories which upset the New York Japanese of Zipangu, and which might astonish other New Yorkers, would in fact work best where the readership ('upscale' as it might be) would not be particularly well-informed about Japan. You would not find them, it was suggested to me, in the *Los Angeles Times*, which 'has to cover Japan as if it were part of the LA metropolitan area'. Sonni Efron, Tokyo bureau chief at that paper, thought that particular formulation might be too strong; but she agreed that because so many of the paper's readers in California have either business or kinship connections in Japan, and have been to Japan themselves, her bureau's coverage of Japanese affairs had to be a bit different from that of her East Coast colleagues. She would not get away with so much surprise, real or feigned, and there were other kinds of stories which were perhaps of greater concrete interest to the California readers. She had worked for several weeks on a story of genetically modified foodstuffs and Japanese resistance to them; this was a topic of interest to California agribusiness (Efron 1999a). And a colleague of hers in the bureau was doing a story on the weak presence of venture capital in Japanese business, contrasting the situation with that in Silicon Valley. The *Los Angeles Times* style of Japan reporting, however, did not necessarily keep it out of controversy either. Precisely because of those diverse linkages across the Pacific, its Japan coverage also tended to generate comment and feedback. After Efron had done a portrait of a well-known right-wing ideologue at the University of Tokyo, a conservative Tokyo newspaper had responded critically under the headline 'The Insolence and Arrogance of a Great American Newspaper'.

Family and Gender: The News of Youngish Correpondents

Påhl Ruin, the neophyte stringer for *Dagens Nyheter*, was a little impatient with the tendency of Japan correspondents to dwell on difference, and hoped to do some stories where similarity would be the main theme. But he was still thinking about how to do it. One might say that in one distinctive way, this is in fact a recurrent contemporary theme especially of American foreign correspondence, as its representatives in different corners of the world report to people at home on 'Americanization', especially in consumer habits and popular culture. There is no dearth of such stories out of Tokyo either.

It is perhaps in one wide genre of feature stories, recently quite conspicuously cultivated by Japan correspondents, that the play of similarity and difference becomes particularly evident: that of family and gender. Påhl Ruin (1999e) reports on being on the streets of Tokyo on weekdays, on parental leave and in the company of his firstborn, looking for another father attending to a baby; he never saw one. And he proceeds to describe a Japanese government campaign to get men to spend more time with their children, and the mixed reactions to it. In another article, the focus is on Fuchino, an 84-year old woman, living in her son's household, and the main point of the story is that every third household in

Japan is still made up of three generations – but more and more women, especially as they hold on to jobs of their own, simply refuse to manage domestic lives of this kind. Jordan and Sullivan (1999a) of the *Washington Post* have a similar story on the limited domestic involvements of fathers, and Jordan (1999a) also writes on the aversion of Japanese couples to child adoption. In yet another story, Jordan (1999b) reports on an effort to start a national fund-raising network for female political candidates – international women's right groups, she notes, have criticized Japan for having 'far fewer female politicians than many less advanced countries'. Sheryl WuDunn (1997), on a reporting trip to Korea, finds that young people reject the old practice of marriages arranged by parents – and turn instead to dating services, which offer a somewhat similar service of suggesting socially compatible partners. Nicholas Kristof (1996), also on a Korean assignment, describes the continued prevalence of marital violence – many Korean men, readers are told, still somewhat routinely beat their wives. And from Tokyo, again, WuDunn (1996, 1998) notes that Japan appears still to be in no hurry to legalize the Pill.[20]

Why are there all these stories relating to family and gender coming out of Japan? Certainly the most obvious reason is that, against a background of shared modernity, this is again an area where Japanese society is noticeably different from western Europe and North America. Difference is news here, when reported over a distance, and it is a kind of difference to which just about every reader can relate personally. Gender inequality (with some rather kinky expressions) and gender segregation together form the basic story, together with inter-generational cohesion in families, and changes away from that baseline allow further variations on the theme.

Even so, one may wonder if these interests are not also of special interest to some foreign correspondents. If the correspondents had more often conformed to that stereotype referred to before, of greying lonely men, would they have been doing these stories? Less likely, it seems. One factor may well be the influx of women into the foreign correspondent corps in recent times – and not necessarily the female counterpart of the stereotype male correspondent, but often young women engaged in their own family lives, like Mary Jordan, Sheryl WuDunn, and Sonni Efron (and a great many others in various postings around the world). To them, one may surmise, family and gender differences between Japan and the west may also be what is especially striking at a personal level. It might at times affect the way they go about their professional lives as well. Efron noted that having children could be an asset – people in the street are more willing to talk to someone pushing a stroller. And when she took her children to the park on Saturday mornings, she could get a sense of what the Japanese mothers assembling there were concerned with, as they chatted while the children played. So could it even be an advantage to be a woman correspondent? No, not in Tokyo, on the whole; she could not go out and drink with bureaucrats or politicians on Friday evenings, when their tongues might loosen, and there are still very few women in prominent positions in Japan to whom she could have comparable access. This, she summarized, was still a society of 'gender apartheid'. Nevertheless, she could as well use the particular insights available to her as a woman and mother.

The increasing number of women correspondents, however, is hardly the entire explanation either, so far as the interest in family and gender stories is concerned. It would also seem probable that a fair number of youngish male correspondents, growing up in Europe and North America in a period of changing patterns of personal relationships and with a great deal of public discourse over such issues in their home countries, would also be drawn to such reporting during their stays in Japan. Kevin Sullivan and Nick Kristof seem not to have been noticeably less involved in gender and family issues than their co-worker spouses, and then there is also Påhl Ruin, whose wife is not in the news business, using his experience while on parental leave in Tokyo. All of them, too, seem to be drawn to stories on Japanese schooling (see, for example, Jordan and Sullivan 1999b). Sullivan, when I talked to him, smilingly acknowledged that being of more or less the same age and in the same stage of the domestic life as the *New York Times* couple could perhaps sometimes influence his and his wife's work – when they identified a topic, they might try and do the story sooner rather than later, because it was quite likely that Nick and Sheryl would be attracted to the same idea.

All this, of course, is not to say that stories on family and gender are entirely the province of correspondents who are either women, youngish, or both. *The Economist* (for example, 1999b, 1999c) occasionally does similar stories which, despite being unsigned, one may assume are the work of Nicholas Valéry, of a somewhat older generation in journalism, although a person of wide-ranging curiosity and insight. What might perhaps be argued, however, is that shifts in the demography of foreign correspondence might favor such stories; and that someone like Valéry, after all, may also pay some attention to what younger colleagues in Tokyo find of interest.

Conclusion: The News of Gradual Change

When I met Valéry, it was a couple of weeks after *The Economist* had published his cover story on the Japanese defense debate. He had persuaded the editor in London of the value of the story about a month in advance, and it had taken a few weeks of thinking, but he knew the debate was coming up in the Diet, so that he would have some 'spot news', something that just happened, to hang the story on.

Several Tokyo correspondents spoke about this issue – what were the time frames of 'news', how could one maneuver with them within the conventions of news reporting? Valéry reflected on famous past attempts to grasp the nature of Japanese culture and society. Ruth Benedict's *The Chrysanthemum and the Sword*, from the end of World War II, had been interesting, but wrong; the more recent *The Enigma of Japanese Power* (1989), by the veteran Dutch Tokyo correspondent, Karel van Wolferen, had been quite good, but had perhaps overemphasized the weakness of the center in the Japanese political system. Valéry had told him that changes were occurring at the peripheries. Now he saw the present as 'the beginning of the end of denial', and thought this was the big story to be told. For decades, Japanese society had been built on the premise of expansion, but this no longer worked; it had actually been in a phase of maturity since 1973. The senior Japanese generation, people in their sixties, were slow to recognize this, but there were people a generation younger who had understood it.

But then how does one deal with such changes? Valéry's own handling of the defense debate story suggests what seems to be a fairly typical way: you identify, perhaps even beforehand, some event which will provide a peg for the longer-term story. Sonni Efron of the *Los Angeles Times* similarly felt that many stories of Japan were matters of process – you kept watching them, not quite sure when to actually do them. One of her predecessors in the bureau had said they were like a toothpaste tube: you have to decide yourself when to stop squeezing. She took some particular interest in technology stories, but she found it very difficult to predict precisely what innovations would have the greatest long-term impact, and the experts often disagreed among themselves. It was, she thought, the opposite of what had been her experience as a Moscow correspondent: in Moscow, when she was there, one could be sure of what was the story of the day, even as information was unavailable or incorrect. In Tokyo, there was plenty of information, but what was news was not obvious.

Handling time frames, at various levels, conceptually as well as practically, is clearly a typical preoccupation of newspeople. How do you deliver the goods when it is fresh, how can you represent a process through an event, how do you turn something that is far away, but perhaps fairly constant, into news? When I encounter such concerns among the foreign correspondents, I am reminded of Fernand Braudel's (1980) identification of three types of speed in the writing of history: the history of the long time span, the *longue durée*, where things seem to be stable, repetitive, or at least very slowly changing; a medium-term, 'conjunctural' history, of periods between a decade and a half-century; and *l'histoire événementielle*, event history, the history of the short time span. When some newspeople speak of 'being present when history is made', we may assume that they have the *histoire événementielle* in mind. Here is the 'breaking news'. In the case of many feature stories, where something may be new to the readers (or listeners, or viewers) simply by being far away, and previously unknown to them, but may otherwise be in a more or less stable state, we seem closer to Braudel's *longue durée* – and to what anthropologists, in a similar reporting situation, have referred to as 'the ethnographic present'. This can be discerned in many of the stories of Japanese difference.

But in between, and in the concerns identified by Nicholas Valéry and Sonni Efron in their Japan reporting, is medium-term history. Looking at foreign correspondence out of Japan, we can perhaps recognize it in a range of stories. When Efron (1999b) reports on the passage of Japan's first freedom of information law, she sets it against the background of twenty years of struggle by

146

citizens' groups – and one gets some sense of cumulative change away from the old opacity of Japanese power. When Påhl Ruin (1999f) describes the revolt of Japanese youth, rejecting ideals of life-long employment and loyalty to the corporation, and shifting to expressive cultural styles, we sense that a generation is rearranging its relationship to the economy. When Mary Jordan and Kevin Sullivan (1999b) begin a story on 'classroom chaos' with a visit to Miss Sato's collapsing second-grade class, where 'one child has broken windows four times, hits other children, walks on the desks, urinates off the veranda and spits on the floor. Another scribbles all over the room and lies down on the desktops', it is made clear that something other than individual misdemeanors is involved. An old authority structure is failing. And when the same writers find that 'Japanese Retirees Head Back to Work', it becomes obvious that what they identify as the world's fastest aging and longest living population is fitting itself into the economy, and into family life, in changing ways (Sullivan and Jordan 1999). We realize perhaps, too, that many of the stories on family and gender are not just about difference, but about the making of history as well. Indeed, it may be that the medium-term change, rather than Japanese 'weirdness', is now becoming the big news from Japan, and that it is under the Tokyo dateline we will find some of the most thoughtful experimentation with the news of gradual change.

Notes

1 I am grateful to the Tercentenary Fund of the Bank of Sweden for its support of my study of foreign correspondence. Previous publications relating to the project include Hannerz (1996:112 ff.; 1998a; 1998b; 1998c). For invaluable help in making contacts in Tokyo, I especially want to thank Professor Harumi Befu and Professor Fumio Kitamura.
2 In the Foucault-inspired terminology of George Marcus (1998: 203ff.), this is a study of another regime of power/knowledge.
3 According to Yuji Yoshikata, Subsaharan Africa correspondent for the *Yomiuri Shimbun*, whom I met in Johannesburg in 1998, his paper has over fifty foreign correspondents; the *New York Times* has about forty. The networks are, of course, differently weighted regionally, so that for example the *Yomiuri Shimbun* has a greater proportion of its correspondents in southeast Asia than any European or American paper would have.
4 I am grateful to Professor Kitamura, former Director of the Foreign Press Center, for these figures.
5 For some recent comments on the Tokyo foreign press corps, see Neilan (1995) and Mayes and Rowling (1997).
6 See for example my earlier article on the correspondents in Jerusalem (Hannerz 1998c).
7 On the kisha clubs, see van Wolferen (1989:93–95); Neilan (1995:313–315); Hall (1998:45 ff.); and deLange (1998).
8 The volume published by the Foreign Correspondents Club of Japan (1998) to celebrate its fiftieth anniversary offers detailed information on the history of the organization. See also comments by Neilan (1995:310–313).
9 I am indebted to Robert Neff, Contributing Editor of *Business Week* and President of the FCCJ at the time of my visit to Tokyo, for discussing the work of the organization with me and for showing me its facilities.

10 All three, admittedly, work for the print media, and all three are male. There will be some discussion of gender issues below, however, and the choice of these three is also linked to the exemplification of themes of reporting which follows.

11 I believe Kevin Sullivan, working for another news organization, was making no conscious allusion to the Gwertzman memorandum when he told me that the imagined reader he wrote for was his mother – intellectually alert and generally well-informed, although without any special interest in Japan (at least until her son and daughter-in-law went there).

12 Articles originally published in the *New York Times,* the *Washington Post* or the *Los Angeles Times* will usually be cited here in the versions appearing in the *International Herald Tribune*, which largely relies on the foreign correspondent network of these papers and which has been more easily accessible to me in Europe. The titles of the articles may or may not be the same in the two versions.

13 When, somewhat later in 1999, the Diet adopted the flag and the anthem as national symbols, *Frankfurter Allgemeine*, the German newspaper with the largest foreign correspondent network, also devoted a substantial report to the historical background and the current Japanese debate (Schneppen 1999).

14 Enz was not alone among the correspondents I talked to in suggesting that Japanese public figures would feel little compunction about such different pronouncements. Perhaps it is useful to see this against the background of Moeran's (1989:18–19) comments on the contextualizing of sincerity in relation to public/private, frontstage/ backstage divides in Japanese speech.

15 I have the formulation from Shmuel Eisenstadt.

16 For their experiences in reporting on China, see Kristof and WuDunn (1994).

17 I have discussed Kristof's Kobe reporting elsewhere (Hannerz 1998a).

18 In relation to MacLachlan's discussion of the tendency of Japanese media to deemphasize criticism and controversy in covering the handling of the earthquake by Japanese authorities, it may be noted here that Kristof was one of the foreign correspondents who gave some attention to such issues.

19 Foreign correspondents in Japan seem rather often to dwell on *manga* comic books. These may well be a central feature of contemporary Japanese popular culture; yet one may wonder if one reason for this attention could be that for those not fully literate in Japanese, these publications offer windows of opportunity through which at least some views of Japanese life and fantasy may be glimpsed.

20 In later coverage, WuDunn (1999d), as well as other correspondents, would contrast the slowness of the Japanese authorities in accepting contraceptive pills with their immediate approval of Viagra – what did this suggest about the political strength of male and female interests?

Part III

Advertising

Figure 9 Bombay billboard
(Photo courtesy of Dermot Tatlow)

7

CREATING ADVERTISING IN JAPAN

A Sketch in Search of a Principle

John L. McCreery

Discovering Japanese Advertising[1]

In *Discourses of the Vanishing*, Marilyn Ivy (1995) describes the creation of Discover Japan, an advertising campaign created by Dentsu Incorporated for what was then the (as yet unprivatized) Japan National Railways. Her description of how the campaign was created is taken from an account by Fujioka Wakao. In 1970, when Discover Japan was created, Fujioka was the account executive in charge of the campaign. Ivy's synthesis of Fujioka's description of how the campaign was developed proceeds along the following lines.

We learn first that the planning began with discussions about the meaning of travel. The starting point was the word *tabi,* an indigenous Japanese term associated with Edo-period pilgrimages:

> Tabi brings up associations of solitary pilgrims traversing remote mountains; it is a word appropriate for describing the journeys of Japan's famous spiritual poet-travelers, the monk Saigyō and the haiku master Bashō.
>
> (Ivy 1995:37)

The Dentsu team concluded, however, that in the Japan of the 1970s, few Japanese had ever had the chance to embark on a true journey of self-discovery (*tabirashii tabi*). Then they realized that while their Edo prototypes were men, the only people in Japan with the time and money for travel were young, unmarried women.

After market research confirmed that young women who travel imagine themselves as 'just like movie heroines', the team developed commercials in which pairs of young women appear as if on stage at travel destinations that represented the very essence of traditional Japan. Modern young women would see themselves leaving home and traveling into the Japanese countryside where they could discover their true selves. The ultimate destination not shown in any commercial was, of course, home again. There these young women would eventually assume their proper roles as Japanese wives and mothers, reproducing the essential Japan of which they would now be the true embodiment.

My purpose in this paper is not to quarrel with Ivy's interpretation of the larger cultural significance of Discover Japan. But as someone who has worked for thirteen years for Hakuhodo Incorporated, Dentsu's largest Japanese rival, what I find unconvincing here is the smoothness with which the campaign's development appears to unfold. Where are the unsuccessful alternatives? What became of the quarrels, the struggles, the late-night battles by which they were sifted and shaped into the proposals – never just one – that were shown to the client? How were they presented to the client? Who made the final decision? And why?

I recall, however, that Fujioka is one of Japan's most famous and successful account executives. The story we have just heard is precisely the kind of tale that great account executives (or the marketing planners or creative staff who may do the actual work) incorporate in presentations and then, when campaigns are successful, in press interviews and in books and articles which serve as promotional tools both for themselves and their agencies. As descriptions of the actual processes by which campaigns are created, they are, at best, highly sanitized history. One could, perhaps, following the lead of Joy Hendry (1993), describe them as a kind of verbal wrapping that focuses attention on the author's intention while artfully concealing the substance of what they are talking about.

My purpose in this essay is to peel away the wrapping and sketch, albeit very roughly, what goes on back stage at a Japanese advertising agency as advertising campaigns are developed, produced and delivered to the public whose members, unless they take some special interest in the matter, will see only the polished surface of the finished print ad or TV commercial, floating free like a fetishized commodity from the messy muddle of industrial and artistic processes, corporate politics and frequently tense interpersonal relations through which it has been created.

Getting Behind the Scenes

A useful place to begin – and an excellent source of comparative data – is Brian Moeran's description of the *Ikon Breath O₂* contact lens campaign in Chapter 4 of *A Japanese Advertising Agency* (Moeran 1996a:133–68). In contrast to the Ivy/Fujioka account of the Discover Japan campaign, here we get a good deal closer to the everyday realities of agency life. Where Ivy begins by unpacking the meanings perceived as inherent in a key word – *tabi* in the case of Discover Japan – Moeran begins with a clear understanding that creative work in advertising is:

> A curious amalgam of different sets of values which are continually subject to a process of negotiation, not just between the Agency and its client, but also between different members of the Agency's account team *and* between superior and subordinate in the client's organization.
>
> (Moeran 1996a:140)

In the case of *Ikon Breath O₂*, the creative team was juggling: first, with a client proud of a real but difficult-to-explain technical advantage in its contact lenses and opticians who, for the product to succeed, would have to recommend it; second, with a target audience of young women more attracted by lifestyle imagery than technical explanations; and third, with strict government regulations concerning the use of superlatives and claims of a medical nature. The copywriter favored use of the client's technical jargon, the words 'corneal physiology', not because he felt that it would be meaningful to the audience but instead because it would be sufficiently new and different to cut through the clutter of bland clichés normally used to describe contact lenses. The creative director was holding out for 'hard/soft', a paradoxical formula, he suggested, with imagistic appeal to the target. Both to resolve this conflict and to move the technically oriented client to a more marketing-savvy position, the account executive cleverly asked the client to poll its own female employees for reactions to the technical terminology. Their revulsion quashed the idea and opened the way for a new round of proposals.

The choice of the celebrity featured in brand advertising was equally complex. The agency pushed for a celebrity instead of an ordinary model on the grounds that only a celebrity could provide the instant recognition required for effective communication in an ad-saturated marketplace. The celebrity should be a young woman to appeal to the primary target. In addition, because she would appear in both print and TV she would have to look good in both media. Besides providing a beautiful face, for the TV commercials she would have to act. (There were, I am sure, also client preferences for one or another actress in play.)

There were also the material complexities of having to plan simultaneously point-of-sale materials along with the TV and print advertising. The former had to be produced more quickly, but the image they conveyed would have to be consistent with that of the TV and print advertising produced later. A last-minute change in the latter, for example, in the choice of celebrity, would totally disrupt production of the former.

Imagine yourself in the role of the account executive in charge of pulling all this together, ensuring that the advertising gets produced on time, negotiating payments that will earn the agency a profit, and keeping the client happy as well. If you find yourself imagining ulcers, you won't be wrong.

Is Valid Understanding Possible?

In a classic, empiricist frame of mind, one imagines a program of systematic research in which a whole series of ethnographers working in different agencies pile up enough case studies like that provided by Moeran to provide the empirical ground for a theory of how the creative process works in Japanese advertising. Combined with similar research in other parts of the world, this work would support the development of a general theory of creative process in advertising agencies around the world.

153

The scope of the enterprise is daunting. Hakuhodo, the agency where I worked, produces on average 2,000 TV commercials a year. I have never been able to find anyone who knows precisely how many pieces of print advertising, billboards, point-of-sale materials, direct mail and, now, Web pages, the company produces. Hakuhodo, mind you, is only Japan's second largest agency.

When I open the July 1997 issue of *Brain*, Japan's leading marketing trade magazine, and turn to the results of the 35th annual Tokyo Copywriters Club Awards competition, I find that the total number of works submitted in the regular division (excluding point-of-sale and other collateral materials) was 4,198. The entries in this contest are divided into thirteen categories by industry.

A Liquor and tobacco
B Food and beverage
C Department stores, supermarkets, specialty stores, fabrics and fashions
D Cosmetics, pharmaceuticals, science, personal products
E Home electronics, AV equipment, computers, OA equipment, communications equipment, office equipment, telecommunications services
F Precision machinery, production materials, housing and real estate
G Shipping, transportation, tourism
H Automobiles, motorcycles, bicycles, motorboats, tires, gasoline, and other transportation related products and services
I Recreation, sports and sports equipment, events, concerts
J Financial institutions, insurance, government, education
K Mass media, publishing
L Naming, catalogs, pamphlets
M Others

As an advertising professional, I note, first, that this list can be described as a typology of sponsors with distinct communication needs and separate regulatory environments. Liquor and tobacco advertising is legally confined to messages to adults. Food and beverage advertising is often directed at teenagers or at housewives concerned about what they feed their families.

This same list is also a typology of skills. Thus, for example, photographers who specialize in food or fashion are in a very different business from those who are experts in automotive or sports photography. Copywriters who write in the high, serious tone preferred by financial institutions are a different breed altogether from those who use trendy slang to pitch soft drinks. Both may find themselves at sea if asked to write about high technology.

I also note the remarks by Akiyama Shō, chairman of the Tokyo Copywriters Club, who is speaking about the newcomer (*shinjin*) awards and taking advantage of the opportunity to preach to the younger generation.

Advertising is not movies. Nor is it writing fiction. Advertising progresses by finding its own modes of expression. One has only fifteen seconds in which to speak. The message must be spoken in a single line. Beneath its surface, however, is a huge intention, the product of planning, imagination, calculation. Advertising is only the visible peak of marketing. Thus, as a form of expression it is different from movies and fiction. It might be described as 'saying through labor in the middle of the night things which cannot be said in the open light of day'.

Akiyama continues with an inventory of the types of appeals a young copywriter might want to consider:

Realistic. Psychological. Exciting. True. Humorous. Raw. Gentle. Nagging. Unexpected. Human. Artificial. Factual. Relaxed. Insightful. Poisonous. Helpful. Playful. Despairing. Hopeful. Hilarious. Blind spots. Strange. Mathematical. Revealing. Lonely. Familiar. Manhattan. Each is a possible approach . . .

(Akiyama 1997:33)

One suspects somehow that the number of possible ads and the number of possible paths to reach them are, like the number of possible human genotypes, larger than the number of electrons in the visible universe. To point to one case and say, 'There, that's how it's done' is, to put it simply, absurd.

Speaking as a practitioner-observer, I also cannot help being aware of the blinders that being a practitioner imposes. As Jib Fowles observes, advertising is in fact what its Frankfurt School critics called it: one of the culture *industries*. Except for the smallest boutiques, advertising agencies are complex, multi-tiered organizations. 'Those toiling within these organizations are specialists, contributing only fractional pieces to the eventual product, which can be said to originate in no single person' (Fowles 1996:17). The result is that no single person who works in advertising ever knows all that went into producing a particular campaign.

Even the account executives responsible for overseeing the whole process cannot be everywhere at once. If they are off talking to the client, they don't know what actually went on in creative or marketing staff meetings. Every meeting, including those in which the whole team participates, involves negotiation. The reports of other meetings heard when people get together are inevitably edited summaries, often from individuals with conflicting points of view. Critical exchanges take place in hallways or between key figures who speak to each other privately precisely because they don't want everyone involved privy to all that is going on. From a business point of view, it suffices at any particular stage for the process to move ahead. What matters at the end of the day is that an ad or commercial is produced, the client is happy, the agency is paid. There is no motivation for anyone to keep track of every detail of how these results are achieved.

There is, moreover, motivation for mystifying the process. Agencies are paid large sums of money for doing work described as *original* and creative. As I have pointed out elsewhere, in brainstorming sessions in Japan there is no more damning comment than *mō furui* (literally 'already old'; in other words, *passé*). There is no simpler way to kill a proposal than to point out that its words or images have already been used, either for the product in question or for one of its competitors. Once used in print or on TV, both words and images must wait for several years (or be transferred to another, sufficiently different product category) to be seen as fresh again (McCreery 1995:322–3). I would add here that nothing is more damning in evaluations of creative staff than to say of someone that he or she is 'one-pattern', in other words, too used to doing things in one particular way, which as it becomes hackneyed, loses the freshness that earns the label 'creative'.

What, Then, Can We Say?

The awful warnings sketched above are not intended as a counsel of despair. We may not be able – and I would say never will be able – to predict precisely the creative ideas that an agency's creative staff will come up with in response to a particular marketing problem, which of their proposals their clients will choose to produce, and which of those actually produced will be taken by consumers and affect their behavior in clearly identifiable ways. We may still be able to understand in some detail how advertising is created and recognize the critical choices that have to be negotiated in producing an advertising campaign.

A useful starting point is Moeran's (1996a) proposal that we put to one side the semiotic analysis of individual ads or campaigns conceived like works of art as separate and unique products and focus instead on the processes by which advertising is produced. I have argued elsewhere (McCreery forthcoming) that when we try to conceptualize those processes the work of Victor Turner (1974) and Pierre Bourdieu (1992) provides some of the elements we need.

Turner's 'social drama' provides an overall framework. The curtain goes up when a breach of everyday routines calls into question the central moral principles on which social life depends. The breach leads to a crisis. Those involved take sides. Then, however, others with a stake in keeping the breach from becoming irreparable step in. If all goes well the relationship threatened by the breach is reaffirmed. The parallel steps in the world of advertising are: orientation that starts a project; the mobilization and interaction of the staff who will carry it out; the moves to fix directions that occur as deadlines draw near; and, finally, the presentation itself.

Strictly speaking, the summons to an orientation that starts a new project is not a breach of regular, norm-governed social relations. It is, in principle, a normal step in the business transactions that link the agency and its client. Why then does it feel like a breach? The answer, I think, is simple: each and every presentation is a crisis that may either strengthen or destroy that relationship. The processes involved in putting together a presentation are inherently and intensely political.

Like Turner's 'drama', Bourdieu's 'habitus' reminds us that those involved in putting together a presentation are rarely, if ever, involved in making wholly rational decisions. The perfect information required for perfectly rational decisions is never at hand. Confronted with the need to make decisions and mobilize support for them, the actors involved in this process fall back on dispositions that are partly personality, partly deeply engrained habits; plus an understanding of the situation that may be as idiosyncratic as it is common sense.

Both Turner and Bourdieu employ the term 'field' to describe the fluctuating environments in which social dramas and struggles for position take place. Borrowing an image from Bourdieu, we may liken the actors in a social drama to players in a soccer game, who must struggle to keep track of not only the ball and the goal, but also the other players, their own positions on the field, and the clock that is counting down the minutes left to play – all factors that are constantly changing once the game is underway. We must note, moreover, that since preparing a presentation is, indeed, a political process, there is also the real possibility that someone is going to change the rules.

The Advertising Process

Broadly speaking, the process of creating both individual ads and full-blown campaign composed of many ads involves six steps. The client's *orientation* sets the agency team in motion. Having received the orientation, the marketing, creative, sales promotion or PR staff required to do what client has requested begin *brainstorming*. The ideas which emerge from the brainstorming are brought to meetings where the *presentation plan* is assembled. As the presentation plan is being finalized, production of presentation materials begins. This *presentation production* phase typically continues until the last possible moment before it is time to *make the presentation*. If the presentation is successful and the client buys one of the agency's proposals, *production of the finished ad* can begin.

It should be noted, first, that all of these steps including the last – the production of the finished ad – may be repeated if there are setbacks. At any moment before the presentation is made, an agency superior's negative reaction can send the planners back to brainstorm some more. If the client rejects the presentation and decides to give the agency another chance, the same thing will happen. In the worst case, a second orientation may be required. Generally speaking, overall concepts come first, followed by working out details. Both, however, are up for grabs until deadlines are reached. Why not do this? Why not do that? New ideas are constantly being tossed out and either accepted or rejected.

Deadlines are real and can be deadly. Presentation production takes time. Producing the finished ad takes time. Smart account executives also leave time enough to make a second presentation if the client rejects the first. Clients, conversely, are often forced to accept ads that they don't really like very much because they, too, have their deadlines. The product launch is scheduled, the factories are piling up inventory, the distributors are poised to move the product into the showroom or onto the shelves. If the advertising isn't ready, careers are on the line.

A Simple Case

The simplest advertising jobs are small, one-off print ads. Budgets are typically low. Creativity is limited to whatever can be done with stock photography, words and layout. In these cases, only the account executives receive the client orientation directly. They then meet informally with the creative staff assigned to the project to tell them what needs to be done.

In a Japanese agency setting, the creative team will typically include an art director, a copywriter, and one or two individuals from the production company that will, if all goes well, lay out and produce the mechanicals from which the films used in printing the final ad will be shot. For a project this small, there will be no marketing, sales promotion or PR planners involved.

Thus, for example, I once found myself – I was the copywriter – sitting at a table with an art director and the designer from the production house he used. On the other side of the table were two account executives whose client was the Bridgestone Tire Company. The job was very simple indeed. Bridgestone was the sponsor of the Silver Bridge concerts. An ensemble of young Japanese musicians was to be taken to New York to perform at Carnegie Hall. What Bridgestone wanted was a one-page, English-language corporate ad for the concert program.

I am often asked where creative ideas come from. In this case the idea we sold popped into my head as we were leafing through the company's annual report, and I noticed a photograph of the undercarriage of an air liner landing at an airport. I was moved to ask, 'Is there any chance that the airliner that carries the musicians to New York will land on Bridgestone tires?' 'Of course', said the account executives, 'they will be flown over on Japan Airlines, and Japan Airlines uses Bridgestone tires. Bridgestone is one of the world's largest suppliers of airplane tires'. 'I've got it', I said, 'the headline is "Another way Bridgestone supports the arts"'. We also developed a couple of other ideas, playing with familiar clichés like building bridges and harmony, but this was the one the client bought.

The brainstorming and presentation planning took less than an hour. Producing the comp (semi-finished mock-up) for the presentation took another day. The presentation went smoothly. All that was left to do, then, was to resize the photo, which the client had in its archives, write a paragraph of body copy, finish the layout, do the separations, color proof the separations, and get the film to the printer. Except for the body copy (my responsibility), managing all that was the art director's job.

In this case the creative team was happy. The project had gone smoothly, the client was pleased, and the ad itself approached the illusive ideal of communicating a serious idea from a fresh and engaging angle. That wasn't just our opinion; later the ad won a silver medal in a local advertising contest.

It's Rarely that Simple

At the other extreme are major new product launches that involve multiple media: TV, radio, newspapers, magazines, transit posters and outdoor billboards, point of sale and, sometimes, direct mail materials. Further complexities are added when the presentation is competitive, with several agencies competing for the business. Huge amounts of money may be at stake. I remember being told (I was not privy to the actual figures) that to launch Caffeine Free Diet Coke in Japan, Coca-Cola spent around ¥2 billion, or – assuming ¥100 to the dollar – US$20 million. For the launch of Pure Silk, a premium fabric softener, Nippon Lever spent only ¥600 million or, using the same calculation, around US$6 million. My agency colleagues claimed that this figure was a bare-bones minimum.

There are also many more people involved. The agency creative staff is expanded to include a senior creative director and TV commercial planners, plus multiple copywriters, art directors and designers. Marketing, sales promotion and public relations staff are pulled in. Senior account directors appear together with multiple junior account executives. The pressures are intense.

In this kind of situation, it is common for all of the senior and many of the junior people involved to be taken to the client orientation, to hear for themselves what the client has to say. The first meeting following the orientation will be the occasion on which all those involved try to sort out what they have heard. This task is not a trivial one.

One hears that in places outside Japan where the headquarters of giant, fast-moving consumer goods companies (P&G, for example) are located, marketing plans are generally produced in-house with agency account executives serving as consultants to the product or brand managers on the client side. When the marketing plan is finalized, the account executive prepares a brief for the creative staff at the agency. The brief is prepared in a set form that varies somewhat from agency to agency, but generally includes the following items.

- The *target*: a description of the audience to whom the advertising is directed (always demographics, sometimes psychographics as well);
- The *advertising objective*: what the campaign is supposed to accomplish (unaided or aided recall, understanding of key sales points, emotional identification, trial, a certain percentage of increased sales);
- The *proposition*: the essential core of the message that the audience should take away from the ad;
- The *rationale*: a brief explanation of why communicating the proposition to the target audience should achieve the advertising objective;
- The *support*: a short list of items that can be mentioned as evidence for the proposition;

- The *creative guidelines*: these include both a list of items that have to be produced, for example, a series of TV commercials or print ads for certain specified newspapers or magazines, and a list of dos and don'ts. The latter may have to do with issues – for example, the use of a logo – covered in a formal corporate identity manual, or with client aesthetic preferences. They should always include taboos whose violation will cause the client to reject a proposal automatically.

The brief may be accompanied by supplementary information on the target, the product, competitors and overall market trends that will help to focus the creatives' work.

At least in the case of clients that I have worked with in Japan, there is wide variation in the quality of orientations. Some are well-organized and contain most of the information described above. Many are sketchy and ambiguous. It is not unusual to find that on the client side there are people from several different divisions of the company. A common pattern is to have both people from the advertising division and people from other divisions directly in charge of producing, selling and distributing the product. Their remarks are often inconsistent, reflecting the organizational interests and personalities of the individuals in question. A large agency team also has its own divisions, politics and personalities to deal with. That is the point of the meeting that follows the orientation, to forge some kind of consensus on the agency's perception of what the client is asking for.

As soon as that meeting is over the account executives will rush off to check with key people on the client side to make sure that no fatal misunderstanding has occurred. Still, mistakes do happen. One especially disturbing possibility is that, even after the orientation, the client may change its collective mind. The politics on the client side are never-ending. That, as much as anything else, explains why the account executives in charge of a project are expected to be in – at a minimum – daily contact with the client and to keep their colleagues up to date on what is going on.

Brainstorming, Presentation Planning and Production

These phases of the process typically overlap. There is an ebb and flow of activity as creatives and other planners slip away to come up with ideas, then regroup in meetings where the shape of the presentation is hammered out. Then, as the presentation plan begins to take shape, orders start going out to the suppliers who produce the materials required for it.

But even this is too simple a description. Most individuals who work for a Japanese advertising agency are involved in several projects at once and juggling their responsibilities as they move from one meeting to another. Days are frequently filled with meetings, leaving only the wee hours of the night or time stolen from other work in which to think independently.

The role of junior people is to come up with lots of ideas. A phrase I learned shortly after I joined Hakuhodo sums this up: 'one night, a hundred proposals' (*hitoban hyaku an*). Older, more jaded, creative hacks keep files of old ideas that can be recycled as needed. In either case, most will go in the trash. Some copywriters and art directors show up at meetings with large stacks of proposals. Others show up with nothing; they sit mute and apparently mentally constipated until something moves them. I was never able to predict which would come up with the winning ideas until I had gotten to know them as individuals. Fluency was not a predictor of quality.

A key question in planning meetings is how many proposals to present. For major projects, the usual range was three to five. Competitive presentations are frequently limited by the client to a certain number of proposals or, more often, to a fixed amount of time. Choosing which ideas to present and the order in which to present them is always a deeply political decision.

As deadlines approach, pressures mount. Comprehensives and storyboards are prepared by 'sketchmen', and those who are both quick and talented find themselves in high demand. Often decisions are forced by the fact that the sketchmen in question have to have a decision by a certain hour on a certain date or they won't be able to fill the order. Major competitive presentations can involve the preparation of 'stealamatics' (cobbled together from existing film) or 'animatics' (illustrations video taped and mixed with music and narration to simulate a TV commercial). Documents integrating the overall communication strategy with marketing, creative and media plans must be assembled. These preparations also take time.

The sifting and sorting that goes on in presentation planning meetings turns on several key issues. As Moeran's *Ikon Breath 0_2* example illustrates, there may be tension between those who think that what is most important is communicating effectively with consumers and those concerned to do what they think the client wants. The TV planners and art directors, copywriters and marketing, sales promotion and PR planners involved may all have different positions on these issues. The marketing team may want the creatives to 'stay on strategy'. The creatives may want the marketing team to rewrite the strategy to fit what they see as a brilliant creative idea. The sales promotion group may argue for a different idea altogether, on the grounds that it is more suitable for point-of-sale materials. Meanwhile the account executives stew over what the client is likely to say.

At the end of the day, a combination of seniority and a strong personality usually carries the day – until, that is, the test results are in.

Presentation and Testing

Let us suppose that the presentation has gone off without a hitch. The presentation planning and production of presentation materials was completed on time. The presenters perform well, and the client is inclined to accept one of the agency's proposals. There is still a lot of money to be spent, and those who have to spend it are justifiably nervous about their decisions, even in the unlikely event that all those on the client side are united in liking the proposal in question. Especially in the case of a major new product launch, the client may ask to have the agency's proposal tested. It is now common, moreover, when large amounts of money are at stake for agencies to pre-test their proposals and incorporate the results in their presentations.

There are many testing methods, but they all fall broadly into two categories: group interviews or theater tests. In the case of group interviews (also called 'focus groups'), the comprehensives for print advertising and/or the storyboards, stealamatics or animatics for TV commercials are shown to groups of six to eight consumers recruited from the target audience in question. Theater tests involve larger samples who are shown the same materials and asked to fill out questionnaires. Alternatively, when TV commercials are being produced, subjects may be asked to twist a small dial as they watch a stealamatic or animatic to indicate their level of interest.

Group interviews are a good way to achieve quick negative results. Thus, for example, I remember a case in which a team with which I was working proposed some ads for a major German automobile manufacturer. The creative team loved its proposals. So did the European marketing manager in charge of the project on the client side. Since the proposals were, however, a bit unexpected and would have to be approved by headquarters, group interviews were laid on in hopes of bolstering the case for their use.

As it turned out the groups hated the ads. The tastes of Japanese luxury car owners in their 40s and 50s were, it appeared, quite different both from those of Japanese creatives in their 20s and 30s and those of the marketing manager to whose preferences they had tried to conform. It was back, then, to the drawing boards.

Theater tests are more often used after proposals have been tentatively accepted, in an effort to 'fine-tune' the advertising. Unless totally positive, their results are detested by creatives who feel that their superior creative intuitions have been impugned. But it can't be helped (*shō ga nai*); the client is god.

It is also, I must note, a fallacy to assume that because an idea is well thought out and the presentation carefully planned and produced that the presentation itself will go off without a hitch. Shrewd presenters describe the strengths of each proposal in simple, easy-to-understand terms, then try to engage the client in discussions of which strengths are most important to them. Skillful presenters can, in effect, turn on a dime in response to client feedback, dropping a point when an eyebrow is raised or pursuing a line when smiles appear. Sadly, however, creative genius and good presentation skills do not always coincide in the same individual. Nothing can sour a presentation more rapidly than a prima donna's doggedly defending an idea that the client has plainly rejected.

162

Then, Finally, Production

All of the processes sketched above are aimed at a single goal, securing the client's approval to proceed with production and placement of the advertising in question. It would, however, also be a mistake to assume that once the client's seal is on the contract the agency's work is done. For now is the time that the ideas the agency presented must take concrete material forms. Producing those forms is the job of artisans who are, surprisingly enough, brought together on an ad-hoc project basis.

In the case of the simple print ad described above, producing the mechanical required only a designer to do the layout and a typesetter to produce the text. Now that desktop publishing has become widespread, the designer and typesetter may be the same person. A printer hired by the agency produced the color separations and films delivered to the program publisher, who assembled the entire program, and arranged with another printer to print it. Throughout the process the agency art director was responsible for color proofing and checking printing quality.

TV commercial production is a much more complex business. As an illustration, I will simply report here on the production of one commercial in which I happened to be involved. The campaign was the European launch of the Canon EOS Autofocus Camera system. Early versions of the product were expensive and required an up-scale image. The proposition was that this revolutionary new autofocus camera system was faster than the competition, whatever the length of the lens. To communicate this proposition, we had sold the client on the idea of producing a commercial in which an obviously wealthy father is shooting pictures of his daughter, an equestrienne who is jumping her horse over obstacles on a show-jumping practice course.

As it turned out, the commercial, to be aired in March, would have to be shot in January. The story board had suggested blue skies, but in January there is no outdoor show jumping in Europe. That's how I found myself, as a perk for having helped to sell the campaign, sent to watch the commercial shot in Florida in the USA. I remember being surprised at how the shoot was organized. There were only two of us from the agency, the planner who had planned the commercial and myself the copywriter. A Japanese film production company supplied a producer, an assistant producer, and a free-lance Japanese director hired for the occasion. A coordination agency based in New York set up auditions for the models and hired the assistant director, the stylist, the make-up artist, the cameraman and the grips. All were free-lancers who had, however, run across each other on other shoots. We came together for a week in Florida, shot the film, and then disbanded.

Back in Japan, the film production company engaged a narrator (having first submitted voice samples to the agency and client). Meanwhile the rushes, the raw film from the shoot, had been edited. The rough edit was shown to the client and a final selection of the footage to use was negotiated. The narration was recorded and mixed with the music and the footage selected to produce the commercial that was then delivered to Sky Channel.

This was, I learned later, a relatively simple commercial to produce. Large productions can cost a million dollars or more and involve hundreds of people. A client who sees the rough edit may reject all the available footage, producing a catastrophic crisis if the people involved in the shoot have to be reassembled. More tense moments can occur in the final editing and mixing.

And then, of course, everyone is waiting to see what happens. If the product's sales go up, the client is happy and the agency eager to claim credit. If awards are won, that's icing on the cake. If the product's sales don't go up, there is furious back-pedaling and looking for excuses on all sides. As Jib Fowles (1996:9), for example, notes, the successes are the exceptions and not the rule.

Learning From Failure

This essay began with a smoothly told, second-hand tale of a justifiably famous and highly successful campaign. It ends with a first-hand account of the muddle and confusion of an unsuccessful presentation in which the author was recently involved. The second of these descriptions is, I suggest, far more representative of everyday life in the advertising business.

The client, identified here as *Ōgatasha* (Big Car), is one of Japan's largest automobile manufacturers. The agency's goal, as described in the orientation, was to produce a combined TV and print campaign for southeast Asia. It would air on satellite TV and appear in major international and local print media. Our primary target was affluent families, and the message to be communicated 'safety'.

Ōgatasha had a great deal at stake in this campaign. As the Japanese economy, stagnant since the early 1990s, teetered on the edge of recession, domestic sales were sluggish. A smaller, more agile competitor with an image tightly focused on a 'sporty', 'high-tech' appeal was eroding its market position in the southeast Asian market. Plus, all this was only background to the Asian financial crisis of 1998. The crisis had shattered consumer confidence, depressed auto sales throughout the region, and radically transformed the field for all of the players in *Ōgatasha*'s marketing operations.

Instead, then, of simply handing the assignment to one of its agencies – the previous pattern for campaigns in the region – *Ōgatasha* invited seven agencies to participate in a competitive pitch.

All presentations are social dramas. As Moeran (1996a:92–6) has pointed out, moreover, competitive pitches are, in effect, tournaments of value whose results will strengthen the position of the winners and also, of course, damage the position of the losers. In this case, the agency was especially eager to win. Top level policy called for improving the agency's position in Asian markets, where its network was long-established but, sad to say, regarded as weaker than that of the agency's largest rival. Thus it was that the agency took a step as radically different in its own way as *Ōgatasha*'s decision to open the business to competition. It assigned not one but three creative teams, each headed by one of the agency's most famous senior creative directors, to work on the campaign.

It is not, perhaps, so terribly unusual for agencies in other parts of the world to hold internal competitions before work is presented to the client. In the Japanese agency world as I have experienced it, this step represents a radical breach of protocol. It did, in fact, create serious problems in putting together the presentation. For us, however, it provides an opportunity to explore how creative teams headed by three distinct and powerful personalities approached the same creative problem.

Ōgatasha's brief was clear: the campaign theme was 'safety'. But what does 'safety' mean? As a functional claim, automobile safety is usually divided into two types: 'active safety' and 'passive safety'. 'Active safety' refers to features of an automobile that enable the driver to avoid accidents. 'Passive safety' refers to features that protect the driver and passengers when an accident occurs. As an emotional claim 'safety' implies confidence, security, comfort, and – especially when extended from driver to passengers – the fullfilment of responsibility.

Thus, for example, a famous commercial for Audi links active safety to fatherhood and a father's responsibility for his children. In the opening scene a telephone rings, a man rises from his bed. As he takes the call he looks excited. He throws on his clothes, runs down the hall to where he wakes a sleepy little girl and takes her in his arms. In the next scene we see them in a new Audi. The little girl is asleep in the back seat, all properly buckled up in a seat belt. We see her through the eyes of her father, who has glanced back to see how she's doing. Perhaps she looks so sweet that he allows his eyes to linger. In any case, at the moment his eyes return to the road, a milk truck comes shooting out of a side street. Reflexively, he turns the wheel to avoid a collision. The Audi slips smoothly around the truck. The camera cuts to the last scene, where father and daughter are at mother's bedside, welcoming a new baby to the family. The Audi's agility has turned a potential tragedy into a celebration of family life.

Ōgatasha's orientation included a sample of recent Volvo advertising in which the message 'Protect your most precious investments' is combined with the image of two toddlers, happily riding in their safety seats in the backseat of a car. In this ad, where the functional claim is focused on passive safety, Volvo artfully links the safety of its cars to worries about family financial security in the wake of the near collapse of Asian financial institutions. It is hard to think of a better example of updating a long established brand image (Volvo = safety for your family) to take advantage of breaking news. That would be a problem for the agencies' creative teams.

Ōgatasha's advertising in southeast Asia had been positioning the company as one proud to share its customers' 'Asian values', a concept rooted in the proposition that healthy societies require strong, patriarchal families. Marketing points to the need for consistency in message to 'grow existing brand assets', and *Ōgatasha's* main business is selling large numbers of mass-market family cars. It was not, then, surprising to find that 'safety for your family' was the safety message the client wanted. The creative problem, however, was how to present this entirely conventional and often-used message in a way that would seem eye-catching and persuasive and add value to the client's claim. Three different creative directors would have three very different approaches, each representing a habitus shaped by his own personality and experience.

Director A is famous for brilliantly conceived product demonstrations, Director B for commercials conceived as highly emotional family dramas, Director C for lavishly produced, visually gorgeous ideas, where a primary focus is entertainment. Each would consider a wide variety of ideas suggested by either more junior members of their teams or production companies who hoped to be the ones who would actually produce the commercials. In the end, however, each would choose to develop ideas that fit his own personal style.

Director A, with whom I have worked off and on for several years, is at his best when given a product with a small but clear technical advantage to dramatize. Unfortunately for him, *Ōgatasha* makes a wide range of vehicles which, while they offer the full array of currently available safety technology, have no innovations to announce. His approach, then, is to settle on a frequently used image that clearly communicates a concern for automobile safety but to do something innovative with it. His proposal turns on the idea that *Ōgatasha* cars have become so safe that a crash-dummy's once exciting life has become – boring. To me, it seems witty.

Director B has turned for help to an agency affiliate in Taiwan and picked up one of their ideas, a family melodrama that begins when a middle-aged couple in Taiwan receive a phone call from their daughter who is studying in the United States. She announces that she is coming home – with her new American fiancé! Tension rises as her father and mother wait at the airport. The father can barely contain himself when the fiancé turns out to be a large, blond, long-haired artist. He slips into sullen silence which is only broken when the fiance, trying to make conversation remarks 'I also drive an *Ōgatasha*', and the daughter echoes 'A new *Ōgatasha*, because it's so safe'. The two men have found a bond in their common concern for the daughter's safety. To me the implicit racism in this proposal is offensive. I can, however, understand how shocked many conservative Asian parents might be when confronted by this situation.

Director C wants entertainment. After canvasing possibilities that include Godzilla stubbing his toe on an *Ōgatasha* as he tramples New York City in a soon-to-be-released movie (rejected because of the costs involved), he settles on the idea of using computer graphics to create a spectacular amusement park in which all of the cars on the ferris wheel, the roller coaster, and other rides have been replaced with *Ōgatasha* vehicles. I think it looks like fun, an opinion I share with my Japanese colleagues.

While these decisions are being made, however, tension is steadily rising. In an effort to appear more international, the agency has mobilized its affiliates and production companies they recommend in southeast Asia and Australia. Their proposals trickle in, but many reach us only at the last minute. They also reach us in many different styles, some very rough indeed, which makes it difficult to do straightforward comparisons. Endless time is consumed in trying to visualize what is being proposed and debating the merits of one proposal versus another.

We are all supposed to be working together to decide which proposals to present. It is clear, however, that none of the creative directors will give way to the others. One is openly angry at being compelled to participate in an internal competition that he feels insulted by. The others are only more discreet about their dissatisfaction. In the end a compromise is reached. Each will get to present one of his proposals. This decision turns out to be a bad one.

Ōgatasha had given the agency only one hour to do its presentation. Since time will have to be allocated for introductions and the marketing team's review of the orientation, the creative directors each had only ten minutes to present his proposal. We are talking about individuals who are used to being in complete control of the creative portion of a presentation and having a half-hour or more in which to speak. During the presentation it was all too clear that each was too squeezed for time and that no firm consensus had been reached on which proposal the agency would recommend.

Following the first presentation, the ideas proposed by Director A and Director B were out of the running. Director A's bored crash dummies had been dismissed as 'too highbrow'. Director B's had also died. Being seen as a 'Chinese' idea had aroused fears that it might not work well in Malaysia and Indonesia. The agency was asked to brush up Director C's idea to strengthen the connection between the entertainment and the message. But following re-presentation, it too died. The victor was a proposal from the agency's archrival. It featured small, fuzzy animals and was seen as 'easy to understand'.

Note

1 This essay is dedicated to the memory of Kimoto Kazuhiko, the creative director who hired an anthropologist and turned him into a copywriter. He taught me many things, but the one I remember today is this, 'In our business, there is only one rule. If the client gives the agency business because you are here, you can break all the other rules'.

8

CITIZENS HAVE SEX, CONSUMERS MAKE LOVE

Marketing KamaSutra Condoms in Bombay

William Mazzarella

> Kama is the perception of the power of illusion materialised in an object, since from perception is born desire, attraction, ardour. The tendency to possess oneself of these objects is eroticism [*kama*].
>
> Yashodhara (12th century commentator on Vatsyayana's *Kamasutra*)

This is a story about the marketing of a premium brand of condoms called KamaSutra.[1] KamaSutra was launched at a time when the Indian government had just been forced to adopt a new IMF-imposed regime of economic 'liberalisation'. The 1980s had seen a boom in urban middle-class consumption; by the time of the reforms in 1991, the idea of consumption as a driver of economic growth and all-round social well-being had become a central feature of the new dispensation. The turn towards consumerism in the 1980s coincided with the erosion of the national political near-hegemony of the Congress Party, a party which since Independence in 1947 had managed to serve the interests of its urban middle-class constituents while keeping up a populist rhetoric of democratic socialism.

Here I am not concerned with why this dispensation passed; rather, I examine a particular manifestation of what, for large sections of the affluent classes, was offered in its place – namely, an aestheticised version of national development and the public sphere, one that focused on consumer goods as the markers of individual self-realisation and collective progress. While the 'exploding middle classes' constituted one of the great Indian media obsessions of the 1980s, somewhere around half of the population of India continued to live in poverty, however conceived. Mobilized year after year in political speeches and oppositional attacks, statistics like these inevitably became routinised and banal. Nevertheless, the visceral evidence of poverty, mutilation, and degradation increasingly and ironically constituted a hideous double of the billboard images of consumer affluence, wholeness, and well-being that cluttered every metropolitan skyline and thoroughfare.

It fell to the advertising industry to develop the images that would elicit an *aesthetic* response to the new 'liberalising' dispensation, thus legitimating it on a level more libidinally powerful than the abstractions of economic discourse.[2] KamaSutra happened to fit the bill perfectly: as the quintessential luxury product, its eroticised packaging spoke to the aspirations of the consumerist avant-garde. On this level, it was a response to a marketing problem: how to turn a universally disliked object into a desirable lifestyle accessory. At the same time, its material form – the fact that it was, after all, a condom and as such associated with the quintessential state project of family planning – allowed the language of sex and pleasure that the brand was built around to be extended into a universal critique of the post-Independence polity. Indeed, for its makers, KamaSutra was an argument for, as it were, the public efficacy of publicity. It seemed to demonstrate how an affluent minority could be confirmed in the pleasures of its distinction, while at the same time having the very sign of its affluence convey an egalitarian promise.

Beyond the *Cordon Sanitaire*: Locating Advertising

In her seminal book *Decoding Advertisements*, Judith Williamson declares the following methodological creed:

> I am simply analyzing what can be *seen* in advertisements ... Analyzing ads in their *material form* helps to avoid endowing them with a *false* materiality and letting the 'ad world' distort the real world around the screen and page.
>
> (Williamson 1978:11)

Williamson goes on to offer a range of exemplary techniques for understanding the structural composition of advertisements, but her conclusions are, in my view, limited precisely by the imposition of this analytical *cordon sanitaire* – between a self-sufficiently signifying 'world of ads' and a 'real world' that is apparently only cognisable in its 'reality' when protected from the onslaught of ideology that advertisements represent. Williamson's model offers a certain interpretation and extension of Karl Marx' famous theory of the fetishised commodity (Marx 1971 [1887]), one that implies that it is only through a deconstruction of this realm of commodity signs that we can get at the truth of our social relations (cf. Burke 1996: Introduction; Miller 1997: Chapter 6 for related critiques). The risk here is that lending an analytically isolated structure of signs (Jean Baudrillard's notion of 'the code' is another case in point) such interpretive priority will end up granting it precisely the kind of power over our imaginations that Williamson's analysis seeks to contest.

I do agree, however, with Williamson, Baudrillard and others that advertisements tend to exhibit certain characteristic structural features that enable them to communicate – that is, to activate desire, identification, and agency – in particular ways. One of the most basic ways in which ads communicate is by their simultaneous appeal to inclusivity and exclusivity. They employ signifying elements that are broadly intelligible to all those who are able, at a minimum, to imagine themselves as consumers. At the same time, they order these signifying elements into discreet 'lifestyle' clusters, which are both horizontally defined, allowing a 'totemic' kind of classification (see Sahlins 1976: Chapter 6; Moeran 1996: Chapter 3), and vertically arranged, giving rise to the hierarchical 'invidious distinction' that Thorstein Veblen (1899) and, later, Pierre Bourdieu (1984 [1979]) have discussed. This double ordering encourages habituation and aspiration simultaneously; either way, the aim is to channel consumer desire along a complex web of social identification and distinction.

Baudrillard outlines the historical conditions under which such a system of classification proved useful (presumably the immediate reference is to French modernity):

> ... The extension of competition, the largest social migration in history, the ever-increasing differentiation of social groups, and the instability of languages and their proliferation [...] necessitated the institution of a clear, unambiguous, and universal code of recognition. In a world where millions of strangers cross each other daily in the streets the code of 'social standing' fulfills an essential social function, while it satisfies the vital need of people to be always informed about one another.
>
> (Baudrillard 1988:20)[3]

I have doubts about the 'unambiguity' of this 'code', as well as its purported tendency to supplant all other systems of social classification ('of birth, of class, of position'). Nevertheless, I think there is a strong case for arguing that, at the very least, commercially-mediated imagery provides an important – if ambivalent – classificatory idiom for our everyday encounters. Moreover, as Rosemary Coombe points out in her work on the trademark, 'its paradoxical promises of standardisation and distinction' authorise this system of difference and distinction through a legitimating assurance of *quality* (Coombe 1996).

In the realm of advertising, claims about the quality of the product are at once an assurance of, and an 'alibi' for, the promised quality of the consumer's consuming experience. It is therefore all the more important that the analysis of this promise is not reduced to an over-simplified 'culture industry' model, in which the interests of capital are simply read off (and thus tautologically confirmed as analytical categories) from an analysis of ad content.

John McCreery and Brian Moeran – both contributors to the present volume – have each developed participant-observant approaches to the production of advertising which effectively highlight the complex, situated, and unpredictable processes through which the visible forms with which we are all familiar are assembled and disseminated (McCreery 1995 and in the previous chapter here; Moeran 1996 and Chapter 12 in this volume; see also Schudson 1984). Daniel Miller's (1997) anthropological study of the local articulations of global capitalism in Trinidad contains invaluable reflections on the politics of producing local advertising in the context of transnational flows of capital, goods, and images. I am particularly indebted to these authors' insistence on contesting simplistic critiques (and heroic narratives) through a fine-grained attention to the micropolitics of advertising practice. At the same time, the value of such fine-grained ethnographic research surely lies in allowing us to reach a *critical* understanding of the complex relations that obtain between production culture on the one hand (including individual practice, institutional frameworks, and wider social constraints), and capital on the other.

An anthropological engagement with the advertising industry militates against understanding advertising or the people that produce it as mere mouthpieces of 'underlying' ideological interests. But that is not to say that the connections between the statements my informants gave me were not motivated and, in their effects, ideological. My analytical dilemma, then, has revolved around reconciling the complexities of my informants' practices and motivations with a strong consciousness of the ways in which these practices tend to reproduce certain troubling social relations of power.

As a profession, advertising richly rewards analytical and creative thinking; by the same token, it offers little time and few incentives for self-reflection to the men and women making a frantic living in the belly of the beast. In this it is not unique, of course; most high-powered and competitive professions discourage leisurely contemplation.[4] Yet the advertising industry – especially in its media and account planning functions – is unusually invested in constructing its own image of society and subjectivity, an image that, for professional reasons, tends towards the positivistic. It is to that extent, in the context of its everyday operations, impatient with modes of critique – one might say that it has no *use* for them – that question the epistemic boundaries of its own project. At the same time, the forms of my informants' involvements with their products – among them the KamaSutra campaign – was a complex blend of personal aesthetics, professional commitment, cynicism and ideological justification, a blend in which each element stood in a relation of counterpoint to the others. At first glance, this marriage of work and self appeared to be a happy one – the very image of unalienated labour. Yet it was predicated on a separation of domains – a personal, aestheticised relationship to particular products and campaigns was kept quite distinct from a rather objectified relationship to the 'society' into which these products and campaigns were launched (and in this, it mirrored the kind of separation that I discuss above in relation to Williamson's analytical approach to advertisements). In what follows I explore the tensions and contradictions that arose when this distinction was breached, when a complex combination of factors encouraged an agency to make the aesthetics of a particular campaign speak to the totality of social life.

A Marketing Man's Dream Come True: the Launch

In October 1991, the Bombay-based glamour magazine *Debonair* sold out its print run in a matter of days. That month's issue quickly became a collector's item, changing hands at premium prices. But it wasn't the editorial content that

Figure 10 On the 21 Kisses. For the Pleasure of Making Love.
(KamaSutra ad campaign)

sparked this enthusiasm. Nor did it appear to be a direct result of the customary photo-features of half-naked women, inserted in between a characteristically eclectic assortment of literary efforts, surveys, and social commentary. What was happening was a marketing man's dream come true: by all accounts, readers were actually buying the magazine for the advertisements it contained. That month, a company called JK Chemicals (JKC)[5] had launched a new product – a self-proclaimed 'premium condom' called KamaSutra. And as part of the attendant media blitz, their ad agency, Lintas, had taken out every single page of advertising space in *Debonair*.

The ads that were featured in *Debonair* that month were in part the same ads that ran elsewhere: blue-tinted photographs of a half-clad couple, clutching each

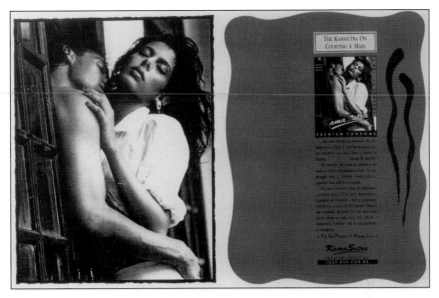

Figure 11 On Courting a Maid. (KamaSutra ad campaign)

other in a variety of urgently passionate poses. The aesthetic parameters were clearly derived from the visual repertoire of fashion shoots and the glossier end of rock videos, suggesting candidly captured yet carefully stylised moments. The man was invariably positioned in a supporting role as the ardent source of the female model's pleasure. Both of them had closed eyes, the man's face usually half-hidden, while the woman's head was thrown back, suggesting submission to a pleasure heightened by the discerning deployment of a KamaSutra condom. Each ad featured one of a series of quotations from the text of the *Kamasutra* itself, by way of hints for the sophisticated lover. In at least one case the text directly implied that the acquisition of the product might be the key to a woman's desire: '... The man should do whatever the girl takes most delight in, and he should get for her whatever she may have a desire to possess'. Invariably signing off with the baseline 'For the pleasure of making love', the copy of the ads specifically sought to position the condoms themselves as a source of enjoyment.

But the centrepiece of the issue amounted to a veritable KamaSutra advertising supplement, in the form of a multi-page photo-essay entitled '... And Then Came KamaSutra (Or the beginnings of a New Sexual Revolution sparked off by a condom)'. In addition to the ads that were also run elsewhere, the text of the copy was interlaced with topless shots of the female model featured in the main ads, Pooja Bedi, as well as of two other women. Several of these pictures were published in the foldout format that *Debonair* used for its regular photo-features, but differed from the usual fare in that they echoed the smooth production values of the main KS ads, thus giving the impression that

173

KS could bring a whole new level of gloss to erotic objectification. Lest the process remain at the level of looking, the text of the copy suggested that the refinement connoted by the brand in turn offered nothing less than self-realisation. First, a quasi-history was evoked, which would allow the brand to appear as a contemporary rediscovery of a timeless truth:

> Over 3000 years ago, the Egyptians used linen sheaths. Casanova used condoms made out of animal intestines. World Wars I & II saw condoms issued in standard service kits for men in the armed forces. The Beatles and Rock'n Roll and the sexual revolution ignored the condom to the dark side of the moon [*sic*]. And for years, there was an uncomfortable silence. And then came KamaSutra. The condom. Dedicated to the partners of love-making. And their pleasures.

Note the manner in which the passage used stereotypical images of western postwar popular culture to cue the period which in the Indian context tacitly refers to the post-Independence years, here a time, apparently, of 'uncomfortable silence'. The body of the text went on to explain that KamaSutra condoms were specifically designed to enhance pleasure, that they were in themselves objects of desire, inseparable from sex, and to stress that it was up to the consumer to take the initiative:

> The fact is that KamaSutra condoms are created for love-making. Pure fact. And that KamaSutra condoms are especially textured. Contoured. Dotted. On the outside. Also ultra-thin. And that the attraction begins with the aura around the KamaSutra condom itself. However, a lot will depend on you. And the ambience in which you open the pack. And the manner in which you decide to wear KamaSutra. Or let someone else put it on for you. It's just the beginnings of the desire called KamaSutra.

The final lines presented the decision to purchase the condom as the first step in the consumer-citizen's duty to inaugurate a national erotic revolution:

> The stage is set. The location is upto [*sic*] you. The fires have been on low for too long. KamaSutra condoms have been launched in October 1991, all over the country. It's your revolution. It's your condom. It's KamaSutra.

Amrita Shah was at that time the editor of *Debonair*. In November 1997, I asked her about the public stampede for the issue. She told me:

> I was completely taken aback. I couldn't work out why this was happening. I mean, it wasn't as if we were featuring anything more explicit than what we had run before. But it got to the point where we were actually considering a second print run. The models in the launch campaign were girls that we had already featured in *Debonair*. So what was the big deal?

It was a question that I had asked myself many times, ever since I came across the KS ads on my first visit to Bombay in January 1997. At that time the campaign was in its fourth phase, and was, in terms of publicity value, old news. When I quizzed friends and acquaintances about the campaign, it was clear that many of them had developed what ad people refer to as a 'blind spot'. They were full of recollections of the launch, as well as the public uproar that had followed; how the Advertising Standards Council of India had denounced the ads and, most gratifyingly, how Lintas had *gotten away with it all*. However, most of them were only vaguely aware that KS was advertising again. But to my relatively unjaded eyes, this latest incarnation raised several fascinating questions: what did it mean for a contemporary Indian premium consumer product to be marketed through the use of an ancient Indian treatise on the science of the senses? Could parallels or comparisons be drawn between the intended audience of Vatsyayana's *Kamasutra*, the *nagaraka* (basically, the well-to-do man-about-town),[6] and the figure of the affluent urban Indian premium-brand consumer – crudely, the 'Indian yuppie' – that was in the process of being delineated in advertisements, press commentaries, and corporate conference rooms all around me? Was the whole phenomenon in fact less to do with the selling of erotica than with the eroticisation of selling in a wider sense?

'It Just Looked *Classy*': the Aesthetics of Self-Recognition

My giddiest interpretive extrapolations were quickly checked upon my return to Bombay in the autumn of 1997. One advertising art director shook his head and clicked his tongue impatiently: 'Don't over-intellectualize it. What was important about the campaign was that, for the first time, Indians were being told that sex is fun. That and the pictures. Don't read too much into the words. They're just the product of some copywriter's overheated imagination'. His friend, a writer from another agency, nodded in agreement. 'That's right. From a marketing point of view, what was clever about the campaign was the way it took away the embarrassment of going to the roadside stall and asking for a pack of condoms'. (All the ads had featured the line 'Just ask for KS'). A second writer, seated on the other side of the bar table, sipping his mug of beer thoughtfully, ventured: 'I think what KS meant was that if I use KS, I would be a better lover'.[7]

Despite the disclaimers, however, certain themes kept recurring. A KamaSutra user understood that sex was 'fun', that it was 'nothing to be embarrassed of', and that the sex that they were having, when they used KamaSutra, was sophisticated, premium-quality sex. During these conversations, and at many other times when I talked to people inside and outside the media industries in Bombay, read the 'lifestyle' articles in the press, and just generally kept my ear to the ground, another word cropped up with striking regularity: 'evolved'. The 'new' post-liberalisation consumer was a more 'evolved' consumer, markets were more 'evolved', attitudes were more 'evolved', perhaps even 'basic values', although most marketing people remained skeptical about drastic change on this level. Initially, I ignored the word, thinking that it was little more than hype, the complacent congratulatory discourse of a social class that liked to see itself as the avant-garde of the new 'consumer society'. But gradually I came to realise that this notion of evolution hid a deeper current: the harnessing of desire through the commercial medium of a range of premium consumer goods brands, all connoting quality, sophistication, class. It wasn't just about sex, it was about consumption more generally; one of the aspects of KamaSutra as a brand was that it used a discourse of sex – or, more precisely, '*making love*' – metonymically to naturalise the idea of self-realisation through consumption.[8] An imagined world was at issue – one in which being 'Indian' did not mean having to be separated from the luxuries and markers of social distinction that were available in other, 'more evolved', places.[9]

A few evenings after my discussion with the admen, I was talking with a business journalist friend at what has become one of the epicenters of Bombay yuppiedom, the bar of the Bombay Gymkhana Club.

> I think what was so powerful about the campaign was that it managed to be extremely upfront about sex – the baseline, after all, was 'For the pleasure of making love' – while at the same time making it *elegant*. That was very new in India. Previous campaigns had all been very coy – unlikely situations, giggling couples, with the product logo and descriptor virtually hidden. Or the imagery had been smutty, like the pictures on the boxes of the imported condoms that you buy on the roadside.

'It just looked *classy*', a copywriter friend told me. 'It was like something out of *Playboy*'. Frank Simoes – one of the *enfants terribles* of the Bombay advertising world of the 1960s, and a veteran of sex-in-advertising – elaborated on the theme in an essay published a couple of years later:

> This was no quickie piece of plebeian latex for brief encounters of the furtive kind. This was the ultimate 'pleasure enhancer'. If no romantic evening was complete without the Jag, the champagne and roses, candlelight and violins, the perfumed suite with velvet drapes, making love would never be the same again once you slipped on a Kama Sutra, or, *noblesse oblige*, 'Let her put it on for you'.
>
> (Simoes 1993:143)

For many of those who had been impressed/excited by the ads, the fact that public watchdogs as well as 'conservative opinion' had denounced the ads as (in the words of the Women and Media Committee of the Bombay Union of Journalists) 'highly irresponsible, voyeuristic and sexist' (Pillai 1992) merely served to confirm their own sense of social and aesthetic progressiveness. But how did a *condom*, of all things, come to be a marker of social distinction?

From Anathema to Accessory

In the autumn of 1991, a journalist, commenting on the launch of a different upscale condom brand (one which, unlike KamaSutra, died a quick death),[10] remarked: '[they are] selling the notion that sex is fun, safe, and somehow upmarket to young, high income yuppies' (Sengupta 1991). Indeed, this would not have been a bad way to describe the man who was put at the helm of the business venture that gave rise to KamaSutra. For Gautam Singhania, the 24-year-old scion of one of the most prominent industrialist families in India, 'the condom project', as it was referred to in the beginning, was a chance to stretch his entrepreneurial wings.[11] JKC, which was run by his father, had been casting around for a small investment opportunity for him, something on the order of five or six million US dollars. It was the end of the 1980s, and several factors had conspired to make the condom market an attractive proposition. Under the Board of Industrial and Financial Reconstruction, ailing industries, many of them in 'backward' areas, could qualify for grant money and tax incentives from the government. A factory site in the depressed city of Aurangabad[12] appeared ideal for the project, particularly since the Singhanias had been able to strike a deal with a South Korean supplier for some hi-tech condom-manufacturing equipment. Condoms seemed a promising bet both for the domestic market, where free government distribution required a supply of 700–800 million pieces a year, and for export, where the labour-intensive nature of condom production put India at a comparative cost advantage.[13] Lastly, the contemporaneous emergence of AIDS as a major issue seemed set to give the previously stagnant commercial condom market a fillip.[14]

Knowing next to nothing about the condom market, Singhania and his associates at JKC entrusted the promotion of the entire project to Lintas (Bombay), a large advertising agency that had already done work for the Park Avenue line of suitings, a division of the prestigious Raymond brand, one of the most visible companies under the J K Group umbrella. Lintas found itself faced with a not entirely thrilling prospect: the billings for the account were rather meagre (at least by its standards as one of the top two agencies in India),[15] and there was a widespread impression that the free and subsidised condoms distributed by the government under the brand-name Nirodh had been instrumental in creating a great deal of popular resistance to the product category as a whole. One contemporary account describes it thus:

> In the beginning there was Nirodh, a non-lubricated ... government-manufactured condom that was as thick (and sensitive) as a rhinoceros-hide. Its sickly-yellow colour ... was enough to put anyone off sex for ever. Little wonder that even today condoms are a good substitute for balloons in rural areas.
>
> (Kankanala 1991:52)

Here, then, was the marketing problem: the condom did not only have to be made attractive, it had to be transformed into a *premium* branded product. Consumers had to be enticed to pay for the brand as well as the product. How was this done?

'It Will Be Sex!': Contested Origin Stories

My initial round of research into the origins of the KS brand position – magazine articles, casual conversations – had thrown up the kind of seamless heroic narrative that John McCreery so usefully problematises in the previous chapter. The official hero of the story was Alyque Padamsee, then close to the end of his reign as CEO of Lintas India. In this guise, he appeared as the Legendary Adman, routinely revolutionising marketing through inexplicable flashes of inspiration. As he told me:

> [The government condom, Nirodh] acted as a deterrent to sex, because as soon as you thought of Nirodh, you lost your erection! If you lose your erection, you can't put on a condom. The logic is simple, but nobody seemed to have stumbled upon it. So I said, 'How can the male think of the condom as a pleasure-enhancer?' Nobody wants to sit down to a sumptuous meal, and then be told that you have to take medicine before it. Kills your appetite.[16]

By the time I got my audience with Padamsee, however, I had already spoken to a number of the other key players in the KamaSutra story. And in the process I had discovered that the 'attraction [that] begins with the aura around the KamaSutra condom itself' had a complex and contradictory parentage.

Adi Pocha, now the head of a film scripting/production house called Script Shop, was the creative director on the KamaSutra account. He told me that the idea for a pleasure-enhancing condom had come to him in the course of brainstorming in preparation for a pitch for a *different* condom account at Lintas (Calcutta) where he was at that time creative head, about eighteen months before the JKC project landed at his new job in the Bombay office.

> I'll explain what the exact thinking was. If a guy is into sex, and he doesn't wear a condom, chances are he's doing it for a child. Or, just because he can't care less. But if a guy wears a condom, that means he's only into sex for the pleasure. Right? Because there's no other functional benefit of sex with a condom ... But a condom is perceived as inhibiting pleasure. So we said 'Why don't we turn that around on its head, and see if we can associate some amount of sexiness with a condom. So that a guy who's considering buying a condom says "OK, if I've got to wear a condom, why don't I at least go for the sexier one?"'[17]

Pocha's recollections were typical of an agency creative in that they revolved around the problem of getting a daring idea past the cautiously conservative instincts of his colleagues in suits:

All these guys said 'you're crazy! How can you position a condom as an aphrodisiac?' To Alyque [Padamsee's] credit, when I surfaced it at the brainstorm, Alyque said [in expert impression of theatrical Padamsee cadences]: 'Yees, my boy! That's briiilliant! Just go with it!' And then of course everybody just piled onto that. Then in Bombay, when this whole KamaSutra thing – of course it was just a piece of rubber at the time – when the whole thing came up, again there was a lot of resistance from servicing [the account executives]. There was a lot of ... I won't mention names, but there was a lot of people who went into, you know 'let's water down the position a bit, let's make it love instead of sex', and 'let's have this woman reading poetry' and, you know, stuff like that. And again, to Alyque's credit, he stuck by me right through and said: 'Nooo! It wiiill be sex!' And that was it. Once Alyque had spoken, everybody just kind of fell into line.

Whether Jayant Bakshi was one of the 'suits' that Pocha remembers struggling with is unclear; however, he *was* the executive put in charge of the KamaSutra account (subsequently taking it with him when he left Lintas to form his own agency, HeartBeat Communications). By the time I met him, Bakshi had developed a whole genealogy of the brand in which the appearance of KamaSutra appeared socially inevitable:

The understanding of what will work for KamaSutra, the brand as we now know it, started off as a learning in 1976, which is a good fifteen years before the brand was finally launched.[18]

Bakshi had formed part of a task-force, drawn from several agencies, to work in consultation with the Government of India on a project to devise more effective methods for the communication of family planning messages to urban and semi-urban populations.[19]

... In fact one of the biggest problems that family planning had ... was that we used to call it 'family planning'. After successive representations by the advertising field, we began to call it 'family welfare'. We started positivising it ... The moment you said 'family planning' people said 'don't talk to me about it!' So when we were launching KamaSutra it was that understanding.

What Bakshi was saying was that governments in the post-Independence era, attached as they were to centralised regulation, had understood little of what motivated people to 'buy into' a programme – whether political or commercial. Here then, was an opportunity for private sector 'communications professionals'. And family planning became the paradigmatic example of the disastrous consequences, in a modern polity, of not understanding that people needed to be seduced by appealing to their own desire for pleasure.[20] One of the cruellest manifestations of the authoritarian resolve of the 'emergency' declared by Indira Gandhi in 1975–77 had been the ubiquitous sterilisation camps. Doctors with quotas to fill left scars on the collective memory as well as on citizens' bodies. Bakshi:

> They would go into these areas, they would conduct a camp, they would invite people to the camp, not always by self-volition. Some of it was also forced. And they would say 'No, no, no, you have three children', *brakk!* [makes emphatic chopping motion], 'You have to get into the camp!' So they put all these guys in there, women and men, irrespective of age, irrespective of caste, and then had them go through vasectomy or tubectomy or coerced them sometimes into having copper-Ts inserted, and so on and so forth. Consequently ... the people didn't think very kindly to receiving advice on any sort of device or usage of contraceptive methods. They also didn't think very kindly of the government ... What these people used to say was 'Look, if the government has done nothing for us, then who is the government to tell us what to do?'[21]

Communications for condoms during this period, Bakshi and others argued, had similarly not made any concessions to seducing their audience; rather the emphasis was on getting across an unequivocal message, through slogans like '*do ya teen bachche bas!*' ('two or three children are enough!'), or 'You have two, that will do!' Even the name of the product, Nirodh, a Sanskrit-derived word meaning 'restraint' or 'control', seemed admonitory.[22]

> It doesn't work like that, and in family planning ... it had an adverse impact. This doesn't come across from any attitudinal survey. It comes when you travel from, you know, shantytowns to ivory towers. What we attempted to do was position KamaSutra for the pleasure of making love. Trying to tell couples that this was going to enhance sexual pleasure, and therefore they should use it. Not keep talking about the fact that 'It's for your own good, therefore do it'.

Nirodh metonymically represents the government as a whole ('As soon as you thought of Nirodh, you lost your erection' – and, as Bakshi suggested, if you *listened* to the government, you could well stand to lose more than that), while KamaSutra stands for the pleasures of the consumer's market. Impotence and humiliation were thus trumped by virility and sensuous self-assertion.

It was not, however, just the origin of the brand idea that was contested. For Adi Pocha, KamaSutra was only *representationally* radical; all it was meant to do was to steal market share from the closest competitior in the product category (then, as now, Kohinoor). Bakshi's narrative suggests a greater ambition: shifting the very terms of public communication. Despite this difference – to which I shall return – everyone was agreed on the immediate problem at hand: how to incite and maintain the elusive erection.[23]

Erotics and Legitimacy: Articulating the Brand

The product had to be made sexy, but this eroticisation also had to be 'tasteful'. Overtly, this meant making it acceptable for public consumption. But equally important was that these aesthetic considerations should serve effectively to position the product as a sign of social aspiration and a marker of distinction.[24] The brand name KamaSutra had the advantage of being almost universally recognisable as a code for eroticism, and at the same time officially and culturally legitimate. With characteristic dramatisation, Alyque Padamsee remembers how it came about:

> One of the first names that had emerged was Tiger. It seemed apt. It had all the right connotations of virility and excitement, and seemed to lend itself to interesting visual imagery. But the drawback was it was too male-focused ... Then, during a brain-storming session, somebody came up with the name Khajuraho [the name of the temple town where the famous 'erotic' carvings are located]. This led, naturally and immediately, to Kama Sutra. And the moment that happened, suddenly everbody sat up. Instinctively, we all knew that we'd got what we wanted. It was a winner. There was no need to search any further. The name KamaSutra had everything. As a brand name it was universal. It telegraphed sex without actually mentioning the forbidden word. It was daring, yet culturally it was wholly acceptable.
>
> (Padamsee, nd)

The client, too, was pleased with the marketing possibilities. As Aniruddha Deshmukh, the executive director of JKC (now JKC-Ansell) explained to me:

> See, the advantage of KamaSutra as a brand name, if you look at it simply as a brand name, is that it cuts across all language barriers. It's a brand name which is understood very clearly in south, in north, in east, in west. So that was a distinct advantage. It cuts across all income barriers ... Everyone in India was aware of Kamasutra as a cultural heritage.[25]

The fact that the word 'Kamasutra' connoted an officially approved version of public culture offered legitimation as well as the suggestion that KamaSutra, the brand, might help to *restore* a heritage that had been hijacked by the guardians of public morality. Adi Pocha, the creative director, stressed this 'proactive' implication of the positioning:

> We thought that if we do something as radical as this, because in the Indian context that would be very radical, we'd need some kind of ... something that would prevent people from jumping down our throats. So then we came up with the idea of using 'Kama Sutra' as the brand name, since that's part of Indian heritage and Indian culture. It legitimated it. See, Indians are very hypocritical about sex, OK? We have a population of

181

some nine hundred million people; we must be knowing *something* about sex! But we don't like bringing it out in the open, we don't like talking about it. It's not considered good to be sexy. I think it's just a phase that our civilisation is going through. Because at one time we were extremely sensual and erotic. I mean, if you look at the *Kamasutra*, it's as erotic and as advanced in sexual thinking as you can get. So all we said was: 'Let's just go back to the fact that that's what we genuinely are, let's *use* that. Put the name KamaSutra on the condom, and then let the hypocrites try and attack us'.

Once again, the question of who this 'we' that the condom was supposed to address remained ambiguous. This ambiguity was key: the 'inclusive' aspect allowed the name both to function as a 'cultural' legitimator for the brand and – in a wider sense – to suggest that the marketing exercise (of which the advertising was but the most visible part) was in fact performing a socially progressive function. Meanwhile, the 'exclusive' aspect was subtly signalled by the fact that texts like the *Kamasutra* were historically aimed at defining aristocratic behaviour;[26] to that extent, the brand image stood for the limited democratisation of formerly aristocratic pleasures through premium-level consumption.[27]

The visuals, for their part, needed to supplement this delicate balance with the burden of attracting the attention and desire of consumers. For hard-hitting sex appeal, Pooja Bedi, an actress friend of Gautam Singhania's (who also happened to be the daughter of a thespian associate of Alyque Padamsee's) was chosen as the female model. The agency was hoping that the tabloid attention that she had already generated would 'rub off' onto the campaign.[28] In Padamsee's words, she was 'quite a bit of a starlet, and something of a sex bomb'. 'She had a fairly amorous existence', Jayant Bakshi remembered, 'and in fact one of the reasons when we took her as the right choice was to do with being able to get a rub-off from her personal life'.

At the same time, this tabloid notoriety needed to be aesthetically channelled into something more refined; to this end Lintas brought in a Delhi photographer called Prabuddha Das Gupta who was known for his monochrome 'art' nudes as well as his mainstream advertising and fashion work. He remembered his meeting with Lintas:

They had a brief and they even had some picture references which they had pulled out of [Western] magazines [...] There wasn't anything in India that was like that [...] They wanted this whole feeling of, kind of, spontaneity and sensuality [...] Not the carefully created, beautifully lit kind of thing, but more of a kind of shot-from-the-hip and caught-as-they're-doing-it kind of thing. [... A]gain you come back to 'the blossoming middle classes' – that's where it was targeted at. And for these guys, for this set of middle class people, for aspiration they would immediately turn their heads westwards. So that was decided, that 'we are going to make it western-aspirational', as in ... what was happening at that time? Calvin Klein, maybe.[29]

Padamsee describes how, all through the planning of the campaign, Gautam Singhania had a constant catchphrase: 'I want you to make my eyes dance with delight!' (Padamsee, nd). To this end, he had suggested Pooja Bedi. Adi Pocha remembered being dispatched to meet her: 'I really liked her, because she really kind of *exuded* sexuality. She's talking to you and, you know, you can see it and feel it'. Nevertheless, it seems that it was precisely the intensity of this voyeuristic gratification that gave Prabuddha Das Gupta second thoughts:[30]

> I do remember at one point I wasn't particularly comfortable with the idea of Pooja Bedi. ... [B]asically I think it was ... Well, Pooja Bedi is a very voluptuous sort of woman. Big breasts, wide hips. I mean she, if anybody, fits in more with the traditional notion of an 'Indian woman' [...] It didn't have anything to do with personal preferences, but I just thought that at that point – maybe I was wrong, because the pictures worked – was that that sort of voluptuousness might tend to lead it more towards a sort of vulgarity, you know? I wanted someone with a less obviously [...] voluptuous body. Which would, to my mind, keep it well on this side of what would be called ... I guess, 'good taste'. For want of a better phrase.

Indeed, the pictures *did* appear to have worked. As Alyque Padamsee told me, 'KS' had apparently become a kind of shorthand for desirability ('and if it's desirable, then it's buyable') among kids in elite Bombay colleges: 'We had tape recordings. We did a kind of *vox populi* in colleges, and we found that girls would describe a man as "he's quite KS", meaning "he's quite sexy"'. It was, however, one thing to suggest that the product had been successfully eroticised, and quite another to offer it as a metaphor for a whole new model of sociality. Yet this is precisely what some of my informants tried to do. In the following section I examine the manner in which this was done.

The Erogenous Public Sphere: KamaSutra as Dubious Public Service

It has been said that, in a democracy, one's man's preference is another man's prurience (and the gendering of this *bon mot* is not accidental). In the face of opinion suggesting that advertising for luxury goods in a country with staggering levels of poverty and deprivation was in itself little short of obscene, the advertising industry had for some time been building its own case.

In his 1983 Union Budget speech, then Finance Minister Pranab Mukherjee declared that he was imposing a 'disallowance' on the tax-deductibility of a proportion of certain kinds of business expenses, among them advertising. The aim, he argued, was to:

> Discourage conspicuous consumption at the individual and corporate level, inculcating an atmosphere of austerity and providing a disincentive to unproductive, avoidable and ostentatious spending in trade and industry.
>
> (Kumar 1984)

The Indian advertising industry had faced similar initiatives before (in the mid-1960s and again in the late 1970s), and had on those occasions appealed chiefly to economic rationales: advertising helps expand markets, thus theoretically bringing down prices and creating jobs and so on; the industry also conflated the rhetoric of democracy with the image of consumption, trumpeting the consumers 'right to choose'. These two arguments were recycled in 1983–84, but this time they had been inserted within a much wider critique; the nascent 'consumer boom' allowed (and required) advertisers and their agencies to suggest that the government's earlier economic policies were misguided insofar as they were part of a more profound misrecognition of human needs and desires.

The advertising industry framed it in terms of 'communication'. As we have seen in Jayant Bakshi's recollections of his time on the family planning task force, bad communication led to poor response and, ultimately, to alienation and stagnation. What the government had been dispensing, Padamsee told journalists, was mere 'information'. 'You have to put electricity into the information to make it communication' (Thakur 1985). The point was not simply, in other words, to inform, but rather to *motivate*. The 'electricity' would serve to 'connect' recipients with the content of the communication in an active way, encouraging them to let their own desires bring them to an engagement with the communicated material. Thus the difference between commercial and political speech was erased: 'motivation is the only difference between advertising and propaganda' (*Telegraph* 1988).

The locus classicus of this fusion – and again a field that Alyque Padamsee managed to dominate in the media – was 'public service advertising', which underwent a boom in the 1980s, even instituting its own annual awards competition in 1984. Globally, public service advertising is often dismissed as little more than a cosmetic and sometimes hypocritical effort on the part of the advertising industry to improve their public image; an agency might win creative awards for their imaginative anti-smoking billboards while at the same time generating excitement in the trade press for their pioneering cigarette branding initiatives. Be that as it may, Indian public service advertising in the 1980s also enabled ad agencies to claim communicative expertise in a sphere traditionally monopolised by the government, and thus to counter the perception that all they were good for was pushing product.

It is in this light that one may interpret JKC Managing Director Gautam Singhania's statement to a journalist at the time of the KamaSutra launch:

India has been one of the largest contributors to the world population. With only 2.4 per cent of the world area, we account for about 15 per cent of it! Besides this there is also a high incidence of sexually transmitted diseases. It is a proven fact that of all the ways of contraception, condoms are the most reliable not only in birth control, but also in preventing diseases. And talking of AIDS, it's not a problem of the future or anything. KamaSutra with its bold advertising is our contribution to doing social good. The 15 crore (Rs 150,000,000) investment that we have made to set up the factory in Aurangabad is a very small sum, considering the amount of good that we can do.

(Menon 1991:19)

Here there is a telling condensation: the discourse of public service advertising – and hence the implication of 'social good' – is allowed to 'rub off' onto KamaSutra, the premium condom, both because it could be interpreted as a family planning device, and because it uses bold advertising, which has already been established as the key to effective mass communications. The paradoxical implication is that a public service could be performed admirably by the promotion of a specific branded consumer product, even though that product is quite obviously pitched at the higher end of the market. A conversation with Aniruddha Deshmukh of JKC confirmed this contradiction. I asked him why they had not chosen to market KamaSutra on an anti-AIDS platform, given that growing awareness of the epidemic had been one of their reasons for getting into the condom business in the first place. While conceding that condoms as a generic category could, indeed should, be marketed on such a platform ('So it's there in the back of the mind that *all* condoms are good against AIDS'), he opined that the lifestyle connotations of someone *choosing* a particular brand on the basis of its protection against AIDS – and thus himself being identified with that ('It would be a giveaway to his lifestyle') – would not be socially acceptable:

If you have a condom, which you're promoting saying that this is very good as a prevention against AIDS ... saying that it has got nonoxynol–9 or something like that, and if you have consumers buying that, it's a very strong indication that here's a person who's promiscuous or is visiting commercial sex workers. Now that's not accepted over here as yet. So you would have a very, very, very, very limited segment for that ... We don't believe that there is a segment that you can market a condom to on those lines.

A product that will not generate profits through volume will have to play on the 'added value' of premium positioning. Since premium positioning must imply social distinctions, a premium branded product can only contribute *incidentally* to alleviating a generic 'social problem'. The reporter who interviewed Gautam Singhania at the time of the launch apparently recognised this, and summed up the situation succinctly:

> ... Gautam Singhania has discovered an erogenous place in the market which, when stimulated, he hopes, would yield pleasurable results.
>
> (Menon 1991:19)

'I'm Going to Express Myself, I Need a Condom': Advertising in a Time of Liberalisation

If such extravagant claims on behalf of KamaSutra were in fact transparently unsupportable, then why should the industry bother making them? What was at stake for Lintas, and for the industry as a whole? In this concluding section, I examine what happened when the aesthetic parameters that resolved the inclusion/exclusion paradox on the level of the brand were extended to a justification of consumption more generally, in tandem with the discourse of 'liberalisation' as universal social tonic.

We have seen how, in the 1980s, the advertising industry started claiming a wider social efficacy for its communicational expertise, one that was directly oppositional in relation to the government and its long-suffering publicity wing, the Directorate of Advertising and Visual Publicity. In addition to the legitimating functions that I have mentioned, this expansiveness was also motivated by infrastructural incentives: the first wave of consumer goods deregulation coincided with an across-the-board pay hike for the salariat, and from 1982 onwards (when colour transmission was introduced) television became a crucial advertising medium.[31] It brought unprecedented reach for audio-visual commercial messages; indeed, it has been estimated that in 1985, a new transmitter was being set up somewhere in the country every other day. It brought the possibility of staggering new levels of billings for the ad industry (as well as revenues for the government). And it meant, for the first time, that mainstream advertising in India really had become a question of *mass* communication. As a consequence, the advertising industry found itself speaking, more than ever, to a truly generalised public (see also Mankekar 1999: Chapter 2 for a discussion of this moment).

Ironically, at the same time as this mass mediated sphere of publicity was being consolidated, Indian politics were becoming increasingly fractured, as interest groups and regional lobbies that had previously been more or less contained within the near-hegemonic dispensation of the Congress Party started to gain increasing leverage at the centre. Rajiv Gandhi's tenure as prime minister (1984–1989) encapsulated this contradiction: a technocratic discourse emphasising efficiency, managerialism, and 'taking India into the 21st century' was juxtaposed against fumbling attempts to coordinate an ever-more divided political scene, spiralling debts, and a fiscal crisis that directly precipitated the IMF intervention of 1991.

As the ad agencies' clients in general embraced the new economic rhetoric of *laissez-faire* that the government was obliged to adopt (even as it in fact proceeded with caution on the reforms), the agencies, in turn, found themselves obliged to support their clients' interests. Herein, however, lay a problem: apologias for economic liberalisation are largely able to disguise the massive and ongoing state intervention that underlies the dream of the perfectly-functioning, transnationally-coordinated 'logic' of supply and demand behind a pseudo-scientific and transcendent discourse of 'structural adjustment'.[32] The proof of the validity of the liberalising promise of 'trickle down' (the theory that stimulating economic activity in the upper reaches of society will cause wealth and employment to 'percolate' downwards) can be almost indefinitely deferred, by citing market imperfections and so on.

Advertising complements the theory of trickle-down with a dream of constant upward mobility, embodied most classically in 'aspirational' advertisements, whose images of exclusivity nevertheless offer an inclusive promise. In a time of liberalisation, the visibility, presence, and concretion of advertising lend tangibility and libidinal focus to the abstraction of economic discourse. But the fact that publicity relies precisely on visibility makes advertised imagery much more vulnerable to critical evaluation than the economic ideology that it is required to support. Unlike the deferred realisation of trickle-down, advertising is always on trial in the present. So while it may be deployed to legitimate one ideological abstraction – that of the 'free market' – it remains accountable to another: 'public opinion', manifested in terms like 'common decency,' 'public morality,' and 'good taste'.

According to questions raised in parliament in the autumn of 1991, and complaints passed through the Press Council and the Advertising Standards Council of India (ASCI), the KamaSutra campaign fell foul of all these yardsticks. It apparently sought to satisfy 'voyeuristic sensibilities which exceed common decency' (Pillai 1992), and to promote 'sex itself' rather than family planning and the prevention of sexually-transmitted diseases. Moreover, it was deemed 'vulgar and indecent in the context of an Indian morality' (Prakash 1993). Of course, Lintas fully expected there to be an outcry following the launch of the campaign, and wanted to make sure that they could turn it to its advantage. Indeed, it had quite consciously stoked the fire; there were teasing advance leaks to the press, like the report that Pooja Bedi had apparently demanded a 'no-nipple clause' in her contract. And in an immediate sense, it was successful: a move on the part of a member of Parliament to have the campaign banned got snarled in the gaps between inefficient ministries; the official reprimands from the Press Council as well as the ASCI could enforce no more stringent legal requirement on Lintas and JKC than that they 'amend' the campaign, which in practice meant little more than reshuffling the existing campaign; the fact that the national state-controlled television network, Doordarshan, banned the spots generated more publicity than damage, since Lintas in any case could target its audience more effectively through localised cinema and cable screenings.

The sheer sex of it – the factor that had caused all the hullaballoo – was also Lintas' most effective rhetorical strategy in defense of the campaign. I have discussed how the idiom of 'making love' came to naturalize the idea of self-realization through consumption; I have also shown that the sexiness of KamaSutra was used to set it off from Nirodh, the government condom. But the problem of exclusivity remained, and so finally the universality of sexual activity was made into the basis of a general parable about the difference between government speech and commercial speech. As Jayant Bakshi told me:

> Men and women copulated, or had sex. They never really *made love*. It was more either a procreative necessity, or it was a diversion, or it was, you know, 'I have to do this because what else?' or 'I'm expected to do this'. In many cases, in fact, the parents and the grandparents used to check, about fifteen years ago, after the wedding night with the children, 'Did you have sex?' Not 'Did you *enjoy* sex?' Nor 'Did you have a satisfying night?' No, no – 'Did you have sex?' Because, you see, what they wanted to know was, the boy was OK and the girl was OK. And somehow the certificate of that was the penile action. 'Did you manage to penetrate the vagina?' – and it's all over![33]

This scene of gerontocratic inquisition dramatises the ideological confrontation between the stereotypical government official – the census-taker or the family planning agent with his quota to fill, bored and hurried, interested above all in a quantitative result – and his imagined other: a service-oriented consumer industry representative, intimately solicitous about the qualitative evaluation that the customer may have of his or her 'experience'. Liberated by KamaSutra, the masses throw off the shackles of prudery: 'It's your revolution. It's your condom. It's KamaSutra'. Suddenly the aesthetic positioning of the product appears progressively inclusive:

> ... Quality suffered in this country. Service suffered in this country [...] I think a *latent* desire was always there with people to try and express it [dissatisfaction], and I think one of the expressions was this case [the KS campaign]. And coming as it did on the heels of this liberalisation movement, I think it just fitted. It seemed that, at a very large level, the time was just right for somebody to say: 'Hey, I'm going to express myself – I need a condom!'

Here is the apotheosis of the consumer-citizen: the civil franchise of the *right to choose* triumphs serenely over the arduous, contradictory, and messy procedures of representative democracy. An alchemical transformation has been effected: through the magic of the aesthetic object, individual interest and desire is sublimated into an objectively collective project. In the stark words of Kenichi Ohmae (1990:3), management guru and apologist for global deregulation: '... when individuals vote with their pocketbooks [...] they leave behind the rhetoric and mudslinging'. The Government of India, at least in its overtures to foreign investors, was by the mid-90s also painting a picture of a nation unified by consumer goods. In an official brochure, it excitedly proclaimed: 'Indeed, leading brands of trucks, scooters, soaps and detergents, batteries, cigarettes, footwear, etc., have become as much of a unifying force in India as some of the obvious national symbols!' (Government of India 1995).

The power of libidinal investment in the image of a product – the power of desire – appears as a more efficient route to self-realization than a public sphere characterized by mere verbiage, 'rhetoric and mudslinging'. For KamaSutra, the political presence of the great suffering masses did not, as one might have expected, pose a threat to such universalising discourse; indeed, it became evidence of the need for sterner measures, even for the abolition of a democratic system that, like the governments it put into power, had proved ineffective.[34] Remarking on the vast differentials in resources, one Bombay ad person told me:

> ... There's a tremendous dichotomy and I think [it] will need to be addressed by this country. By the same token I'm admitting that you cannot address the dichotomy because one or two per cent of the people want to ... 99 per cent of the people are either oblivious of it, or at least a good 70 per cent of them are just not in a position to express it. For one reason or another ... I think what you really need in this country is stability with a single political and economic will for a *minimum* of ten years for the country to even begin to turn around and do some of the things that everybody believes we should be doing.

A corollary of this view is that the idea of a collective public sphere becomes nonsensical, a Procrustean imposition upon voices and interests that are neither commensurable nor even coeval. In this way, the vision of a newly egalitarian collective space defined through goods hides an exclusivist orientation behind populist rhetoric: while a product like KamaSutra can become a sign of the *possibilities* of universal communication and collective aspiration, it would, according to its makers, be unreasonable to expect that its 'evolved' imagery could at present find favour with more than a progressive minority. As Jayant Bakshi put it to me:

> William, I am convinced about one thing: ... that India lives in more than one generation at any one point in time ... If you just walk the roads of Bombay and don't even go any further, you will realise that we are actually living in more than one generation. Just in this very city. And it is therefore unfair ... either for them to expect or for me to be able to deliver, at any point in time, any material in this country which will not be objected to by at least a few. So it's *extremely* difficult.

Paradoxically, the persistent presence of the dispossessed, within this discourse, becomes at once the justification for the expansion of the ambit of the advertising industry *and* the explanation for the impossibility of holding it accountable for its products. Moral responsiblity is limited to the immediate family. Work becomes a matter of personal integrity, but an integrity that is largely bracketed off from the social relations that make the work possible and that it seeks to address:

189

I think at the end of it, one has to be just honest to one's work. We, at any point of time, as marketeers [sic], market a particular product for a group of people. We never market it for the entire universe. While doing so, what we have to consciously try and exercise is a responsibility which says 'I will not consciously, I will not knowingly affect the sensibilities of the other'. Whether they be religious, whether they be economic, whether they be social, whatever it is. I quite honestly can hold my hand over my heart and say that we've done that as far as KS is concerned. So I for one continue to tell everybody, without any compunctions, that there is no single KS campaign which I would not discuss at home, or I have not discussed at home, or which my children don't know about from the time that they were eight years old. And only time will tell, you know, whether that was the right way or the wrong way.[35]

Conclusion: the public paradox of advertising

At a very early stage of my fieldwork, I asked a top executive of one of the big Bombay agencies whether he didn't feel that there was some contradiction in expressing concern at the mushrooming of 'Pizza Huts on every corner' and at the same time being professionally committed to encouraging such a development. At first surprised, he quickly adopted an expression of pity, as if the depth of my naivete had just been exposed. Evenly poised, he replied: 'A *long* time ago I learned to separate the personal from the professional'.

On one level, my informant's response merely illustrated the problem which Max Weber (1946 [1918]) long ago identified as characteristic of modern vocational practice: the unbridgeable gap between the instrumental rationality required to succeed in a particular undertaking and the value-rationality required for an ethical orientation to the world as a whole. But we may perhaps go further and suggest that the practice of advertising, as the herald and handmaiden of consumerist dispensations worldwide, at once attempts to address this dilemma *and* reconfirms its inescapability.

KamaSutra was presented by some of its proponents as emblematic of the therapeutic role that advertising-led consumerism could play in a polity suffering from an alienated relationship between abstract ideals of social justice and modes of implementation that apparently bore no relation to the interests and intimate concerns of the citizenry. Precisely the affect-intensive and embodied quality of the eroticized images used in a campaign like KamaSutra helped to figure consumer goods advertising as an efficient way to engage with the 'true' needs of the citizenry as a whole. Because KamaSutra, in its guise as a condom, could draw upon a discourse of generalized public service, it suggested an *inclusive* effacement of the distinction between the normative discourse of the political sphere and the instrumentalities of the market. By the same token, in its capacity as a paradigmatically 'aspirational' brand, KamaSutra demonstrated how the consumerist dispensation could also furnish smaller groups of consumers with the more *exclusive* satisfactions of aesthetic distinction, legitimized as culturally-appropriate 'self-realization'. The measure of its success could be taken either according to the quantitative index of sales or the more qualitative dimension of 'buzz' – notoriety, sensation, spectacle.

The purported 'directness' of the striking advertising image appeared to transcend the need for cumbersomely discursive public debate and 'artificial' economic planning, while at the same time conveniently naturalizing the distinguishing aesthetic conventions of a national-cosmopolitan elite. And yet precisely the 'integral' power of such images, magnified by their public ubiquity, resulted in a kind of ethical crisis, in which the executive power of public dissemination enjoyed by the publicity industries and their clients was in no way accompanied by an adequate public discourse on the implications of the very *form* of visually-driven publicity as a contemporary institution.

The limitations of both the advertising industry's own tendency to establish *content* guidelines (see Goldman 1992: Chapter 2 on this topic) as well as the conventional and defensive moralism of the criticisms generally launched by official watchdog organizations is in itself a symptom of this crisis. Faced with the magnificent and terrible power of their own tools, for which such grand social claims are constantly made, many advertising professionals will, unsurprisingly, attempt to limit the scope of their own responsibility: 'at the end of it, one has to be just honest to one's work'. Finally separating 'the personal from the professional', the realm of value from that of instrumentality, the advertising industry finds that ultimately it cannot support its own progeny.

I am keen to avoid misunderstanding on this point: I am in no way attempting to *criticize* advertising professionals (or indeed the industry as a whole) for adopting this stance. Rather, I have focused on the advertising industry precisely because its professional predicament so clearly illustrates some of the key dilemmas of a world in which both politics and commerce are increasingly mediated through commercialized image-repertoires. The particular conjunc-tures of Indian public culture in the 1980s and 1990s threw these themes into especially sharp relief: the competing social ontologies of market and state, the tension between national integrity and cosmopolitan aspirations, and – lending an exceptional ethical urgency to these conflicts – a polity in which the distribution of resources, and everything that follows from that, was so markedly skewed.

But of course the story of KamaSutra describes something more than an 'Indian situation'. Insofar as the *Kama sutra* could be mobilized as a national cultural artifact, it enabled my informants to construct a local legitimation for a set of translocal processes. In the process, however, the consumerist dispensation was not merely 'translated' into an Indian idiom, but was rather created anew, with particular possibilities and vulnerabilities unknown to its manifestations elsewhere. And it is precisely at this delicate intersection between the universalizing ambitions of the commodity form and the invariably local conditions of its implementation that the publicity industry professional and the ethnographer of contemporary media-capitalism confront each other.

Notes

1 The bulk of the narrative refers to events that took place in 1991. It has been reconstructed out of a combination of recollections and archival materials that I collected during my fieldwork in Bombay in 1997–98. The research on which this chapter is based was funded in part by the Social Science Research Council, in the form of an International Dissertation Research Fellowship. I would like to thank the SSRC for its generous support.

  I would also like to acknowledge the extremely helpful critiques and comments that I have received on this paper from Lawrence Cohen, Jennifer Cole, Vikram Doctor, Brian Moeran, Christian Novetzke, Peter Phipps, Allan Pred, James Watson, the members of the 1998 *ConsumAsian* workshop in Hong Kong, as well as the two anonymous reviewers for the present volume. A more extended discussion of the themes presented in this paper appears in Mazzarella (2000).

2 I use the term 'aesthetic' here in the double sense so usefully highlighted in Eagleton (1990) on the one hand, a rarefied discourse of high culture; on the other, a universal and profane corporeal experience:

  That territory is nothing less than the whole of our sensate life together – the business of affections and aversions, of how the world strikes the body on its sensory surfaces, of that which takes root in the gaze and the guts and all that arises from our most banal, biological insertion into the world.

  (Eagleton 1990:13)

3 Compare the passage cited with the following one, taken from Veblen (1899:96):

  The means of communication and the mobility of the population now expose the individual to the observation of many persons who have no other means of judging of his reputability than the display of goods (and perhaps of breeding) which he is able to make while he is under their direct observation.

4 See Ohmann (1996) for an illuminating series of encounters between academics and media professionals, in which this issue – the question of self-reflexivity – is a recurring theme.

5 JK Chemicals is one of the main companies of the JK Group, named after its founder, the late Juggilal Kamlapat Singhania. The JK Group was in 1988 divided into three separate corporate entities, each headed by one of J.K. Singhania's sons – Padampat, Kailashpat, and Lakshmipat – and *their* sons. The three family groupings were given control of, respectively, JK Synthetics along with cotton, jute and iron companies; Raymond (leaders in high-end men's suitings and body-care products); and JK Industries, which included JK Chemicals.

6 Alain Danielou, the translator of the unabridged English edition of the text – which palimpsestically interweaves Vatsyayana's fourth-century work with a twelfth-century commentary by Yashodhara and a modern one by Shastri – offers the following characterisation of the *nagaraka*: 'a wealthy, cultivated bourgeois male who is an art-lover and either a merchant or civil servant living in a large city' (Danielou 1994:7).

7 This was in fact explicitly part of the product promise. One of the ads in the third series of the campaign, run in late 1994, read (in part): 'Be it the well known treatise or the celebrated condom. KamaSutra holds only one promise. To make you a better lover. The first tells you how to do it, the second helps you do it better'.

8 Interestingly, Mohandas 'Mahatma' Gandhi's description of his own path to celibacy also posits the harnessing of one's sexual desire as metonymically standing for a relationship to the world in general. But for Gandhi, self-realisation, and the 'potentiality' that came with it, would only come through the renunciation (or perhaps sublimation) rather than the indulgence of one's desires. Consequently, for him using contraceptives amounted to taking the easy way out, since it didn't deal with the fundamental problem of mastering (rather than being mastered by) desire. As recounted in his autobiography, his internal debate started with the problem of how his relationship with his wife could be based on pure motives if it consisted 'in making my wife the instrument of my lust? So long as I was the slave of my lust, my faithfulness was worth nothing'. At the same time, he admits that he fell short at first because his motivation was none the highest.

> My main object was to escape having more children. Whilst in England I had read something about contraceptives . . . If it had some temporary effect on me, Mr Hill's opposition to those methods and his advocacy of internal efforts as opposed to outward means, in a word, of self-control, had a far greater effect, which in due time came to be abiding. Seeing, therefore, that I did not desire more children I began to strive after self-control. There was endless difficulty in the task.
>
> (Gandhi 1982 [1927,1929:195])

Gandhi, however, also expanded a personal and pragmatic economy of desire into a political and ideological project: the birth of an independent India. Hence the double meaning of the term *swaraj*, which connotes 'self-governance' in both the personal and the geopolitical senses.

9 See Mazzarella (2000: Chapter 3) for a discussion of 'auto-orientalism,' namely the manner in which upscale representations of 'ancient' Indianness are deployed in contemporary aspirational advertising for Indian products.

10 In fact, the fate of these condoms (branded Adam) was sealed in part by the emergence of KamaSutra, as the industry closed ranks under fire and exiled one of its own as a true exemplar of bad taste. Adam had committed the mistake of using humour rather than sex appeal (admittedly, rather crude humour – the ads featured scenes of a virile cartoon caveman dragging off his female partner by what appeared to be her hair).

11 In April 1998, I attempted to schedule an interview with Mr Singhania. His secretary, however, was of the opinion that since I had already spoken with Aniruddha Deshmukh, the executive director of JKC, I had 'the whole story'.

12 Incidentally, the name Aurangabad would also have seemed auspicious for anyone reflecting upon it: the Persian word *aurang*, from which it is derived, combines the meanings of 'emperor's throne' with 'building for manufacture' and 'warehouse'.

13 Latex, from which most condoms in the world are made, is a labour-intensive material to deal with, in part because it is an agricultural commodity, and therefore its consistency cannot be regulated by any formula, as with petrochemicals. This becomes a particularly critical factor in the manufacture of condoms, since a pinhole-free surface with a thickness of just .06 or .07 mm has to be maintained.

There were two large-scale producers at that time: Hindustan Latex (HL), a public sector company – and the largest manufacturer of condoms in the world – and TTK-LIG, a private operation, which had evolved out of the earlier London Rubber Co. The commercial market amounted to a total of around 400 million pieces annually, including the subsidised government brand Nirodh (which commanded 56 per cent of the market by volume, primarily supplied by HL). There was only one substantial non-subsidised branded player, a TTK brand called Kohinoor (20 per cent of the market at that time) which was being marketed on a relatively conservative family planning platform. So the field seemed relatively open for a new entrant, particularly if it could be positioned differently. Another TTK brand called Fiesta had acquired a five per cent market share with a campaign that had been quite risque for its time (the mid-1980s), in which the theme had been 'different colours for different days of the week,' thus to some extent preparing the ground for a more eroticised approach. In addition, around eleven per cent of the market was taken up by the imported southeast Asian condoms that my journalist friend had mentioned, selling in quasi-pornographic packaging, under brand names like *Push Me*, *Sexy Girl*, and *Happy Hours*. (These figures on market share are from Irani 1991 and Annuncio 1993. The latter emphasizes that although these 'pornodoms' accounted for around eleven per cent of the commercial market by volume, they represented as much as 22 per cent of the market by value).

14 Lobo 1991 estimates that the AIDS 'scare' had caused a twelve per cent per annum growth in the commercial condom market in the late 1980s and early 1990s.

15 The launch campaign ended up wildly overshooting promotional budgets, although even accounts of the original budget vary. Padamsee claims that it was Rs 3.3 million; in Doctor and Sen (1997) Jayant Bakshi, the executive in charge of the account, estimates it at Rs 6–7 million, and suggests that around Rs 11.9 million were actually spent on the launch.

16 Interview with Alyque Padamsee, Bombay, 3 February, 1998. All subsequent quotations from Padamsee, unless otherwise referenced, are from this conversation.

17 Interview with Adi Pocha, Bombay, February 3, 1998. All subsequent quotations from Pocha are from this conversation.

18 Interview with Jayant Bakshi, Bombay, 27 November, 1997. All subsequent quotations from Bakshi, unless otherwise referenced, are from this conversation.

19 This particular group of professionals went out and did field interviews in cities and towns with populations of more than 50,000 people, Bakshi told me. At no point during this initiative, and the one that followed in 1979–1980 (unlike earlier advertising industry involvements in government family planning initiatives in the mid-1960s) was there a serious move to engage the advertising industry in communicating with people in rural areas.

20 Here there is a direct parallel to the new mode of social integration advocated by the bourgeois revolution in eighteenth-century Europe. As Terry Eagleton (1990:23) puts it: 'the compulsion of autocratic power is replaced by the more gratifying compulsion of the subject's self-identity'.

21 Interview with Jayant Bakshi, Bombay, 28 January, 1998. While the sterilisation camps came to be identified with the authoritarian excesses of the 'emergency', the period was not without its own moments of tragicomedy, especially for those not directly affected by it. Raj Thapar remembers in her memoirs:

> Little decorated vasectomy plants sprang up on every street, adorned with tins of cooking oil as giveaways – this, which had disappeared from the market – and with loudspeakers throwing out suggestive film songs . . . At the Irwin Road camp one evening there was a macho looking man at the mike singing a little ditty – in English, with a broad Punjabi accent: 'Come have yourself vasectomised, make your family systematised', whatever that may mean. I realised that it could only be aimed at me – certainly none of the fruit-sellers around were familiar with English, so who else, thought I, as I looked up and down the street. No one.
>
> (Thapar 1991:419)

22 Ardashir Vakil, in his fictionalised memoir of a Bombay childhood in the early 1970s, describes the scenario:

I walked back to the corner of Carmichael Road, where the paanwallah on the corner still had his shop open. I had forty paise in my pocket. I thought I might find something to eat. In the front of his shop I saw a box of Nirodhs. I had no idea what they were though I had seen the advertisements saying, 'Hum do, Hamare do' (The two of us and our two children), which the round cartoon faces of mummy, daddy, smiling son and pig-tailed daughter. The model family.

(Vakil 1998 [1997]:124)

23 The market research that Lintas conducted around this time confirmed their hunch: it showed that although awareness and even one-time trials of condoms among members of the target group (at the time of launch, defined as urban middle-to-high income males, 25–40 years old) was as high as 80 per cent, continued usership was a dismal two to three per cent.

24 The presence in the market of the southeast Asian pornodoms was both a significant business irritant and an opportunity to draw aesthetic delineations which positioned KamaSutra on the side of tasteful 'erotica' and the pornodoms on the side of exploitative 'pornography'.

25 Interview with Aniruddha Deshmukh, Bombay, 13 January, 1998. All subsequent quotations from Deshmukh are from this conversation.

26 The *Kamasutra* was originally compiled by the fourth-century scholar Vatsyayana, and has, like most major 'Hindu' texts, since then spawned a vast supplementary literature of commentaries and interpretations. Its introduction into European Victorian society through the selective translation into English of Richard Burton contributed to its popular and prurient reputation as an 'oriental sex manual', a reputation which persists among contemporary Indian middle-class professionals, the intended audience of the KamaSutra ads. Although much of the text of the *Kamasutra* is indeed concerned with sexual practice, the refinement of sensual pleasure (*kama*) through sex is to be pursued in relation to the other major goals of life – *dharma* (a famously complex term which is often translated as righteous or ethical action, in relation to one's position in life) and *artha*, the management of material interests. Consequently, the *Kamasutra*, before launching into its famous sequence of sexual recommendations, dwells in detail on interior decoration, education, leisure, and care of the body.

27 In fact, one might argue that there are structural parallels between Vatsyayana's exhaustive enumeration of sensual possibilities and the multiplication of possibilities for high-end consumer gratification through the profusion of product variants offered under a brand umbrella: one of the more recent KamaSutra ads, from the 96-97 phase of the campaign, seemed explicitly to play on this correlation. The ad presented the range of products as a kind of mirror for sexual self-understanding. The layout showcased the entire KS range, which by that point included eight different packages of variously textured and 'scented' condoms. There was by now even a bumper pack of 15 for the insatiable. Beneath a headline demanding 'What kind of lover are you?' the viewer could follow arrows through a flowchart linking the various packs, thus arriving at the product that was perfectly matched to his predilection: 'Are you the moody type? Do you keep it simple, stupid, flowing with the tide, or do you occasionally swim against it? Are you fussy? Are you flexible? Are you driven by wild fantasies? We believe your condom choice can help come up with an answer'.

28 See Brian Moeran's discussion in this volume of the multidirectional quality of such publicity tie-ins.

29 Interview with Prabuddha Das Gupta, Bombay, 20 April, 1998. All subsequent quotations from Das Gupta are taken from this conversation.

30 The cheap thrills didn't stop there, as Prabhudda Das Gupta recalled:

I still remember this one incident [laughs] – I think this was the first day we were shooting – there was some six people from the agency that were present in Goa at the hotel. I was horrified! And when we were setting up this room shot, I noticed that somebody was bringing these chairs into the room . . . Before I knew it, they were, like, all six were beginning to sit down on these chairs . . . I think I took Adi aside and I told him: 'If you want any of these pictures to even begin to work, you'll have to dispense with this audience participation [laughs] that you seem to have in mind!'

31 Television was first introduced in India, on a very small scale, in 1966. It was primarily conceived by the government as a tool for propaganda and 'nation-building', although even at this time the advertising industry was lobbying the government to let it get a toe in the door. Advertising was first admitted in 1976, although it was at that time restricted to still pictures in monochrome with voice-overs. National television remains government-supervised to this day, although the 1980s saw the growth of local cable networks and commercial pan-Asian satellite television, courtesy of the Hong Kong-based Star network appeared in 1991. See Shah (1997) and Gupta (1998).

32 See Ferguson (1993) for a brief discussion of the relationship of what he calls the 'scientific capitalism' of the international lending agencies and indigenous models of wealth in sub-Saharan Africa.

33 Interview with Jayant Bakshi, Bombay, 28 January, 1998.

34 See Chatterjee and Mallik (1997 [1975]) for an analysis, framed in neo-Marxist terms, of the political dilemma of the 'Indian bourgeoisie': a political economic history that suggests totalitiarianism as the path to hegemony, coupled with a reliance on political alliances and an ideological legitimation that require the continuation of democracy. The idea that full democracy is in fact inimical to the realisation of historical destiny is of course a centrally constitutive strand of modern thought, and goes back at least to Hegel.

35 Interview with Jayant Bakshi, Bombay, 28 January, 1998.

9

DRUNK ON THE SCREEN

Balinese conversations about television and advertising

Mark Hobart

Healer: It is as it says in the song I have written down. The *Sapta Timira* signify seven forms of benightedness, of darkness surrounding the heart. For you should know that excess stirs up confusion and bewilderment, and makes life fruitless ... There are drunk people: there are people who get besotted with appearance. Beauty (or handsomeness) infatuates them. Appearance, wealth, ability, status, youth, drink, winning (power). Those are the Seven Intoxications. '*Sapta*' **is** '**seven**', just so you know.

1st person: Don't joke – and in English too!

Healer: That's **seven**. What's *timira* in English?

2nd person: It's darkness.

(From *Guna tanpa guna*, Hindu Religious Rostrum series performed by Sanggar Gintanjali Apgah Denpasar, broadcast December 28, 1994)[1]

Consumption, in so far as it is meaningful, is *a systematic act of the manipulation of signs*, a *total idealist practice* ... which has no longer anything to do (beyond a certain point) with the satisfaction of needs, nor with the reality principle ... [It is] founded on a *lack* that is irrepressible.

Baudrillard (1988a:22–25)

That the silent majority (or the masses) is an imaginary referent does not mean they don't exist. It means that *their representation is no longer possible*. The masses are no longer a referent because they no longer belong to the order of representation. They don't express themselves, they are surveyed. They don't reflect upon themselves, they are tested ... Now polls, tests, the referendum, media are devices which no longer belong to a dimension of representations, but to one of simulation. They no longer have a referent in view, but a model.

Baudrillard (1983a:20)

> When an individual watches a TV ad he or she is watched by a discourse
> calling itself science but in fact disciplining the consuming subject to the
> ends of rationality and profit.
>
> Poster (1990:49)

The masses are increasingly the target of television advertising in Asia. Who
they are, however, in many countries remains largely unknown. And what the
masses think – as opposed to the simulations market research imposes on them –
seems mostly a matter of supreme indifference to manufacturers and even
advertisers.[2] In Indonesia, for instance, insofar as the masses are presumed to be
economic subjects, at best they have been imagined as passive subjects, who on
a good day are capable of applying practical reason to the procuring of selfish
ends in pursuit of pleasure. The rest of the time they are bogged down in
superstition, communalism and hyperconformity (Heryanto 1999). So there are
limits on what needs to be known about them. No sooner is this said than the
argument's implausibility is evident. Such economic rationality is not only a set
of *a priori*, and so universalist, assumptions (von Mises 1960), but profoundly
rhetorical (Brown 1987; Klamer 1987). Such assumptions are comfortable
because they provide an uncomplicated and largely unfalsifiable framework for
explanation. It also gives the impression of being able to distance, tame and
represent the masses (Baudrillard 1983a). Economic events in Pacific Asia in
1997 and 1998 should have shown the palpable inadequacy of such models. So
self-justifying and self-enclosed are these models, and so vested the interests of
some in defending the *status quo*, however implausible, that I doubt much will
change.

This is not to suggest advertisements are not economically important. On the
contrary,

> If cost is the criterion, ads must be regarded as among the most important
> elements of the economy. Ads are also in a central structural position in the
> economy, overlapping the means and relations of production. The major
> problem of the capitalist economy since the 1920s shifted from production
> to consumption ... When an individual watches a TV ad the health of the
> economy is at stake.
>
> Poster (1990:47)

In that case are my remarks about advertising agencies in, say, Indonesia not far
from the mark? After all, is not a significant proportion of their budgets spent on
market research? Why my scepticism?

Audiences and consumers are not however natural objects, but differently
constituted, as Foucault put it, in different régimes of truth. Market research
researches markets – a contested enough notion in itself. What such research
tells us, incidentally, about what humans think depends inevitably on the
presuppositions of the analysis itself. The ontology of mind and its relation to
choice and action is a thorny philosophical issue. So it is hardly surprising that

advertisers' research is prediction-driven and tends to rely on pre-psycho-analytical, mechanical, behavioural and statistical models. The ends of market research would seem to dictate closure.

> The standpoint of market research is limited by the instrumental yearnings of the corporations. The goal of increased profits for the corporation actively interferes with the critical analysis of TV ads. The competitive stance of the firm structures the discourse of market research into the position of the rational subject: the world appears as a mute other that is to be pushed that way or pulled this way. The only question is which configuration of images will do the best job. The position of the firm structures knowledge as a neutral window opening onto a world of discrete interacting objects. The subject remains the desire of the firm and science is its procurer. If the desire of the firm is cancelled, no justification remains for discourse to constitute the world as a mechanics of interacting objects, as a pullulation of causes and effects. Knowledge as a ratio or table of causes/effects is thus connected to the presumption of a rational, autonomous subject, no doubt a male one, a fantasy of desire as profit.
>
> Poster (1990:49)

There are, of course, other ways of imagining humans as subjects – political, religious, historical – just as there are of construing differences according to place, race, class, gender, sexual orientation and so forth. Such constructions remain, however, the preserve of an élite, be it political, economic, media-based or academic. The objects of these accounts – the masses, ordinary people, you and I when we watch television – are mostly presumed to be passive subjects (Hobart 1997a). Such subjects are capable of responding to laws, orders, exhortations, enticements, advertisements, but either they are unable to reflect critically on the conditions under which they live or, if they do, it is a matter of little importance.

In this chapter I wish to consider what a number of Balinese villagers had to say about their engagement with advertising. I shall argue the strong case that, in Bali, people who see themselves as poor (*Sang Tiwas*), insignificant little people (*wong alit*) and part of the masses (*rakyat*) have an understanding of what is going on, what we might call 'implicit theory', which differs from, but in ways is at least as important as, that of their lords and masters, academic experts and others. What is more, this understanding suggests different and subtle ways of understanding how advertising works and how people are implicated in contemporary mass media.

My suggestion that Balinese intellectual practices should be treated seriously in their own right and even juxtaposed critically to the monolith of scientific knowledge on occasion elicits howls of indignant outrage.[3] So let me outline what I am trying to say and what not. I am not proposing some romantic return to a pure and original native knowledge (see Hobart 1993).[4] It never existed. We need, though, to distinguish natural scientists' necessarily extrapolated and textualized accounts of their theoretical worlds from their scientific practice and its consequences (Feyerabend 1975, 1987). Anyway, as Foucault pointed out (1972; and even Habermas largely accepts, 1987) the human sciences face the rather different problem that human beings are at once the subjects and the objects of their own knowledge. The result is a potentially vicious inflationary spiral of ungroundable knowledge, exemplified by the rapid expansion of the human sciences. Without independent conditions of judgement, analysis depends upon the critical evaluation of the presuppositions and implications of the approaches in use. If Quine was forced to admit that there were no epistemological grounds to choose between Homer's gods and atoms (much though he preferred the latter [Quine 1953:44]), why the thinking subject-matter of the human sciences should be excluded from having a rôle in explanation is unclear. That is not to imply that they meet on equal terms. Far from it. Natural scientific knowledge especially is hegemonic. My interest is in the practices through which it is articulated – the outrage that questioning evokes being itself arguably a defensive articulation.[5]

As introducing the notion of articulation (see Laclau and Mouffe 1985; Laclau 1990; Hall 1996; Slack 1996) suggests, I wish to shift discussion away from what Bakhtin called the 'theoretism' of much human scientific thought to reconsider our uses of theory as a set of intellectual practices which produce and reproduce knowledge itself (see Hobart 1996). Reviewed in these terms, the intellectual practices of academics, market researchers and the people being studied necessarily overlap, engage with and affect one another.[6] Knowing as a situated act is a relatively minor theme in western philosophy, which has remained in thrawl to visual or spatial metaphors of knowledge (Rorty 1980; Salmond 1982). Indian philosophers, however, have taken the issue seriously. As Matilal noted, in Nyaya philosophy, knowing is a process which:

> Is set in motion by doubt and ends in a decision ... The end-product takes the form of a mental episode called *prama,* 'knowledge' (a knowledge-episode). It is such a cognitive episode (*jñana*) as hits the mark! ... Indian philosophers viewed a world or constructed a world of a series of cognitive events rather than collected a mass of true propositions.
>
> Matilal (1986:100, 105–6)

As Balinese have been for close on a millenium part of this philosophical discourse, it would seem *force majeur* or plain ethnocentric to declare them unqualified in principle from commenting on their own thought. That this involves a counter-articulation to the prevailing hegemony should not worry critical thinkers, though it may well upset pillars of the *ancien régime.*

Background

Because I shall let a number of Balinese speak reflectively about themselves at some length, in order to appreciate what they were saying, I need to sketch in some theoretical and ethnographic background.

Of the approaches to consumption and consumerism, despite his tendency to over-generalize his arguments, I find the work of Baudrillard the most stimulating and perceptive. Perhaps it is significant that his key work, *La Société de Consommation* took twenty-eight years to be translated (1998).[7] On advertising, I am still feeling my way. On television and mass media, working in a Balinese village, where issues of audiences loom large, my starting position is with the work of critical media scholars like Ien Ang (1991, 1996) and David Morley (1992). The conclusion to their arguments is the importance of ethnography. I would argue further, though, that it also involves the inclusion of the objects of inquiry as agents, whose reflection on their lives is the condition of changing them, not just as patient subjects of others' knowledge. If the slogan 'media practices' is not to be vapid, a new kind of critical ethnography is required which includes people's appreciation of the circumstances of their own practices.[8] Much has been written on the human subject in media, especially film, studies. I am disturbed by the ethnocentric nature of much of this theorizing, Lacanian or otherwise; as I am by the continued exclusion from those analyses of those whose thought and lives we take it upon ourselves to study. I hope that what follows will make it clear that they are abundantly qualified to participate. Following John Hartley (1992), I take it that good practice in media studies is of necessity interventionist. Impressive as it may sound, scientific neutrality here is a disingenuous posture that has unacceptable implications.[9]

The conversations on which this paper is based took place in August 1997 in the highland Balinese village where I have worked since 1970. They were part of a long series of discussions during my annual visits, since I became interested in 1990 in the mass media in Indonesia. This interest was sparked by Balinese themselves, who pointed out to me that the spread of television was having an enormous impact on their lives, more significant than tourism or the government's development policies. By the late 1980s, public life around coffee and food shops in the village square, to which people had previously repaired after work in the rice fields and in the evening, had largely ceased. People, including teenagers, mostly preferred to stay at home and watch TV. This affected my research, because villagers rarely ambled round any more for a drink and a chat as they had in the past. When I caught up with them, usually watching television, they would often muse about its impact, because television was a topic of increasing concern, the implications of advertising being high on the list (Hobart 1999, 2000).

Almost every household in the village where I work (which is neither particularly affluent nor poor by Balinese standards) now has at least one radio and a television set. Poorer families own black-and-white sets which receive only the state television channel (TVRI), but more people now own colour sets which can also receive five terrestrial commercial channels, as well as over twelve satellite stations (although only one family has yet bought a dish in the settlement itself). Such sets cost over half a million Rupiah in 1997 before the monetary crisis (US$200 or more, and the dishes $500). Quite how the less well-off pay for these is a question which exercises local Balinese themselves. Much work, whether carving, sanding and painting statues, or making offerings and cooking, is compatible with watching, or at least listening to, television which, in most households, is on from morning to late at night.

The conversations, from which extracts follow, are part of my work in progress on television as a social practice in Bali. The mass media are part of a congeries of practices, many if not most of which happen when the television set is not even on, be it cooking in time to watch a TV programme, saving to buy a video recorder or buying a product as seen on TV. I live with an extended family and spend much time watching television with them, and watching and listening to them while they do so. The relevant members of the family are as follows. The head, Ktut Sutatemaja, aged about 60 at the time of writing, is my main research assistant. He was a long-distance truck driver, actor and later became village head responsible for customary and religious matters. His wife, Mèn Sinduk, in her early 50s, runs a general shop. Her daughter, Ni Sinduk, in her late 20s, at her mother's urging married Ktut Sutatemaja's eldest son (by a different marriage, but they are notionally brother and sister). She recently completed a degree at the Academy of Performing Arts in the provincial capital and is an accomplished actress-dancer. Her husband, Wayan Suardana, is a secondary school teacher and does most of the work on a project to record Balinese television programmes, which I started in 1990.[10] Mèn Sinduk's recently widowed mother, who spent every day as a petty trader in the market, had also moved in.

In a pavilion, conveniently near the kitchen for the women, is the television set. It is turned on during the day if someone has leisure time, and almost every evening from about 7 p.m. is the focus of family life until they go to bed one by one. Until July 1997, they had made do with a black and white set, which could only receive state television (TVRI). Few people, however, watch this channel. If they cannot afford colour sets, which receive five commercial channels with a far more varied and glossy fare, they often go round to the neighbours who have. When I presented the family with the old 21 inch Sony set used by the Television Project, its effect on family life was immediate. The adolescent boy in the family now stays in most evenings; television is on much of the day; members of the family do work when possible while watching; and the women in particular watch much more than they did. The advertisements are a favourite, not least as a topic of conversation. No family I have seen watches television in silence: it is an interactive occasion.

In the conversations about advertising excerpted below, the household head was always present; and his daughter-in-law usually was, because she was quite interested in talking about television and the other topics we tended to discuss. Other family members dropped in and out. Two other key figures were also often present. One was an old actor in his early 90s, 'Gung 'Kak, a minor scion of the local court, and a great deal clearer in mind despite his age than I often am. The other, Déwa Pekak, was a wealthy high caste farmer and lover of shadow theatre

202

and conversation. I have worked with both on and off for many years. The elderly actor in particular is an old friend of the ex-headman and they frequently have conversations when I am not there about much the same issues which we discuss. I recorded four discussions about advertising in all in the summer of 1997.[11] Each was fascinating; but I deal largely with the first as it was that which took the most reflective turn. Feminists might well argue that this was because of the dominance of elderly males. If you look at the transcripts carefully, this underestimates the role of the young woman.[12] I would suggest the quality of the argument has more to do with the fact that three of the main people were, or had been, actors. And actors, rather than, say, priests, are still the traditional intellectuals in Bali.

As far as I can judge, the conversations on which the research is based are extensions of discussion that takes place on various occasions, rather than radically different kinds of activity. There are, however, important differences. These discussions have an interrogative twist: I ask questions in a way Balinese would often not. By virtue of my being an academic, my presence there as part of research, often with a cassette recorder, provided a direction at moments to conversations that they would probably not have otherwise. I say 'at moments' because, despite leaving a tape recorder running, the speakers often gave every appearance of ignoring me. (This is less obvious in the extracts chosen here, because I have selected moments when they were addressing my questions to them). It is a matter of degree. On their own account, when you spend so much time chatting in a group, issues of status diminish, although they do not disappear. I would suggest that they are unlikely to disappear for the family, who earn a significant proportion of their total income from the Television Project, even if that is largely unconnected with my day-to-day research. Finally, by showing interest and asking questions about television, the people I work with, at least intermittently, think about television in different ways in their lives.

The idea, though, that there is some pure, authentic 'response' to television advertisements, some state of being which transcends practices of viewing is a utopian fantasy.[13] On the other hand, the idea that there is a 'dirty' response in terms of how many units are sold per broadcast is equally fanciful. For practical, as well as theoretical reasons, you can never know why. No matter how ardently advertisers or media studies specialists might wish it, there can be no generalized account of Balinese, Indonesian – or anyone else's – response to television or to advertisements (see Ang 1991). It is to precisely these issues that I now turn.

Caveat Spectator

Over the years several themes often came up in conversation. Villagers were acutely sensitive to the differences of power between ordinary viewers and metropolitan élites. The latter are widely presumed to organize deals among themselves. So even the scheduling is a form of advertising for those with connections or cash. How programmes promoted lifestyles, and advertisements sold goods to people who often did not really want to buy them, was a constant theme. Explanations ranged from situated worlds (if you stand near a waterspout you get splashed) to theories of imitation (cf. Smith 1995).[14] A favourite was telling stories against yourself about how you had been fooled into buying some product you saw advertised on television.[15] That in itself is an interesting comment on how poorer Balinese saw themselves implicated in advertising practices.

Earlier on the evening of the first conversation, we were watching television when there was an advertisement was for a refrigerator, which I found rather unoriginal and ignored until my host became excited and remarked how clever the presenter was. Later I asked about it.

Self:	You were just talking about the fridge advertisement. Can you explain it again? I'm not sure I really understand.
Ex-head:	It's about what's said in the fridge ad, the one who speaks – what's his name? The one in the SiDoel films who plays Kong Aji. (*SiDoel Anak is a series which has the highest audience ratings in Indonesia. It is one of the few about ordinary people's lives.*) Now he's talking about the fridge. 'Hah! Now this is good. It holds a lot and is economical on electricity'. Now, after that it goes: 'New, durable!'
Self:	Hmm.
Ex-head:	Now the presenter is clever.
Old Actor:	Hah!
Actress:	Emerald, Emerald. That's the brand name.
Ex-head:	What?
Actress:	Emerald.
Ex-head:	Well, Emerald or whatever. That's understood. As long as goods are new, of course they're good. But, after a few months, a few years, what then?
Old Actor:	There's a time limit, of course.
Ex-head:	The presenter is consummate; what he says is ingenious. It's so he can't be attacked by those who buy it. If, after three months, it breaks down, can the purchaser hold him responsible for saying it's durable? That's smart, that is.
Old Actor:	That's someone who's good at being ambiguous.
Ex-head:	Using 'Hey! New durable!' It's funny; it's articulate.
Old Actor:	A clever person, who also has a silver tongue.

While much of what the participants said I had heard in some form in other conversations, it was not chance, I think, that this one was only picked up by viewers who had themselves been actors. It is the art of being careful, or deliberately ambiguous, in your choice of words to convey one impression, but say something different, which is appreciated by the more discerning, more mature listeners. Such mature speech, *raos wayah*, is much used in public fora and, of course, in theatre. There was appreciative recognition of a Javanese, fellow professional. The presenter had managed to square his obligations to the advertising agency which hired him and to the more discerning among the viewers to whom he was supposed to sell the fridges. If people chose not to think about what they heard, that was their problem.

Selling Words, Not Images

As the discussion continued about how words were used to persuade, I interjected that surely it was the images – the endless procession of desirable looking commodities – which made advertisements really enticing.

Self:	It isn't just in words that television advertisements promote their goods. There are images. There are pictures.
Ex-head:	It's showing what the items are like, to inform people who don't know about them.
Old Actor:	About the products.
Ex-head:	In (advertising) literature, for example, you have to specify what it is that you are talking about. That is so that people know about the goods in question, that according to the ad they are good.
Self:	If so, the purpose of advertisements is so you will know about the product in question?
Ex-head	You are only able to know about it. It's just an image. You do not yet know it, what it is really made of, what its real worth is. You just know about the image ...

This line of argument surprised me initially, I think because I had slipped into what is at least my idea of British media priorities, namely images over text. It might seem that the downplaying of images was because, as stage actors, they depended on the word. However, during the opening scene of a popular drama performance by perhaps Bali's best-known troupe in March-April 1991, one performer had slapped down his long-time partner for stating as a fact what he had seen on television. He was reminded sharply that it was just an image, *lawat*, the same term the ex-headman used. Nor is it the case that Balinese, or at least the actors, eschew images for words, which would be rather odd in a society famed for its visual sensitivity and panache. This time, though, the commentators were saying what is widely held to be so. In Bali '*wysiwyg*' is '*wysiwys*': what you see is what you see, not what you get. There is a more serious point here. Images are suggestive, but you tend to need words to tell you the significance of what you have seen.

Selling Words, Not Goods

The conversation continued with me still confusing image and reality, and being corrected again. (Ethnography is largely a battle by the people you work with to overcome the analyst's ethnocentric and professional prejudices. If you are lucky, they win – sometimes).

Self:	Now, if I understand advertisements on television, they show a comfortable existence – the good life – so people will want a lifestyle like that?
Ex-head:	They don't show the good life. What they show – better what they put forward – is an existence they say is good. But that is not yet for sure.
Old Actor:	What's good.
Ex-head:	Yes. Is it actually good – is it really like it is presented – or not?
Old Actor:	That's so.
Ex-head:	Now, I'm speaking from what I've heard, I don't know it personally. I've just heard word. Don't believe what you see, because you've never tried it. But, as to the products, the advertisements will make all sorts of claims about them. The sort of person who buys is the sort of person who has no need to make their money work any more, isn't that so 'Gung 'Kak? 'Hey! Let's just buy one. The ad said they were marvellous'. Huh. That sort of person.
Old Actor:	They've never bought one before.
Ex-head:	In other words, buy something to try it out.
Old Actor:	As I said. Never bought one, let's have a trial ...
Ex-head:	Now, if I think about it, if a patent medicine-seller turns up: 'This medicine, that medicine. *(In other words, whatever its name is, it cures lots of diseases)*. Rub your eyes, they disappear.[16] However, in fact what you're selling is the words. You aren't really selling the goods if you are a patent medicine-seller. People say they sell speech.
Old Actor:	It's generally known that. Of course what medicine-sellers trade in is sounds.
Self:	Is there a point to what they say?
Ex-head:	Just a lot of hot air. There's nothing of substance.
Old Actor:	Nothing at all.

The commentators make the point that beautiful images and elegant lifestyles do not speak for themselves. They require mediation. (Note that mediation here is not instantiation, as if often assumed in Cartesian and idealist models). The remark about 'the sort of person who has no need to make their money work any more' is interesting. The ex-headman is neither an economist nor a businessman. In fact he has six years of elementary school education. It is more a comment on contemporary Balinese society, where rocketing land prices accompanied and enabled a spectacular boom in consumption unrelated, as many Indonesians are finding out at the time of writing, to the conditions for balanced economic growth. While a conspicuous set of people, right out to the remoter villages, was selling land and other assets to be able to buy the widely-available consumer items, a much smaller group was gravely concerned about the consequences.[17]

As usual in conversations in many places, it is what is not said that is as important as what is. Here the unstated theme is: what sort of state have you to be in to try something out for the hell of it? And what sort of person must you be to indulge in such wasteful consumption when others around you are near starvation? Hence the repeated reference to 'the sort of person (who)'. As the context makes clear, they are the sort of people who either cannot, or no longer, bother to distinguish the image from the reality, or who are so besotted they need to buy something simply because it is there. In short, they are benighted, intoxicated. There is a close parallel between Balinese and English, *peteng* being 'night', so that *kapetengan* is literally 'benighted'. In contemporary Balinese usage, seven kinds of intoxication are recognized (see below), only one of which refers to strong drink, drugs and so on. It is a far broader, and more interesting, category.

The whole analysis rests not upon ever more dazzling exegeses about the ultimate nature of the image, of the media, of the umpteenth late capitalism, but upon a recognition of human proclivities, as known by people in the village. By contrast to the largely mechanical models of the subject in market research, Balinese discourse treats the subject explicitly as a site of transformative processes, *triguna* (see below). Is there much difference in falling for the wonderful claims made for patent medicines and for television advertisements? Then comes the twist. Images are imaginary. What you are actually buying is not what the salesman's patter was about, but the words themselves in all their insubstantiality and seductiveness. Having ploughed through tedious tomes on theories of consumption, am I alone in finding a deftness, an analytical sharpness, a sense of history and irony in the Balinese conversations which the former mostly lack?

Something more general is at issue here. My companions were engaged in a disquisition on seduction. As Baudrillard has argued at length, seduction both undermines and refuses the inscription and hypostatization of the discourse of production, which indefatigably strives, and fails, to negate the workings of seduction. The paradoxes, fantasies and elusiveness of desire, what motivates particular humans on particular occasions, make a different sense within the twists and turns of dialogic interaction than when laid out on the slab of hypothetico-deductive thought.[18] It is in this sense that Balinese thinking requires attention, not in the forlorn hope that they will write the ultimate treatise on human nature which, as Collingwood (1945) noted of Hume's attempt (1739), is an impossibility because the notion is indissolubly linked with reflective human interaction and so is dialogic.

The End of Advertisements

The next step raises a practical point, which turns out to be a rather subtle issue in pragmatism.

Ex-head:	No one ever advertises things which are really first class.
Old Actor:	Ah! It's true, they don't. But why not? Some ads have great lines, but it's far from certain the product is any good.
Actress:	It's like Dad says, if the product is really good, then you don't need to advertise it, like Sony products. There are never any ads on television for them.
Old Actor:	Of course, everyone knows that.
Actress:	Everyone knows if goods are really good.
Ex-head:	There is no way of knowing if the product is any good from advertisements. The cost of hiring people to make ads is extremely expensive, 'Gung 'Kak.
Old Actor:	Hiring them?
Actress:	It's very costly. They say you have to pay them for every time it's broadcast.
Ex-head:	How much for so many people? You get very rich through doing ads; you earn an enormous amount. So you have to stick your neck out and pay god knows how much to run an advertisement. Instead, why not give out samples for everyone to try? If the product were really good, they'd hand them out on request. That would really help.
Old Actor:	In other words, people would promote them by passing on the word.

This is by no means the end. If it is insubstantiality and seductiveness, exemplified in the word and the image, which you are buying, then the divorce of the sign from the object is not only complete, but the sign becomes its own reality. Without post-structuralist academic credentials, the commentators have reached a related position to Baudrillard's famous rescension of Foucault's *The Order of Things*.

This would be the successive phases of the image:

– it is the reflection of a basic reality
– it masks and perverts a basic reality
– it masks the *absence* of a basic reality
– it bears no relation to any reality whatever: it is its own pure simulacrum.

Baudrillard (1983b:11)

Whereas Baudrillard retired into unsituated abstraction with his image of the image, the commentators are capable of coping with a heterogeneous reality.[19] Not all representations are simulacra: that would be too easy. The problem is that the different phases of the image co-exist. The good products sell partly because they are not simulacra. The seduction of the image is its own limiting condition. There is also the seduction of the real, which succeeds because it proves to be on the whole what critical investigation said it was, in this instance Sony television sets. To achieve his effect, Baudrillard has to ignore his own analysis of seduction by creating a new grand narrative of the image and seduction. For Balinese, if something works, people tell one another.[20]

Baudrillard argued, rather cogently, that in the world of mass media there are two orders: 'an operational system which is statistical, information-based and simulational' and a 'system of representation' based upon a 'philosophy of the subject: will, representation, choice, liberty, deliberation, knowledge and desire' (1988a:209, 214). Instead, however, of pitching one against the other to produce at best an interminable stand-off, at worst a vicious vortex, in their conversation the Balinese, recognizing these possibilities, pointed to a route out of the academicism. The recognition of reality, statistical or subjective, depends as C.S. Peirce (1984) and the commentators noted, upon a community. In the latter case you talk over with others what it was that actually worked.

Beauty in a Bottle

There are no advertisements which the Balinese I know are more rueful about being taken in by than those to do with personal appearance. Shampoo advertisements were the favourite. Only after buying one or two brands, they said, did it become obvious that the models who posed for the ads were chosen for their beautiful hair to begin with! The actress, a beautiful woman – but one whose skin was a very slight shade darker than that considered attractive – turned to her use of skin whiteners which were much promoted during 1997.

Actress:	I tried it because the woman in the advertisement was beautiful.
Ex-head:	The one who was using it?
Actress:	The one they used in the ad. They showed her first and the effect of whitener. To begin with she's presented as dark, after using whitener, she gets whiter, whiter, whiter until she's white. After seeing it, why not try it out once? I wanted it there and then.
Self:	Did it work?
Actress:	No! My skin was just the same. It didn't get any whiter.
Self:	After that did you try any more?
Actress:	No. The bottle's still half full. I never used it up.
Self:	Did you try another brand?
Actress:	Oh, no!

The theme, familiar to Balinese and one to which I shall return in the conclusion, is the central role of people's vanity, which drives them to spend money even if they know it is going to be wasted. As the actress remarked: when she saw the advertisement, she wanted the whitening agent instantly. You rarely buy a line a second time if the first was a failure and recommendation by friends displaces the lure of the advertisement.

Do Advertisements Force Viewers to Buy?

As the evening wore on and what people had to say was emerging more fully, my questioning moved from jogging the conversation along to being more openly interrogative. A common concern in daily life is whether a person was forced into an action, a possibility which is strongly disapproved of on the whole. So I asked what seemed to me the obvious question.

Self: Now it's like this. If products are being hyped the whole time, are people in some way forced?

Ex-head: That's being forced.

Old Actor: That isn't being forced. You can't call that forced.

Ex-head: Yes?

Old Actor: As a person I am not forced by that. It's perfectly all right if you have some way of showing that it's useful, so that people are pleased.

Ex-head: That's a form of forcing people, what you've just said.

Actress: Now if they just show advertisements again and again, but if I've bought whatever and it was no good, I'm not going to buy it again. But I can enjoy watching the advertisement by itself.

Old Actor: That isn't good. (*This sentence could mean several things. It is impossible to tell for sure which.*)

Ex-head: Whatever way you look at it, that means being forced. (*He switches to Indonesian. From the style it would seem a publicly rehearsed case against advertisements.*) 'Being coerced by advertisements'. (*Reverts to Balinese.*) You aren't being forced to buy! It's not that. You're not forced in that sort of way. It's when you don't, you don't trust something, but you find yourself using the words, talking about it, that's what we're calling force.

Actress: Now listen. It's not just about people buying. It's about believing what you watch. Now you've never bought whatever it is, then you think: 'Well let's give it a try'.

Ex-head: That's it.

Actress: Because they keep repeating the ads.

Ex-head: That's what we mean by being forced. It isn't just one person. (*He switches again for the next sentence to Indonesian.*) Many people are coerced by advertisements.

Old Actor: Now, suppose it is just the three, or four, of us, for example. Now, there are advertisements as I see it, Tuan (*that is, me*). Now I'm not denying that there are all sorts of advertisements, whether they are worth anything or not. People are only reasonable in – what's it called? – demonstrating what their products can do, using words. 'This is what my product

210

is good for'. Now that's very useful. But whether that product is any use to you, I have no idea. I am not denying people promote products that way. But, now, if it were me for example who was going to buy it, I would be very careful indeed before doing so.

Actress: You'd be careful buying whatever it is, but you'd just enjoy looking at the ad. Like 'New. Durable!' you can enjoy listening to it. But you don't feel like buying the product.

As happened often, there was an interesting disagreement. The ex-headman instantly adopted the idea of forcing and a position common in media studies' work on media imperialism. What matters is the structure within which the viewer is constrained. By contrast, the actress, while recognizing the impact of repetitive exposure to an advertisement, brought her own experience to bear. No amount of repetition will make you buy something that does not work. She also neatly split appreciating the product from appreciating the image, the beauty, the cleverness of the advertisement.

The old actor instead took a nuanced position, often assumed by wiser theatre actors. Responsibility for action, here purchasing a product because it is heavily promoted, lies in the end not with the advertiser or producer, but with the viewer. Companies quite reasonably wish to inform the public of their products. Indeed it is useful. That you should then go and buy the product is something quite different. That depends on the personal exercise of critical judgement. However much they might wish otherwise, advertisers can only partly – and partially – structure the conditions under which you have preferences or make choices: they cannot decide for you. Philosophically the coercion argument is incoherent on the matter of responsibility and so agency. Interestingly, the old actor parallels Ernesto Laclau (1990) who noted that, if decisions are structurally determined, the possibility of the human subject at all is eliminated.

If you think that I am over-interpreting what Balinese have said and am attributing a degree of reflection to their thought which is not warranted, I would beg to differ. That we may not be so reflective is no excuse for projecting, ethnocentrically, our habits – indeed prejudices – onto others. The old actor and ex-headman are both traditional intellectuals and quite aware of the complexity of the issues they were addressing. 'All men', as Gramsci (1971:9) famously remarked, 'are intellectuals ... but not all men have in society the function of intellectuals'. It may require the participation of a trained academic like myself to put the arguments into a format acceptable to the dictates of style of late twentieth century academia. Much of the theory is obviously implicit, but then much theory is in academic argument (Collingwood 1940; Quine 1953). We only reveal the tip of a treacherous iceberg. All that says is that ethnography is the product of a complex agent, comprising the ethnographer and her interlocutors. As Collingwood (1940:34) noted, much that passes for research is based on the idea that knowledge is:

The simple 'intuition' of 'apprehension' of things confronting us which absolutely and in themselves just are what we 'intuit' or 'apprehend' them as being. This theory of knowledge is called 'realism'; and 'realism' is based upon the grandest foundation a philosophy can have, namely human stupidity.

Seduction

As the evening grew late and conversation seemed to be drawing to a close, I asked a leading question. It was bringing Baudrillard to Bali.[21]

Self:	If I look around for an analogy to the way advertisements coerce, is it like seduction? If a man softens up a woman?
Ex-head:	Now that's refined coercion. Seduction. It fits, it's seduction.
Self:	What do you think, 'Gung 'Kak?
Old Actor:	Now if you say that, if it's like someone trying to seduce someone else, as Ktut said. I feel it's right.
Actress:	That kind of forcing isn't brutal. It's subtle force, isn't it?
Ex-head:	A refined way.
Old Actor:	Now in a refined way, for example. If everyday people say it too often, of course you get a feeling that you want to give it a go. In fact, of course you have to have money.

Whether it emerges in the transcript or not, my suggestion was immediately appealing. Young men's attempts to seduce women, *and vice versa,* are a favourite theme. It also provided a way out of the dilemma about agency. The person being seduced has to comply, and contributes actively in her or his own seduction (see Hobart 1990). Advertisements cannot seduce you unless you collaborate.

No Cash, No Desire

The reference to seduction reanimated the whole discussion. My host's son had turned up and his wife started to tell the story of how he went out one day without telling anyone and bought a gas hob, because a poor relative had bought one, whereas he was a high school teacher (and moreover had a very good income from the Television Project). His father remarked wryly that his son was caught in the new trap, *Géngsi* (the need for prestige, being one up on the neighbours). 'What was he feeling?', the father asked. His daughter-in-law, the actress, replied:

Actress:	He just wanted to buy it.
Ex-head:	Hah! He just wanted it! Now after being desperate to buy it, what if you don't have the money? How do you feel then?

Actress: If you don't have the money, then that's it. If you don't have the money, you aren't really going to feel strongly about getting a gas hob. It's because he's got a good job, he had the money to use to buy it. If he hadn't, he wouldn't have. We'd have used the usual (*paraffin*) stove. There would be no point in wishing for it. Of course he didn't feel so strongly about it. The point of the gas hob is that because he had the money, he wanted to buy it.

At the end of the previous extract, the old actor had remarked that advertisements made you want to try out something, but only if you had the money. The actress developed the point. If you cannot get hold of the money, you do not want something. Desire is not a primordial condition of human beings (Deleuze and Guattari 1983). It is the product of the relationship between an image, an object, an occasion, an inclination, the means and a decision, the willing of an act. You might fantasize about something, but there is no point. So you do not wish for, or want, it.

Drunk on the screen

According to Thatcherism 'greed is good'. Capitalism is naturalized by declaring economic activity to be based on rational choice, rational choice on egoism and egoism on greed. That the connections do not work well (for example, Hindess 1988:29–41; and as the Soeharto régime belatedly found out at the nation's expense) does not prevent them, like advertisements, from being recycled endlessly. The old actor's point was that that is no reason to accept the argument.

I take it that explanations of complex processes like contemporary capitalism, advertising and mass media are underdetermined. That is, there are several explanations which fit the facts, albeit in rather different ways (Quine 1960). Additional criteria are required to decide between explanations (Hesse 1978). Politicians and economists may be interested in those explanations which make their policies or theories look attractive. As an anthropologist I am interested in explanations which avoid ethnocentricity and are commensurable with people's understanding of the conditions of their lives. I am therefore more interested in accounts that permit people critically to reflect on themselves as agents, not just the practices which may tend discursively to produce the passive subjects or objects of others' actions, such as advertising.

Balinese bring a considerable arsenal of religious and philosophical ideas to bear on the explanation of human action. I shall mention only two, which bear directly on advertising. My sources are from television. Hinduism is a state-recognized religion in Indonesia and most Hindu broadcasts are produced by Balinese. Understanding the earth-shaking economic and social changes taking place, hardly surprisingly, is a preoccupation. As with the old actor's analysis, the trend is to locate the areas of antagonism within the person or between

213

people, rather than displace them onto external structures, that objective reality loved of scientism.

One of the best known classical frames of reference is the *sadripu*, the six inner enemies, which each human has as part of their being. These are *kama,* desire, the pleasure of the senses; *kroda,* anger, passion; *loba,* greed, covetousness; *moha,* infatuation, darkness of mind, ignorance; *mada,* intoxication, whether by passion, drink, fury or whatever and *matsarya,* envy or jealousy (Zoetmulder 1982; *Sadripu* Téater Nusa Denpasar, broadcast February 24, 1993). Here at last, surely we have greed (and desire, for that matter), and a framework which bears at least a passing resemblance to the seven deadly sins.

Although the *sadripu* are widely known, they are too general to be applied usefully to the critical analysis of human action on specific occasions. They are overshadowed, in religious broadcasting in the nineties at least, by a different explanatory grid: the *Sapta Timira*, the seven forms of benightedness, or intoxication. It is these to which Balinese broadcasters appeal in addressing the problems of the contemporary world.[22]

Let me quote from the programme entitled *Mada*, intoxication (the fifth of the *sadripu* listed above):

> *Surupa* is a person being intoxicated with beauty, or with handsomeness. *Dana* is being overwhelmed by money. *Guna* is when someone is inebriated with their own abilities. Cleverness, of course, also intoxicates. *Kulina* is obsession with status and title. After that *Yowana* is being infatuated with youth. *Sura* is being intoxicated on strong liquor, like Pan Suba (a figure in the story) who gets drunk to the point of being *Sura.* Finally there is *Kasuran,* that's getting carried away by victory. So, for example, winning at gambling is also a cause of intoxication.

Why so many Balinese feel so ambivalent about the island's most famous tourist resort, Kuta Beach, starts to make sense. It is the place which best instantiates all seven *Timira* at once on a daily basis.

From the excerpts above, it should be clear that, as Balinese talk about them, advertising has on the whole far more to do specifically with forms of intoxicating than with the other inner enemies. In different ways, different genres of broadcasting address different kinds of intoxication. The most widely spoken about when discussing advertisements is *surupa* – the intoxication is double. It is not just your own appearance, which impels purchases of shampoo, skin whitener, clothes and so on. More broadly it is intoxication with the attractiveness of the actors in the advertisements.[23] Obsession with youth is another, if less remarked upon, feature of advertisements, as *kasuran* is in quiz shows and televised sports.

I do not wish to force the issue, but Balinese have a wide vocabulary to talk about their engagement with television. This relates to quite distinctive complexes of ideas about the nature of the human subject (cf. Wikan 1990). Indian Samkhya had developed an intricate account of the subject and its dispositions as part of a world of transformative material processes, the *triguna* (Larson 1987). Quite how generally Balinese versions of the *triguna* were used in, say, the precolonial period, by whom and on what occasion, I am not in a position to say. It seems to be the dominant frame of reference in Hindu religious broadcasts and is often referred to in theatre. The theory is not just dialogic, but treats humans as continually making and being remade by the world about them. It is an account of the subject which fits post-structuralist approaches far better than the atomist theories prevalent for example in psychology.

Advertisements make people drunk. That is why they feel they must buy things suddenly. The image of intoxication is significant. It presupposes choice and its forfeiture, excess and loss. There is a recognition of the threat to one's self-command (not self-control, with its mechanistic image of the subject) and the impossibility, in a world of transformative process, of total command over oneself anyway. This account of intoxication also presupposes the dangers of a false appreciation of oneself and its relation to the world, and a disjuncture between a desired or imagined object and reality. It is a relational term, but one that involves rupture and so signals the end of dialogue, now replaced by narcissistic monologue (the favoured form of theoretism) or vacuity. The primary relation is now to the subject's own longings. But this in turn presupposes a double other. The first is the imaginary being who really appreciates your beauty, wealth, prowess or whatever. (In Bali even drunks used to get drunk together in *tuak*-drinking groups.) The second is those others, Peirce's community, who both appreciate its allure – *kapetengan* is an inevitable part of being a sentient human – and misery; and form the conditions of the possibility of recognition of intoxication.

Drunkenness in Bali can also be contagious. Balinese are bitterly aware of their proclivity to *nuut lubukan*, to walk in the footsteps of those who have gone before, never veering from what others have done before. No one even knows the number of 'artshops', homestays and paraphernalia thrown up in an epidemic of *Dana* across what was once, by their own admission, a rather lovely landscape. There were never remotely the customers to justify the riot of intoxication, which was itself cut short by the riots across Indonesia as an economy itself built upon intoxication imploded. Much of the development turned out to be a simulation.

Put this way it sounds as if intoxication in whatever form is out-and-out bad. That, however, would be to impose a quite different, and puritan, metaphysics upon what Balinese are arguing about.[24] The point was made nicely by the rich farmer, who turned to me one day during a conversation and remarked that he was mad. To my astonishment, the others all chimed in laughing and announced that they were mad too! The farmer put me out of my misery by expatiating. He was mad about *bricolage*. He was mad about repairing things and messing with odds and ends. The old actor was mad about theatre: it did not matter how old he was, how bad the weather or how far away the show, he would be there. Everyone is mad about something: something intoxicates them. Meditative abstinence is

215

for saints. And there have never been many of those around, not least because so fierce a negation of ordinary mortal frailties sets up the likelihood of a correspondingly ferocious reaction into excess. To be mad or drunk may be bad, but it is human. Anyway those who proclaim their restraint or advocate it to others all too often, sadly, turn out later to have indulged in excess themselves. Advertisements simply tap into human frailties.

To return to advertising, it is not simply that watching the television screen makes you intoxicated by what you see. A striking feature of advertisements is the ecstacy which is supposed to overcome actors when presented with a cold-relief pill, on pouring chilli sauce all over your food or given the chance to wear a proprietary sanitary pad. What is distinctive of advertisements as a television genre, perhaps not just in Indonesia, is that it is not just the viewers, but the actors too who are drunk on the screen. That it no longer matters that it is a simulation is part of the point of advertisements.

Television advertisements are part of a new emerging régime of pleasure. Ideas of pleasure, gratification, happiness, and the conditions for their achievement, are highly discursively specific (Foucault 1986a, 1986b). The pleasure theory of human drives nicely fits capitalist ideology, because it is linked to an Enlightenment theory of the psyche as an internal market to start off with, a model now being displaced by consumption as ecstacy (Ferguson 1990; or as Balinese prefer, inebriation). The disciplining discourse which television advertisements aim to impose is connected with the imperative of seeking pleasure almost as a moral and civic duty to further Indonesian economic development. As Baudrillard remarked caustically:

> The best evidence that pleasure is not the basis of consumption is that nowadays pleasure is constrained and institutionalized, not as a right or enjoyment, but as the citizen's *duty* ... The consumer, the modern citizen, cannot evade the constraint of happiness and pleasure which in the new ethics is equivalent to the traditional constraint of labor and production.
>
> Baudrillard (1988b:46, 48)

And as he has been at pains to make clear, what is consumed are signs of difference, driven by a desire for social meaning. Were it not so, consumers would have long ago been sated. This is why advertisements are as much about consummation as consumption.

What my Balinese companions had to say about televised advertising involves presuppositions broadly similar to those in Baudrillard's analysis. They continually stressed the overwhelming importance of the image and the need to think critically about its relation to the object, which is never fully revealed. They were also quite clear that their moments of enjoyment came about from appreciating the images for themselves, an aesthetic consummation. As they were fairly poor people who could not buy most of what they saw, to what extent was this vicarious pleasure or even, as mall walking is supposed to be, an act of resistance? No doubt it is that in part, although quite how you tell I do not know.

216

From what they said, however, it has another aspect. Where the school-teacher was evidently caught up in the civics of consumption, the others were articulating the counter-case for a quite different account of the subject. It is a subject placed in a complex dialogue of seduction, excess, intoxication and often, by virtue of the human condition, inevitably disappointment. If nothing else, I hope that the analysis of these conversations has made the point that, if we imagine our discursive ideas about consumption, pleasure and the human subject are universal, we are likely to miss much that is of interest and importance. There is more in heaven and earth than is dreamed of in writing about advertisements and television.

Notes

1 The programme was in Balinese. Words in bold however were in English in the original; italicized words are Old Javanese.

2 I have yet to carry out research on the practices of Asian advertising campaigns (such as those described by McCreery and Mazzarella in the previous two chapters. However, extrapolating from work done elsewhere, I would advance a double 'null hypothesis'. First, the relationship between advertising and sales is sufficiently complex and indeterminate that even the crude formula 'provided it sells the product' cannot be the yardstick for evaluating the efficacy of advertising campaigns (Schudson 1984). Second, sales may well be as much about 'keeping the score' between rival metropolitan advertising companies, whose prime constituency is the world of national and transnational media, as it is about the interests of the commercial companies for whom they work.

3 Juxtaposing and allowing the intellectual practices of the objects of study to comment and reflect on the thinking and practices of their knowing subjects upsets many scholars. The objections take two forms. The first is that I do not need continually to invoke philosophers in order to legitimate what Balinese have to say. Encouraging a normally forbidden, recursive reflection on our own thought is not however primarily about justifying Balinese thinking. It is to question the hegemony of our own thinking and decentre it. It is also to enable the antagonisms (in Laclau's sense) of different congeries of intellectual practices to engage to whatever outcome. The second objection is the inverse of the first. It is that academic thinking is *a priori* so superior to any native thought that the exercise is inevitably fruitless, inappropriate, indeed polluting. Danny Miller's response to this chapter was that: 1) Balinese had nothing to say that was profound; and 2) viewers in other parts of the world could come up with parallel ideas. I leave it to readers to judge the first comment for themselves. The second merely reiterates what I am arguing, namely that academic objectivations of people as viewers, masses and so on involve serious misrecognition – indeed denial – of what they are doing.

For some reason, this juxtaposing seems particularly to upset north Americans. I do not know if this is because they still see themselves as the dominant world power and their knowledge as correspondingly hegemonic and sacred, whereas we Europeans have come sadly to learn that the world all too often exceeds, and fails to conform to, our theories. My own theoretical position here links work in history and philosophy with that of Foucault, Baudrillard and the post-Gramscian critiques of Laclau and the cultural studies' debates in Britain.

4 Nor am I reiterating the romantic media studies' thesis of the active viewing subject, who determines her conditions of engagement with the media. As the Balinese

commentators made clear, that argument confuses activity and agency. What this does suggest though is that, at least for Indonesia, arguments like Stuart Hall's about the degree to which mass media are hegemonic are overstated and the familiar product of armchair theorizing.

5 This argument obviously echoes critiques of the hegemony of Euro-American science by scholars like Haraway (e.g. 1991) and Latour (e.g. 1993). The difference is that, of necessity, they remain part of, and must work within, the ensemble of intellectual practices they are criticizing. The issues of incommensurability and radical translation, let alone potentially quite different kinds of intellectual practice, are marginal to their main concerns.

6 So juxtaposing such practices is merely undoing the original hypostatization by which knowledge was made to emerge as a transcendental system in the first place. As the Frankfurt Critical School made clear, knowledge is always directed to a purpose, even if this purpose is non-technical, but interpretive or emancipatory (Habermas 1978; Apel 1979).

7 Glossing the title as *The Consumer Society* significantly puts the stress, as Anglo-Saxons prefer, on the individual rather than upon the practice of consumption – thereby also missing the *double entendre* on consummation so central to Baudrillard's analysis.

8 Elsewhere I have considered the problematic relationship of anthropology to cultural and media studies (see especially Hobart 1997b). A crucial issue is the relevance and kind of ethnography. The present piece is arguing for a shift in degree, if not in the kind, of ethnography to incorporate and acknowledge the constitutive dialogue which underlies the final inscribed accounts.

9 For this reason I exclude passages from the conversations which would provide advertising companies in Indonesia with what viewers consider effective ways of overcoming their critical judgement. Here I echo my Balinese colleagues: advertising should inform about the existence and merits of goods and services, but not attempt to preempt preference or choice.

10 For a brief account of the television project, see Hobart (1999).

11 The first, which is the one discussed mainly here, was with the elderly men and the actress on August 8. The second, on August 17 (National Day), was when I returned to the theme after watching television with my host, his son and daughter-in-law and the old actor. Four days later the whole family and some friends were raptly watching a film. So I recorded the advertisements on a VCR and played them back afterwards, while recording their comments on a cassette tape. The next day I found the three women in the family (great-grandmother, grandmother and daughter) working together and asked them about advertisements while they worked and chatted.

12 A problem is that village women are busy, they have little time to break and often prefer to talk while they work. On many topics, they were the best commentators. On television they tended to be less so, perhaps because they only really started watching after the colour set changed household dynamics.

13 The point has been made forcefully by Johannes Fabian (1990), who has argued ethnography to be one performance among the many which are going on at the same time. His argument however still implies inherent dissimulation. For this reason, I prefer Judith Butler's account of performance as simply what there is (Butler 1990, 1994).

14 Significantly, accounts of identification which have been so central to much film and cultural studies did not feature. I spent much time last summer discussing identification with actors as well as audiences. It is remarkably hard going actually to formulate questions about identity in Balinese. And when you do, you easily land up going round in circles. When they finally understood what I was driving at, everyone I spoke to gave identification short shrift.

15 Seduction by advertisements (a theme I develop below), as with other embarrassing moments, is conventionally supposed to happen to someone else, never to you. That Balinese were enthusiastic to admit to getting carried away has, as I argue towards the end of the chapter, to do with ideas about seduction and intoxication.

16 This sort of sales talk is the butt of popular jokes. There is apparently a well-known sales pitch which is meant to imply that whatever the illness, it will disappear in the wink of an eye. As the patter has come to be condensed, what it literally says is: 'Rub your eyes and your eyes will disappear!' Conveniently nothing is actually claimed for the medicine.

17 The collapse of the rupiah, the implosion of the Indonesian economy after May 1998 and the decline of the tourist trade have tended to prove my host right in his decision to forego lavish spending and buy rice land when everyone else was in an orgy of selling theirs. Once, of course, rich consumers had made their money work or they would not be as rich as they are.

18 On the applicability of dialogic analyses to the study of Bali, see Hobart (2000). The choice is between what you can make of the sort of thing the commentators were discussing above as against the finding, say, that 92 per cent of young people between sixteen and twenty years of age from a particular Asian country said that they did not respect politicians. (This, as near as I can remember it from a lecture during the original conference in Hong Kong, is the percentage who asserted this wholly unremarkable pseudo-fact during interviews made under unknown, but doubtless 'carefully controlled, objective' circumstances.)

19 It does not follow, as some participants at the original *ConsumAsiaN* workshop on 'Asian Advertising and Media' took it, that the commentators were arguing that the product is seen as no more than an image. That is a classical problem of European representationism. Quite the contrary, the problem to Balinese is that people easily conflate image and object and confuse the complex relationship between them. Unless you happen to bump into something, most of what you encounter happens to be images. The formal philosophical issues have been laid at some length in Nyaya-Vaisesika (see Potter 1977; for the problems of its applicability to Bali, see Hobart 1985).

20 Incidentally, if I – by way of the commentators – appear to be taking issue with Baudrillard in particular, it is largely because he actually said something interesting and worth engaging with.

21 He is in vogue in the Faculty of Arts at the provincial state university. I must confess I am partly, but by no means wholly, responsible for this through my work on media studies in Indonesia. The excitement he generates there is interesting.

22 Inevitably perhaps accounts vary, primarily over whether bravery or concern with winning should be separated from *kasaktian*, unusual efficacy (conventionally glossed as 'mystical power'). Other programmes in the Hindu Religious Rostrum series of broadcasts make it clear that *timira, kapetengan,* or *kagelapan* all signify intoxication, *kamabukan,* for example *Karma wesana* broadcast November 3, 1993; *Peteng pitu* broadcast September 21, 1994: 'The seven forms of benightedness or *sapta timira* are seven kinds of darkness or seven kinds of drunkenness' (*Peteng pitu atau sapta timira adalah tujuh macam kegelapan atau tujuh jenis kemabukan*).

23 Balinese are often quite open about their sexual attraction to television actors .

24 This is not to say that some people do not subscribe to anti-recidivism, even encratism: for example, the producers of some Hindu religious broadcasts. To what extent this is a reaction among public presenters of all the major religions in Indonesia against the conspicuous excess of the last years, and to what extent a more specifically Hindu-Buddhist response to the preachings of the more puritanical schools of Islam, is an interesting question.

Part IV

Producing Consumption

Figure 12 Miss Chinese International Beauty Pageant
(Photo courtesy of Dermot Tatlow)

10

SO CLOSE AND YET SO FAR

Humanizing Celebrity in Japanese Music Variety Shows, 1960s–1990s

Carolyn S. Stevens and *Shuhei Hosokawa*

'You really can't talk about music on this show, can you?' (Shin'ya, drummer of Luna Sea)

Hey! Hey! Hey! Music Champ, June 8 1998

This chapter provides an analysis of televised Japanese music variety shows, as influenced by methods of consumption and prevailing commercial and aesthetic tastes.[1] It begins with a brief history of music television, beginning in 1958, and then explores the development of these trends in contemporary programs. We see reductions in the focus on musical performance and in the way that the MC, a non-musical participant, has risen in importance. A case study is also included to provide industry insights into the program production process. The paper concludes with a discussion of the changes in the definition of music celebrity-hood. There is a gradual disintegration between public and private; the star is no longer a one-dimensional, glamorous figure. The audience actively participates in interpreting and even determining the star's performance and thus, part of his/her image. We argue that the music television program has transformed over the years into a medium that supports and encourages this process.

Changes in the presentation and perception of celebrityhood have also affected the production of Japanese music television shows. Audition shows in the 1970s changed the way the audience viewed not only the product of stardom (the performance) but also romanticized the production process (the selection of amateurs). Despite their sometimes melodramatic tone, these shows did much to bring the business into the living rooms of middle-class Japanese families. In the 80s, celebrities were hunted down to the corners of the country if their songs happened to be in the Best Ten that week, illustrating the power of the television industry in setting marketing trends. However, in 1989, some celebrities struck back at the industry, with the band boom (where artists had more professional control over their images as songwriters and producers). Currently, the industry and celebrities seem to have struck a balance, as most of the suffering that the stars experience takes place publicly at the hands of other stars (in the role of MC).

Most striking among the changes are shifts in the level of professionalism and the transparency of the shows' production processes, resulting in a decrease in formality and a collapse of the perceived distance between the means of production and the audience's perception of the product. In this context, intimacy can be used to describe this decreased emotional distance between viewer and performer. Intimacy in this context has been described as 'the interconnectedness of selves enmeshed within social lives' (Yano 1998). Here, the practice of consuming both aesthetic and emotional products, as illustrated in the music television show, is part of the social life that connects viewers to each other as well as providing a sense of.

These trends described below indicate the changes in how music is consumed and highlight a preference for informality and surprise (versus formality and expectation). This suggests gradual changes in this particular field of cultural production, according to Bourdieu's model (1993a) of the structure of positions and spaces in cultural spheres. Though the actual physical distances between producer and consumer of television programming have not necessarily changed, tactics for attracting audiences utilize an appearance of decreased distance between these positions. Winning ratings away from other shows is the goal; manipulating their icons (the celebrities themselves) and presenting them as approachable is the strategy.

Television as text is a highly contested area of investigation, where researchers compete to define the most viable method to interpret this slippery mode of communication.[2] Meyrowitz (1985:75, 82–3) sees visual, electronic media images such as television shows to be less encoded, more contemporal, and more transparent than printed images, making the analysis more difficult to pin down in terms of audience composition and interpretation. However, most television analysts agree with the claim that television texts are open to different interpretations that are not necessarily competitive but are complementary, suggesting that meanings work together in the minds of active, not passive, viewers (Livingstone 1990:6, 20). John Hartley and Ien Ang argue the notion that audiences are created by the medium and are further defined by their relationship to the medium. This can be measured in terms of ratings (in contrast to Ang's more abstract concept of the social world of actual audiences) (quoted in Moores 1993:2–3). However, authoritative theoretical models in this field are rare as investigators have been unable to create a controlled experimental environment for viewer testing and must combat the temptation to make inferences from correlational data (Livingstone 1990:15–6). This research takes as a starting point Ang's 'emotional realism' (in contrast to empirical realism), a key concept to describe the result of viewer interpretation (Livingstone 1990:46). The investigators have interpreted the texts using a combination of emic and etic perspectives. Moores (1993:3) writes that 'the ethnographer ... conceptualizes media audiencehood as lived experience', defining the television program as an experience comprising visual and audio symbols which is consumed during a certain time period and in a certain environment, and is conditioned by other complementary media such as magazines and newspapers.[3] Television viewing is not isolated from other interactive experiences, nor is it isolated from knowledge provided by other media sources. Rather, it is embedded in daily experiences and human interactions, as a part of individual practice.

Television plays such an important role in the development of popular music that it has even been seen to constitute its definition: one term for popular music, *kayōkyoku*, has been loosely translated as 'trendy pop music that thrives on television publicity' (Cahoon 1993:1286). Japanese music television here is defined as broadcasts of live or pre-recorded performances and interviews with popular music stars.[4] This study conforms most closely to the definition of a music show as a musical variety show, rather than one that consists wholly of video clips (for example, *Music Tomato* [TVK]) or live concert performances (*Pop Jam* and *Futari no Big Show* [NHK]). Another feature is constancy. Annual shows such as the NHK's *Red and White Singing Contest* (shown on New Year's Eve) and music award ceremonies are important to the wider relationship between the music and television industries. This chapter, however, focuses on the weekly broadcast show.

In the title we used the term 'humanizing' to refer to a process of perception, rather than to the quality of that perception. This describes a process of creating fictive relationships between audience members and stars through an effect of familiarity, closeness and intimacy (a concept discussed further by Koichi Iwabuchi in his analysis of Japanese idol dramas in Taiwan earlier in this volume). In opposition to cult icons, these humanized stars have often transparent public images and the public perceives them as the girl or boy-next-door. Celebrity TV appearances are crucial to the creation of this illusion and their survival: television is pivotal to the process.

From Professionalism to Amateurism: Getting Closer to the Audience

The 1960s

Japan's first weekly music television program was *Mitsuko no Mado* (*Mitsuko's Window*, NTV, 1958–1960). This show featured film star Kusabue Mitsuko as host to a program of song, dance and light comedy. Kusabue was best known for her stereotypical maternal film roles; therefore her fictive personality was well suited for a family-oriented program. This show's success may have influenced NHK's casting decision in hiring Nakajima Hiroko as MC for *Yume de Aimashō* (*Let's Meet in a Dream*, NHK, 1961–66). Nakajima was not a celebrity but an amateur often criticized for her stiffness and over-refined facial expressions and gestures. However, she gave the program freshness and naivete. Stars of *Yume* included the original interpreter of the *Sukiyaki Song*, Sakamoto Kyū, and Kuroyanagi Tetsuko.[5] Sakamoto was one of the first television star-singers. His acne-scarred face provided a sense of familiarity to viewers tired of slick images.

225

Kuroyanagi was young and fast-talking, with a sharp sense of humor.[6] Both these young performers became icons in Japanese popular culture; one through his untimely death in a plane crash and the other through her public longevity.

Shabondama Holiday (*Soap Bubble Holiday*, NTV, 1961–72) was another music variety show with a cast of regulars who entertained weekly guests. The influence of US programming was apparent in the Ed Sullivan and Lawrence Welk flavor of the enduring *Yume* and *Soap Bubble Holiday*; this American character of television content could also be identified in Japanese serialized drama, game and talk shows and news programs. Japanese music variety shows had a clearly articulated format with four major components: introduction / songs / skits / commercials. This format was taped in a studio, and though broadcast live, musical performances were all lip synced. In other words, though the performers were live on television, what the audience heard was a prerecorded, fabricated performance. Some artists pushed this contradiction to the limit, using lip syncing as an expressive tool rather than a musical one. Sakamoto Kyū's songs on *Shichiji ni Aima Show* (*Let's Meet at Seven O'clock*, TBS, 1963) demonstrate the use of lip syncing to express actively emotion, rather than as a pretense for performance. At times Sakamoto didn't even pretend to sing, but coyly covered his mouth with his hand or merely grinned through an entire chorus.

The early 60s saw the rise of another type of program: the audition show. *Hoi Hoi Music School* (1962–65, NTV) showed the audience attempting 'entrance exams' for this fake school. The program showcased public talent before a panel which included show business professionals. Since only a handful of participants achieved professional status, the program was not taken as seriously as the audition shows in the 1970s (see below). Therefore, *Hoi Hoi* tended to be humorous, as did other popular programs such as *Avec Uta Gassen* (*Duet Singing Contest*, 1962–1968, NTV) and *Kazoku Sorotte Uta Gassen* (*Family Singing Contest*, 1966–1980, TBS). Yet, the audition format show gradually became professional in the late 60s when several competitions for electric guitar bands featured slick performances. Although only a few groups (Savage and the Purple Shadows, for example) could make the successful transition from amateur to professional, the program itself was an important development in the history of Japanese popular music. The band contest program, broadcast during the dinner-time slot, intensified competition among amateur bands all over Japan. Furthermore, the show exhibited an emerging student music culture. This widely recognized platform for professionalism was unprecedented in previous youth music genres such as jazz, country and western, rockabilly and rock' n' roll where newcomers were recruited from local nightclubs. Finally, the audition show forced performers to change their strategies for success. They could not rely purely on their music and their ability to reach a live audience; they also had to calculate their mass visual appeal.

Shows in the 60s focused primarily on slick, professionally packaged entertainment and auditions that encouraged public participation. Like their

American counterparts, music shows were not just performance-oriented but encompassed varied forms of entertainment. The producers of these shows clearly demarcated the distance between the stage (as consumed by viewers) and the process by which the shows were delivered to the public. *Yume* and *Soap Bubble Holiday* were concerned with professionalism in its strict sense. These shows tended to be recorded live (thus requiring an expert, reliable cast). Audition shows were usually broadcast from large scale public halls or from television studios with audiences because the house presence encouraged the performers' feeling of being on a grand stage, as well as transmuting the interaction between the performers and the live audience to television viewers through broadcast cheers and applause.[7] The consciousness of the different spheres of professional and amateur status was important to the definition of popular music.

The 1970s

Among many music variety programs televised in the 70s, *Star Tanjō* (*A Star Is Born*, NTV, 1971–83) was symbolic of the decade.[8] This show created top adolescent stars, who became the prototype for Japanese idols: Yamaguchi Momoe, Mori Masako, Sakurada Junko, and Pink Lady, among others. *Star Tanjō* was broadcast on Sundays at 11 am, and was recorded live from a public hall, not a studio. Like its predecessors, it was a family-oriented program. However, it represented a new step in music programming in that it reduced the distance between the audience and the concept of 'stardom' by familiarizing the viewers with the process of stardom.

On *Star Tanjō*, producers invited A & R executives from top record companies and artists' management agencies to attend the broadcasts, cast as competitions. They merely raised their hands if they wished to sign on a performer. Although a self-righteous press often criticized this process as promoting human traffic, this scheme of open access to professionalism was a new concept in Japanese television and the wider entertainment industry; it stimulated a huge wave of public interest in music television programs. Here, the position of producer in this cultural field became transparent to the consumers, a sphere that had been hitherto hidden or disregarded. In the 70s, the viewers became more involved through witnessing the process.

Over 20,000 applications from young women were received every week during the show's hey-day. The most notable stars from this period were Mori Masako, Sakurada Junko, Yamaguchi Momoe (all three were about fourteen at the time of their 1972 debut), Iwasaki Hiromi, Nakamori Akina and Koizumi Kyōko. Girls in their early teens became the exclusive pool from which audition participants were drawn.

The structure of *Star Tanjō* put the viewing audience in a dual position. They could identify with the performer as an amateur, yet they were also viewing the performers through the judges' discerning eyes. The audience thus learned to judge the business value of a singer. Viewers witnessed the moment the star was born and then followed her path from the girl-next-door to a national heroine. This process increased the viewers' identification with the stars, especially for female viewers of similar ages. This program served to bring the Japanese showbiz machinery closer to the public as well, making its viewers feel a part of the entertainment world.

There were also industry issues at hand when the popularity of *Star Tanjō* skyrocketed. Previously, Watanabe Productions had had a virtual monopoly on television programming, including *Soap Bubble Holiday* and other prime-time shows. Indeed, the connection between the so-called Nabe Pro and NTV was so strong that at times artists contracted to the agency could not appear on other stations' programs. However, while Watanabe Productions displayed only the results of star training and management, *Star Tanjō* took the initiative in displaying the making of stardom. To counter the slick singers and comedians of Watanabe Productions, *Star Tanjō* created a strategy of unprofessionalism, uncovering the raw material of stardom. This program became a springboard for Hori Productions (which handled Mori Masako and Yamaguchi Momoe) and Sun Music (which managed Sakurada Junko and later, Matsuda Seiko and Miyako Harumi). The emergence of these two agencies induced the decline of Watanabe Productions and paved the way for the rise of other management companies that thrived in the 80s such as Johnny's Entertainment, an assembly-line producer of male teenage idols.

Star Tanjō represented a Japanization of the music television show, moving away from the American style of music variety and shifting its focus to the process of celebrity-making. Its western counterpart, *Star Search*, served a similar function, but the publicity and the hype surrounding the US version were not nearly as intense as in Japan, and its commercial value was lower. *Star Tanjō* created a specific image of artists in the 70s and canonized the process of stardom in the symbolic representation of an adolescent idol, highlighting the process by showing artists as inexperienced innocents naively chasing a dream. Though this process was first constructed as a strategy to win ratings from other established shows, the outcome was a collapsing of the distance between the viewer and the star. This image was presented to the viewer in the home and contrasted with different perceptions viewers had of stars consumed in other media, such as radio, records and film. The television screen presented 'closeness', not only physically but also emotionally.

The 1980s

The 80s were the supreme era in Japanese music television programming. Audience ratings for music shows during that decade were over 40 per cent, illustrating the intense audience interest during this period. This is compared to 20.9 per cent, the highest audience rating for the top 1998 show (*Nikkei Entertainment* 1998a:46). Shows in the 80s included *Top Ten* (NTV), *The Best*

228

Ten (TBS, 1978–1989; this show once boasted the famous 40+ per cent audience rating) and *Music Station* (Asahi). One emerging characteristic of 80s shows is the prevalence of ratings, which reinforced the links between television programming and consumption practices.

The Best Ten was a 'professional' show, yet it was far from its static relation, *Yume*. Broadcast live from a television studio, it had a quick tempo and dynamic structure, urged on by the rhetoric of live interviews and reports from backstage on the concert tour. Thus, the 'intimate' atmosphere that arose from *Star Tanjō* was preserved and further developed. *The Best Ten* integrated the professional timing of the 60s' shows with an element of surprise. Performers were selected by viewer mail; these requests were ranked and the top ten performers sang in order of their popularity. The audience could see the singers' expressions of joy (when their songs ascended the chart) or regret (when they declined in popularity). When a singer was unavailable, a live camera crew chased after the performer and broadcast a live spot. A member of a popular 80s band remembers the difficulty appearing week after week on the show, merely because their song had been nominated (currently, performers only appear periodically to promote new releases). For busy celebrities, this was a nerve-wracking process and it demonstrated the power of the television producers over artists and their managers. The structure of this show demonstrated an emerging rift in the field of production, between television producers and music producers (the artists themselves).

The Best Ten was thought to be an authentic hit chart, as authoritative as *Oricon*, the weekly journal of the music industry. The show's ratings eventually declined partly due to segmentation of taste and market, bringing into question its authority as the best. The resulting cancellation of this program was often interpreted as the end of the era of groups and singers who could appeal to a wide ranging audience and the beginning of strictly youth-oriented bands.

The Best Ten perhaps best represented the peak of integrating music television programs into the overall show business landscape. However, another eighties' show, *Yūyake Nyan Nyan* (*Sunset Meow*, Fuji, 1986–88), radicalized talent scouting and further dissolved the boundary between the professional and the amateur, and between the industry and the audience. Broadcast from 5 to 6 p.m., it was a constructed after-school gathering of the *Onyanko Kurabu* (*Pussycat Club*, with all its sexual connotations). All the performers were students at a fictitious entertainment girls' high school. These girls sang, danced, played games and chatted before the camera; variety was re-incorporated into the music show, using 'amateurs' as actors. Some of them were featured as soloists, and like Kudō Shizuka, went on to become million-selling recording artists and popular television actresses. Thus young Japanese women were intensively involved not just in music consumption but also in media production. Music production and consumption in the feminine sphere were fused.

The program was notorious for its hype, fully utilizing the power of the press and record companies. According to the show's producer, the program didn't sell music so much as girls as commodities (Ofisu Matsunaga 1990:89–96). This strategy worked: *Onyanko Club* members' singles topped the charts for months. However, sociologist Inamasu Tatsuo (1989) has argued that the girls and their fans were not as passive and manipulated as many social commentators believed; instead, they actively participated in and helped to construct the 'game' initially set into motion by the show's producer, Akimoto Yasuo. Discussing Akimoto's methods of star fabrication that had hitherto been concealed, Inamasu stresses the girls' awareness of the delicate balance between hype and self fulfillment:

> In speculating and going behind the scenes, [Akimoto] forced a false perception of the world on the public under his own control, and many [the performers and the viewers] supported the concept of this constructed world
>
> (Imamasu 1989:195)

However, one should not ignore the fact that Inamasu is remarkably uncritical of the show and the process of instant celebrity-dom. It is likely he took this position, supporting both the fans and the producers of this show, to criticize a self-righteously left press. Critics condemned the *Onyanko Club* for manipulating young, inexperienced women and the fans for blindly consuming them. However, Inamasu's critique tends to celebrate the dominant reading of this particular media event and to overemphasize the differences in the viewers' reception and interpretation modes in the 80s and the 90s. Furthermore, his ideas, based on Baudrillard's simulation theory, appear to simplify matters when he claims that Japanese idols must be fake to be genuine and argues that fiction is more real and more appealing than reality.

Amateur band contests had disappeared from television screens, but returned once in 1989 when *Heisei Meibutsu Ikasu Band Tengoku* (*Paradise for Cool Bands*, nicknamed *Ikaten*, TBS, 1989–91). This show, televised at midnight, featured up-and-coming bands from every corner of Japan. This signaled the end of an approximately two-decade absence of amateur competitions on Japanese television. The delay in the rise of rock bands can be partly explained by the obstinate power of the songwriting/production assembly-line in the Japanese music industry, another important field of production in this cultural area. There was an established division of labor between lyricists, composers, and arrangers who had exclusive contracts with record companies. Amateur rock bands (who wrote and arranged their own music) had the potential to break down this system, so they had been excluded. This show symbolized a shift in the power structure of industry: artists who produced and performed their own music were gaining recognition and control over their business activities.

In the 80s, television producers took the adolescent female singer, reminiscent of the *Star Tanjō* era, and re-worked her into a schoolgirl-*cum*-sexual target. This idealized immature sexuality is still seen today, in the promotion of schoolgirl groups such as SPEED and MAX. Idoldom was still important to music production and the fascination with the process of creating stars continued; however, variety was re-introduced on the *Onyanko Club*. The close of the 80s saw the rise of rock and the introduction of this musical genre to mainstream television culture for the first time. Though a latecomer, *Ikaten* was important because previously rock music was not considered suitable for television viewing. The standardization of rock music marginalized other traditional forms of popular music (such as *enka* and *chanson*) and paved the way for mainstream acceptance of hard rock bands in the nineties (such as the 'visual-type' bands, Glay and Penicillin[9]).

Conclusion

Comparing formats and content over the decades illuminates changing modes of producing and consuming Japanese music television. In the 60s, it was a completely new area, and program content was able to cover a great deal of territory: music, dance, comedy, and sometimes even social comment. The television studios and artist production companies shared a close relationship. Shows in the 70s marked territorial lines between audience, professional and amateur and then proceeded to break them down. 80s and early 90s programs narrowed their purpose to serve as an important marketing tool for many different performers who thus had to compete for exposure. Due to conflict in this field of production, the increasing power of the performer, and the rise in other forms of music consumption, music shows went into decline, and in response to this, the remaining shows needed a new strategy. In the late 90s, the real stars of the music show are not the musicians but the MCs, who control the discourse mercilessly. Music is no longer as important to the music show. Personality, talk, surprise and informality attract viewers in the 90s.

Talk Makes a Comeback: Contemporary Music Shows

Industry experts note that the early 90s represented a period of stagnation in music television. Though Fuji Television began broadcasting its hit *Hey! Hey! Hey! Music Champ* in 1994, it is generally thought that music television did not gain momentum until 1997, meaning there was an approximately eight year blackout in the genre. Since the size of the popular music industry had not decreased and since Japanese youth were not at all disinterested in music and television, many wondered why music variety television faded in this way. One reason was the shift in musical tastes; audiences moved from manufactured pop music to authentic rock. Another theory explaining to the genre's decline focused on the traditional 'one director/one idea' production structure where the director had complete artistic control over his program (*Nikkei Entertainment* 1998a:46). This ended up alienating many performers who had their own opinions about how they wanted to be presented to the public. A rock critic suggests that the 1985 marriage of ultra-idol Matsuda Seiko and a diversification in taste had a hand in taking public attention away from the music television show. Once idols were no longer a major presence on television, there ensued a cultural vacuum. In the late 80s, the cute idol was no longer the idealized feminine type, as both female and male consumers began to take interest in diversified icons such as models, television talents, adult video actresses, and female pro wrestlers. These different images were difficult to compress into a single format.[10]

Technology also changed music consumption. The 1988 appearance of three-inch CD singles was a blow to the dominant idol music genre since the single's seven-inch jacket had been an important visual tool for idols whose images were then translated into a televised format (Igarashi Tadashi, personal communication). After the boom in music programs had ended, concert attendance, radio and 'pay-for-listen' satellite radio services became main venues for consuming music. Moreover, young viewers, accustomed to singing trendy songs in karaoke boxes (see Mitsui and Hosokawa 1998), were less interested in listening to the latest songs than in singing them.

Music shows did make a comeback in the latter part of the decade. In January, 1998 the top ten music shows were:

1. *The Yoru mo Hippare* (slang for Hit Parade; NTV), 20.9 per cent audience rating;[11]
2. *Hey! Hey! Hey! Music Champ* (Fuji TV) (Also known as *Hey3*), 19.9 per cent;
3. *Sokuhō! Uta no daiji-ten* (*Latest News! The Big Dictionary of Music*; a pun on the concept of the top 'ten' and the Japanese word for dictionary; NTV), 19.4 per cent;
4. *Music Station* (Asahi TV), 16 per cent;
5. *Utaban* (a compound of the two kanji for 'song' and the first syllable of 'bangumi', or show; TBS), 13.3 per cent;
6. *Love Love Aishiteiru* (*Love, Love, I Love you*; Fuji TV), 12.9 per cent;
7. *Futari no Big Show* (*A Pair's Big Show*; NHK), 11.5 per cent;[12]
8. *FAN* (NTV), 10.2 per cent;
9. *Music Fair '98* (Fuji TV, 1964 to present), 9.3 per cent;
10. *CDTV* (anagram for *Count Down TV*; TBS), 8.2 per cent.

Many shows focus on the singers' verbal interaction with hosts (or with each other). The number one show *The Yoru mo Hippare* (hereafter, *The Yoru*) and *Love Love Aishiteiru* are karaoke parties for stars, allowing the audience to participate in a slice of their fabricated personal lives. These shows illustrate the importance of karaoke practice in the current consumptive modes of popular music in Japan.

Entirely different in structure and emotive atmosphere from *The Yoru*, *Hey3* and *Utaban* symbolize comedic modes of popular music consumption. These two shows are hazings where the MCs deliberately unnerve the guests with joking banter. Guests who can keep up with the pace win the audience's cheers; guests who break down into tears under pressure gain shouts of sympathy from the studio audience, who then reprimand the MCs for their insensitivity. *Hey3* is notorious for not briefing its guests on the hosts' questions. During these hazing sessions, the studio audience interacts with the performers through the practice of calling out comments, similar to the shouting in kabuki performances. This symbolizes the television audience's reactive role to the televised discourse. The hosts of *Hey3*, the manzai comedy team of Matsumoto Hitoshi and Hamada Masatoshi known as Downtown (discussed by Joel Stocker in the following chapter), are the real stars of the show. Matsumoto plays the buffoon role, harassing the guests, while Hamada, the straight man, acts as mediator between the guests, the audience and his partner. During one striking scene, Matsumoto makes a member of the all-girl group, SPEED, cry on stage. The mostly female audience boos him relentlessly: Hamada joins in the condemnation and actually jumps off the stage into the audience, joining in the jeering at his partner. The topsy-turvy social interaction blurs the roles of and the boundaries between star, host, and audience.

Downtown's verbal gags are often highlighted by oversized subtitles that redundantly transmit verbal messages, emotional onomatopoeia, and contradictory subtexts in the interaction. This technique was probably inspired by the visual rhetoric of comics, and is now very common in Japanese comedy shows as well as in the music television genre. The semiotic redundancy certainly leads to reception of a preferred reading of the image and voice. Moreover, when words that infringe on the broadcasting code are mentioned (see MacLachlan's earlier chapter on news broadcasting), a beep or electric tone is inserted but the rest of the utterance is preserved. It is possible that Matsumoto consciously uses the prohibited words to show the viewers how they can transcend respectability to ridicule conservative codes. Furthermore, this practice underscores the live quality of these shows by segregating the studio audience (which can hear the entire utterance) from ordinary viewers (who only hear the annoying alarms).

Ranking has remergeed as an important function of Japanese music television.[13] Nearly all Japanese music television shows rank CD single and album sales, CD rentals, and karaoke, radio and internet requests. The paradox here is that the more a program relies on an established chart (such as Oricon), the more its line-up becomes similar to that of its rival programs. There are two ways a show can distinguish itself from other programs: by creating an original chart (although it may not reflect real sales), or by featuring 'superstar' musicians who are not necessarily represented on current charts (see Asō 1998). *Hey3* is quite meticulous about calculating these rankings; in averaging the various categories, it creates what it calls the perfect ranking. Though based on sales, some people suspect that some rankings are manufactured (because rankings from show to show in the same week may vary). Rankings also symbolize the selling of music to the audience. The rankings, which tell audiences what is 'hot', act as a tool to produce a feeling of shared taste. Hit charts directly support the consumer system, highlighting the most fundamental motive of music television.

One might argue that musical performance has declined in importance because of the flood of 'image' songs on the Japanese hit charts since the 1970s. Today, approximately 90 per cent of top ten songs are theme songs from prime-time trendy dramas (of the sort discussed by Iwabuchi earlier in the book) or commercials for a variety of products. Although only snippets of these songs are broadcast on television, their influence on the general music market is overwhelming because of high youth audience rates. Commercial songs, for all their brevity (about 30 seconds), pour out of every channel except NHK. Since the song title and the name of singer are usually credited, the commercials often look like fragmented music videos, yet are specifically referencing certain commodities. This may also explain the limited popularity of music video programs in Japan (see Hosokawa 1990). Because of the availability of visual clips in other genres, the audience expects more variety, less music and more familiarity with the human side of artists. This is seen in imperfect vocal performances. Because the sound systems and mixing equipment in many television studios are inferior to concert hall standards, bands will use recorded backings, thus faking their musical performances. However lip-syncing is no longer a widely used technique. Performance (sometimes including off-key notes) is also humanized, in contrast to the 60s expert musical and comic presentations.

Another point relevant to the discussion of music television in the nineties is problems with nomenclature. For example, *TV Pia*, a bi-weekly television magazine, doesn't list *The Yoru* as a music show, but as a variety show. Interestingly, one of the top ranked shows in general listings, SMAP x SMAP is categorized as a variety show, but music is an important element of the show's structure.[14] Despite the vitality of Yoshimoto Kōgyō described by Stocker in the next chapter, some industry commentators argue that SMAP's management office, Johnny's Entertainment, is the only agency systematically training and producing 'comedians' (*SPA* 1998:36). Increasing competition between television shows in other genres such as variety and talk shows force producers to find continually new ways to attract new audiences. Competition in any genre of Japanese television programming is fierce, and this affects the way all shows, including music shows, are produced and presented.

The MC: Creating and Controlling the Discourse

The emerging importance of talk in music television is most clearly seen in the atmosphere created by the MCs. In the 60s and 70s, MCs consisted of a dominant male supported by a female partner.[15] These MCs were trained professionals who presented a punchy, comic image to the audience. However, their expressive code was limited for they kept close to the formula of gags / skits / introduction / performance. The precise role of the MC was dependent on the presence of a studio audience (for example, the MC spoke to a live audience on *Soap Bubble Holiday* while the hostess spoke to a camera on *Yume*, partially explaining Nakajima's stiffness).

The MCs' performances on *Hit Studio at Night* by Maeda Takehiko and Yoshimura Mari marked a shift in the importance of their roles in music television shows. Both were talents, or celebrities known for their interviewing skills and familiar personages rather than for their musical or stage expertise. Maeda was especially popular among women because of his daily midday program, targeted at housewives and working women during their lunch break, called *Ohiru no Wide Show* (*Wide Show at Noon*, Fuji, 1968–1971). Both shows showed Maeda to be relatively intelligent if somewhat curious and laughable. He was certainly not as serious as other male presenters of other wide shows who were usually recruited from a pool of retired and conservative NHK newscasters. The smart conversation between Yoshimura and Maeda, complete with flattery, sarcasm and humor, unveiled their guests' 'true face', and this sustained *Hit Studio*'s popularity, until it was finally cancelled in 1990. *The Best Ten* deployed Kume Hiroshi and Kuroyanagi Tetsuko (of *Yume* fame) as MCs. Kume (currently the lead newscaster of the immensely popular evening *News Station*), was younger than his predecessors, and he interacted more sharply with Kuroyanagi's quick repartee than had Maeda with Yoshimura's frilled feminine speech. The verbal combination of Kume and Kuroyanagi matched the quick flow of the program, implying an urgency that compelled viewers not to miss even one song from the nationally acknowledged *Best Ten*. Another important function of attractive and talented MCs was that they could transcend segmented audiences; while some viewers might not enjoy a particular week's top ten choices, they could still enjoy the MCs' banter.

The informal talk style of Kume and Kuroyanagi fits with Norman Fairclough's conversationalization of public discourse, or the fragmented and sometimes incoherent exchange of phrases between two presenters. A key characteristic of this process is synthetic personalization or 'the simulation of a personal relation between a spoken or written text and an audience' (in Moores 1997:224). This synthetic personalization goes further in the 90s where we see presenters chatting with the singers, rather than 'presenting' them as such. Consequently, the flow of each program is more similar to a 'talk show' than to the classic music variety show. The living room setting of *Hey3* and the hyper-fast pace of Matsumoto's utterances speak eloquently as evidence of this change. In nearly all shows, we see MCs in more powerful positions, while their guests appear vulnerable. The MCs are at home on the television while the guests represent the 'outside' sphere of artistry.

Changes in the strategies of MCs reflect a correlation of music television with other Japanese genres such as the wide show in the 80s and comedy shows in the 90s. As the MCs come forward as spotlighted personages, they have more freedom to express their stage personalities. Their initially limited modes of expression have gradually expanded until boundaries of propriety can be broken. One may argue that the stardom of MCs such as Downtown has changed the way the public views music. For example, these shows have facilitated hard-edged rock bands' break into the mainstream music scene. Though their music is loud and aggressive, Downtown's harder-edged comedy makes them appear relatively gentle and non-threatening. However, not all shows conform to non-conformity; different shows cater to different tastes. *The Yoru* is more conservative while *Utaban* (which sometimes features harsh treatment at the hands of MC Ishibashi Takaaki, mediated by the gentler Nakai Masahiro of SMAP) spans the continuum between the more conservative and the radical.

The Yoru as Humanized Formality in a Party Environment

The Yoru consists of a cast of regulars and guests who perform the weekly top ten hits of other artists, as well as a finale which features one special guest who sings a medley of his or her own songs with current hits. This show promotes not only interpersonal interaction between stars but also utilizes the element of surprise in entertainment. This is achieved by putting together mismatched combinations of song and singer. Guests are rising stars, past idols, actors and even sports personalities who are asked to perform songs that belong to others. These performances topple set boundaries created by, for example, age and gender. A middle-aged man is greeted by squeals of surprise and joy when he sings a tune made popular by a teenage idol; women sing male songs; groups sing solo numbers. This practice allows songs to belong to anyone and to be enjoyed in any number of ways. After a performance, the artists sit in front of the camera with the MCs and the other guests to discuss their performance with typical comments such as 'I was so nervous!' and 'I really love the song, but it was hard! I made mistakes!' Despite such professions of nervousness, the MCs uniformly reassure them with phrases like 'You were great!' This feel-good interaction is an important component in the show's atmosphere and appeal.

The medley finale of *The Yoru* is a battle for control of the microphone between singers who change songs as well as genre with each verse. The audience thrills to the clever twists between songs that are connected by similar lyrics or musical styles but span several decades of musical history. This is truly staged spontaneity as the singers know what they will sing next but pretend to be shocked as another grabs the spotlight from them.

Despite this playfulness, *The Yoru* does not ignore social convention observed at functions like company get-togethers and year-end parties. Guests greet each other with polite care and all rise when a performer finishes and all sit together, much like a Japanese classroom. Older performers are treated with respect, seen through language and their interaction with younger guests. Senior artists are treated as representatives of a revered musical history to which the younger members pay homage. In this sense, *The Yoru* very much underscores traditional relationships between junior and senior members of the entertainment industry and in larger society.

The producer of *The Yoru*, Tsuchiya Yasunori, has had over twenty years' experience in the field and worked on previous hits such as *The Best Ten*. He claims that talk is what saved the music show and points out that, even during the

80s, audience ratings dropped significantly during music performances but rose during talk segments. Then, singers talked before performances. They often were too nervous to present themselves convincingly. On Tsuchiya's show, on the other hand, the performers sing first, making it easier for them to relax during their talk segment. Furthermore, the presence of a studio audience sometimes unnerved performers because they could not always anticipate its reactions. According to Tsuchiya, such uncertainty threw the timing of show, which is normally tightly scheduled because of commercial breaks. Eliminating the audience, therefore, has helped to create a more comfortable atmosphere for the stars.

Tsuchiya suggests that talk in music shows has a humanizing effect on the representation of singers because it is easier for viewers to interact emotionally and sentimentally with them while they are talking rather than when they are singing. This further underscores the slow ascent of MTV-type video programs. A musician concluded that the tendency to see video clips as a western creation (and viewing them as a western 'custom') is the origin of MTV's difficulties in breaking into the Japanese market. Japanese artists do record videos but these are not used widely on commercial television; they are sold in stores to fans. Approximately five seconds of clips are shown on television during rankings to identify individual artists while the hit chart is read. However, they do not show human interaction. Video clips merely show a finished product (the song, or the artist's image), while music television, through talk, shows the process of delivering music and imagery to the audience.

To capitalize on talk, *The Yoru* has moved towards an anxiety-reduced format. It is a closed, professional karaoke party, conscious of the camera, the clock and the studio walls. This production strategy reminds us of Goffman's metaphor of the stage and performance. The social interaction taking place in the television studio is 'molded and modified to fit into the understanding and expectations' of the audience (Goffman 1959:35). The producers create a false sense of spontaneity. The audience can peer into the stars' exclusive space, and thus satisfy an increasing interest in the backstage and unrehearsed reality.[16] The backstage world is considered more authentic, more real, and therefore more satisfying to the audience. However, on *The Yoru*, this is an accident; there is no unrehearsed reality as all are professionals who come in, do their job and leave. The unrehearsed reality thus becomes a mere creation of the audience.

In *The Yoru*, we see how television backs up karaoke practice as it provides further visual information for the consumer. One may argue that the relationship between karaoke and television viewing is so important that in some cases the two activities are fused. The karaoke atmosphere of *The Yoru* exhibits a familiarity of persons, informal (but polite and supportive) interpersonal relations, and the performance of music that is not one's own. Much in the same way as the home drama on Japanese television is said to simulate the ideal home, *The Yoru* represents the ideal karaoke box. The stars' social life becomes a social fact through the television and other cooperative media.

Making Money With Music: The Economic Structure of Music Television Shows and Viewer Habits

Broadcasting in Japan is a 'dual' system, superficially similar to the United Kingdom's public/commercial dichotomy, but the commercial networks more closely resemble US television stations, due to strong influences during the immediate postwar era.[17] Virtually all of NHK's income comes from subscription fees while the commercial networks work with fees paid by program sponsors and companies who buy commercial time. Television advertising comprises one third of the entire nation's total advertising expenditures (Gotō 1991:6); this is a higher ratio than most European countries (Dunnett 1990:170). Competition between commercial stations is quite intense as, the wider the area a network can cover, the more prestigious (and high-paying) sponsors it can attract.

Unlike commercial networks in Europe and Australia, Japan imports only three per cent of its programming, primarily from the US (Dunnett 1990:171), which means that there is a plethora of domestic competition in programming. Despite this intense fight for creativity, foreign critics disparage Japanese programming, claiming that directors and producers respond to the viewers and to the demand of the advertisers that their message reach as many viewers as possible (Dunnett 1990:172). It is also noted that generally Japanese TV shows are cheaper to produce than their US counterparts because of a smaller domestic market and limited export opportunities (although Iwabuchi's paper earlier in this book makes a strong argument for potential changes in this trend) (Dunnett 1990:174).

The domesticity of the Japanese television market parallels the situation in the recording industry. De Launey (1995:205) notes that sales of western artists in Japan are dwarfed by domestic artists: Sony's international repertoire only accounted for thirteen per cent of its total Japanese sales in 1990; in 1993, 25 per cent of MCA Victor's Japanese sales came from only ten of the label's domestic acts, while 800 or so international titles make up the remainder. The domesticity of the Japanese music industry is striking considering the worldwide success of acts such as Madonna, Michael Jackson and U2. The native-ness of both the television and music industries is a concept that influences both the production and the consumption of popular culture in Japan and the commonality of tone and atmosphere in the two industries makes for tighter bonds between them.

The amount of time the average Japanese spends in front of the television appears unclear. This is most likely due to the differing definitions of what it means to watch television: is the viewer paying close attention to the show? Or, is the viewer talking on the phone, reading, doing chores, eating, or surfing the internet while the TV is switched on? Some say that the average Japanese person watches almost four hours of television a day (Dunnett 1990:169). Merry White (1994:57) notes that watching television and time spent in front of a television might be different, finding that 64 per cent of families (and 80 per cent of senior high school students) watch TV while eating meals. Painter writes that current statistics indicate that the average household in Japan has its television set (or more often, sets) turned on for an average of between seven and eight hours per day (1996:198).[18] This would make for an attractive situation for advertisers: they have an immediate venue for reaching potential customers. And, as Moeran (1996a:242) notes, television is one of the most advantageous methods of communicating a message to an audience due to the 'combination of sight, sound, motion and colour, to viewers of virtually every age, gender and socio-economic status all over the country' – although he also points out that it is one of the most expensive forms of advertising.

Current music television shows are aimed at a youth audience. A recent study found that 48.4 per cent of all elementary students questioned watched music television shows. 37.1 per cent of junior high school students, 32.4 per cent of senior high school students and 50 per cent of university students counted themselves as music television audience members (Inamasu 1995:93). Because of this specialized audience, there are links between certain industries and music shows. It seems obvious that record companies would advertise during these shows. Commercials for new singles and albums flood music television shows, but few take on sponsor status. *Hey3* is the only contemporary show which has attracted record companies as sponsors; the producer of *The Yoru* claimed that the relationship was 'just too close'. *Yume*, broadcast on NHK, was free from advertising though *Soap Bubble Holiday* was very much influenced by its sponsor, 'Milky Soap'. Commercials for *Soap Bubble Holiday* were sometimes incorporated into the show as the regulars read scripted lines for the commercial breaks, blurring the lines between show and commercial.[19] Today's shows seek and gain sponsors that target their products towards a young, primarily female market.[20] The sponsors' idealized audience also consumes a great deal of junk food and buys electronic goods. This contrasts with the wholesome, family images of sponsors in the 60s.

A production assistant explained the relationship between the station, the producers and the various companies, which were divided into two categories: those featured as sponsors (who enjoyed 'time advertising') and those who paid for discrete commercial time ('spot advertising') (Moeran 1996a:243). Her show is 100 per cent financed by sponsorship fees. High ratings allow the station to negotiate favorable conditions when contracting sponsors. The management (*eigyō*) section usually handles negotiations with the sponsors, but at times a producer will play a personal role – especially when s/he goes to discuss new plans for program development with sponsoring executives.

However, sponsors have no power over producers' creative activities. Producers do worry about showing competing products' commercials during one program, and are careful about not damaging a company's image by placing a commercial right after a scene which denigrates the product it advertises (showing a car crash before a commercial for automobiles, for example). Sponsors are companies that buy the show and its image while commercial spots are considered contracted time sold individually; record companies tend to avoid sponsorship of music shows because they feel that short, sharp and frequent spots during music shows are more effective than the labeling of sponsorship.

As one can see from the list of sponsors of current music television (see endnote 11), company names appear more than once: McDonalds and Ōtsuka Seiyaku sponsored two of the top shows, supporting Moeran's claim (1996a:236) that Japanese television attracts a great deal of money from a relatively small number of advertisers. Again, though the company names differed, the products advertised fell within relatively narrow categories: foods and drinks, pharmaceuticals, and cosmetics and toiletries (Moeran 1996a:236). Moeran went on to analyze sponsors as those who take on sponsorship to 'improve a company's *corporate image*, whereas spot advertising tells people ... about its *products*' (1996a:243, emphasis in original). Taken the fact that record companies tend to use the spot advertising technique, we can surmise that commercials for CD singles and albums are not really about the artists' *image* but the *product*. Thus the Japanese music variety show becomes a separate and important venue for creating and maintaining artist images in the public sphere.

Shifts in viewing habits have affected the meaning and the function of music television. *Soap Bubble Holiday, Yume* and other 60s and 70s shows were created for family viewing and were broadcast at dinner time. This sense of family increased ordinary appeal but viewing was shared with others. It was structured family time entailing sometimes hierarchical relationships. Like an ideal dinner conversation, the shows in the 60s and 70s were humorous but kept with social convention. Skits were cheeky but appealed to an intergenerational sense of humor. Young rising stars were presented in such a manner that older members of the family might find them appealing. Though music shows catered to current trends, the shows' concepts were timeless: song, dance, simple costumes and sets, light comedy and professional show biz *à la* Ed Sullivan.

80s shows were shown during prime time, geared mainly towards teenagers not only as audience but also as performers. Costumes, sets and special effects were a large part of the total presentation. Much in line with Inamasu's the-faker-the-better reasoning, dress symbolized the idol more eloquently than did the music. Matsuda Seiko and the female duo Wink appeared wearing elaborate, wedding-cake style outfits complete with gloves, hats, boots and other accessories that emphasized their fabricated status as celebrities. Interestingly, this glamour was not an elite fashion statement that might distance the stars from real life. Rather, it was kitsch, tacky and even a bit sleazy. Cheap gorgeousness, typified by polyester lace and brightly colored plastic accessories, brought the female celebrity close to home. This closeness is reiterated by the current popular female duo, Puffy, whose natural-ness in fashion is contrived yet familiar to many Japanese young women who live in T-shirts and jeans.

Today, women in their thirties remember 80s music shows as a complete visual, audio and social experience. Though they might not have wholly emulated the frilled feminine look on television, discussing the music, costumes and styles presented on television with friends the next day at school was an important part of creating and maintaining friendships. These shows thus provided the fodder for adolescent human contact, seen at night but re-lived in verbal exchanges the following day.

Current shows are mainly shown after 9 or 10 p.m. This also means that the programs are not intended to act as bridges between generations, but are targeted specifically at segmented audiences. Consumers feel jaded in a glutted market; thus programs need an element of surprise. Catching a star off guard is more hilarious than a carefully produced skit. Surprise shortens the distance between viewer and viewed.

'The Imitation of Life': Omnipresent Celebrity-hood and Humanization

What makes celebrities *célèbres* is the widely shared knowledge and belief that everyone knows them. The celebrity has no other public identity than the one seen on television, the most diffused audio-visual technology in Japan. A celebrity's specific attributes will vary, but inarguably the mass media are one of the most decisive forces creating and sustaining the existence of all celebrities. Jimmie L. Reeves (1988:149) describes the celebrity as a commodity which 'contributes to the production, maintenance, repair and transformation of social reality by animating a ritual of social typification and individualization'.[21] The celebrity lifestyle, though distant from the everyday life of consumers, touches the public in intimate ways in the way it influences their perception of the world around them.

Before the advent of television, Japanese music stars had a much narrower vocabulary with which to express social values. Television has helped to expand this vocabulary not only by including visual elements in music consumption, but also by incorporating other media genres (talk shows and comic book text, for example) to further expand the typification process. The changing boundaries in music television programming allow celebrities flexibility in creating and delivering these identities to the public. Producers facilitate this process by creating show formats that give celebrities the space to develop and sell their personalities.

To win ratings, television producers need new strategies to attract audiences. In moving the spatial and ideological boundaries that television programs and television stars occupy, music television producers have been able to present a format that appeared human, familiar, and informal. However, this change has not occured in a vacuum. Other genres such as straight variety and talk shows have also been affected by programming strategies. Common to all genres are changes in the definition of celebrity, which is juxtaposed with the spaces and boundaries between the daily life of the viewer and the viewer's relationship to the 'celebrity' as mediated by television programs. Bourdieu (1993a:45) writes that:

Adjustment to demand is not the product of a conscious arrangement between producers and consumers. It results from the correspondence between the space of producers, and therefore of the products offered, and the space of the consumers ... In other words, obeying the logic of the object competition between mutually exclusive positions ... the various categories of producers tend to supply products adjusted to the expectations of the various positions in the field of power, but without any conscious striving for such adjustment.

In a sense, this speaks to the power, albeit limited, of the consumers; they do not blindly consume shows produced by showbiz elites.

Why do music stars utilize television as opposed to other methods of media transmission to support their audio careers? Television is the most coercive form of media in Japan. Programming is overwhelmingly domestic (in both senses of the word: it is home grown and is consumed in the home). Television is thus humanized, and is no longer 'larger than life' (this is in comparison to film, which continues to attract audiences using large screen action and effects). Images projected on the television screen are presented in the home on a smaller scale, and this designates the reality of television celebrity-hood in the sphere of closeness, humanism and familiarity. Music magazines and radio are still viable media, but television reaches a wider audience and has a long history of cooperation with the music industry.[22] The links are already there; they are molded and guided to present a product that is familiar to an audience.

The more stars expose their pseudo-private lives on television, the more they imitate the lives of the anonymous audience – traveling, cooking, chatting, weeping, laughing, mourning, and singing. The audience intrudes on their privacy just as much as stars invade the private lives and domestic space of the audience. According to sociologist Ishida Saeko, Japanese celebrities form an immense body of information constructed and magnified by the media (Ishida 1992:263). Stars are characterized by the constant consciousness of being seen, by the gaze of a mediatic Other (= public), by the public-ization of private life and by an eagerness to control one's self-image (Ishida 1992:267). The talent book is just such an example of the celebrities controlling and authorizing their self image. Audiences are, by contrast, characterized by a constant desire to watch the object of a mediatic Other (in other words, celebrity), by the privatization of 'public-ized life', and by an eagerness to control their own self-image in their own processes of socialization.

What does this say about celebrity-hood in the sphere of music? Today's television shows present stars who are amiable, with occasional faults. The imagined distance between audience and star determines the latter's relationship with the public. The audience wants not only to adorn and celebrate but also to mock the star, further domesticating celebrity identity. Even if we consider stars to be ordinary, they merit our attention through extraordinary emotion, as illustrated in the frequent crying sequences in *Hey3*. The public and personal tragedy of the SPEED member in one particular episode caused the audience to sympathize with her, as well as drawing jeers and laughter at the hosts. Personal experience is transformed into tragicomedy. The show demonstrates psychological methods to deal with setbacks: sympathy, blame and, finally, laughter. These contain and disperse uncomfortable feelings both on stage and in the studio audience.

Tsuchiya says that popular music in Japan used to be everybody's music: in other words, popular music was more or less unified so that the audience was familiar with the field. Thanks to the near-daily prime time broadcast of shows in the past, the general public was well-versed in the discussion of artists, musical trends and professional practice. However, today's plethora of artists, bands, movements and fashions in Japanese popular music is staggering, and audiences need more information in order to be able to act as discriminating consumers. Talk is one measure by which fans can discriminate between artists, so that their consumption of music is ordered and contained – again domesticating the star as a commodity to be bought and sold.

Although the criteria for musicianship in Japan are malleable, music professionals and audiences alike bemoan the current state of Japanese popular music: 'real talent' such as that of Yamaguchi Momoe is gone; today's stars have looks but less than perfect pitch. Tsuchiya notes that the definition of singer has changed: no longer is it a matter of music. Now it is an expression of character. During a March broadcast of *Utaban*, viewers witnessed host Nakai Masahiro, the leader of an idol group with dozens of number one hit singles and the winning team captain of the *Red and White Contest*, barely able to carry a tune when asked to sing a cappella with his guests. Yet he was voted the number one celebrity in Japan (with a combined audience rating of 84.8 per cent for his nine regular music, variety, talk, news and other genre shows [*Nikkei Entertainment* 1998b:59]). Because he is an intimate part of many people's daily lives, he is so close and yet so far – a 'star'. Popular music becomes a tool to achieve celebrity, and television is an effective and an affective technology to deliver it.

Although talk is becoming more and more important to the Japanese music show, the celebrity's status as a singer should not be completely dismissed. Singing is one of the most emotionally-charged, bodily-haunting human acts. It accentuates the materiality (or 'grain') of the voice by an aesthetic articulation of sound produced more expressively than other methods of utterance, such as speaking. If talk conveys the personality of the stars, singing transmits their bodies. Simon Frith notes that popular music:

> Provides us with intensely subjective sense of being sociable ... It both articulates and offers immediate *experience* of collective identity.
>
> (Frith 1996:271, emphasis in original)

In the Japanese construction of celebrity, music is constitutive of a star's fictive personality and is a centripetal force in a multifaceted popular culture.

Notes

1 The authors would like to express their gratitude to The University of Melbourne's International Exchange Agreements Collaborative Research Awards Programme, and to Brian Moeran and Lise Skov of *ConsumAsiaN*. They also thank Igarashi Tadashi, Iwabuchi Kōichi, Omodaka Naoko, Seki Yoshibumi, Shibata Kaoru, Takamizawa Toshihiko and Tsuchiya Yasunori for sharing their industry insights.

The following video references were used for this chapter:

- **Collections**: NHK Videography *Yume de Aimashō* (five volumes), 1991, Take Shobō; *Crazy Cats Memorial* (four volumes), 1995, Toshiba EMI, BVS 357; *Sakamoto Kyū Shichiji de Aima-Show TBS*, 1995, Toshiba EMI, TOVF–1229; *Welcome Back The Peanuts – 20 Years On*, n.d., King Video.
- **Weekly Broadcasts**: CDTV (TBS); Enka no Hanamichi (TV Tokyo); FAN (NTV); Futari no Biggu Show (NHK); Hey! Hey! Hey! Music Champ (Fuji); Love Love Aishiteiru (Fuji); Music Fair '98 (Fuji); Music Hammer (Fuji); Music Station (Asahi); Pop Jam (NHK); SMAP x SMAP (Fuji); Sokuhō! Uta no daiji-ten (NTV); The Yoru mo Hippare (NTV); Utaban (TBS).

In addition, the following reference materials were used for dating shows: Iyoda Yasuhiro et al. 1996 *Terebishi Handobukku* (*A Handbook of Television History*), Tokyo: Jiyū Kokuminsha.

2 Our argument employs historical text analysis. Shows were viewed on videotape, while some were viewed in 'real time' or were based on recollections of the authors' experiences and those of industry experts (see Gobuichi 1995). Interviews with producers, their assistants, a music writer and a musician also helped to illuminate the process of delivering these programs to the public.

3 Japanese newspapers are published twice a day and the television schedule is the only section that appears in both editions, showing the importance of evening television viewing in Japanese family life.

4 MTV or pay-for-TV stations that broadcast music videos produced by the artist's recording company, constitute a separate category of music television which is not included in our definition. Another category is theme songs for made-for-TV dramas and television commercials, but these are of different performance quality and should be considered separately. Narato (1995:85–6) makes the argument that the decline of music shows led to the necessary proliferation of theme song tie-ups with commercials and television shows.

Enka, a genre of Japanese popular music, is another visible element in Japanese music television, but lies outside our definition of music variety shows for several reasons. Firstly, *enka* singers are trained vocalists who take pride in exemplary musical performance. They do not need to project their personality to sell CDs; they sell their musicianship. Secondly, the narrative of *enka* does not fit the mode of instant consumption that is easily communicated through television. Rarely do *enka* songs deal with topics such as love in an abstract sense, making it difficult to communicate messages in short sound bites.

5 Another *Yume* regular, E. H. Eric, played the strange foreigner role in skits (half Japanese, half French, he most likely had a high level of cultural literacy in real life). Eric's bumblings as the tall, awkward foreigner underscored the still important communicative and cultural gaps between the Japanese and the US Occupation forces (who had left in 1952 but whose presence was still strongly felt at bases scattered throughout the country). One of the more striking scenes from a 1962 show shows a guest and Kuroyanagi Tetsuko playing with toy models of US tanks, showing that Japanese were still conscious of war and its symbols in their land. These messages

probably resonated with the elder viewers, while the younger viewers focused on music.

6 She is still one of the best known figures in contemporary Japanese television, due to her long-running daily talk show, *Tetsuko's Room*.

7 The annual *Red and White Contest* is similar in construct, utilizing the grandness of the NHK Hall stage.

8 For more on *Star Tanjō*, see Aku Yū (1993, 1997).

9 This category refers to a wave of popular rock bands that vary in musical style but all capitalize on heavy make-up, elaborate costumes and hairstyles, and varying degrees of transgendered identification. Some critics see visual bands as an outcome of a rich Japanese theatrical tradition such as kabuki and *Takarazuka*; others place the phenomenon more closely to western glam acts such as David Bowie and KISS. Early visual bands include X (later, X-JAPAN), while more contemporary examples include Sharan Q, Shazna, Luna Sea, Glay and Penicillin. Sharan Q and Shazna offer a more mainstream pop sound, but other visual bands may categorized as hard rock or heavy metal. The mainstreaming of rock on music television is a process by which visual and audio images are supplemented by personal talk, which is then transformed into emphasized, viewable images through subtitled utterances. Talk deconstructs the images presented on stage (which are aggressive, over-the-top and loud) and presents a sociable persona more in line with traditional Japanese celebrity-hood, allowing the hard rock star to gain mainstream fame.

10 Igarashi Tadashi, personal communication, June 1998.

11 However, the number one music television show dropped to number eighteen when ranked against other variety and drama programs (figures drawn from the Kantō area; *Nikkei Entertainment* 1998a:46).

12 *Futari no Big Show* (NHK) is one of the few current shows that concentrates on musical performance. It features two veteran singers who sing and interact (without MCs). Another is *Enka no Hanamichi* (*Gorgeous Road of Enka*, TBS, 1978-present), a half-hour program where two *enka* singers perform in a studio setting (without MCs) that reflects the nostalgic atmosphere of the songs.

13 This is not a new component, as early shows such as *The Best Ten*, *Kayōkyoku Best Ten* (*Best Ten Songs*, TBS, 1965) and *Yoru no Hit Studio* (*Hit Studio at Night*, Fuji, 1968–1990) introduced a countdown section, foreshadowing the 80s and 90s shows with rankings.

14 Johnny's Entertainment, which manages male idol acts such as Shōnentai, SMAP, Tokio and V6, produces many weekly shows, ranging from after school to prime time slots. These focus on male idol performances but also incorporate talk show, variety, sports and even cooking show elements.

15 Early MCs included *Hoi Hoi*'s Suzuki Yasushi (the buffoon) and Kinomi Nana (a straight woman), two young singers. *Soap Bubble* was emceed by the all-male band the Crazy Cats (fronted by Ueki Hitoshi) and the female twin duo, the Peanuts.

16 This can also be seen in other genres in the plethora of NG (no good) special programs or scenes shown after the broadcast show.

17 Cable television plays a smaller part in the overall broadcasting scene; originally instigated to compensate for poor reception in mountainous areas, commercial cable systems are slowly infiltrating the consumer landscape. This unfamiliarity with the technology may in part explain the difficulty MTV has in permeating the field.

18 For his part, Moeran (1996a:241) writes that the average number of hours spent watching television in Japan is only 8.5 hours per week. The differences in calculations are most probably due to the flexible definition noted here of what 'watching' television means.

19 For the most part, commercials today are separate visual entities from the show, although shows like *Love Love Aishiteiru* tend to blur this line by exclusively showing commercials that feature the two of the show's MCs.

20 *Hey3* sponsors in early 1998 were Unicharm (feminine products), Toys Factory (a domestic record company) Toshiba EMI, Sony Music Entertainment, McDonalds, Sega, Nike, Pokka (soft drinks and snacks), Otsuka Seiyaku (sports drinks such as Pocari Sweat), Morinaga Seika (snacks and soft drinks) and Calpis (soft drinks). *Utaban* sponsors were Lion (health and beauty aids), Edwin (a jeans maker) and Glico (candy and snacks). Sponsors for *The Yoru* were Shiseido (cosmetics), Lawson (a convenience store) Kirin (soft drinks and beer), Lotte (a candy and snack company), Ōtsuka Seiyaku, JACCS (credit card) Honda and Nestle. *Love Love* is wholly sponsored by Panasonic, which features commercials starring the show's youthful hosts. Sponsors for *Music Station* included P&G, Santen Seiyaku (eye drops), Kinchō (insect repellent), McDonalds, Kobayashi Seiyaku (personal and household sanitary goods), DDI Pocket (pagers), UC Card (credit), Coca Cola, Calbee (snacks).

21 Social typification serves to 'define and maintain "appropriate modes"' of social participation, reconciling the tension between individualism and conformity (Reeves 1988:150).

22 The print media's role should not be underestimated in this discussion. Photo albums and 'talent books' demonstrate the extent of celebrity overexposure in Japan. Using colloquial language, singers write about their semi-private lives and the secrets of their success, as well as their own interpretations of life, love, family and other basic social values (80s idol Go Hiromi, Downtown's Matsumoto Hitoshi and Luna Sea's vocalist Kawamura Ryūichi are some recent best-selling authors). Usually, the content of talent books is not as important as the name of the author (despite the fact they are often ghost-written by others 'the faker the better' mentality at work). This is contrasted with the unofficial biography so popular in the US and UK where the text, written by a third party, makes books sell.

11

YOSHIMOTO KŌGYŌ AND MANZAI IN JAPAN'S MEDIA CULTURE

Promoting the Intersection of Production and Consumption

Joel F. Stocker

In this chapter, I will analyze the relationship between corporate media production and consumption in urban Japanese media culture by discussing the case of a large Japanese media production company and its school for media entertainers, in the context of the popularity of the company's local form of comedy. Run by Yoshimoto Kōgyō, Ltd. (Yoshimoto), the Osaka 'New Star Creation' (NSC) entertainment school acts as a dynamic site where corporate comedy production plans and comedy fans' consumption practices coincide.[1] This specific case illustrates a general trend: across the globe, corporate media producers increasingly promote audience participation in various aspects of the production, circulation, and promotion of cultural goods and services in diverse local settings, and consumers increasingly seek out this complex participatory relationship in cultural production for their own ends, if not entirely by their own means. To put it another way, production and consumption are mutually determined, and promotion serves to strengthen this association.

By presenting this perspective, first of all, I intend to dispute the tendency in media research to center on consumption practices, largely in western societies, while presenting corporate production either in terms of abstract social formations that menace democracy and local individual autonomy, or as little more than a distant backdrop to commercial products which are taken up as a resource in sundry ways by meaning-producing consumer audiences. Swanson points out, for instance, that revisionists have reworked critical theorists' strong conception of media dominance into one focusing on the audience as an 'active producer of meaning', with the following result: 'connections have been attenuated between the political economy of mass media, the production of media content, and audiences' interpretation, consumption, and use of content' (Swanson 1996:54). Although researchers have touched upon the importance of the connections between media production, consumption, and circulation (for example, Hall 1980:128; Baudrillard 1983; Ang 1990:240), few have focused on the nature of the connections between these different aspects of the media at the local, detailed, everyday level. Furthermore, as has been noted in the

Introduction to this book, the relative lack of participation in media research to date by anthropologists (since Powdermaker's [1950] early anthropological study of Hollywood film studios), in particular, is quite odd since, on the one hand, ethnographic methods have been employed in disciplines that do focus more on the mass media; and, on the other, anthropology has a tradition of employing interdisciplinary perspectives (cf. Spitulnik 1993; Abu-Lughod 1997).

A second aim of this essay is to apply the above perspective to the recently popular topic in Japanese studies of Japanese cultural diversity. In a discussion of Osaka cultural localism, I will link this issue of 'diversity' to the Japanese media industry, as well as to the everyday cultural practices of the Japanese as media consumers. Japanese media processes play a very significant role in the cultural production of forces of both heterogeneity and homogeneity in Japanese culture. Furthermore, media production practices and everyday consumer practices themselves are diverse and complex. That is, they are ambiguously defined, negotiated, and enacted in forms usually consistent with companies' talent and consumer development, profit-making, and branding goals, but also with media audiences' eagerness to participate in corporate production and in social arenas not directly related to the consumption or reception of traditional media products such as television programs. Moreover, many of the *processes* of mediation involved in producing, marketing, and consuming culturally unique professional comedians and corporate comedy, for instance, appear to be similar to those that take place in other parts of the world. In other words, Japanese culture is not only not homogeneous; the cultural production of Japanese diversity, even if locally distinct, is similar, and likely to be tied, to cultural processes and changes occurring elsewhere – many of them, furthermore, substantially mass-mediated and thus a part of a 'media culture'. One thing at stake here is whether or not Japanese cultural diversity is actually differentiation within a media culture that elides the non-marketable (that is, socially, culturally sensitive) aspects of social groupings through incorporation or expropriation. But, again, this question of whether the mass and popular media are liberating or oppressive is difficult to understand in the binary terms of media-versus-consumers or audiences and, either way, usually appears merely to establish the observing scholar as hero (of the common people or of intellectualism). Nevertheless, diverse individual, group, and institutional identities and relations are increasingly negotiated in sites located between cultural production by the corporate media and cultural production by the people who live and consume in simultaneously mass- and micro-mediated social worlds.

Thirdly, I will demonstrate some ways in which this ambiguity in media production and consumption practices takes shape. For example, what a media company may consider to be part of a consumption sphere it has produced may be viewed by consumers to be part of that company's production sphere in which the fan can become a star or insider. Either way, both positions construct new and distinctive cultural spheres for corporate marketing and audience pleasure, as well, to be gained through imaginative enterprise and entertainment. Yoshimoto's New Star Creation in second-city Osaka is in such a dual position. As we will see, the circumstances of Yoshimoto and its Osaka entertainment school, students, and comedy fans, illustrate important aspects of Osaka's struggle to produce and market local goods and services, and of Japanese young people's search for alternative types of consumption as well as self-expression.

Media Entertainment: Promoting the Local, Selling it Nationally

In Japan, 'Yoshimoto' is synonymous with lowbrow, popular, mass-mediated, second-city 'comedy' and commercial, not 'cultural', second-city 'Osaka'. One explanation for Yoshimoto's Osaka entertainment school's relative success is that Osaka is a city where media producers – production companies, talent agencies, local television stations, and so on – are known to cultivate and cater to the desire among many locals to perform in public, especially through the mass media. Neither of these tendencies or reputations had to come first: Osaka as an entertainer-training ground, or the penchant for Osakans to perform and become public entertainers. Rather, both seem to issue from the ongoing and dynamic production and consumption relations in the second city of Osaka which add a certain kind of diversity to Japanese culture. In this regional media culture in which the lives of Kansai people are greatly embedded, many people and institutions significantly distinguish themselves by playing on the fact that Osaka and the Kansai region overall are *not* Tokyo and the Kanto region; that is, not the central source of Japanese cultural authority and political economic power, but a region of people (many not 'natives') and institutions able to grasp on to and successfully sell alternatives to 'standard' Japanese culture. The tenacious pride of Hanshin Tigers fans is one example of how active consumers can be in making products of the entertainment industry – baseball – into an expression of local difference – in particular, in opposition to the Tokyo Giants and the Kanto region.

This brings us back to the subject of Osaka's comedy entertainment, which has become a key and highly visible, contradictory means for giving humorous, reflexive voice to Osaka's second-class, second-city status. Osaka and the Kansai region are not unique in doing battle with the overwhelming central power of urban Tokyo and in having to deal with a stagnant regional economy that resorts to strategies of cultural promotion to bolster tourism and other forms of entertainment in the face of few other avenues tending to political economic strength and independence. Osaka and Kansai localism is indicative of the circumstances surrounding the promotion of regional differences throughout Japan. This sort of intranational cultural particularism also serves as a handy tool at the international level for Japanese leaders who, for example, attempt to deflect the cultural universalism of American leaders asking the world to follow the supposedly universal principles of American democracy, capitalism, and militarism. Mass media provide means of expression that utilize currencies of particularism, localism, universalism, and so forth. Osaka, as the media center of the Kansai region and number-two media power in Japan, works at going up against and conforming to Tokyo as no other regional culture can within Japanese media culture. Yet, Osaka's media entertainment exposure appears to have another side to it, mainly represented by Tokyo-led popular opinion of second-city Osaka, much but not all of it negative. The view that Osakans (or Kansai-area people) are natural born comic entertainers has become a common one in Japan, especially, in my experience, among people from the Tokyo area. And this view is frequently recited as the reason why, firstly, so many Osaka-area people are television entertainers; secondly, even Osakans overheard on a street corner sound like comedians doing a routine; and thirdly, Osakans are often obnoxious or intrusive, which rubs 'us' the wrong way. In many respects, this sort of mutually constructed regional antagonism – and, at times, admiration – forms a politically safe and socially entertaining set of ostensible cultural differences that generate senses of Japanese 'diversity' while potentially significantly eliding discourse on the deeper social divisions within Japan. Therefore, for instance, Japanese comedians commonly deal with differences in age, sex, gender, region, and Japaneseness (in relation to other countries' peoples), but very rarely bring up the topic of ethnic or class differences within Japan, even though many entertainers are from working or lower class backgrounds and quite a few are rumored to be Korean Japanese (the issue, as noted in an earlier chapter by Liz MacLachlan, is not ordinarily discussed in public). Through books, newspapers, television, radio, and other media, academics may also popularize regional cultural differences without problematizing the manner and means of the construction of those differences. This practice can be seen in ethnologist Michitarō Tada's celebration of Osaka as an original site of Japanese diversity, openness, and creativity. Historically, Osaka 'was the place where various native elements *as well as* cultural influences from overseas merged and combined to form a unique, new, hybrid culture' (Tada 1988:40, original emphasis).[2] In recent years there has been somewhat of an Osaka culture 'boom' among young Tokyoites who enjoy Osaka-produced Yoshimoto comedians on television and theater stages, show an interest in certain aspects of Osakan culture, its dialect, and cityscape, and, in some cases, travel (along with others from all over Japan) to Osaka to study at the Osaka NSC.

About the time the Kansai region began to sink into an ongoing industrial decline in the 70s, the fortunes of Yoshimoto began to improve as its comedians became salable commodities on Japanese television – a national phenomenon that in its growth became, not surprisingly, more localized. On the one hand, Kansai leaders have in the same period heightened their efforts to promote Kansai and Osaka tourist sites (one of which is Yoshimoto's local Namba Grand Kagetsu theater). On the other hand, in a nod to Tokyo's financial and representational power, local Osakan entertainers still must eventually make the move to the Tokyo media industry in order to become truly national stars, even while Yoshimoto remains headquartered in Osaka, and despite its status as Japan's largest production company. The business community in Tokyo where media power is concentrated has received the company rather coolly. Yoshimoto became successful nationally in the 80s and 90s, but has had to struggle to market itself because it is a second-city business with a fairly localized product in a very expansive, globalizing industry. In addition to the factor of the defiant pride in Osakan culture seen locally, often joined to a sense of irony about the contradictory views surrounding it, the appearance of Yoshimoto comedians on national broadcasts and the interest shown by Japanese youth (including Kansai-area suburbanites) in Osakan culture as an 'exotic other' have been key to the development of a Yoshimoto-brand comedy and comedy entertainment school.

The expansion of mediated localization

Yoshimoto Sei and Kichibē, the founders of Yoshimoto in 1912, had acquired what people at the time referred to as an 'entertainment kingdom' (engei ōkoku) of variety halls in urban Japan after less than a decade in show business. This blue-chip company has been a dominant presence in comedy entertainment in Japan ever since, with branch offices in Tokyo, Sapporo, Fukuoka, and Nagoya and over 200 salaried employees. Yoshimoto specializes in rakugo comic storytelling, shinkigeki comedy theater, and manzai fool-wit comedy acts.

Arjun Appadurai in Modernity at Large (1996) argues that 'production fetishism' (replacing Marxian commodity fetishism) paints transnational relations of production as locally occurring relations. In the case of Japanese manzai, the local corporate production of this genre was fetishized nationally as it became established – mainly by Yoshimoto – through mediatization between the 1930s and 90s. This process linked it locally to Osaka and prompted the everyday practice of manzai-like humor by the local people at the same time that images of Osaka and Yoshimoto manzai were transmitted nationally, and even abroad (to entertain Japanese military troops and, back home, to transmit news from the nation's colonies and war-fronts) (Akita 1984; Yoshimoto Kōgyō 1992; Sawada 1994). Yoshimoto-brand comedy has been strongly localized by Yoshimoto and its entertainers, as well as by the Japanese media industry in general, in part through the utilization and elaboration of stereotypes of Osakans as fast-talking, dialect-speaking, downtown-rooted merchant and yakuza gangster characters who possess a vulgar sense of humor embedded in everyday topics (see Kuroda 1991, 1994), as popularly portrayed in manzai fool (boke) and wit (tsukkomi) comedy roles. Although Yoshimoto is (still) trying to shed its image as a production company that built its entertainment kingdom with yakuza muscle, its executives themselves, long notorious for being ruthless tightwads, utilize the above stereotypes to promote the company's overall image by, for instance, portraying their business style of crassly focusing on making money, not art, into a seemingly light-hearted, joking characteristic of

251

'Yoshimoto'. This fact reinforces the company's brand image as a central representative of Osaka, which has long been known as the 'capital of money', where people use '*Mōkarimakka*?' (Profiting?) as a daily greeting. The name for early industrial Osaka was 'the capital of smoke', but, largely due to Yoshimoto which has as one of its playful mottos, *shōbai wa shōbai* (our business is selling laughs, or, it pays to sell laughs), Osaka has become known as the 'comedy capital' (*shōto*).

Moreover, as seen above, the company itself has been developed as a character, something imaged as an animate being thoroughly Osakan. For instance, during the opening of Yoshimoto's Ginza 7-Chōme Theater in 1995 in Tokyo, the billboard outside the theater advertising Yoshimoto's arrival in the heart of downtown Tokyo depicted a round-headed old man sporting a wide, sly grin exposing his lone two front teeth and vocal chords. Hands outstretched, grasping a mini Tokyo Tower in both hands between his legs, he sat on his knees like a child, playing with the captured tower. The sign read: 'Really, I like Tokyo' (*Hontō wa Tokyo, suki nan desu wa*). The regional differences, antagonism and competition Yoshimoto and its characters had employed for years were hinted at in this phrase, a mixture of Tokyo (*hontō*) and Osaka dialects (*nan desu wa*). Moreover, in the visage of a venerable (centuries' old Osakan merchant culture) yet childish (Osakan comedy) man who with a big grin had placed Tokyo's city symbol, Tokyo Tower, provocatively in his hands, the billboard further suggested the Osakan company's venerable yet playful status as a comedy company.

In my interviews with Osaka-born Yoshimoto employees, I found that, without exception, they portrayed themselves as people who possess unique 'Osakan' qualities that they also find in Yoshimoto as a company, as well as in many of its performance characters. In an interview with the Los Angeles Times, Yoshimoto spokesperson Noyama at the time described the shinkigeki comedy theater actors in this way: 'Yoshimoto characters are talkative and overly kind, to the point of butting into other people's business ... They speak frankly and are easily seduced by money' (Holley 1995). According to one of Yoshimoto's top executives who himself has written a book about the special human characteristics (that is, the Osakan-ness) of the company, the production company ultimately would like to make all of Japan into Yoshimoto (Kimura 1995). Toward this end, Yoshimoto has developed in-house and co-operated (with television stations), multi-media production and distribution capabilities in downtown Osaka and Tokyo, and places in which imagined local space and history can reveal themselves in the form of, for example, entertainment schools, a pop culture museum that acts more like an amusement center (within larger entertainment districts), Yoshimoto goods shops, and export abroad of the form of its cultural productions. It has also taken part in promotional campaigns surrounding most of the key events and development projects sponsored by the Kansai economic block. Disney, Inc., on a smaller scale at the moment, is Yoshimoto's executives' ideal.

Yoshimoto Manzai

How did manzai comedy in particular become strongly associated with Osaka and Yoshimoto? And why has it been so popular in Japan in the last two decades, to the point of becoming the primary subject at two Yoshimoto entertainment schools with altogether 500 to 900 annual attendees in the last few years?

Manzai to a great extent has been formed, consolidated, and expanded by Yoshimoto since the early 30s via live stage and the mass media. The Yoshimoto brand of manzai derives from a little-understood confluence of older performance genres (for example, blessing-ritual manzai, improvisational *niwaka kyōgen*, *Mikawa* manzai, and *ondo* singing) that by the late nineteenth century had become the most variegated vaudeville genre in urban Japan (see Mita 1993; Bensky 1998). Since the late 20s, when manzai surpassed rakugo story telling as the number-one theater act in Osaka, manzai comedians have formed the cornerstone of Yoshimoto's entertainment corps. To be precise, what is now popularly known as manzai broke from the motley manzai of the early vaudeville years in 1930 when the comedy duo Yokoyama Entatsu and Hanabishi Achako, working for Yoshimoto, shed the old-fashioned-appearing variety show manzai of the day by putting on western suits and distilling manzai into a dialogue-based form of stand-up comedy, involving a fool and wit whose comical dialogue revolves around contemporary events and life styles. Manzai became similar to the dialogue- and slapstick-oriented double acts of American vaudeville and film performance styles of the first half of the twentieth century (similar, as well, to comedy acts found in Britain in the same period).[3] Finding success through this type of manzai during the 30s, an earlier period when aspects of Osakan culture were relatively popular in Tokyo (Horie 1994:127), Yoshimoto utilized its network of theaters, as well as radio and film appearances by its entertainers, to build the company and to transform manzai into a nationally recognized, mass-mediated Yoshimoto brand of comedy.

A key turn in the post-World War II fortunes of manzai occurred in 1970 when over 64 million people visited Osaka for the Osaka Expo. People from all over Japan flooded Osaka-area vaudeville theaters and millions of tourists gained a familiarity with manzai as a 'unique' regional popular art. Although many vaudeville theaters closed down in the years following Expo 70 (Inoue 1992), Osakan television and radio companies established a number of manzai and rakugo comedy competitions from the mid-60s to the early 80s that helped to strengthen the presence of comedians in the mass media. In this way, the local media entertainment industry took an important step towards promoting manzai and rakugo in the media, working in their genres and as all-purpose entertainers. Furthermore, the creation of formal competitions offered a more presentable, less low-brow image of Osakan comedy and helped to promote Osaka as a 'unique' (that is, marketable) local culture coinciding with the Osakan business community's preparations for infrastructural developments (for example, the Kansai International Airport) and celebrity tie-ins (such as advertisements on projects featuring Yoshimoto entertainers) from the early 70s to the present day.

Although there have been several manzai 'booms' since the first recognized boom of the early 30s, the popularity of manzai team comedy did not significantly rise again until the early 80s, when the conditions surrounding the production and consumption of manzai changed most dramatically. Manzai entertainers approached the status of pop-culture idols through stage-based television appearances due to the creation of a number of shows, such as Fuji TV's pioneering *The Manzai* which broadcast the stage routines of manzai performers.[4] Most of these comedy duos had gained experience in Yoshimoto's theaters in Osaka, while a few were from the cabarets and variety halls of the red-light district of Asakusa in Tokyo. As we have seen in the previous chapter, fan-idol relations grew rapidly across a number of pop culture genres in Japan by the late 70s and early 80s (see also Kinsella 1996). *The Manzai* started a nation-wide manzai boom within Japan's burgeoning media culture, featuring such entertainers as Yoshimoto's Shinsuke Ryūsuke duo, who exhibited a new style that came to be known as *ochikobore* manzai (dropout manzai). In contrast to the status-quo manzai which had largely worked between and within lower and middle classes, manzai pairs in the 80s became representatives of a new generation of Japanese youth then emerging as a powerful consumer group eager to consume mass-mediated forms of 'difference' in a society viewed by many Japanese as having become deeply immersed in middle-class, mainstream norms. Yoshimoto comedians generally were marginal in language, geography, social class, and vocation, and not many had experienced widespread fame in previous decades. Just as the margins of society were being swallowed up by Tokyo-led middle-class suburban norms,[5] the mass media came to reproduce the socially marginal for youth culture consumption in the form of these fast-talking, street-smart manzai pairs. 'Classic' (Yoshimoto-style) manzai stemmed from the tradition established in the early 30s, which emphasized the personal dilemma of mutual incomprehension that occurs between the wit and the fool while they discuss the daily happenings surrounding the work place, family, sports and other urban happenings. Although the basic form did not greatly change, the routines of the young manzai comedians of the boom period contained more social sarcasm, grotesque humor, references to pop culture stars (musicians, actors, and so on), brief skits, outrageous parody and cynicism directed at the very entertainment apparatus of which they had become a part.

During the large-scale manzai boom period of the early 80s, the television industry found at least a temporary audience for manzai performed on television, but this state of affairs did not necessarily create long-term work for Yoshimoto comedians. For a start, popular comedians exhausted their polished routines after a couple of years under heavy media exposure. And then, more importantly, the demand for televised manzai routines itself lessened as their novelty wore off. Manzai comedians were, however, soon featured in other forms of comedy television, such as *Oretachi Hyōkinzoku* (We Are The Comedy Tribe, Fuji TV,

1981–1989), 'emphasi[zing] ad libs, running gags, and free-form parodies of popular songs, TV shows, and commercials' (Schilling 1997:259).[6] In addition, Yoshimoto was able to sustain and extend interest in Yoshimoto comedy through forms of what became participatory comedy consumption in downtown Osaka.

Television and manzai

The Japanese entertainment industry is a fairly close-knit, intricately webbed world, with two major centers of media production and consumption, Tokyo and Osaka, and until recently only a limited number of stations and programming.[7] Televised manzai and more generalized comedy shows (co-)produced by the company and its hundreds of comedians are what come to mind when one thinks of manzai these days in Japan. Young Yoshimoto comedians with manzai training have had a strong presence on Japanese television in a variety of capacities since the 80s. Thus, the name Yoshimoto is to comedy entertainment what the top talent agency Johnny's Jimusho (Johnny and Associates) is to pop music bands, and what the all-female Takarazuka Revue is to pop musical theater: the most economically productive and pop culturally visible presence in an industry niche, with far-reaching influence in the world of media entertainment and the promotion of multi-talented personalities in Japanese media culture. However, unlike pop idol production companies since the 80s (as we have seen in the previous chapter by Stevens and Hosokawa), Yoshimoto has not lost control over media production itself to Japan's media conglomerates. On the contrary, it is doing more production work than ever before and is also expanding into new areas of media production through subsidiary companies and the broad development of both the hardware and the software of cultural production and distribution. The company has reported consistently higher earnings each year since the beginning of the early 80's manzai boom when the company grew rapidly, essentially doubling sales from 1980 to 1989 (Yoshimoto Kōgyō 1992:277), and again in the 90s despite the ongoing recession.

Across the television channels and genres of Japan, comedians trained in, and with a knack for, spontaneous-appearing conversation and joking comprise a large percentage of Japan's endlessly circulating personalities. There are still television shows featuring manzai routines (*konto* 'skits' and stand-up), but since the early 80s 'boom' the most famous manzai comedians have rarely directly practiced their art even in a mass-mediated form. Instead, they have shuttled endlessly between regular appearances on (an average of three to eight weekly) television talk, variety, quiz, infotainment and music shows, with perhaps the occasional drama. They are members of Japan's tight-knit media personalities world where novelists, sports heroes, foreigners, music idols, film actors or directors, journalists, intellectuals, politicians and other publically recognized figures participate in televisual gatherings as 'friends' on disposable – that is, one-run – shows guided by an affable host(s) and cheered on by a live audience. The shows are highly structured in terms of performer roles and show themes and 'are so stereotyped as to become parodies of themselves' (Stronach 1989:154). The core of most shows, especially entertainment shows outside of drama and 'serious' news programs, consists of light banter and antics among a group of recycled pop culture personalities (cf. Schilling 1997:11–13). So far as the production company, television station, ad agency and sponsor's points of view are concerned, comedians are desirable performers on the small screen between, around, and in television advertisements because they are relatively inexpensive and versatile (cf. Yoshikawa 1989:82). Comedians also may find it difficult or unattractive to rely solely on live stage performances, given today's mass media-intensive entertainment industry; it may since the 80s have been an important path towards media exposure for comedians, but it would not have gained comedians a significant audience without television shows to feature them (Inoue 1992).

Particularly since the 80s, therefore, Yoshimoto's performers have appeared in the productions of a wide variety of television-related media companies. The majority of them are manzai performers by trade and, with over 600 performers in all, Yoshimoto has become a powerful talent agency, as well as the largest production company in Japan. It has maintained its focus on comedy and its image as 'the comedy company' due to its renewed investment in comedy stage management in the 80s and 90s and its adept brokering of the nation-wide popularity of a number of its rakugo and manzai stars. Indeed, the company's New Star Creation schools, live theaters, special events, tours with the stars and other forms of comedy production and publicity have gained much of their momentum from the ubiquity and popularity of humorous (some would say silly or offensive) television shows featuring Yoshimoto comedians. The popularity of manzai comedians, together with media images of manzai comedians' lifestyles, has been such that many talent agencies and production companies based in Tokyo and normally managing other types of entertainers have themselves in recent years begun to nurture young manzai aspirants in their facilities (see Sekiguchi 1996:88–89).

Yoshimoto's NSC School in Osaka

Until the late 70s, manzai audiences were mainly working and middle-class families from Kansai, as well as elderly tourists, who went to the theaters to enjoy live stage-performed manzai, but probably never themselves considered pursuing manzai as a career. The new young consumers of the last two decades, however, have been fans of manzai entertainers performing across many media and genres and have gathered both in downtown Osaka, and more recently Tokyo (since 1995), in order to become professional comedians-in-training by participating in the Yoshimoto-supplied NSC classes. The Osaka NSC was established in 1982 and a performance theater (Shinsaibashi 2-Chome Theater) for graduates of the school in 1986.[8] The establishment of this school signalled a shift from manzai comedians trained by veteran Yoshimoto manzai comedians in master-apprentice relationships, to general entertainers who happened to be manzai comedians, trained by manzai scriptwriters and other teachers at the school in year-long manzai, skit, voice, acting, and dance classes.

The creation of the Osaka NSC was basically a move by Yoshimoto production and advertising staff to study the early 80s' popularity of mediated manzai more closely by getting to know the young consumers who had newly emerged as a considerable force in the market place, and to draw on these same people as a potential pool of new talent as manzai-trained entertainers who could apply their talents in the mass media market. For their part, fans felt they were getting what they wanted finally – a taste of live manzai on stage in downtown Osaka and the possibility of fan-into-performer success stories. Yoshimoto staff did not at the time, however, plan to promote the school itself as a site of consumption or to use the school as a symbol of the company theme or brand (in other words, to emphasize the company's most general selling points). But the rise to fame of the manzai duo DownTown's Matsumoto Hitoshi and Hamada Masatoshi in the late 80s, half a decade after their graduation from the First Class of Yoshimoto's NSC school in 1983, dramatically increased interest in the NSC and Yoshimoto and Osaka *Minami* (downtown South Osaka). Since the DownTown phenomenon, Yoshimoto staff have strategically promoted the unexpected long-term, hands-on interest in manzai performance and solid fan support for the NSC graduates at the local theaters by trying to strike a balance between the consumption and production of manzai. Thus, for example, the company expanded the number of students in Osaka from a couple of hundred to 600 per year from 1999 (and has similar plans for its Tokyo school from the year 2000), but at the same time raised its standards for proceeding to the level of performing in front of paying audiences. In this, Yoshimoto has tried to encourage the participation of a broad spectrum of students – from those who drop out as soon as their fan interest in the place fades, to those who have the talent and charisma to go on to stage performance in front of live audiences. On the one hand, admission fees, tuition, and the number of months of prepayment required, along with enrollment numbers, have gone up considerably in the 90s; on the other hand, the school has been unable to produce any nation-wide stars in the last decade, other than one pair of manzai comedians from the class that graduated in 1990 – the duo Ninety-Nine.

NSC students

In the 80s, as an outgrowth of manzai's popularity, hundreds, and in the 90s thousands, of Japanese youth enrolled in the NSC, for the most part to study manzai comedy as a means toward becoming general media entertainers. Yoshimoto has the largest and most organized training facilities for comedy entertainers in Japan. The Osaka NSC is an alternative form of vocational education, located in the downtown setting where many vocational schools have been established in the last decade, especially those having to do with media production – photography, advertising, modeling, fashion design, computer programming, and even a vocational school for the training of porno-film actresses. According to interviews and surveys I conducted, most of the students said they were following in the footsteps of Japan's manzai teams active on television. And close to half of the fans at the Shinsaibashi 2-Chōme Theater, where many NSC graduates first performed in public, themselves expressed a desire to become manzai comedians. The personal histories of the students I came to know at the NSC also indicate that viewing manzai performers on television inspired them to attempt to go beyond consumption and into production.

In a media-dominated world where commodities seemingly have become detached and alienated from their producers, thousands of these comedy fans have sought hands-on experience, personal adventure, close friendship, exciting conversation – the dream of being both consumer and producer in a uniquely personal yet consumer-shared experience. Many comedy students at the NSC, who themselves began as and for the most part remain fans of Yoshimoto's manzai comedians, seek an intimate proximity to production, so that they can independently make their own way in life, create their own meanings and their very own selves. Their chances of success are near zero, but the situation is remedied by the heady possibility of their achieving national fame and recognition (appealingly) against the odds. Comedian aspirants dream of having their own television shows and strive to attain media stardom, although many of them appear to find satisfaction, not to mention a wide community of similar-minded people, in merely giving it a try. For most of the young comedian aspirants, manzai performance is supposed to be only the first step toward a diverse media career that may not involve recognizable manzai performance. As a stepping stone for the rise of a handful of top-earning media stars and as the place where want-to-be media television personalities and eager fans at least play out their dreams of celebrity, the NSC has played an important role in the company's goal of expanding into the shifting currents of Japanese media entertainment services.

For most of the 90s, 225 or more people gained admission annually to the NSC in Osaka. Between seven and nine hundred hopefuls usually applied, and 600 or more aspirants were chosen to compete in the auditions. The official age for admission is from sixteen to 24 years old, and the minimum of a junior-high level of education is also officially required. Nevertheless, as the school director asserted in an interview:

> If a person can convince us that he or she is over fifteen and under twenty-five, we won't ask any questions. The kind of talent it takes to convince us that you deserve to get into the school is what counts.

At the time of my research, close to half the enrollees overall dropped out, many in the first couple of months, many others within six months. At the beginning of a school year, on average a little over one-third of the students was female, and generally younger than males at the school. Most students were from the Kansai area. In interviews, the latter frequently mentioned the importance in their lives of manzai-style humor, the give-and-take of fool and wit roles. For example, many students told me they were able to create friendships, become popular, or make up for scholastic underachievement by using humor. Some of them entered the NSC before graduating from high school (going to both schools), or dropped out of high school, or even entered the NSC straight out of junior high school. Many applicants came on their own from beyond the Kansai area to audition at the school, but usually had a harder time in convincing the school's staff that they were tough enough to stick with the life of the comedian in downtown Osaka, and either failed the audition or quit at some point due to financial strain or failure to find a niche. Most NSC students had to do full or part-time work at a convenience store, fast-food restaurant, or bar to make ends meet. In addition to the financial and regional barriers faced by students, parents usually expressed embarrassment and opposition towards the whole idea of their son or daughter going to the famous, and infamous, Yoshimoto entertainer school. In general, would-be comedians who were more easily accepted into the school and lasted until graduation were those who had: firstly, already found a manzai partner before applying at the school; secondly, come from the Kansai area; thirdly, used savings or parents' money and had a job; and fourthly, had no intention of acting as mere fans hoping to meet someone famous.

Courses at the NSC normally run from April for one year. Dance, music, and comedy theater (shinkigeki) students as well as manzai comedy students enroll in the year-long program at the NSC. There are five types of courses offered: manzai, skits, acting, dance, and voice. The aim is to produce entertainers familiar with the fundamentals of performance in general, although most of the people who have made it into the school aspire to become manzai comedians, and so concentrate on preparing for and attending the manzai and skit classes. Students normally go to two to four classes per week, each of which lasts one and a half hours. Up to 1999, there were normally three manzai instructors, and one instructor for each of the other types of performance. Manzai classes emphasized the actual performance of manzai, watching other students perform, and listening to teachers' brief critiques. The majority of the students who made it through the whole year of study in the mid-90s had already chosen their partner(s) before entering the school; typically, like DownTown before them, they were fellow class clowns who had known each other since their junior or senior high school days. Partners may also have performed manzai together at a school or cultural festival, a yearly event common at high schools, colleges, and in neighborhoods.

The legendary DownTown and the NSC

During the manzai boom period, Yoshimoto managers saw the importance of generating and maintaining a distinctive product and, thereby, brand name for the company (cf. Moeran 1996a:130). Moreover, they realized that its products must be highly generic, representing the company as a whole, and highly mutable, to fit shifts and variations within media culture. The entertainment school (NSC), even though not established toward this end at first, nevertheless assisted the company in attaining these goals. The young comedians graduating from this school have been dubbed 'no-brand' manzai comedians (that is, comedians not affiliated with a particular master's tradition and name [cf. Mita 1993:35]), and lack the security of an influential teacher, performance lineage, or personal tutoring that comes with a traditional manzai master-apprentice relationship. They have emerged from this production company's comedy school with no choice (and no other goal usually) but to aim for immediate and extensive experience and exposure on stage and eventually on television. In effect, their masters have been the manzai comedians they have watched on television, the manzai scriptwriters who serve as teachers at Yoshimoto's entertainment school, and also young fan-peers whose preferences get heard through fan clubs and attendance at local performance venues. After the weakening of the master-apprentice relation with the advent of the NSC, Yoshimoto itself became the *brand* – supported by the 'no-brand' stars who eventually emerged from the school, and who have seen themselves as more individualistic and free-spirited than past Yoshimoto comedians trained under 'masters' (representatives of performance lineage 'brands'). According to Andrew Wernick (1991:107):

> The aims and results of star-making are part and parcel of the brand-imaging of the cultural products, and companies, with which stars are creatively associated. Thus capitalists will seek to optimize the promotional value of the celebrified creators or creations they utilize through long-term arrangements which stabilize the link.

Yoshimoto focuses on its stars as the most important currency of the marketplace, its most valuable source of variation in the endless search for new faces and material that will keep up with or be one step ahead of the times.

The media entertainers who have had the greatest influence on young Japanese comedy fans of today are a pair who call themselves DownTown (Matsumoto Hitoshi and Hamada Masatoshi). They have worked for Yoshimoto since 1983, when as young men they graduated from the Osaka NSC. The story of their rise to fame has been repeated in enough mass media forms to be dubbed a legend. DownTown grew up on the cusp of the emergent media-saturated culture, from a very young age watching Yoshimoto's *shinkigeki* comedy theater on television every weekend, and also going to the company's local comedy stages. As for most people who have grown up in the Kansai region, professional comedy (*owarai*) and humor (*warai*) were both a significant part of their everyday lives within Kansai's large, regional media culture.

DownTown first gained local fame at the Shinsaibashisuji 2-Chōme Theater. After appearing on various local television shows, the duo's big break came when they captured two regular shows in Tokyo in 1988, and made it onto a long-running, nationally broadcast afternoon show called *Waratte ii tomo* (Fuji TV, 1988) – the same show that established Akashiya Sanma's enduring presence on national television in the mid-80s. According to his manager in the early years, Sanma was the first Yoshimoto comedian (a rakugo storyteller by training, from Nara) to use Kansai dialect on national television without creating any sense of incongruity while interacting with entertainers speaking Tokyo-dialect. By the late 80s, DownTown had become manzai idols in Osaka, eagerly followed by thousands of adoring young female fans who grouped around the pair's independent style and off-the-wall sense of humor, and, yes, their cuteness (see Kinsella 1996). Fans eagerly joined Yoshimoto's 2-Chōme fan club, called *Chū* (Smooch). They idolized DownTown despite the pair's verbal put-downs of 'girl audiences who don't really understand our comedy'. Like other manzai teams who have made it onto the small screen, DownTown quit performing formal manzai dialogue routines in the early 90s, and turned their full attention to television talk and variety shows (as we saw in Stevens and Hosokawa's discussion of music programmes such as *Hey3*).[9] Matsumoto claims that he stopped doing manzai because no one understood it, and now that everyone wants to hear their manzai 'it's too late'. Nevertheless, on one of their first national television shows, *Gaki no Tsukai ya Arahen* (Not a Task for Kids), the Downtown duo spent most of their time standing on stage in front of an audience telling funny stories in a 'free talk' version of manzai. Many of their stories in the early years of the show, like their manzai routines, were based on episodes taken from, or fictitiously framed within, their everyday adventures as kids and as young adults growing up in Amagasaki (a working-class city located between Kobe and Osaka) and Osaka, and told in their childhood language, Kansai dialect. Although DownTown's seniors in the entertainment industry seemed to see in them the demise of entertainer protocol, in fact much of their appeal on television variety and talk shows has, it seems, revolved around their bad-boy, irreverent treatment of public personalities (on shows like *DownTown DX*) who 'should' be treated with more respect. In their comedy, DownTown have recalled vulgar scenes of their youthful camaraderie; made fun of the elderly (such as old ladies from the Kansai region) and mother-son relations; lampooned celebrities and other public icons; played with popular images of the yakuza, salarymen, and foreigners; created fantasy characters suggestive of ludic and absurd manga and characters in animation films; and (perhaps their one bow to Yoshimoto tradition) focused much of their attention on sex and bodily excreta.

According to my research on fans of Yoshimoto comedians, males in their teens to twenties, on the one hand, tended to watch comedy entertainers on television and videotape at home, and go to large special performances, but did not go to regular performances at local theaters. On the other hand, females in the same age range tended to go to live performances, participate in fan clubs, and watch comedy entertainers on television. These were the two main sectors of Japanese youth culture making up the audiences of manzai-trained comedians, as well as the students of manzai, in the 80s and 90s. I found that many students' personal stories very much paralleled depictions of the DownTown legend. For example, they were influenced by mediated and live comedy and humor as children, inclined to romanticize the special nature of Osaka dialect and the rawness of downtown Osaka, were willing to work hard in pursuit of popularity and fame through humor. Most noticeably, they practiced a manzai derivative of DownTown's style. There is a small public park a block and a half southeast of the school where many of the manzai comedy students practice, just as DownTown are reported to have done when they were students at the NSC. The practice-in-the-park idea has been sacralized by the success stories of DownTown and is associated with tenacious perseverance and brash self-confidence. Nonetheless, no other NSC graduates have found a fame that approaches that of DownTown. At the turn of the century, the NSC students who graduated in the mid-90s find themselves for the most part unable to develop the audience following they need in Osaka for their live performances to lead to the desired sustained exposure in local and then national mass media. Some have moved on to Tokyo to try to find stage time at one of the many small performance venues there, but only a few have found even limited or local notoriety in any city, while most are pursuing other things such as vocational training, university, the same old convenience store job, office work, or have merely become unemployed manzai performers.[10]

Media Culture and Yoshimoto

As we have seen, the everyday social world is immersed in consumption practices linked to the mass media and media production. In his formulation of urban popular culture, Theodore Bestor (1989:2) says that:

> Most forms of popular culture are associated with commercialized mass production and consumption, but lifestyles (although they may be defined by the sorts of commercialized consumption they promote) are not themselves direct products of commercial cultural production in quite the same sense.

But it is precisely those associations, however direct or indirect, which may prove to be the most interesting and relevant to study. Moreover, 'popular culture' too much suggests a grounding of social practices in the culture of 'the people' or fairly contiguous, folk-like urban communities (Traube 1996). Yet, what Douglas Kellner says of capitalist countries in general appears to hold true of Japanese media, as well as of the local history of Yoshimoto's comedy:

> A media culture has emerged in which images, sounds, and spectacles help produce the fabric of everyday life, dominating leisure time, shaping political views and social behavior, and providing the materials out of which people forge their very identities ...
>
> (Kellner 1995:16)[11]

In a media culture, the issue of whether or not a culture has a social grounding in 'the people' is not as pertinent as the question of how products, professional producers and their means of production, as well as audiences or other cultural producers, together with institutions, are caught up in the very production and circulation of each other's social practices. Yoshimoto invites people to identify with certain 'Yoshimoto' places, people, genres, and styles taken up by consumers as part of 'lifestyles' constructed and practiced, for instance, by young entertainer aspirants by means of the NSC school and its vicinity (the old Osaka Minami entertainment district). This 'invitation' gets played and worked out particularly in the ambiguous areas where commercial production and consumption overlap. People's lifestyles may not be the 'direct products of commercial cultural production' (in Bestor's words) but many people do spend a great deal of their time and energy constructing their identities and daily practices out of, and within, production/consumption/promotional sites such as the NSC school within Japanese media culture.

The consumption of a given media production crosscuts the consumption of other products and of other social relations. The main categories of consumers in the case of Yoshimoto's comedy are live studio audiences, amateurs who participate on media shows, theater and special event audiences, fan club members, performance (vocational) school students, readers of print media (newspapers, magazines, books, and so on) devoted to comedians, as well as users of place, language, and fashion associated with the manzai comedian. The Osaka NSC and the Osaka downtown area have developed into significant sites where Yoshimoto comedy fans can turn themselves into potential professional media entertainers, or at least into 'insider' fans who participate in an 'Osakan manzai comedian' lifestyle that includes consumption of the urban streets of downtown Osaka, Osaka dialect, and Osaka comedy.[12] Although most of the Osaka NSC students are from the suburbs and urban centers of the Kansai region, great efforts are made by young people from all over Japan every year to participate directly in the lifestyle of the cultural commodity that is the manzai comedian. As we have seen, Yoshimoto has in recent years expanded the production-like possibilities of this phenomenon for a number of reasons, including that of promoting the company brand at large.

Consumption, Production, and Promotion

Recently the nature of the most generalized category of media consumer, that of the 'audience', has come under scrutiny in both business and academic media studies. Ien Ang sheds light on why 'well-chosen ideas of consumer agency', as Arjun Appadurai (1996) puts it, are necessary from the point of view of corporations:

In industry and advertising circles there is talk of the diversification, fragmentation and demassification of the audience. They have become acutely aware that audiences are not gullible consumers who passively absorb anything they're served, but must be continuously 'targeted' and fought for, grabbed, and seduced. The shift in institutional awareness throughout the rapidly globalizing media industries, which intensified during the 1980s, signifies the emergence of the spectre of the 'active audience' at the very heart of corporate concerns. It is common industry wisdom that it is *never* possible to predict the success or failure of a particular film or programme, despite all sorts of safety valves such as formulaic production, use of stars and celebrities, and market research.

(Ang 1996:10; original emphasis)

And, at the same time that the nature of the audience is being interrogated, the consumer and consumption in general are being declared the most influential, widespread social force of the postmodern world (for example, Miller 1995). From a pessimistic media-dominance point of view, Masao Miyoshi (1993:747) declares:

Even without the formation of TNCs [transnational corporations], the world has been turning toward all-powerful consumerism in which brand names command recognition and attraction ... Cable TV and MTV dominate the world absolutely. Entertainment and tourism are huge transnational industries by themselves.

As we have seen, Yoshimoto's and consumers' practices suggest that 'consumption' often takes place in contexts traditionally viewed as falling into the production sphere, but that it actually occurs in a promotion-permeated arena in between traditional consumption and production contexts. The promotional arena of the NSC schools, for example, produces and thereby links both performers and consumers (one as the other) – an audience that to some extent consumes itself as commercial product even while learning how to become a product for public consumption. Another example of the promotional and popular overlap of production and consumption is to be found in the numerous television shows made in Osaka since the early 90s which highlight amateur participation in comedy-oriented situations and settings: for instance, the Kansai-local manzai-competition shows *Bakushō Booing* (KTV), *Sungee Best 10* (ABS), and *WaChaCha Live II* (KTV) which aired in the mid-90s, and, more recently, *Bakushō On-Air Battle* (NHK-G); manzai stage performances showcased on *Yoshimoto's Hamaguri Ōmon Theater* (KBS) and *Ōwarai Nettowāku* (YTV); the unique, long-running national show *Tantei Knight Scoop* (KTV), and talent search shows such as *Terebi Mensetsu* (1995, YTV).[13]

Ien Ang (1996:22) asks: 'which strategies has [television] developed to persuade people to become members of the TV audience?' It is a question that can include the study of the ways in which audiences follow products from one medium to another, and in which fans, in line with corporate domains of production, seek to participate more fully in the life of a product, even to the point of becoming one themselves (especially common in the case of performance genres). In different ways, for both professional media producers and certain media audiences, there can be profound connections between consumption practices and production and promotion practices. For example, once Yoshimoto managers saw that their young comedians were taking off on national television shows, they took steps to try to harness that popularity even though they had not directly created the initial demand. A senior executive producer in the Production Division analyzed the circumstances of the manzai boom period in the following way:

> In the 80s, live houses and small theaters cropped up in response to the demand of young audiences for close-up experiences with comedians. Yoshimoto staff people could not explain why Osakan comedy was so popular, or why it was taking off not only on television but at small venues. But the company wanted to do as much as possible to continue the trend. That is why the NSC was established, and later the Shinsaibashi 2-Chōme Theater. Besides, Osaka production companies and television stations generally supply Tokyo's television key stations with talent, particularly comedy talent, which happens to be easier to produce for general entertainment jobs on television than it is to produce, for instance, a band for the music industry.

According to my interviews of Shinsaibashi 2-Chōme Theater fans in Osaka, part of the attraction of the live theater for manzai fans had to do with television-generated nostalgia for live performance. As Wernick (1991:115) notes: 'the displacement of live performance by recording, of auratic culture by the mechanically reproduced, has led to a countervailing nostalgia for the living, the authentic, and the original'. Furthermore, not only has the NSC's presence made comedy production that much more visible, it has made it more deeply commodifiable, in a new space ostensibly within the production sphere. This presents to anyone who wants to pay an audition fee the possibility of not only expressing one's funniness but actually of becoming a famous comedian. The manzai audience has thus been stabilized, further defined, and perhaps strengthened and expanded in a border area between production and consumption spheres, in the less directly television-based but still television-linked venues of the school, the theater, and the tourist experience of the surrounding urban amusement area of downtown Osaka. Media companies generally attempt to categorize and quantify consumers through the ongoing, contingent processes of consumption, but also through the processes of production. They seem to be linked together more and more through, and *as*, corporate promotional activities. Alongside the production and promotion of other companies' goods, which include the 'consumer' as a good to be produced and consumed in the corporate world, media companies tend to promote their own cultural goods (Wernick 1991:101), including corporate image (their ultimate 'good'), because they have myriad ways of doing so as organizations that specialize in packaging and mediating people, programs, ads, and material products.

Production companies act as suppliers to advertisers and television companies. Yoshimoto solicits contact between consumers and entertainers, and cultural goods and services, through its theaters, training schools, and other live performance-related institutions. These are, then, a means of obtaining knowledge both about basic performance production and about consumption. For it is precisely the entertainer who, as in the case of Yoshimoto's stable of performers, must perform and promote herself as a main product or service of her own, as well as of client companies, in front of audiences. The entertainer is mediated by, and mediates between, corporate goods and services and the consumer, and also the consumer and the 'human face' or performative aspect of corporate identity. In the case of manzai comedy, both the consumer and the consumed are intangible, meaning-producing human beings with performative abilities, value-added 'software' that lends itself to fuzzy borders between one sphere and the other. Image-events – that is, advertising, television and radio shows, live acts, press conferences, newspaper and magazine interviews, fan clubs, and so forth – contribute to the associations between the various domains of commodities or cultural goods, as well as to those between entertainers and audiences. As Brian Moeran also shows in the following chapter, there is a potential cycle of 'mutual admiration' as each can be used in promotional activities for the other.

Conclusion

A serious challenge facing researchers of contemporary urban media environments and their communities is that of investigating how the media consumption that occurs in particular contexts – such as daily conversation, shopping, dining out, and fashion – may be linked to media production, circulation, and promotion in complex yet discernible ways. For example, how can we go about analyzing the connections between different domains of culture, such as those between comedy in everyday conversation, on television, in theaters, and in comedy classrooms? Any particular location, activity, object, person or group – whether the shopping arcades, old entertainment districts and live theaters of downtown Osaka or the pottery, land, and *sake* of rural Japan (cf. Moeran 1997) – is incorporated into capitalist systems of tourism, marketing, media, and national policy-making. Japan's media industries, government agencies, and educational institutions comprise the basic institutional structure for cultural productions centering on Japanese ethnicity, regional character, gender and sexuality, age, ethnicity, and other forms of identity and difference (see Mouer and Sugimoto 1986). This includes the production of commodified cultural 'diversity' that has an impact on consumption in so many ways. The culture industries therefore have a great deal of influence in the construction of common sense or taken-for-granted images of Japan, as well as in the formation and maintenance of media culture.

Yet, the active participation of people in their everyday lives in the consumption of media goods cannot be overlooked. The problem with debates that contrast monolithic institutions and the people is that media audiences and media text consumption, media industry producers and production processes, and media products and their marketing and distribution, tend to be placed in separate, demarcated areas of investigation. Failure to engage in more integrated research diminishes our potential understanding of significant phenomena such as the commodification of culture, consumerism, globalization, media culture, and promotionalism. The latter, so pervasive today in every media process, signals a major shift in the way the world operates. For promotional culture, as Wernick calls it, blurs the past distinctions in media research between production and reception, text and context, commodity circulation and culture, base and superstructure (see Wernick 1991:19). Consequently media researchers must closely attend to the connections between those formally separate domains that in practice overlap. We must take a closer look at the means of promotion being practiced in media entertainment, at how the production and consumption of goods and services can often be seen as a process in which they contain, shape, and advertise one another.

This essay has in large part been about how Yoshimoto and fans of its comedy manage the production-consumption continuum, more often than not wrapped in promotionalism. With the advent of the Osaka NSC and the 2-Chōme Theater, Yoshimoto took one step towards a system of producing manzai entertainers who could see real action very quickly (ready for prime time or, if not, then local late night television), appeal specifically to younger audiences, and not require high overhead costs: in other words, a 'system' adaptable to the demands of a media-, youth-, and tourist-oriented consumer culture. By promoting the growth of young stage performers, Yoshimoto has been able to use its theaters to access information on contemporary fan preferences – the kind advertising marketing divisions pursue in their market studies. Production companies thus try to stay on top of the problem of market innovation by infusing the production sphere with young and youthful employees, temporary workers, as well as fee-paying students, performers, and fans. Yoshimoto's entertainment schools and small live professional stages have made it possible for young comedians to be cheaply and fairly effectively introduced by Yoshimoto into what has become the primary market for comedy since the late 70s: television. The desire to become professional manzai comedians may have been the first reason many students auditioning at the NSC in the mid-90s moved to downtown Osaka. But many also had a desire to live in and experience the real Osaka – the people, places, and language of downtown Osaka – even if their auditions were unsuccessful. The area surrounding Yoshimoto's headquarters has thus come to be developed by the company, and treated by NSC students, as a series of amusement park-like spaces. Yoshimoto promotes fan involvement in its trademark goods through their participation in an array of products and promotional spheres that also involve or have ramifications concerning basic production processes: entertainment schools and auditions, fan clubs, television shows with live audiences or amateur participation, television shows centered on location-shots with locals, radio call-in shows, participatory museum exhibits, corporate branding on a broad variety of consumer products, and even vacation tours with the stars. Manzai comedians, who in previous incarnations have been a part of Osaka's urban entertainment history from at least the late nineteenth century, thrive today more than ever before on television and radio, as well as in performance halls, movie theaters, and so on.

Media-saturated, corporate-sponsored – yet not necessarily 'mass' – cultural relations increasingly occur along or cut across local to global levels. Similar to trends discernible in other commercial media-saturated countries, media production and consumption of entertainment in Japan have in significant ways merged as a result of everyday corporate and personal promotional efforts visible in the Japanese media market and media culture. Relations between consumers and producers, as well as those between different production and marketing processes, are obviously broad and complicated in the case of production companies and consumers of their products. Media production companies sink or swim according to whether or not their entertainers and production staff supply media distributors and advertisers with entertaining shows and ads that appeal to consumers. Production companies like Yoshimoto endeavor to manage the many types of interaction they and others differently promote between the company, its stars, fans, non-employee production-related people, and aspiring comedians, including the students of its entertainment schools. In Japan, comedy celebrity has worked as a promotional currency and over the decades become a national media phenomenon that nevertheless is locally grounded and elaborated. The significant change that has occurred is in the way in which production and consumption have coincided as a means of consumer expression, as well as of corporate promotion.

Notes

1 The author carried out ethnographic research from 1995 to early 1996 on the Osaka 'New Star Creation' (NSC) entertainment school. The NSC's official name is Yoshimoto Sōgō Geinō Gakuin.
2 Koichi Ōtani's (1994a, 1994b) work provides a more recent and egregious example of the same phenomenon.
3 Manzai is ordinarily performed by same-sex pairs or married couples, but three-to-five person teams also exist.
4 A comedy boom hit North America at about the same time, in the early 1980s, ushered in by The Second City theaters in Chicago (1959) and Toronto (1973), which have had a great impact on the North American entertainment industry, including television and film. The development of regional comedy styles and training facilities at these theaters is somewhat similar to Yoshimoto's. A Second City theater was also established in Detroit in 1993.
5 By the 80s, Tokyo had become more dominant than ever over the rest of Japan, and both Tokyo and Osaka had greatly reduced inner-city residential populations,

increased levels of commuting and inner-city high-rise businesses, with the majority of their populations living in suburbs (see Hanes 1993:87).

6 Stronach (1989:153) describes the show as 'adventurous enough to be ranked second by Japanese mothers among the shows they would least like their children to watch'.

7 In a country with nearly a 100 per cent diffusion of television sets, the Kanto and Kansai regions together comprise close to 50 per cent of Japan's population and over 50 per cent of its broadcast television audience.

8 The 2-Chōme Theater, a small performance stage (134 seats) in which the recent graduates of NSC tested their abilities, was closed in March, 1999, and replaced by baseYoshimoto, a larger theater that opened in the fall of 1999 in Osaka. A Tokyo NSC was established in 1995.

9 It can take months to write and polish a good routine. Once used a few times, it will have to be thrown away because it has been heard by most audiences due to the effective reach of the electronic media.

10 Those who are not established entertainers at Yoshimoto, in the top 40 on the company list, are not likely to be able to make a living as an entertainer alone.

11 Others, such as Willis (1990) and Silverstone (1994), have made similar points.

12 For programmatic portrayals of this 'lifestyle', see, for instance, Nishida's novel *Ōsaka Dream* (1993) and books written by the comedians themselves (for example, Matsumoto 1994, 1998a, 1998b, 1999) or by 'research groups' (such as the Nihon DownTown Chōsadan, Tokyo DownTown Kenkyūkai, and Tensai-jinbutsu o Hyōkasuru Kai) that recount DownTown's rise to fame. Tsutsui (1997) has presented an account of how young people in the Kansai region take up fool and wit manzai dialogue, illustrating how dynamic the relationship between mass media performance and everyday interaction among media audiences can be.

13 Media directors and writers working in the Kansai area commonly assume that even the average Kansai person can perform well in front of the camera or can be made to appear funny.

12

PROMOTING CULTURE

The Work of a Japanese Advertising Agency

Brian Moeran

In a television interview with Sarah Ferguson aired in Hong Kong in December 1997, the American presenter Larry King found himself being presented with a birthday gift. This he began to unwrap and, in order to fill in the pause in talk occasioned by his having to do something other than look at his interlocutor or the camera, King told the duchess to 'say something'. This she duly did: a full minute of promotion for one David Tang, who was a 'close friend' and a 'lovely man', and whose new store, Shanghai Tang, just happened to be opening in Manhattan that week.[1] In the meantime, Larry King unwrapped – and, at the duchess' bidding, put on – a purple velvet jacket, before (again at her bidding) rolling up the sleeves to reveal a gaudy green silk lining for which Shanghai Tang – best described, perhaps, as a purveyor of high-class, oriental kitsch – is well known.

One of the things about promotions is that everybody knows that they are *there*, but hardly anyone knows *how* they manage to get where they are. As Michael Schudson (1984:13) has said:

> We live and shall live, barring nuclear or other disaster, in what has been called 'promotional culture' … The promotional culture has worked its way into what we read, what we care about, the ways we raise our children, our ideas of right and wrong conduct, our attribution of significance to 'image' in both public and private life. The promotional culture has been cultivated and indulged in. It has been ridiculed and reviled. It still needs to be understood.

We might justifiably ask, therefore, what we should make of the above promotional incident. Had the whole thing been arranged in advance, or had we witnessed a rare moment of spontaneity in television? Was King really at a loss for words when, seemingly suddenly, presented with a birthday gift on air? Or was he trying to find out how good his guest might be as a TV presenter, since she had already expressed an interest in doing work of this kind? Did Ferguson just happen to say the first thing that came into her head when put on the spot (and that was a reference to Shanghai Tang because she had attended the opening of the Manhattan store the night before)? Or had she rehearsed the whole incident in advance?

And what about the gift itself? Was this something she had bought because she felt it suited Larry King and would be an appropriate present for him (which, given his normal shirt-sleeved appearance, seemed unlikely)? Had she bought the jacket at all? Or had she been given it by her good friend David Tang precisely because she was going to appear on *Larry King Live* and both knew it was Larry King's birthday that day? Was the timing of her interview itself fortuitous? Or did she stipulate in advance (with or without the connivance of Tang and/or King) that she be interviewed on the television presenter's birthday, and the day after the opening of Shanghai Tang in New York, so that she could give him a present from the store in front of millions of syndicated viewers all over the world?

These are just some of the questions that arise from one rather obvious instance on a television chat show of what a PR pioneer, Edward Bernays, would have called an 'overt act which juts out of the routine of circumstance' (Ewen 1996:18) – an act finding further life now in scholarly print. Doubtless there are more questions that might be posed – in particular, as we have seen in the previous chapters by Joel Stocker, and Caroline Stevens and Shuhei Hosokawa, concerning the role of those *producing* such promotions. As for their answers, I somehow doubt whether anyone would be willing to reveal all the backstage negotiations that accompanied this super-celebrity endorsement for Shanghai Tang. What is interesting, though, is that this kind of activity routinely goes on in advertising and media activities and that – equally routinely – we accept it without question.

All of which brings me to two issues. The first has to do with the nature of 'promotion' itself in advertising. The second concerns the idea of 'promotional culture' and thus the relationship between economy and culture in contemporary capitalist societies.

First, the word 'promotion' is not usually found in the indexes of the many books in cultural studies now devoted to discussions of advertising, nor, for some reason, in many discussions of marketing (for example, Brown 1995; Costa and Bamossy 1995; Schmitt and Simonson 1997). This is surprising because the '4Ps' model of marketing management – product, price, place and promotion – has been widely used for designing market strategies (Usunier 2000:247). On the one hand, 'promotion is all about communicating with the customer and the wider public' (Bohdanowicz and Clamp 1994:118) and uses advertising, sales promotion, publicity and personal selling to this end. On the other hand, the word 'advertise' refers not only to a type of message placed in some public medium of communication, but to a more general type of speech which calls attention to something in particular (Wernick 1991:181–2). This chapter will address this issue by examining the way in which a Japanese advertising agency makes use of 'below-the-line' promotional ideas to create closer business ties with its clients and thereby gain access to 'above-the-line' advertising in the four main media of television, newspapers, magazines and radio.

Second, an early attempt to highlight the exponential growth of promotional culture during the twentieth century was that by Daniel Boorstin who argued that the whole machinery of contemporary society – he was writing at the beginning of the 60s – was caught up in what he called 'the manufacture of pseudo-events' (Boorstin 1963:47). By this he referred to events that were not spontaneous but contrived; designed to be reported or reproduced (mainly by the media at which they were often aimed); ambiguous in the sense that they may or may not have actually taken place; and intended as self-fulfilling prophecies (Boorstin 1963:22–23). Such 'pseudo-events' began to take over our everyday lives after the so-called 'Graphic revolution', which occurred during the last quarter of the nineteenth century,[2] and which enabled man to move from the written word to the manufacture, preservation, transmittal and dissemination of images (Boorstin 1963:24).[3]

This shift from word to image has led scholars to argue that promotional culture encourages a perceived homogeneous structure of signification, leading to 'artificial semiosis' (Wernick 1991:15), the 'tautology of the signifier' (Baudrillard 1998:124), and thus 'the menace of unreality' (Boorstin 1963:242). The agents of this perceived shift from 'content' to 'form' are advertising and media which not only allow objects to play 'walk-on parts' (Baudrillard 1998:121) between media productions (cf. Wernick 1991:101), but which are linked between and across media products and product lines, as well as by a common cultural pool of images (Wernick 1991:94–5). At the same time as ensuring that each message refers to another message (an automobile factory lay-off to a [different company] car ad to news of a planned new motorway to a drink-and-drive ad),[4] media also themselves refer back and forth to one another (a magazine feature to a film whose star endorses a particular product in a TV commercial that is the subject of discussion on a radio programme) (cf. Wernick 1991:116), in order to impose 'a whole system of segmentation and interpretation of the world upon us' (Baudrillard 1998:122). It is this 'intertext of promotion' (Wernick 1991:95) that Baudrillard (1998:125) sees as preventing any view, discussion, explanation or understanding of events in their historical, social or cultural specificity. Rather, they are reinterpreted according to the same code that both contains ideological and technical structures, on the one hand, and constrains meaning, on the other.

Although Baudrillard (1998:126) warns us against 'interpreting this gigantic enterprise of production of the artificial and cosmetic, of pseudo-objects and pseudo-events, which is invading our daily existence, as a denaturing or falsifying of an "authentic" content', I see three main problems with the approaches to promotional culture as outlined here. First, it is clear from the language used that promotional culture somehow 'devalues' (Wernick 1991:189) culture *per se*. This is most obvious in scholars' use of the prefix 'pseudo-'[5] which, with other tell-tale signs,[6] suggests that – in spite of all their remarkable insights and clear-headed arguments – they hanker nostalgically for a 'purer', 'higher' form of culture untainted by commercialism. Such high cultural elitism inhibits the search for understanding called for by Schudson.

Second, there is the unstated hint that, by becoming 'culturally dominant' (Wernick 1991:184), promotions somehow deprive us, their targeted audience, of 'spontaneity' as they 'invade' our daily lives, 'obliging' us to replace dreams with illusions and ideals with images. In this way, consumers are seen to be passive rather than active agents, powerless to act as cultural hecklers. At its extreme, promotional culture seems to deny the very existence of people and human relationships for it is seen to refer merely to 'a world that is absent' (Baudrillard 1996:176).

Third, and perhaps connected with the above, those who address the problem of promotional culture do so very much from the viewpoint of the *reception* of objects, events and their images. They thus pay comparatively little attention to how those involved in public relations and promotional activities go about their work, although Wernick's discussion (1991:1–19) of Josiah Wedgwood's creation and marketing of the Portland Vase and Stuart Ewen's description (1996:3–18) of his visit to a 99 year old Edward Bernays are important exceptions.[7] This critique can be made of much of cultural studies in general, of course, but it is the springboard for this particular discussion of the *production* of promotions by a Japanese advertising agency.

In an earlier monograph (Moeran 1996a), I outlined the overall structure of the advertising industry in Japan and described the social organization of a Tokyo advertising agency (called the Agency) – focussing in particular on its account services, marketing, creative and media buying divisions. One area of the Agency's activities which make it, and other Japanese agencies, slightly different from European or American advertising agencies is the extent of its handling of what are known as 'below-the-line' activities. Whereas most western agencies are primarily concerned with the procuring of space and time for the sale of advertising in the four main media of magazines, newspapers, television and radio, and leave promotional activities to promoters and other specialists, Japanese advertising agencies devote much of their time and energy to activities that are not directly connected with media buying, but which in fact contribute greatly to it. This kind of work is for the most part carried out by the Agency's Promotions Division which plans, co-ordinates and carries out all kinds of tasks, very often in conjunction with the Marketing Development and Special Promotions (SP) Divisions.

The case studies given here focus in particular on the promotion and packaging of companies (corporate identity), of products, and of events, although each of these – possibly arbitrary – areas tends to overlap with the others to a greater or lesser extent. I hope they will reveal not only how closely enmeshed advertising, media and cultural forms are in promotional culture, but how very often (precisely because it is being promoted) that culture is not all that it seems to be because of the way it is packaged. In my conclusion, therefore, I will examine the ways in which promotions reinforce a particular relationship between economy and culture. Although the Agency concerned is Japanese, and although the examples all refer to ways in which aspects of Japanese corporate and consumer cultures are promoted, my argument is that such practices are in one way or another characteristic of most Asian – and other first world – societies.

Promoting Institutions

Corporate identity is something that, in one way or another, exercises the minds and purse strings of almost all business enterprises all over the world. It is also something that is not new, but goes back to classical antiquity (Marchand 1998:10–11). Department stores were among the first to develop the art of public relations in an attempt to build corporate image (cf. Miller 1981; Marchand 1998:10–15; Moeran 1998), but many other business organizations soon followed suit, as Roland Marchand's detailed historical analysis of American corporations during the first half of the 20th century reveals. It is perhaps hardly surprising to learn, therefore, that Japanese companies are no less concerned with the images which they project and by which they are publicly perceived (see also Moeran 1996a:218–23).

This projection of images takes place in a variety of ways that are far too numerous to detail here. Some of it is straight 'public relations': for example, one-off pamphlets or books for a European national tourist association (put together, printed and distributed by the Agency's subsidiary publishing company); or the regular publication of a monthly magazine for a Japanese credit card company. Some of it is less obviously so: as with the Agency's provision of recipes for a television cooking programme sponsored by a food manufacturer, or the preparation of editorial tie-ups in newspapers and magazines for other clients. Such PR activities are all seen as part of the 'total communications services' rendered by the Agency to its clients.

As a, slightly unusual, example of the kind of work in which an advertising agency might find itself involved, let us look at the way in which an Italian opera company, the Arena di Siena, was brought to Japan for a number of performances of *Tosca*.[8] This event originated in 1987, when senior staff at Asatory Breweries began to consider how best they could celebrate their company's centenary, and invited nine advertising agencies, including the Agency, to participate in a competitive presentation. The ideas put forward in these presentations ranged from the production and sponsorship of special television programmes, to the Agency's suggestion that Asatory Breweries sponsor a Tutankhamen exhibition. Asatory found none of the ideas particularly appealing and as a result limited itself in the meantime to flying its own air balloon and to sponsoring an amateur American football competition (more of which later).

News soon got around about Asatory's interest in linking its centenary with some kind of event to enhance its corporate identity. From April 1988, individual promoters – mostly specializing in particular regions of Europe and the Soviet Union (as it then was) – began to join advertising agencies in making presentations to the company. One such promoter was trying to find a sponsor for the Arena di Siena's version of *Tosca* in Tokyo, but a second promoter was simultaneously trying to sell a British, and a third a Canadian, version of the same opera to Dentsu (at the time, the world's largest single agency) which then approached various clients with these 'sponsorship opportunities' during the early summer of 1988. Eventually, some nine months later, a large Japanese retailer agreed to sponsor the British *Tosca*, with the involvement of the NTV Nihon Television network.

According to gossip, Dentsu told the first promoter that it would also try to sell his idea to a sponsor, but then went straight to Siena behind his back in order to try to secure a separate deal. This plan backfired because the Arena di Siena had an arrangement with a German agent regarding all its performance and music rights, and the German agent had already agreed to give the first promoter far east Asian rights. Dentsu did its best to overcome the difficulties posed by this agreement, apparently, but while it was still negotiating with those concerned in Europe, the promoter in question (who was working entirely on his own) managed to get a direct interview with the CEO of Asatory Breweries who fell for the idea and agreed to sponsor *Tosca* to the tune of ¥1,000 million (US$10 million).

Clearly, as a one-man company, the promoter faced considerable difficulty in organizing an event on such a large scale, so Dentsu immediately suggested that *it* run everything on his behalf. The promoter consulted his new sponsor who said that *he* would decide who was going to run the event. The first the Agency heard of the *Tosca* idea, therefore, was when the senior account director in charge of an Asatory beer account was asked whether he would take over the event. It seemed that the Agency was preferred to Dentsu because Asatory Breweries did not wish to assign its account to an agency that was already handling one other *Tosca* event and was doing its best to get hold of another. Moreover, the fact that Japan's largest advertising agency was reported to be adept at converting sponsor profits into agency 'expenses' did not endear it to this particular corporate sponsor.

Since Asatory had only one or two of its own employees available to work on the event, it asked the Agency to provide people to work for its own marketing division. In August 1988, therefore, the Agency found itself fully involved in preparations for the Arena di Siena's performances and trying to solve a number of problems (not least of which was making sure that the sponsor's funds were properly used and, given that both the German agent and Japanese promoter were small business enterprises, that the Arena di Siena company actually came to Japan). First there was a problem of audiences. In order to pay for the opera company's expenses, the Agency needed to fill a concert hall seating 10,000 people during each of the six performances. Yet there were altogether only 20,000 dedicated opera fans in the whole of Japan. Secondly, there was a problem of concert hall venue, in that some of those with the largest audience capacity (such as the Yoyogi Hall, for example) made a principle of refusing to rent out their premises to business corporations. For this reason, the support of a 'public' institution such as a television network was vital in order to secure the necessary venue. At the same time, thirdly, the three groups involved in the event sorely lacked both manpower and experience to be able to bring things to a successful conclusion and so needed, once more, the backing of a television station which could supply them with event know-how and the means of attracting an audience.

Given this situation, the next step was to decide which TV station to choose. All Japanese TV stations are allowed to use a certain amount of air-time for their own PR (outside the ten per cent air time limit on commercials), and it was this that the Agency hoped and expected a station to make use of to promote *Tosca*. One station that those concerned felt would be fairly active in such PR work was Yamato TV. The Agency decided to negotiate with Yamato because it had also in the past made fairly frequent use of the Yoyogi Hall and seemed to be the best hope for securing this arena for the Siena opera company's visit.[9]

It was this experience that gave Yamato a strong bargaining position during the ensuing negotiations. The original plan was that Asatory Breweries should be the main 'sponsor' (*shusai*), with the promoter and television station as 'co-operators' (*kyōryoku* or *kyōsan*). Yamato, however, objected to this on the grounds that it was the only organization that could provide the venue that both the sponsor and the Agency wanted; Asatory objected to Yamato's stance because it has been a frequent advertiser on the station's programmes over the years. Yamato stuck to its position, however, and said that it could not do everything for free, so Asatory threatened to go to two other stations (not NTV, which was putting on the London *Tosca* with Dentsu).

At this point, the Agency's account director persuaded his client to go along with Yamato Television: firstly, because it *was* the station most likely to be able to secure the Yoyogi Hall as a venue for the opera; secondly, because it had a very strong position within its national media group, so that whatever the station did, the group's national newspaper reported (whereas, with the ANB and TBS networks, the Asahi and Mainichi Newspapers were more powerful than their group TV stations and hence less cooperative); and thirdly, and very importantly, the Agency account director's own connections with Yamato TV went far and deep.

So, it was agreed that sponsor and station act as 'co-sponsors' (*kyōdō shusai*). This meant, though, that the Agency's own position was complicated, since under the original plan it would have acted under its client's instructions as mediator between Asatory Breweries and other institutions involved concerning the actual operation of the event. Now it seemed as though it had two 'clients', only one of whom was paying it a commission. After some discussion, it was agreed that Asatory would retain the Agency which would enter into contract agreements with the promoter and television station on its behalf, while Yamato TV would itself sign contracts with the promoter, the German agent, and Arena di Siena.

Given the size of operations of the two music agents-*cum*-promoters who were acting as go-betweens, there was still considerable worry on the Agency's part that the Arena di Siena might not in the end come. This necessitated the drawing up of two further contracts: one directly with the Arena di Siena, and the other with the German agent. Another major problem affecting the nature of the final contract with Arena di Siena was how to make sure that all six of the main opera singers would come to Japan *and* sing. This proved to be a sticking point for a full three months, but eventually the opera company agreed to the proposal (in March 1989).[10]

Finally, one more contract had to be drawn up between sponsor and television station. This, too, proved to be less than simple because there was an argument about figures. Asatory Breweries reckoned that it would get ¥300 million back in ticket sales, and that its outlay should as a result be no more than ¥600 million yen.[11] Yamato TV, however, calculated that costs would come to ¥1,400 million (of which ¥150 million would be for publicity) so that the sponsor needed to put up ¥1,000 million (the amount it originally agreed to with the promoter). This estimate was accepted by Asatory at the end of 1988,[12] but four months later a medium-sized spanner was thrown in the financial works when the Japanese government instituted a three per cent tax on all items of consumption (including events). This gave rise to considerable argument, with Asatory reckoning that its contribution *in*cluded consumption tax, and Yamato TV insisting on an extra ¥30 million. The account director in charge of ensuring that things went smoothly realized that it was the Agency which stood to lose if both sides stuck to their negotiating positions over interpretation of their contract, and did his best to soothe ruffled feathers. Fortunately, tickets for the opera performances sold much better than expected, with the result that net costs amounted to only ¥900 million. Consumption tax ceased to be an issue.

Given that it had not been involved at the start of Asatory's search for a suitable project to promote its corporate identity, the Agency received only five per cent commission for its part in arranging for the Italian opera company to come to Japan. Yamato TV, however, which was closely involved in the staging of performances, was able to use all kinds of affiliated and subsidiary companies – for lighting, art and design, music, and so on – and make a lot of money in the customary kickbacks, on top of its own commission (which history does not relate). The office that the Agency ran in conjunction with Yamato and Asatory had a dozen or so people working in it – one from the Agency itself, one connected with the promoter, four from the TV station, and eight part-time workers. Between them they arranged six concerts, one of which was shown on television, involving the whole cast of the Arena di Siena, together with 300 Japanese auditioned locally for parts in the chorus, as soldiers, servants, and so on. Altogether 450 people were shipped over from Italy, and – miraculously – everything went smoothly. As a result, both Asatory Breweries *and* Yamato TV benefited from being seen to have helped the Japanese public enjoy a spectacular cultural event while, by acting as intermediary in the success, the Agency improved its corporate image and cemented its relations with both client and media organization concerned.

Promoting Products

Another sphere of activities in which the Agency's Promotions Division has an active interest is in product promotion. This includes the placement of clients' products in all kinds of attention-grabbing environments (a mineral water standing on one side of a television presenter's desk, ready to assuage a thirst caused by studio lights; a soft drink taken from an ice box and gulped down between games by players in a tennis championship; a bottle of alcohol regularly used by the main characters in an action film; and so on). It also includes, of course, advertising in media other than the four main media of television, newspapers, magazines and radio: specifically, outdoor advertising – in particular, billboards which are themselves divided into different categories depending on their location at street level ('city' boards), on rooftops for overhead roads ('highway' boards), and near educational establishments ('campus' boards); transit advertising (mainly train and subway station and carriage ads); and cinemas; but also including telephone, subway, train and other pre-paid cards, match boxes, pens, pencil cases, T shirts, cushions, baggage carts, plane tickets, and all those myriad places and paraphernalia where we find advertising today.

One area of the Agency's interest in product promotion is in premiums. These are often part of advertisements placed in all four media and are of two types. The first is the *closed type premium*, which usually consists of a bag or T-shirt or something equivalent, and for which proof of purchase of the product in question must be provided. This kind of premium is an item of direct exchange. For the most part, it has a retail value of no more than ¥10,000 and legally should not exceed twenty times the value of the product being advertised. The second is the *open type premium*, which is often found in newspaper advertising and which consists of, say, a one-week holiday for two persons, or a new car. In order to win such a premium, people have to fill in a quiz or form of some sort, so that the premium itself is an item of indirect exchange. There is a legal restriction on its value which must be no more than ¥1 million. The usual aim of an open type premium is to improve a product's image, or to make a new product's name more widely known, but in its handout to potential clients the Agency lists 25 other potential advantages of premiums, including revitalization of distribution and the market, getting closer to consumers, increasing 'mind share' and 'topicality', communicating a corporate policy, improving product recognizability, establishing brand recognition in a mature market, and setting up sales opportunities.

The Agency is mainly concerned with closed type premiums, since it is these that usually attract manufacturers who want to know who buys what, where, and when, and closed type premiums provide such information. When such a premium campaign is run, the Promotions Division is contracted to create a post-box address and then analyse all the entries that come in as a result of an ad placed in a particular medium. The manufacturer is thus able to learn comparatively cheaply how its products are distributed by age, gender, occupational group, geographical area, and so on. At the same time, though, precisely because it is handling such information, the Agency is able to update and improve its overall knowledge of consumer tastes (cf. Moeran 1996a:110–16).

One example of the kind of work carried out by the Agency on behalf of its clients may be seen in a Nisshoku instant noodle campaign, which used two popular celebrities, Emori and Kikuchi Momoko, to target middle school, high school and university students, in order to 'refresh' the image of a product which had been on the market for fifteen years (but which still had an annual sales of something like ¥5 billion). The Agency was asked to boost the campaign with a premium idea and to participate in a competitive presentation – the conditions being that the premium offered had to be 'original' and unavailable at department stores, while appealing both to teenagers and to women in particular. The idea that won the presentation for the Agency was to give away to 9,000 people a fox (*kitsune* in Japanese) known as *Donbē* – a name which played on the phrase 'fox noodles' (*kitsune udon*) introduced by Nisshoku some time previously. Since more than this was needed to make the fox both 'original' and different from the cuddly toys available in department stores, the Agency suggested that the fox should be in the form of a pillow, and that it should have an alarm clock inserted in the back of its head. Not only this, but the alarm should consist of the voices of the two celebrities used in the advertising campaign, Emori and Kikuchi Momoko. These would cause the fox pillow to shake all over and awaken the poor sleeper.

The fox itself was made in Korea, where costs were at the time roughly 30 per cent cheaper than in Japan, for about ¥5,000. In order to be eligible to win a fox, applicants were obliged to provide two labels of the instant noodle brand in question. Since each pack cost ¥140, the value of the premium was well below the legal maximum of ¥5,600, but to ensure that there was no problem legally, the Agency took the precaution of arranging with the manufacturer to place a 'dummy' in a department store and to have it photographed with its retail price tag (even though it was not for sale).[13] Together with shipping and storage costs, the total premium campaign thus came to ¥100 million (for which the Agency was then able to charge ten per cent commission). The alarm clock was contracted to Citizen because it happened to have a product on the market that fitted *Donbē*'s head, while Seiko did not.

By the end of the second week of the spot commercials advertising this premium, the Agency had received 29,801 applications for a *Donbē*, with more than 10,000 people writing in on a single day. This figure was seen as only partially successful since Nisshoku had stipulated that the premium campaign should attract 800,000 applications over a three month period of spot commercials on TV. Nevertheless, the Agency stood to gain, whatever the final result, since success in the premium presentation had resulted in its obtaining the

Nisshoku television spot advertising account – itself worth fifteen per cent of its client's expenditure of between ¥3–400 million. In other words, this case study shows how an advertising agency will get involved in aspects of marketing that are not immediately profitable in order to be given a slice of the 'tasty' media buying that often accompanies them.

It is the indirect financial advantages which encourage agencies to take on special promotional work of all kinds. Apart from the kind of 'closed' premium given here, therefore, the Agency is also frequently involved in merchandizing – particularly of products associated with the animated cartoons that it has so successfully devised and sold to television stations over the past three decades, and which have helped it gain access to the otherwise closed shop of television advertising (see Moeran 1996a:233–75). For example, by owning the rights to the popular series *Doraemon*, the Agency has been able to sell all kinds of Doraemon-related merchandise – including a 'Doraemon cheese' to a major dairy products manufacturer. As well as take a two per cent commission on every item sold, the Agency in this instance made the manufacturer's partial sponsorship of the television programme itself a contractual condition. In this way, it was able to ensure that it had one sponsor for a programme series that it had already bought up (*kaikiri*) in advance, as well as to make itself a handsome income from sale of the cheeses in question.

But product packaging goes further than this. What often happens is that the merchandized products are integrated into particular instalments of an animated cartoon. For example, if a particular programme's characters 'take off' in popularity, then the toy manufacturer (Bandai, Sanrio, or whoever) sponsoring the programme will take advantage of that popularity by marketing associated toys and other products. These the sponsor will include in the advertising that accompanies each programme, of course, but it will also try to include plugs for the products in each week's script. This kind of product promotion can also be initiated by the Agency or television station airing the programme. In April 1990, for example, the names of two Bandai robots, *King Skassha* and *Queen Saidoro* (associated with 'lemon squash' and 'cider') were at the last minute inserted into the script of *Lamune & 40* by a production company keen to please the sponsor, Bandai Toys.[14]

Programme scripting of this nature is very much a normal part of children's television programming in Japan (and elsewhere), and helps cement media content with marketing aims. So far as an advertising agency and television station are concerned, there are two sources of income to be gained from airing an animation film: programme income and character income. It is the latter which provides considerable turnover for agency and/or station (depending on the kind of agreement made), as there is voluminous supplemental merchandiz-ing associated with cartoon characters – stickers, notebooks, pencil cases, waste paper baskets, records, CDs, videos, magazines, books, calendars, cushions, towels, kitchen containers – and long-term profits to be made on what can in the end turn out to be relatively little initial investment of money and manpower.

So, when a television station mulls over the numerous ideas put forward by its own departments and advertising agencies in the months before every new programme 'season', it looks not only at whether a particular programme idea is likely to achieve the high popularity ratings its advertisers expect, but at the additional income it may provide. In principle, no station is likely to approve a programme for which the sponsor is seeking an opportunity to sell its new product or product range. What it is looking for is something 'interesting' that will both attract viewers and spark off associated merchandizing (that will in itself create further interest in the programme). It is this 'total package' (Hine 1995) that underlies much Japanese television programming these days, particularly in the realm of children's programmes.

There is one more aspect of the Agency's interest in television animation that should be noted here. Although its success and expertise in developing and producing such blockbuster TV cartoons as *Sazaesan*, *Obake no Q-tarō*, *Candy Candy*, *Dragonball*, *Kyojin no Hoshi* and *Doraemon* have impressed television stations and so been crucial to its ability to buy television time for other programmes and spots for other advertisers, the Agency has always regarded the development of clients' accounts as of the first priority. Every agency has a code by which it assigns to new clients: *S* for 'special', followed by the letters *A*, *B* or *C*, according to the extent to which the account executives concerned think a particular corporation's account can be developed. Thus, it is not the actual volume of advertising so much as the trade potential that interests the Agency, which has used animation films precisely as a means of capitalizing on that potential through linked merchandizing.

Packaging Events

Any advertising agency intent on expanding its business so that it joins the ranks of the Top Ten will have a number of people working on cultural and sporting events, and these are for the most part grouped in the '*bunsupo*' or 'Culspor' section of the Promotions Division (*bun* is short for *bunka*, 'culture', and *supo* for 'sports'). In effect, it is the latter part of the acronym that receives most attention, since – unlike Dentsu or Hakuhodo, for example – the Agency has yet to devote a lot of its employees' time and energy to specifically cultural activities such as art exhibitions. At the same time, as we shall see below, other Agency divisions (even other sections within the Promotions Division) are also involved in the conception of cultural events, and promotion of their sponsors and their products – whether they be an 'Oriental Express' train journey, or a plant-a-tree campaign on behalf of a baby wear manufacturer. As with many activities carried out by the Agency (such as the sponsorship of the Arena di Siena's *Tosca* above), there is no hard and fast allocation of different activities to different divisions. To use a sporting metaphor, the general rule is that those who get hold of the ball should run with it themselves, rather than pass it immediately to those who might be more suited for the job, but who happen at the time to be standing on the other side of the football field.

PRODUCING CONSUMPTION

It is in the promotion of events – rather than merely of corporations and products – that an advertising agency most clearly becomes a kind of 'Cheshire cat' for, in many respects, it acts out the part of the *'kuroko'* black-clothed puppeteer (or 'string puller'), seen but not seen, as it orchestrates its client's every gesture, every move.

For example, in 1990 an audio-visual entertainment company, Frontier, agreed to sponsor a Trans-Eurasian car rally for a fourth year and provided well over US$1 million dollars towards costs of the event, because at the time it made at least one third of all car audio equipment manufactured in Japan and sold something like 70 per cent of this abroad. The Agency's involvement had come several years earlier when the idea of making a film about the rally, with Takakura Ken as the star racing driver, was first mooted and somebody in the Promotions Division came up with a few product placement ideas. Not surprisingly, audio equipment was one of them. The Agency approached Frontier (for whom it handled a comparatively small account at the time) and obtained the corporation's agreement, not only to the inclusion of its equipment in the film but also to acting as main sponsor for the rally to celebrate the 55th year of the company's foundation. As a result, the Agency found itself with a big new account and the creation of yet another department to deal with its new business.

While sponsorship money has been provided by Frontier, the rally itself has been run by a European authority, so that the Agency's main task has been to ensure that its client gets all the publicity possible – by arranging, for example, for a party of a couple of dozen Japanese journalists to fly over to Europe and follow the rally's progress (both on the ground and by helicopter). But in 1990, for the first time in the rally itself, the Agency also found itself involved in merchandising: Frontier's newly marketed satellite navigation system.

Not all in this particular desert has been so cut and dry, however. One of Frontier's largest customers is the car manufacturer, Toyobishi, which fits all its models with Frontier audio equipment. This means that the Toyobishi name or logo also features in photographs, as well as in all kinds of publicity, news, and journalism. Moreover, the automobile manufacturer has also contributed on occasion towards the costs of running the rally – a decision which, because the Agency was handling the Frontier sponsorship, then allowed the Promotions Division to open an account with Toyobishi. So far, so good. However, the Agency's main client is another car manufacturer which is a major rival of Toyobishi and which also participates in the rally, so that the Frontier-Toyobishi relationship can cause a certain sense of unease in both the Agency and the rival manufacturer's camp.[15] Still, one of the intriguing features of the Agency's participation in the Trans-Eurasian rally is the way in which one need has led to another and thus to continuing new business opportunities for the Agency.

Another type of event in which all advertising agencies are closely involved is sports. Almost every major race, match, meeting, tournament and championship – from soccer to windsurfing, by way of athletics, badminton, golf, horse jumping, hurling, motor racing, rugby, table tennis, you name it – is now

282

televised worldwide with its concomitant advertising (on sporting gear, on and around fields of play, on television itself during carefully timed intervals of play). Sporting events, therefore, provide major promotional opportunities for companies that can claim to be 'official sponsors' of this or that event. Although not in the league of an organization such as Dentsu (which is said to run the Olympic Games), the Agency has been involved in various ways in a number of different sporting events, in particular marathon and long distance relay (or *ekiden*) races – both within Japan and overseas (Bali, Guam, and Hawaii). Each of these races tends to be labour intensive over limited periods, so that special 'rooms' are usually set up and extra staff employed for the build-up to, running of, and tidying up after, each marathon (which may not necessarily be of the customary 26 miles, plus so many hundred yards and feet). The Agency thus finds itself heavily involved in the organization of each race, as it ensures not only that the marathon itself is properly conducted with all the fanfare and media hype characteristic of such events, but that everything behind the scenes (from runners' changing rooms to spectators' flags) functions as planned and that sponsors in particular are satisfied with those particular spheres of 'culture' that they have decided – for one reason or another – to promote.

It was its involvement in a marathon race, backed by the Asahi Newspaper, which led to the Agency's first hearing about, then promoting, an American football 'Superbowl' (also backed by the same newspaper). The Superbowl takes place in the middle of December each year, and involves the two winning teams from companies that have participated throughout the autumn in a knock-out competition – one in the Kanto (Tokyo) and the other Kansai (Osaka) regions. Major teams include those from the apparel manufacturers Onward and Renown, as well as that of Asatory Breweries (which sponsors the Superbowl and whose team won the competition in 1989). In the early 90s, the Superbowl attracted large crowds of young people to the Tokyo Dome – a gigantic covered stadium which during the baseball season is home to the Yomiuri Giants – and it was also televised live. Asatory Breweries became the main sponsor as part of its centenary PR build-up in the late 80s, but also following the successful launch of its 'super' lager (for which the Agency put on a successful advertising campaign).[16] The competition itself has been run by an All Japan-American Football Association, while the Asahi Newspaper has acted as non-financial backer.[17]

Prior to the introduction of Japan's professional soccer league, American football was extremely popular in Japan's corporate business world. There were two main reasons for this. In the first place, the nature of the game is 'organizational' in that American football demands close teamwork among different specialists with different areas of expertise, as well as a lot of strategic planning prior to the execution of moves on the field. Most companies, particularly banks, have regarded these as vital attributes for employees who not only develop a sense of company 'spirit' (see Rohlen 1973) from such teamwork, but also learn from strategic thinking about how to practice marketing. In the second place, companies want their employees to attend games like this since they contribute to a sense of company 'oneness' through interaction between players and supporters.

Because ticket sales are the readiest indication of a particular event's success or failure, the Agency does its utmost to persuade people to go and watch the Superbowl. Many of those attending are team supporters (Asatory Breweries contributed 11,000 members of a 52,000 crowd when its team reached the final). The Agency also arranges for all kinds of advertising to be put up in strategic places, so that it is seen by both spectators and television viewers. But at the same time those concerned have to ensure that advertising satisfies strict fire regulations in the Tokyo Dome, so that advertisements – on non-flammable banners, for example – are comparatively expensive. Although income from tickets, pamphlets and merchandizing go to the All Japan-American Football Association (thereby relieving the Agency of risk), the Agency is charged with some merchandizing on behalf of Asatory Breweries and with the organization and running of everything that goes on around the event – preparing programmes, manning reception desks, arranging press conferences, planning parties, conducting the opening and closing (cup awarding) ceremonies, ensuring that important people are photographed in the act of doing important things (preferably with other important people), and organizing a dozen long-legged and short-skirted young ladies to act as companions for VIPs. Most, if not all, of this is overseen by one person from the 'Culspor' Section who has under his command about four dozen people from organizations subcontracted by the Agency for the occasion.

From all these activities the Agency is able to take its commission – usually of around ten per cent, rather than the fifteen per cent or more that it can command for media placement – but at the cost of a large number of working hours put in by members of the Account Services, Creative and Promotions Divisions. One advantage of putting on an event, though, is precisely that it brings together various different divisions in the Agency and allows them to work together as a team. Another is that an event – precisely because it is topical – permits the Agency to secure space in the print and television media on behalf of its client. In this respect, an event contributes towards the Agency's basic advertising activities and is in itself a medium endowed with the image of the sponsoring corporation. In this way, it will differ from the four main media, each of which (like the Nihon Keizai Newspaper for businessmen, for example) has its own image, to which advertising corporations can only subscribe. Thus events act as a means of allowing major corporations to appear in their own, rather than under the umbrella of another's, image.

There is something apart from the direct income that accrues from an event which is of enormous importance to any advertising agency involved in its staging. This merit is in a sense intangible, for, by putting on the Superbowl for example, the Agency is able to provide a venue (*ba o settai suru*) where the presidents and top executives from the sponsoring corporation and the Agency itself can sit together over a two to three hour period and, between the occasional encouraging shout and exasperated boo, discuss their own visions of the universe. In other words, the Agency will get involved in putting on cultural or sporting events because these permit its top management to further cement personal ties. They thus encourage what is generally considered to be the most important thing about Japanese business: the establishment and maintenance of 'human chemistry'. It is the development of such personal ties that leads through the intricate web of individuals' networks to introductions which may themselves lead to further accounts, or to other contacts willing to take a ride in the cultural legoland of the Agency's business plans.

Promoting Agency Business

Let us now try to tidy up the pieces of this chapter by examining some reasons why the Agency allows itself to get involved in such a wide and disparate set of time-consuming promotional activities.

It should be made absolutely clear from the start of this discussion that for an advertising agency promotional activities are in large part *strategic*. This can be seen in a number of different ways. In the first place, there are the marketing benefits that may result. As we have seen in the case of premiums in particular, an advertising agency is able to use promotional activities to improve its own knowledge of consumer tastes as a result of the information that it gains while handling a client's account. For example, one of the accounts handled by the Agency's Promotions Division was low level marketing on behalf of Kanedō cosmetics chain store division. By helping its client in aspects of 'visual merchandizing' (including shop layout, display, colour coordination, general atmosphere, and so on), the Agency also willingly took on finnicky jobs like the design and provision of cosmetic display baskets, two-tone POP umbrellas and mobiles, as well as the printing of leaflets, signs, posters, and Christmas gift catalogues. Its goodwill and success then led to the Agency's taking on some of Kanedō's gift marketing sales promotions, including display kits and advance order cosmetic sets for special events. As a result, it has been able to gain valuable information about the gift market in Japan. Not only does it learn what sort of things people buy on special occasions like Mother's Day (talcum powder, hairbrushes, shampoos), or Valentine's Day (scented soaps, *eau de toilettes*, creams). It also finds out how many of what kind of people buy how much on each occasion, as well as the major gift giving occasions in the cosmetics and toiletries market (with Christmas the clear winner, followed by Mother's Day, mid-year *chūgen* and year-end *seibo* gift 'seasons', and then Valentine's Day).

Thus, as we saw in the case of premiums, the Agency will participate in promotional activities because they provide it with marketing information to which it might not otherwise have access and which it can then feed into its computer base and use in relation to other accounts. At the same time, this information provides the Agency with opportunities to come up with marketing strategies (such as a way to counter the overwhelming predominance of chocolate gifting on Valentine's Day) which may themselves find favour with other clients and lead to an expansion of other accounts.

Another aspect of marketing that we have noted concerns the merchandizing that is often associated with promotional activities (for example, Frontier's satellite navigation system used in the Trans-Eurasian rally). So far as the Agency is concerned, the main opportunities for commercial profit here are in the character merchandizing associated with children's television cartoon programmes, and we have seen how television stations often select certain programmes for their merchandizing opportunities rather than for their contents *per se* (although both are subordinated to popularity and ratings). But one-off events, too, are viewed as potential long-term business opportunities with merchandizing spin-offs. Thus, when it became involved in the organization of the Asia Classical Music Festival in Hokkaido during the summer of 1990, for example, the Agency decided to set up an independent office that would not only liaise between the local festival committee, the conductor's New York office, and sponsor (Yamamura Securities), but which would ensure that it gained access to marketing rights of both performances and recordings (CDs, laser discs, video tapes and so on) of the young musicians attending the music festival once they became better known and regular performers in the world of classical music.

The second strategic business area opened up by an advertising agency's involvement in promotional activities involves access to other kinds of advertising accounts. We have seen, for example, that television programming of all sorts is carried out by an advertising agency with a view to getting a slice of *the* most lucrative aspect of media buying: television. By putting on a programme, an agency is able to buy up time on television stations and sell it (to great profit) to advertisers. But, as we saw in the case of the *Donbē* fox premium promotion for Nisshoku, the Agency was able as a result of its involvement to buy TV commercial space for its sponsor and it was this aspect of the account that was the most lucrative. The same can be said for other events, such as *Tosca* and the Superbowl, organized by the Agency on behalf of its client.

At the same time, we should note that Japanese advertisers are not that gullible; they have learned from experience what kind of games their agencies can play and so will not necessarily fall for promotional plans that are clearly designed to promote an agency's profits rather than a sponsor's image. But agencies also know that would-be sponsors know what they are up to. This is why they try out different proposals that are less obviously profitable (like the Agency's proposal of a Tutankhamen exhibition as part of Asatory Breweries' centenery celebrations), since there is always the chance that a sponsor will fall for a less-obviously greedy agency's proposal and give it the tasty television advertising morsels anyway (as Asatory Breweries did when it charged the Agency with the handling of *Tosca*).

286

This brings us to another aspect of business strategy highlighted by the examples given here: access to new accounts. These are of two kinds. An existing account with a particular client may be developed little by little into new areas – as with the Agency's careful cultivation of Kanedō noted above where, ultimately, the aim was to win an account (through competitive presentation) in the client's big-spending cosmetics and toiletries divisions. Here an agency may direct its attention to low level, less obviously visible aspects of advertising and promotion in the hope of later being asked by the client to handle 'above-the-line' advertising in one or more of the four main media. This is what the Agency referred to as 'marketing in the gap' (*tsukima shōhō*) left by very large agencies like Dentsu and Hakuhodo which did not need to bother themselves with such time-consuming, directly non-profitable activities.

A second kind of account development is through that of an already existing client. This we noted in the Agency's handling of the Trans-Eurasian rally where the sponsor, Frontier, was main supplier of car stereo equipment to Toyobishi. Although hitherto the Agency had not been able to handle business for Toyobishi, its promotional work on behalf of Frontier led to its finally opening an – albeit small – account with the giant Japanese car manufacturer. As with Kanedō, the Agency hoped that it would be able to make full use of this business development potential.

In fact, this did happen almost immediately through an entirely different promotional activity. When the Agency took on the organization of the Asia Classical Music Festival, it found itself dealing with Yamamura Securities, whose CEO only had to make one telephone call to persuade the chairman of Toyobishi to contribute to the event. As a result, the corporation's publicity department was ordered to pay ¥50 million into the Agency's bank account – money which, if the Agency had approached the publicity department on its own initiative (and through networking), would not have been forthcoming because – an account director would have been told – there was 'no money' to be spent on such an event.

This brings us to a third aspect of business strategy opened up by promotional activities: business partnerships and corporate image. We have seen that one advantage for an advertising agency doing promotions is the way in which they can help cement already existing business ties, both between agency and client (as when senior management can sit down for two to three hours during a game of American football) and between agency and media organization (in the case of Yamato TV's handling of *Tosca*). In this respect, promotions merely contribute to maintenance of the tripartite structure of the advertising industry that I have noted elsewhere (for example, Moeran 1996a:21, 2000b).

Under such circumstances, it is not surprising to find that, while often ostensibly designed to enhance the identity of the sponsoring corporation providing the money, promotional activities actually end up contributing to the corporate image of sponsor *and* agency *and* media organization involved. Thus, not just Asatory Breweries, but Yamato TV and the Agency were able to enhance their 'cultural capital' as a result of the successful staging of the Arena di Siena's version of *Tosca*.

Although sponsor and media organization are almost always able to take advantage of public acclaim through further media PR, an advertising agency's ability to capitalize on its success tends to be limited to the field in which the advertising industry operates since it is there that its reputation 'percolates' (as an Indian author once remarked of a Japanese publisher). Successful PR that does improve a sponsor's corporate image, advertising campaigns that do promote sales, below-the-line activities that do help a client – these are what get talked about in the world of advertising where gossip and networking are vital components of business positions, position-takings and negotiations. This is what helps an agency rise in people's estimation from mere 'jack-of-all-trades' (*benriya-san*) to professional organization.

Of course, given that an advertising agency rarely openly provides money for any activity, it is always likely to find itself in a subordinate position to sponsor (although, as we saw with *Tosca*, a media organization can use its access to resources as leverage into more or less equal position of power with a sponsor). There are times, however, when an agency comes up with such a good idea, or manages to create an atmosphere of trust over a long period of time, that it begins to interact with its client in a way that suggests partnership between the two concerns, rather than one merely acting as 'agent' on behalf of the other. This the Agency has managed to do with a handful of big clients. Its aim is to achieve this partnership status with a majority of clients, and promotional activities (like redesigning 270,000 of one manufacturer's retail outlets and introducing automatic vending machines throughout the country) are a major part of this improvement in the nature of the Agency's business relations. In this respect, we can see the close relationship between promotions and packages which 'are about containing and labeling and informing and celebrating. They are about power and flattery and trying to win people's trust' (Hine 1995:25).

Conclusion

In spite – or rather, because – of all these strategic implications accompanying involvement in promotional activities, an advertising agency may appear in the end to be little more than a convenient jack-of-all-trades, arranging anything from annual stockholders' meetings to travelling exhibitions, by way of weddings for famous personalities.[18] In return, it may or may not achieve its strategic aims of developing business opportunities, getting new clients, enhancing its status, or whatever. But of one thing it can be sure. The more involved it becomes with different aspects of promotion, the more an agency can build up a formidable network of business ties with all kinds of disparate organizations – from government ministries to hotels and catering firms, by way of music entertainment, real estate, travel agencies, department and convenience stores, telemarketing, culture clubs, film production, model agencies, and so on.

It is this overall 'know how' which clients want to make use of and which agencies have to develop if they are to survive.

Promotions are a form of *bricolage*, combining familiar ingredients to create novel products and events. The impact of promotions, packaging, branding and advertising used together is, in true Durkheimian fashion, greater than the sum of their individual parts. Promotions are also a 'means of conveying information and changing and sometimes circumventing human relationships' (Hine 1995:75). Together with packaging, they change the ways we understand the world. Arena di Siena's *Tosca*, Kanedō retail chain stores, the Trans-Eurasian rally, the Asia Classical Music Festival, *Doraemon* and other children's television cartoons, are not *like* packages; they *are* packages, and thus 'a tool to control expectations and to assure that the products can be delivered in accordance with those expectations' (Hine 1995:171). Here we see what might be called an 'intentional disinterestedness' as both agencies and clients building up cultural or symbolic capital with a view to transforming it into economic capital as and when appropriate (Bourdieu 1984).

Which brings me to my promised comment on the link between economy and culture. As Thomas Hine (1995:14) has pointed out with regard to packaging, and as Joel Stocker has shown in the previous chapter, promotions form 'a system that links production and consumption'. But just what that link is in the 'uneasy persuasion' of advertising is difficult to describe. After all, advertising is itself promotion. Yet in the advertising world itself, promotions are seen as a *residual* category: below-the-line activities that hopefully, but not necessarily, permit an agency to gain access to its central activity of above-the-line advertising. In this sense, their cultural contents are also residual since the purpose of promotions is essentially *economic*.

It is the way in which what 'should' be *cultural* is somehow transformed into the economic that attracts the attention of almost all those writing about promotional culture and media. For Andy Wernick, 'the rise of promotion as a cultural force signals ... an alteration in the very relation between culture and economy' (Wernick 1991:185) as culture is transformed into 'a mass-producing economic sphere in its own right' (Wernick 1991:100). But does this *matter*? Is culture somehow to be assigned to a commercially pristine state? It would seem so. The very word 'culture', suggests Baudrillard (1998:103–4), is a misleading concept which does no more than provide a 'standard package' of objects, made up of obsolescent cultural ingredients and signs, that consumers should possess in order to be able to call themselves citizens of a consumer society. Thus we have not culture, but cultural recycling (*le recyclage*); not consumption, but consummation (Baudrillard 1998:99–101).

Maybe. But let us also note from this discussion of promotional activities by a Japanese advertising agency that it is those *producing*, as well as those consuming, culture who are 'recycled' as they are 'redesigned' and integrated into a formal system of commodity differences. Thus, both consumers *and* producers are caught up in a system of 'cultural recycling' that was originally intended for consumption. Producers are themselves consumed. Economy and culture thus appear as indivisible elements of a totality, and culture is as economic as the economy is cultural in a country like Japan – which, I suppose, is what Bourdieu is also saying (albeit in different words) in his discussion of cultural production.

In this respect, how the Agency goes about integrating consumers, commodities and corporations by means of promotional activities supports the argument (also discussed in the Introduction) that under capitalism it is the economy that becomes 'the main site of symbolic production', and that 'rational production for gain is in one and the same motion the production of symbols' (Sahlins 1976:211, 215). This has led Marshall Sahlins to argue further that every conceivable distinction of society is used to help distinguish objects (rather than the other way round, as in primitive societies) and so form a system of 'bourgeois totemism' (Sahlins 1976:216). But, as hinted above, such a system is not limited to objects. Rather, as I have tried to show here and in my previous writings on the Agency (Moeran 1996a), such distinctions in society are used also to distinguish organizations, as well as products and consumers. The aim of promotional activities, therefore, is to merge these three distinct totemic systems – of organizations, objects and consumers – into a single integrated 'promotional culture'. If they are successful, we will be able to talk of ProMo for the new millenium!

Notes

1 It has since (July 1999) closed.
2 The inventions cited by Boorstin include dry-plate photography (1873), the telephone (1876), phonograph (1877), roll film (1884), radio (1891) and motion pictures (1900).
3 See also Ewen's (1996:115, 173) discussion of the emergence of public relations in the United States.
4 For a detailed analysis of the relation between advertising and features in a Japanese woman's magazine, see Moeran (1995).
5 Also found in Leo Lowenthal's discussion of mass idols and the 'pseudo-individualization' of heroes (Lowenthal 1968:133).
6 For example, Baudrillard's use of an 'aesthetics of simulation' which is opposed to an 'aesthetics of beauty and originality' (1998:110), as well as his reference (1998:103–4) to the culture propagated by mass media as a 'lowest common culture'. For his part, Wernick (1991:194) talks of promotional culture being 'radically deficient in good faith'.
7 Interestingly, both these discussions are used to *start* their books on promotional culture and PR respectively.
8 For reasons of confidentiality, the names of the opera company and the Italian city with which it is associated, some media events and organizations, and all corporate sponsors mentioned in this paper have been changed.
9 In addition, the promoter himself had approached Yamato TV at one stage during his attempts to sell the opera and the station had shown some initial interest.
10 Matters were further complicated by the fact that the City of Siena was also involved in the running of the Arena di Siena opera company. Needless to say, perhaps, a Japanese lawyer was used to negotiate the contract successfully.

11 There appears to be some faulty arithmetic here. It was estimated that tickets would cost ¥6,000 each on average and that, with Yoyogi Hall's 8,000 seat capacity filled, a single performance of *Tosca* would bring in about ¥50 million.

12 The promoter is said to have taken 30 per cent commission.

13 The practice of making a dummy is carried out by all agencies, as a form of self-protection.

14 *Lamune* is also the name of a *7 Up* type of fizzy drink in Japan.

15 See Moeran (1996a:71–88) for an extended discussion of such rivalry among car manufacturers and consequent difficulties faced by the Agency in the handling of one of its accounts.

16 The sponsorship 'connection' here, for those who might have missed it, lies in the use of the word *super* in both product and event.

17 Backing (*shuzai*) here refers to non-financial media support, typically found among newspaper companies reporting cultural events (see Moeran 1987:35–7).

18 For example, Dentsu 'arranged' the weddings of the pop singers Gō Hiromi and Nitani Yurie, and Itsuki Hiroshi and Kazu Yūko. For discussion of two other mediated celebrity engagements, see Stefánsson (1998)

REFERENCES

Abu-Lughod, Lila 1997 'The interpretation of culture(s) after television', *Representation* 59: 109–34.

Adas, Michael 1989 *Machines as a Measure of Men: science, technology and ideologies of western dominance*, Ithaca, NY: Cornell University Press.

Adorno, Theodor and Max Horkheimer 1973 *Dialectic of Enlightenment*, London: Verso.

Aera 1997 'Honkon, Taiwan, Nihon wa poppu kyōeiken' (Hong Kong, Taiwan and Japan constitute a pop co-prosperity sphere), p.30–38, January 20.

Akita, Minoru 1984 *Osaka Shōwa-shi A History of Osaka in the Shōwa period*, Henshū Kōbō Noa.

Aku Yū 1993 (1997) *Yume o Kutta Otoko Tachi (Men Who Ate Dreams)*, Tōkyō: Koike Shoin.

Anagnost, Ann 1997 *National Past-Times: narrative, representation and power in modern China*, Durham and London: Duke University Press.

Anderson, Benedict 1991 *Imagined Communities,* London: Verso.

Anderson, Michael 1984 *Madison Avenue in Asia: politics and transnational identity in advertising*, Rutherford: Fairleagh Dickinson University Press.

Ang, Ien 1985 *Watching Dallas: soap opera and the melodramatic imagination,* London: Methuen.

—— 1990 'Culture and communication: towards an ethnographic critique of media consumption in the transnational media system', *European Journal of Communication* 5: 239–60.

—— 1991 *Desperately Seeking the Audience*, London: Routledge.

—— 1996 *Living Room Wars: rethinking media audiences for a postmodern world*, London and New York: Routledge.

—— and Jokes Hermes 1991 'Gender and/in Media Consumption', p.307–328 in J. Curran and M. Gurevitch (eds.), *Mass Media and Society,* New York: Edward Arnold.

Annuncio, Charubala 1993 'A barren market', *Advertising & Marketing*, November.

Appadurai, Arjun 1990 'Disjuncture and difference in the global cultural economy', *Public Culture* 2 (2): 1–24.

—— 1991 'Global ethnoscapes: notes and queries for a transnational anthropology', p.191–210 in R. Fox (ed.), *Recapuring Anthropology: working in the present*, Santa Fe, NM: School of American Research Press.

—— 1996 *Modernity at Large: cultural dimensions of globalization*, Minneapolis: University of Minnesota Press.

Apel, K-O. 1979 'Types of social science in the light of human cognitive interests', in S. Brown (ed.), *Philosophical Disputes in the Social Sciences*, Sussex: Harvester.

Asia Times 1996 'Vietnam hints at easing rules for joint advertising ventures', p.13, June 20.

Asian Advertising and Marketing 1997 'A&M Television Profile', p.18, July 25.

Asō Kōtarō 1998 'Rankin kogengaku' (The modernology of ranking), *Rank In*, p.78–82, July.

Augé, Marc 1995 *Non-Places: introduction to an anthropology of supermodernity*, London: Verso.

Bardesly, Jan 1997 'Japanese feminism, nationalism, and the royal wedding of summer '93', *Journal of Popular Culture* 31 (2): 189–205.

Barnard, Henry 1990 'Bourdieu and ethnography: reflexivity, politics and praxis', p.58–85 in R. Harker et al. (eds.), *An Introduction to the Work of Pierre Bourdieu*, London: Macmillan.

Baudrillard, Jean 1970 *La Société de Consommation: ses mythes, ses structures*, Paris: Gallimard.

—— 1983a *In the Shadow of the Silent Majorities . . . or the end of the social and other essays*, translated by P. Foss, P. Patton and J. Johnston, New York: Semiotext(e).

—— 1983b 'The precession of simulacra', p.1–79 in his *Simulations*. Translated by P. Foss, P. Patton and P. Beitchman, New York: Semiotext(e).

——1988 (1968) 'The system of objects', p.10–28 in Mark Poster (ed.), *Jean Baudrillard: selected writings*, Stanford, CA: Stanford University Press.

—— 1988a [1985] 'The masses: the implosion of the social in the media', p.207–219 in Mark Poster (ed.), *Jean Baudrillard: selected writings*, translated by M. Maclean, Oxford: Polity.

—— 1988b 'Consumer society', p.29–56 in Mark Poster (ed.), *Jean Baudrillard: selected writings*, translated by J. Mourrain, Oxford: Polity.

—— 1990 *Seduction*, translated by B. Singer, New York: St. Martin's Press.

—— 1996 *The System of Objects*, translated by J. Benedict, London and New York: Verso.

—— 1998 *The Consumer Society: myths and structures*, translated by C. Turner, London: Sage.

Becker, Howard 1982 *Art Worlds*, Berkeley: University of California Press.

Beilherz, Peter 1991 'Louis Althusser', p.13–19 in P. Beilherz (ed.), *Social Theory: a guide to general thinkers*, Sydney: Allen & Unwin.

Benjamin, Walter 1973 *Illuminations*, London: Fontana.

Bensky, Xavier 1998 *Manzai: metamorphoses of a Japanese comic performance genre*, Master's Thesis, McGill University.

Bestor, Theodore 1989 'Lifestyles and popular culture in urban Japan', p.1–37 in R. Powers et al. (eds.), *Handbook of Japanese Popular Culture*, New York: Greenwood Press.

Birch, David 1993 *Singapore Media: communication strategies and practices*, Asia Paper No. 1 (Asia Reseach Centre, Murdoch University), Melbourne: Longman Cheshire.

—— 1995 'Asianising Asia: constructing public cultures', Keynote Paper at the CSAA Conference, Bathurst (http://www.gu.edu.au/gwis/akccmp/papers/Birch.html).

Blumer, Herbert 1969 (1988) *Symbolic Interactionism: perspective and method*, Englewood Cliffs, NJ: Prentice Hall. (Reprinted by the University of California Press.)

Bohdanowicz, Janet and Liz Clamp 1994 *Fashion Marketing*, London and New York: Routledge.

Boorstin, Daniel 1963 *The Image*, Harmondsworth: Pelican.

Bourdieu, Pierre 1984 (1979) *Distinction: a social critique of the judgement of taste*, Cambridge, MA: Harvard University Press.

—— 1986 'The production of belief: contribution to an economy of symbolic goods', p.131–63 in R. Collins et al. (eds.), *Media, Culture & Society: a critical reader*, London: Sage.

REFERENCES

—— 1993a *The Field of Cultural Production: essays on art and literature*, Cambridge: Polity.

—— 1993b *Sociology in Question*, translated by Richard Nice, London: Sage.

—— and Loïc Wacquant 1992 *An Invitation to Reflexive Sociology*, Cambridge: Polity.

Braudel, Fernand 1980 *On History*, Chicago: University of Chicago Press.

Bremner, Brian et al. 1999 'Fall of a keiretsu', *Business Week*, March 15 (Asian edition).

Brown, R. 1987 'Reason as rhetorical: on relations among epistemology, discourse and practice', in J. Nelson et al. (eds.), *The Rhetoric of the Human Sciences: language and argument in scholarship and public affairs*, London: University of Wisconsin Press.

Brown, Stephen 1995 *Postmodern Marketing*, London and New York: Routledge.

Burke, Timothy 1996 *Lifebuoy Men, Lux Women: commodification, consumption, & cleanliness in modern Zimbabwe*, Durham and London: Duke University Press.

Burns, Tom 1977 *The BBC: public institution and private world*, London: The Macmillan Press.

Business Times 1995 'Foreign advertising agencies in Vietnam', p.11, February 24.

Butler, Judith 1990 *Gender Trouble: feminism and the subversion of identity*, London: Routledge.

—— 1994 'Gender as performance: an interview with Judith Butler', *Radical Philosophy* 67: 32–39.

Cahoon, Keith 1993 'Popular music in Japan', p.1284–85 in *Japan: an illustrated encyclopedia*, Tokyo: Kodansha.

Caldarola, Victor J. 1992 'Time and the television war', *Public Culture* 4 (2): 127–136.

Carey, James W. 1986 'The dark continent of American Journalism', p.146–196 in R. K. Manoff and M. Schudson (eds.) *Reading the News*, New York, Pantheon Books.

Carrier, James (ed.) 1995 *Occidentalism: images of the west*, Oxford: Berg.

Chan, Joseph Man 1996 'Television in greater China: structure, exports, and market formation', p.126–160 in J. Sinclair et al. (eds), *New Patterns in Global Television: peripheral vision*, New York: Oxford University Press.

Chaney, David 1996 *Lifestyles,* London: Routledge.

Chatterjee, Partha and Arup Mallik 1997 (1975) 'Indian democracy and bourgeois reaction', in P. Chatterjee, *A Possible India: essays in political criticism*, Delhi: Oxford University Press.

Chen, Kuan-Hsing 1996 'Not yet the postcolonial era: The (super)nation-state and transnationalism of cultural studies: response to Ang and Stratton', *Cultural Studies* 10 (1): 37–70.

—— (ed.) 1998 *Trajectories: inter-Asian cultural studies*, London: Routledge.

Cheng M. and Tong B. 1993 *Xinwen Lilun Jiaocheng (A Course in News Theory)*, Beijing: Chinese People's University Press.

Ching, Leo 1994 'Imaginings in the Empire of the Sun: Japanese mass culture in Asia', *boundary 2* 21 (1): 199–219.

Chow, Rey 1993 *Writing Diaspora: tactics of intervention in contemporary cultural studies*, Bloomington: Indiana University Press.

Ci Jiwei 1994 *Dialectic of the Chinese Revolution: from utopianism to hedonism.* Stanford: Stanford University Press.

Clifford, James 1992 'Traveling cultures', p.96–116 in L. Grossberg et al. (eds.), *Cultural Studies*, London and New York: Routledge.

—— and George Marcus (eds.) 1986 *Writing Culture: the poetics and politics of ethnography,* Berkeley and Los Angeles: University of California Press.

Collingwood, R. 1940 *An Essay on Metaphysics*, Oxford: Clarendon Press.

—— 1942 *The New Leviathan or man, society, civilization and barbarism*, Oxford: Clarendon Press.

—— 1946 *The Idea of History*, Oxford: Clarendon Press.

Coombe, Rosemary 1996 'Embodied trademarks: mimesis and alterity on American commercial frontiers', *Cultural Anthropology* 11 (2): 202–224.

Costa, Janeen and Gary Bamossy (eds.) 1995 *Marketing in a Multicultural World: ethnicity, nationalism, and cultural identity*, London: Sage.

Danielou, Alain 1994 *The Complete Kama Sutra*, Rochester, VT: Park Street Press.

Davis, Deborah and Ezra Vogel 1990 *Chinese Society on the Eve of Tiananmen: the impact of reform*, Cambridge, Mass.: Harvard University Press.

—— and Steven Harrell 1993 *Chinese Families in the Post-Mao Era*, Berkeley: University of California Press.

—— et al. (eds.) 1995 *Urban Spaces in Contemporary China: the potential for autonomy and community in post-Mao China*, Woodrow Wilson Center Series. Cambridge: Cambridge University Press.

Debonair 1991 October.

De Launey, Guy 1995 'Not-so-big in Japan: western pop music in the Japanese market', *Popular Music* 14 (2): 203–225.

Deleuze, G. and F. Guatari 1983 *Anti-Oedipus: capitalism and schizophrenia*, translated by R. Hurley, M. Seem and H. R. Lane, Minneapolis: University of Minnesota Press.

Dirlik, Arif and Zhang Xudong 1997 'Introduction: postmodernism and China' *Boundary 2* 24 (3): 1–18.

Doctor, Vikram and Subhashini Sen 1997 'A tough, rough and risque market', in *Business World*, September 7.

Dorfman, Ariel and Armand Mattelart 1972 *Para Leer al Pato Donald: comunicacion de masa y colonialismo*, Mexico City: Siglo XXI.

Drucker, Peter 1993 *Post-Capitalist Society*, New York: Harper Business.

Du Gay, Paul (ed.) 1997 *Production of Culture/Cultures of Production*, London: Sage, the Open University.

—— et al. 1997 *Doing Cultural Studies: the story of the Sony Walkman*, London: Sage, the Open University.

Dunnett, Peter 1990 *The World Television Industry: an economic analysis*, London: Routledge.

Dyer, Richard 1992 *Only Entertainment*, London: Routledge.

Eagleton, Terry 1990 *The Ideology of the Aesthetic*, Oxford: Basil Blackwell.

Economist, The 1999a 'Japan's constitution: the call to arms', *The Economist*, February 27.

—— 1999b 'The darker side of cuteness', *The Economist*, May 8.

—— 1999c 'Japan's pretty boys', *The Economist*, July 10.

Efron, Sonni 1999a 'Fight over genetically altered food is bound to have worldwide fallout', *International Herald Tribune,* March 17.

—— 1999b 'Japan's right to know: first freedom of information law is passed after a 20-year battle for open government', *International Herald Tribune*, May 18.

Ewen, Stuart 1996 *PR: a social history of spin*, New York: Basic Books.

Fabian, Johannes 1983 *Time and the Other: how anthropology makes its object*, New York: Columbia University Press.

—— 1990 *Power and Performance: ethnographic explorations through proverbial wisdom and theater in Shaba, Zaire*, Madison: University of Wisconsin.

Fan S.J. and Chen Y.C. 1997 'Jingzheng cai neng jifa huoli: zhujiang tai bankuai lanmu fangan gongkai' (Only competition can stimulate vitality: opening up Zhujiang Television Station programme design), *South China Television Journal* 4: 18–21.

Fang K. 1997 'Ershi yi shiji dianshi fazhan zhan lue - guanyu guangdong dianshi fazhan zhanlue de sikao' (The strategic development of television in the twenty-first century: thoughts about the strategic development of Guangdong Television), *South China Television Journal* 1: 4–12.

Farley, Maggie 1996 'Japan's press and the politics of scandal', p.133–164 in S. J. Pharr and E. S. Krauss (eds.), *Media and Politics in Japan*, Honolulu: University of Hawai'i Press.

Fatt, Arthur 1967 'The danger of "local" international advertising', *Journal of Marketing* 31: 60–62.

Featherstone, Mike 1991 *Consumer Culture & Postmodernism*, London: Sage.

—— 1996 *Undoing Culture*, London: Sage.

—— et al. (eds.), 1995 *Global Modernities,* London: Sage.

Ferguson, James 1993 'De-moralizing economies: African socialism, scientific capitalism and the moral politics of "structural adjustment"', in S. Moore (ed.), *Moralizing States and the Ethnography of the Present*, Arlington, VA: American Anthropological Association.

Ferguson, H. 1990 *The Science of Pleasure: cosmos and psyche in the bourgeois world view,* London: Routledge.

Ferguson, Marjorie and Peter Golding (eds.) 1997 *Cultural Studies in Question*, London: Sage.

Feuchtwang, Stefan et al. (eds.) 1988 *Transforming China's Economy in the Eighties*, London: Zed Books.

Feyerabend, P. 1975 *Against Method: outline of an anarchistic theory of knowledge*, London: Verso.

—— 1987 *Farewell to Reason*, London: Verso.

Fishman, Mark 1980 *Manufacturing the News*, Austin: University of Texas Press.

Fiske, John 1987 *Television Culture: popular pleasures and politics*, London and New York: Routledge.

—— 1996 *Media Matters: everyday culture and political change*, Minneapolis: University of Minnesota Press.

Foreign Correspondents Club of Japan 1998 *Foreign Correspondents in Japan*, Rutland, VT, and Tokyo: Tuttle.

Foucault, Michel 1972 *The Archaeology of Knowledge*, translated by A.M. Sheridan, London: Tavistock.

—— 1986a *The Use of Pleasure*, Volume 2 of *The History of Sexuality*, translated by R. Hurley, Harmondsworth: Viking.

—— 1986b *The Care of the Self*, Volume 3 of *The History of Sexuality* translated by R. Hurley, New York: Pantheon.

Fowles, Jib. 1996 *Advertising and Popular Culture,* Thousand Oaks: Sage.

Fox, Richard (ed.) 1991 *Recapuring Anthropology: working in the present*, Santa Fe, NM: School of American Research Press.

Frank, Andre 1995 *Re-Orient: global economy in the Asian age*, Berkeley and Los Angeles: University of California Press.

French, David and Michael Richards (eds.) 1996 *Contemporary Television: eastern perspectives*, New Delhi: Sage.

Frith, Katherine (ed.) 1996 *Advertising in Asia: communication, culture and consumption*, Ames: Iowa State University Press.

—— and Michael Frith 1989 'Advertising as cultural invasion', *Media Asia* 16 (4): 179–184.

—— 1990 'Western advertising and eastern culture: the confrontation in southeast Asia', *Current Issues and Research in Advertising* 12 (1 & 2): 63–73.

Frith, Simon 1982 *Sound Effect: youth, leisure and the politics of rock'n'roll,* New York: Pantheon.

—— 1992 'The industrialization of popular music', p.49–74 in J. Lull (ed.), *Popular Music and Communication,* Newbury Park, CA: Sage Publications.

—— 1996 *Performing Rites: on the value of popular music*, Cambridge: Harvard University Press.

Gandhi, Mohandas 1982 (1927, 1929) *An Autobiography; or, the story of my experiments with truth*, London: Penguin Books.

Gans, Herbert J. 1980 *Deciding What's News: a study of CBS Evening News, NBC Nightly News, Newsweek, and Time*, New York: Vintage Books.

García Canclini, Néstor 1995 *Hybrid Cultures: strategies for entering and leaving modernity*, Minneapolis: University of Minnesota Press.

GDDSZJT Reform Group (Guangdong dianshi zhujiang tai gaiban xiaozu) 1997 'Daoxiangxing, dazhongxing, jiejinxing, yulexing: xie zai guangdong dianshi zhujiang tai gaiban zhi ji' (Directionality, populism, proximity, entertainment: writing on the occasion of the reorganisation of Guangdong Television's Zhujiang television station), *South China Television Journal* 3: 4–5.

Geertz, Clifford 1983 *Local Knowledge: further essays in interpretive anthropology*, New York: Basic Books.

—— 1984 'Distinguished lecture: Anti anti-relativism', *American Anthropologist* 86: 263–278.

—— 1988 *Works and Lives: the anthropologist as author*, Stanford: Stanford University Press.

Ghai, Yash 1998 'Rights, duties and responsibilities', p.20–42 in J. Cauquelin et al. (eds.), *Asian Values: encounter with diversity*, London: Curzon.

Giddens, Anthony 1990 *The Consequences of Modernity*, Cambridge: Polity.

Gillespie, Marie 1995 *Television, Ethnicity, and Cultural Change,* London: Routledge.

Gitlin, Todd 1980 *The Whole World is Watching: mass media in the making and unmaking of the new left*, Berkeley: University of California Press.

Gobuichi Isamu 1995 *Shabondama Horide: Sutādusto o mō ichi do* (*Soap Bubble Holiday: Stardust, one more time*), Tōkyō: Nihon Terebi Hōsōmō.

Goffman, Erving 1959 *The Presentation of Self in Everyday Life*, New York: Doubleday.

Goldman, Robert 1992 *Reading Ads Socially*, London and New York: Routledge.

Gotō, Kazuhiko 1991 'Introduction', p.3–18 in M. Sata and H. Hirahara (eds.), *A History of the Japanese Television Drama*, Tokyo: The Japan Association of Broadcasting Art.

Government of India (Ministry of External Affairs) 1995 *The Market Beckons* (*Doing Business in India)*, New Delhi: Government of India.

Gramsci, A. 1971 *Selections from the Prison Notebooks of Antonio Gramsci*, edited and translated by Q. Hoare and G. Nowell Smith, London: Lawrence & Wishart.

Gray, Herman 1991 'Television, black Americans, and the American dream', p.294–305 in R. Avery and D. Eason (eds.), *Critical Perspectives on Media and Society*, New York: Guilford Press.

Grimshaw, Roger et al. 1980 'Introduction to ethnography at the Centre', p.73–77 in S. Hall et al. (eds.), *Culture, Media, Language: working papers in cultural studies, 1972–79*, the Centre for Contemporary Cultural Studies, University of Birmingham, London: Hutchinson.

Gross, Larry 1989 'Out of the mainstream: sexual minorities and the mass media', p.130–149 in E. Seiter et al. (eds.), *Remote Control: television, audiences and cultural power*, London and New York: Routledge.

Grossberg, Lawrence 1993 'The formations of cultural studies: an American in Birmingham', p.21–66 in V. Blundell, J. Shepherd and I. Taylor (eds.), *Relocating Cultural Studies: developments in theory and research*, London and New York: Routledge.

—— et al. (eds.) 1992 *Cultural Studies*, London and New York: Routledge.

Gupta, Nilanjana 1998 *Switching Channels: ideologies of television in India*, Delhi: Oxford University Press.

Habermas, Jürgen 1978 *Knowledge and Human Interests*, second edition, London: Heinemann.

—— 1987 *The Philosophical Discourse of Modernity: twelve lectures*, translated by F. Lawrence, Cambridge: Polity Press.

Hall, Ivan P. 1998 *Cartels of the Mind*, New York: Norton.

Hall, Stuart 1980 'Encoding/decoding', p.128–38 in S. Hall et al. (eds.), *Culture, Media, Language: working papers in cultural studies, 1972–79*, the Centre for Contemporary Cultural Studies, University of Birmingham, London: Hutchinson.

—— 1991 'The local and the global: globalization and ethnicities', p.19–39 in A. King (ed.), *Culture, Globalization and World Systems*, London: Macmillan.

—— 1996 'On postmodernism and articulation: an interview with Stuart Hall', p.131–150 in D. Morley and K-H Chen (eds.), *Stuart Hall: critical dialogue in cultural studies*, London: Routledge.

Hanes, Jeffrey E. 1993 'From megalopolis to *megaroporisu*', *The Journal of Urban History* 19 (2): 56–94.

Hannerz, Ulf 1991 'Scenarios for peripheral cultures', p.107–127 in A. King, (ed.), *Culture, Globalization and World Systems*, London: Macmillan.

—— 1992 *Cultural Complexity*, New York: University of Columbia Press.

—— 1996 *Transnational Connections: culture, people, places*, London and New York: Routledge.

—— 1998a 'Other transnationals: perspectives gained from studying sideways', *Paideuma* 44: 109–123.

—— 1998b 'Of correspondents and collages', *Anthropological Journal of European Cultures* 7: 91–109.

—— 1998c 'Reporting from Jerusalem', *Cultural Anthropology* 13: 548–574.

Haraway, D. 1991 *Simians, Cyborgs, and Women: the reinvention of nature*. New York: Chapman & Hall.

Hartley, John 1992 *Tele-ology: studies in television*, London: Routledge.

Hartman, Paul and Charles Husband 1974 *Racism and the Mass Media: a study of the role of mass media in the formation of white beliefs and attitudes in Britain*, London: Davis-Poynter.

Harvey, Paul 1995 'Interpreting Oshin: war, history and women in modern Japan', p.75–110 in L. Skov and B. Moeran (eds.), *Women, Media and Consumption in Japan*, London: Curzon.

Hattori Hiroshi and Hara Yumiko 1997 'Tachannerukano nakano terebi to shichōsha: Taiwan kēburu terebi no baai' (The proliferation of television channels and audience: a study of Taiwan cable televison), *Hōsō Kenkyū to Chōsa,* February: 22–37.

Hendry, Joy 1993 *Wrapping Culture: politeness, presentation and power in Japan and other societies*, Oxford: Clarendon Press.

Henry, I. P. 1993 *The Politics of Leisure Policy*, London: Macmillan.

Heryanto, A. 1999 'Where communism never dies: violence, trauma and narration in the last cold war capitalist authoritarian state', in *International Journal of Cultural Studies* 2 (2): 147–177.

Herzfeld, Michael 1995 'Hellenism and occidentalism: the permutations of performance in Greek bourgeois identity', p.218–33 in J. Carrier (ed.), *Occidentalism: images of the west*, Oxford: Berg.

Hesse, M. 1978 'Theory and value in the social sciences', in C. Hookway and P. Pettit (eds.), *Action and Interpretation: studies in the philosophy of the social sciences*, Cambridge: Cambridge University Press.

Hindess, B. 1988 *Choice, Rationality and Social Theory*, London: Unwin Hyman.

Hine, Thomas 1995 *The Total Package: the evolution and secret meanings of boxes, bottles, cans and tubes*, Boston: Little, Brown and Company.

Hobart, Mark 1985 'Anthropos through the looking-glass: or how to teach the Balinese to bark', p.104–34 in J. Overing (ed.), *Reason and Morality*, ASA Monographs in Social Anthropology 24, London: Tavistock.

—— 1990 'The patience of plants: a note on agency in Bali', *Review of Indonesian and Malaysian Affairs* 24 (2): 90–135.

—— 1996 'Ethnography as a practice, or the unimportance of penguins', *Europaea* II (1): 3–36.

—— 1997a 'The missing subject: Balinese time and the elimination of history', *Review of Indonesian and Malaysian Studies* 31 (1): 123–172.

—— 1997b 'For the motion. Cultural studies will be the death of anthropology', edited by P. Wade, Manchester: GDAT.

—— 1999 'The end of the world news: disarticulating television in Bali', p.265–289 in L. Connor and R. Rubinstein (eds.), *Staying local in the global village: Bali in the twentieth century*, Honolulu: University of Hawai'i Press.

—— 2000 'Live or dead? Balinese understandings of their own theatre', in A. Vickers and Ny. Darma Putra (eds.), *To Change Bali: essays in honour of Gusti Ngurah Bagus*, Denpasar: Bali Post.

Holley, David 1995 'Osaka: the soul of old Japan', *Los Angeles Times* (Home Edition), p.3, 17 January.

Hong Kong Trade Development Council 1998a *Trade Developments: advertising and market research in Chinese mainland*, Hong Kong: TDC, March 1998.

—— 1998b 'Creative ideas grab attention of consumers', *International Market News*, July 1998: 4–11.

Horie Seiji 1994 *Yoshimoto Kōgyō no Kenkyū (A Study of Yoshimoto Kōgyō)*, Tōkyō: Asahi Bunko.

Horikoshi, Yumiko 1995 'Ba o wakimaeta shyuzai o helicopter no gōn' (Reporting that is aware of its own place the noise from the helicopters), *Masu Komi Shimin*, September.

Hoskins, Colin and Rolf Mirus 1988 'Reasons for the US dominance of the international trade in television programmes', *Media, Culture and Society* 10: 499–515.

Hosokawa, Shuhei 1990 'Land of a thousand commercials', p.69–72 in Y.H. Gietema (ed.), *What a Wonderful World*, Groningen: Groningen Museum.

Huang, Yu 1994 'Peaceful evolution: the case of television reform in post-Mao China', *Media, Culture and Society* 16: 217–241.

Hume, David 1978 *A Treatise of Human Nature: being an attempt to introduce the experimental method of reasoning into moral subjects*, edited by L.A. Selby-Bigge, Oxford: Clarendon Press (First edition, London: Noon, 1739).

Huntington, Samuel P. 1996 *The Clash of Civilizations and the Remaking of World Order*, New York: Simon & Schuster.

Hussain, A. 1990 *The Chinese Television Industry: the interaction between government policy and market forces*, London: London School of Economics and Political Science.

Ikels, C. 1996 *The Return of the God of Wealth: the transition to a market economy in urban China*, Stanford: Stanford University Press.

Inamasu Tatsuo 1989 *Aidoru Kōgaku (The Engineering of an Idol)*, Tōkyō: Chikuma Shobō.

—— (ed.) 1995 *Gendai Wakamono to Ongaku: wakamono ni okeru ongaku kōdō no kisoteki na jittai chōsa, 1989–90 chōsahōkoku (Today's Youth and Music: a fundamental survey of youth music trends, 1989–90)*, Tōkyō: Gendai no Wakamono to Ongaku Kenkyūkai.

Inden, Ron 1990 *Imagining India*, Oxford: Blackwell.

Inoue Hiroshi 1992 *Ōsaka no Warai (The Humor of Osaka)*, Suita City: Kansai (Suita) University Press.

Inoue Teruko et al. 1989 *Josei Zasshi wa Kaidoku Suru: kompareporitan nichi, bei, mekishiko hikaku kenkyū* (*Reading Women's Magazines: Comparepolitan a comparative study of Japan, America and Mexico*), Tōkyō: Kakiuchi Shuppan.

Irani, Madhavi 1991 'What is your brand?', in *Times of India* (Bombay), December 8.

Ishida Saeko 1992 '"Yūmeisei" wa dō tsukurarerunoka' (How is the 'celebrity' made?), p.254–296 in *Poppu Komunikeishon Zensho* (*Everything about Pop Communication*), Tōkyō: Parco Shuppan.

Ishii Kenichi et al. 1996 *Taiwan ni Okeru Nihonbangumino Shichōsha Bunseki* (*Audience Survey of Japanese Programme Viewing in Taiwan*), *Discussion Papers Series No. 701*, Tsukuba: University of Tsukuba.

Ivy, Marilyn 1995 *Discourses of the Vanishing: modernity, phantasm, Japan*, Chicago: Chicago University Press.

Iwabuchi, Koichi 1994 'Complicit exoticism: Japan and its other', *Continuum* 8 (2): 49–82.

—— 1995 'Return to Asia? Japan in the global audiovisual market', *Media International Australia* 77: 94–106.

—— 1998 'Marketing "Japan": Japanese cultural presence under a global gaze', *Japanese Studies* 18 (2): 165–180.

—— 1999 'Return to Asia?: Japan in Asian audiovisual markets', p.177–99 in K. Yoshino (ed.), *Consuming Ethnicity and Nationalism*, London: Curzon.

Jain, Purnendra 2000 'Will the sun ever shine in south Asia?', p.187–212 in M. Söderberg and I. Reader (eds.), *Japanese Influences and Presences in Asia*, London: Curzon.

Janus, Noreene 1986 'Transnational advertising: some considerations on the impact on peripheral societies', p.127–141 in R. Atwood and E. McAnany (eds.), *Communication and Latin American Society*, Madison: University of Wisconsin.

Jeffreys, Leo 1997 'Economic effects of the media', in *Mass Media Effects*, Prospect Heights, IL: Waveland Press.

Jordan, Mary 1999a 'Japanese couples' aversion to child adoption changes only slowly', *International Herald Tribune*, June 29.

—— 1999b 'In Japan, a fund-raising effort for female candidates', *International Herald Tribune*, May 10.

—— and Kevin Sullivan 1999a 'Life without father Japanese version: Often absent on the home front, dads remain slow to lend a hand', *International Herald Tribune*, May 8–9.

—— and Kevin Sullivan 1999b 'Classroom chaos: Japan's once-silent pupils erupt', *International Herald Tribune*, January 25.

Kankanala, Ram 1991 'Prophylactic blues', *Gentleman*, October.

Kawatake Kazuo and Hara Yumiko 1994 'Nihon wo chūshin to suru terebi bangumi no ryūtsū jōkyō' (The international flow of TV programmes from and into Japan), *Hōsō Kenkyū to Chōsa*, November: 2–17.

Kellner, Douglas 1995 *Media Culture: cultural studies, identity and politics between the modern and the postmodern*. London and New York: Routledge.

Kimura Masao 1995 *Ki ga Tsukeba, Mina Yoshimoto: Yoshimotoka zenkoku senryaku* (*Before You Know it, Everyone will be Yoshimoto: strategy to make all of Japan into Yoshimoto*), Tōkyō: Keibunsha.

Kinsella, Sharon 1996 'Cuties in Japan', p.220–254 in L. Skov and B. Moeran (eds.), *Women, Media, and Consumption in Japan*, London: Curzon.

Klamer, A. 1987 'As if economists and their subjects were rational', in J. Nelson et al. (eds.), *The Rhetoric of the Human Sciences: language and argument in scholarship and public affairs*, London: University of Wisconsin Press.

Kotkin, Joel 1992 *Tribes: how race, religion and identity determine success in the new global economy*, New York: Random House.

Kristof, Nicholas D. 1995 'Japan's nature: a people tremble in harmony with the land', *New York Times*, January 22.

300

REFERENCES

—— 1996 'Do Korean men still beat their wives? Definitely', *New York Times*, December 5.

—— 1999a 'Japan debates return of rising sun: Government prepares bill to restore controversial flag and song', *International Herald Tribune*, March 29.

—— 1999b 'Warming to "cold pizza", Japan's leader repairs his image problem', *International Herald Tribune*, April 2.

—— 1999c 'Walk this way, or how the Japanese kept in step', *International Herald Tribune*, April 18.

—— and Sheryl WuDunn 1994 *China Wakes*, New York: Times Books/Random House.

Kumar, K. 1993 'Coy public sector', in *Business India*, June 21.

Kuroda Isamu 1991 'Gaikoku toshite no "Kansai" (1) terebi bangumi no naka no Kansai hyōgen' ('Kansai' as a foreign country - expressions of Kansai within television programs), *Kyōyōbu Kiyō* (Osaka Keizai Daigaku) 9: 21–37.

—— 1994 'Gaikoku toshite no "Kansai" (2)' ('Kansai' as a foreign country, Part 2), *Osaka Keidai Ronshū* (Osaka Keidai Gakkai) 45 (2): 43–71.

deLange, William 1998 *A History of Japanese Journalism*, London: Japan Library/ Curzon.

Laclau, Ernesto and Chantal Mouffe 1985 *Hegemony & Socialist Strategy: towards a radical democratic politics*, London: Verso.

—— 1990 'New reflections on the revolution of our time', in their *New Reflections on the Revolution of Our Time*, London: Verso.

Larson, G. 1987 'Introduction to the philosophy of Samkhya', in G.J. Larson and R.S. Bhattacharya (eds.), *Samkhya: a dualist tradition in Indian philosophy*, Princeton, NJ: Princeton University Press.

Latham, Kevin 2000 'Nothing but the truth: news media, power and hegemony in south China', *China Quarterly* 163, September.

—— forthcoming 'Powers of imagination: the role of the consumer in China's silent media revolution' in K. Latham and S. Thompson (eds.), *Consuming China: approaches to cultural change in contemporary China*. London: Curzon.

Latour, B. 1993 *We Have Never Been Modern*, translated by C. Porter, Hemel Hempstead: Harvester Wheatsheaf.

Lee, Chun-Chuan 1980 *Media Imperialism Reconsidered: the homogenising of television culture*, Beverley Hills: Sage.

Lee Kuan Yew 1989 'Singapore and the foreign press', p.117–124, in A. Mehra (ed.), *Press Systems in ASEAN States*, Singapore: Asian Media and Information Center.

Levitt, Theodore 1983 'The globalization of markets', *Harvard Business Review* 61: 92–101.

Lewis, Glen et al. 1994 'Television globalisation in Taiwan and Australia', *Media Asia* 21 (4): 184–89.

Li, Xiaoping 1991 'The Chinese television system and television news', *China Quarterly* 126: 340–355.

Li, Zhen-Yi et al. 1995 '*Tokyo Love Story*: a study on the reason of the popularity and audience motivations in Taiwan', Unpublished undergraduate research paper of National University of Politics, Taiwan.

Li, Zhurun 1998 'Popular journalism with Chinese characteristics: from revolutionary modernity to popular modernity', *International Journal of Cultural Studies* 1 (3): 307–28.

Liao, Ping-Hui 1996 'Chinese nationalism or Taiwanese localism?', *Culture and Policy* 7 (2): 74–92.

Liechty, Mark 1995 'Media, markets and modernisation: youth identities and the experience of modernity in Kathmandu, Nepal', p.166–201 in V. Amit-Talai and H. Wulff (eds.), *Youth Culture: a cross-cultural perspective*, London: Routledge.

Lien, Marianne 1997 *Marketing and Modernity*, Oxford: Berg.

REFERENCES

Lii, Ding-Tzann 1998 'A colonized empire: reflections on the expansion of Hong Kong films in Asian countries', p.122–41 in K-H. Chen (ed.), *Trajectories: inter-Asian cultural studies*, London and New York: Routledge.

Lipovetsky, Gilles 1994 *The Empire of Fashion: dressing modern democracy*, translated by C. Porter, Princeton, NJ: Princeton University Press.

Livingston, Sonia 1990 *Making Sense of Television: the psychology of audience interpretation*, Oxford and New York: Pergamon Press.

Lobo, Austin 1991 'Marketplace: condom marketing has come a long way', in *Times of India*, October 21.

Lowe, Vincent 1987 *Dependency Within Bounds: media and information technology policies within the ASEAN region*, Institute of Asian Studies, Chulalongkorn University, Bangkok.

Lowenthal, Leo 1968 *Literature, Popular Culture and Society*, Palo Alto, CA: Pacific Books.

Lull, James 1990 *Inside Family Viewing: ethnographic research on television's audiences*, London: Routledge.

——— 1991 *China Turned On: television, reform and resistance,* London: Routledge.

——— 1995 *Media, Communication, Culture: a global approach*, Cambridge: Polity Press.

——— 2000 *Media, Communication, Culture* (revised edition), Cambridge: Polity Press.

——— (ed.) 2001 *Culture in the Communication Age*, London: Routledge.

——— and Roger Wallis 1992 'The beat of west Vietnam', p.207–236 in J. Lull (ed.), 1992 *Popular Music and Communication,* Newbury Park, CA: Sage Publications.

McCreery, John 1995 'Malinowski, magic, and advertising: on choosing metaphors', p.309–329 in J. Sherry (ed.), *Contemporary Marketing and Consumer Behavior: an anthropological sourcebook.* Thousand Oaks: Sage.

——— forthcoming 'Finding meaning in the muddle: adapting global strategies to advertising in Japan', American Anthropological Association: City & Society.

McLuhan, Marshall 1964 *Understanding Media,* Toronto: Toronto University Press.

McRobbie, Angela 1998 *British Fashion Design: rag trade or image industry?* London: Routledge.

Mahatir Mohamad 1989 'The social responsibility of the press', p.107–116 in A. Mehra (ed.), *Press Systems in ASEAN States*, Singapore: Asian Media and Information Center.

Mankekar, Purnima 1999 *Screening Culture, Viewing Politics: an ethnography of television, womanhood, and nation in postcolonial India*, Durham, NC: Duke University Press.

Marchand, Roland 1998 *Creating the Corporate Soul: the rise of public relations and corporate imagery in American big business*, Berkeley and Los Angeles: University of California Press.

Marcus, George 1998 *Ethnography through Thick and Thin*, Princeton, NJ: Princeton University Press.

Marshall, A. 1994 'Asian advertising review Vietnam', p.27 in *Asian Advertising and Marketing,* April 22.

——— 1995 'Vietnam', p.26–27 in *Asian Advertising and Marketing*, April 21.

Marx, Karl 1971 (1887) *Capital: Volume 1: a critical analysis of capitalist production*, Moscow: Progress Publishers.

Matilal, B. 1986 *Perception: an essay on classical Indian theories of knowledge*, Oxford: Clarendon Press.

Matsumoto Hitoshi 1994 *Isho* (*Last Testament*), Tōkyō: Asahi Shinbun-sha.

——— 1998a *Matsumoto Hitoshi*, Tōkyō: Asahi Shinbun-sha.

——— 1998b *Matsumoto Hitoshi, Ai*, Tōkyō: Asahi Shinbun-sha.

——— 1999 *Matsumoto Bōzu*, Tōkyō: Rocking On.

302

Mattelart, Armand and Hector Schmucler 1985 *Communication and Information Technologies: freedom of choice for Latin America*, Norwood, NJ: Ablex.

Mayes, Tessa, and Megan Rowling 1997 'The image makers: British journalists on Japan', in Phil Hammond (ed.), *Cultural Difference, Media Memories*, London: Cassell.

Mazzarella, William 2000 *Shovelling Smoke: the production of advertising and the cultural politics of globalization in contemporary India*, Ph.D. thesis, University of California at Berkeley.

Mehra, Achal (ed.), 1989 *Press Systems in ASEAN States*, Singapore: Asian Media and Information Center.

Meyrowitz, Joshua 1985 *No Sense of Place: the impact of electronic media on social behavior*, Oxford: Oxford University Press.

Miller, Daniel 1992 '*The Young and Restless* in Trinidad: a case of the local and global in mass consumption', p.163–182 in R. Silverstone and E. Hirsch (eds.), *Consuming Technologies: media and information in domestic spaces,* London: Routledge.

—— 1995 'Consumption as the vanguard of history: a polemic by way of an introduction', p.1–57 in D. Miller (ed.), *Acknowledging Consumption: a review of new studies*, London and New York: Routledge.

—— 1997 *Capitalism: an ethnographic approach*, Oxford: Berg.

—— 1998 'Conclusion: a theory of virtualism', p.187–215 in J. Carrier and D. Miller (eds.), *Virtualism: a new political economy*, Oxford: Berg.

—— (ed.) 1995 *Worlds Apart: modernity through the pursuit of the local*, London and New York: Routledge.

Miller, Michael 1981 *The Bon Marché: bourgeois culture and the department store, 1869–1920*, Princeton, NJ: Princeton University Press.

Ministry of Trade and Industry 1999 http://www.gov.sg/mti/index.html

von Mises, L. 1960 *Epistemological Problems of Economics*, Princeton NJ: Van Nostrand.

Mita Jun'ichi 1993 *Shōwa Kamigata Shōgeishi (The History of Kyoto-Osakan Arts of Humor in the Shōwa Period)*, Tōkyō: Gakugei Shorin.

Mitsui, Tōru and Shuhei Hosokawa (eds.) 1998 *Karaoke Around the World*, London: Routledge.

Miyoshi, Masao 1993 'A borderless world? From colonialism to transnationalism and the decline of the nation-state', *Critical Inquiry* 19: 26–51.

Moeran, Brian 1987 'The art world of Japanese ceramics', *The Journal of Japanese Studies* 13 (1): 27–50.

—— 1995 'Reading Japanese in *Katei Gahō*: the art of being an upperclass woman', p.111–42 in L. Skov and B. Moeran (eds.), *Women, Media and Consumption in Japan*, London: Curzon.

—— 1989 *Language and Popular Culture in Japan*, Manchester: Manchester University Press.

—— 1996a *A Japanese Advertising Agency: an anthropology of media and markets*, London: Curzon.

—— 1996b 'The orient strikes back: advertising and imagining Japan', *Theory, Culture & Society* 13 (3): 77–112.

—— 1997 *Folk Art Potters of Japan: beyond an anthropology of aesthetics*, London: Curzon.

—— 1998 'The birth of the Japanese department store', p.141–76 in K. MacPherson (ed.), *Asian Department Stores*, London: Curzon.

—— 2000a 'Commodities, culture and Japan's Corollanization of Asia', p.25–50 in M. Söderberg and I. Reader (eds.), *Japanese Influences and Presences in Asia*, London: Curzon.

—— 2000b 'The split account system and Japan's advertising industry', *International Journal of Advertising* 19 (2): 185–200.

REFERENCES

Monzen Yoshiyasu 1995 '1.17 hisaichi no TV kyoku kara . . .' (January 17: From a television station in the disaster zone), *Masu Komi Shimin*, September: 16–17.

Moores, Shaun 1993 *Interpreting Audiences: the ethnography of media consumption*, London: Sage.

—— 1997 'Broadcasting and its audiences', p.214–246 in H. Mackay (ed.), *Consumption and Everyday Life*, London: The Open University.

Morley, David 1980 *The 'Nationwide' Audience: structure and decoding*, London: British Film Insititute.

—— 1986 *Family Television: cultural power and domestic leisure*, London: Comedia.

—— 1989 'Changing paradigms in audience studies', in E. Seiter et al. (eds.), *Remote Control*, London: Routledge.

—— 1992 *Television, Audiences and Cultural Studies*, London: Routledge.

—— 1997 'Theoretical orthodoxies: textualism, constructivism and the "new ethnography" in cultural studies', p.121–137 in M. Ferguson and P. Golding (eds.), *Cultural Studies in Question*, London.

Morse, Margaret 1986 'The television news personality and credibility: reflections on the news in transition', p.55–79 in T. Modeleski (ed.), *Studies in Entertainment: Critical Approaches to Mass Culture*, Bloomington and Indianapolis: Indiana University Press.

Mouer, Ross, and Yoshio Sugimoto 1986 *Images of Japanese Society*, London and New York: Kegan Paul International.

Mueller, Barbara 1996 *International Advertising: communicating across culture*, Belmont, CA.: Wadsworth.

Munro, Donald 1977 *The Concept of Man in Contemporary China*, Ann Arbor: University of Michigan Press.

Mydans, Seth 1996 'Hanoi seeks western cash but not consequences', *New York Times*, p.A3, April 8.

Naficy, Hamid 1993 *The Making of Exile Cultures*, Minneapolis: University of Minnesota Press.

Naisbitt, John 1996 *Megatrends Asia: eight Asian megatrends that are reshaping our world*, New York: Simon & Schuster.

Nandy, A. 1998 'A new cosmopolitanism: toward a dialogue of Asian civilizations', p.141–49 in K-H. Chen (ed.), *Trajectories: inter-Asian cultural studies*, London and New York: Routledge

Narato, Masaya 1995 'The popular music scene in Japan', *Nihongo Jānaru*, June: 85–88.

Negus, Keith 1997 'The production of culture', p.67–118 in P. du Gay (ed.), *Production of Culture/Cultures of Production*, London: Open University/Sage.

—— 1998 'Cultural production and the corporation: musical genres and the strategic management of creativity in the US recording industry', *Media, Culture & Society* 20 (3): 359–80.

Neilan, Edward 1995 'The new foreign correspondent in Japan', *Japan Quarterly* 42: 307–316.

Nikkei Entertainment 1998a 'Ongakubangumi ranritsu jidai no sabaibaru jutsu' (Survival techniques in an era flooded with music programs), p.46–7, March.

—— 1998b 'Terebi no saishin jōshiki' (The newest common sense in television), p.60–79, July.

Nishida Toshiya 1993 *Ōsaka Dorīmu (Osaka Dream)*, Tōkyō: Ōta Shuppan.

Ofisu Matsunaga 1990 *Naze Fuji Terebi Dake ga Nobita no ka (Why did only Fuji Television grow?)*, Tōkyō: Kō Shobō.

Ogilvy, David 1985 *Ogilvy on Advertising*, London: Guild Publishing.

Ohmae, Ken'ichi 1990 *The Borderless World: power and strategy in the interlinked economy*, New York: Harper Business.

304

Ohmann, Richard (ed.) 1996 *Making and Selling Culture*, Hanover and London: Wesleyan University Press.

Ong, Aihwa 1996 'Anthropology, China and modernities: the geopolitics of cultural knowledge', p.60–92 in H. L. Moore (ed.), *The Future of Anthropological Knowledge*, London: Routledge.

Ōtani Koichi 1994a *Ōsaka-gaku (Osaka-ology)*, Tōkyō: Keiei Shoin.

—— 1994b *Ōsaka-gaku - Tsuzuki (Osaka-ology Continued)*, Tōkyō: Keiei Shoin.

Ōtsuka, E. 1991 *Shōjo Zasshiron (Debates on Girls' Magazines)*, Tōkyō: Tōkyō Shoseki.

Padamsee, Alyque nd 'Just say KS', from an unpublished manuscript.

Painter, Andrew 1996 'Japanese daytime television, popular culture and ideology', p.197–234 in J. W. Treat (ed.), *Contemporary Japan and Popular Culture*, London: Curzon.

Parry, Richard 1996 'Vietnam insists the future is red', p.22 in *The Daily Yomiuri*, July 14.

Peirce, Charles 1984 [1868] 'Some consequences of four incapacities', in his *Writings of Charles S. Peirce: a chronological edition*, volume 2, Bloomington: Indiana University Press.

Pickowicz, P. 1995 'Velvet prisons and the political economy of Chinese filmmaking', in D. Davis et al. (eds.), *Urban Spaces in Contemporary China: the potential for autonomy and community in post-Mao China*, Woodrow Wilson Center Series, Cambridge: Cambridge University Press.

Pillai, Ajith 1992 'KS ad found objectionable', in *The Pioneer*, April 10.

Pollay, Richard 1989 'Campaigns, change and culture: on the polluting potential of persuasion', p.185–196 in C. Salmon (ed.), *Information Campaigns: balancing social values and social change*, Sage Annual Review of Communication Research 18, Newbury Park, CA: Sage.

Poster, Mark 1990 *The Mode of Information*, Cambridge: Polity Press.

Potter, K. 1977 *Indian Metaphysics and Epistemology: the tradition of Nyaya-Vaisesika up to Gangesa*, Princeton, N.J.: Princeton University Press.

Powdermaker, Hortense 1950 *Hollywood, the Dream Factory: an anthropologist looks at the movie-makers*, Boston: Little Brown.

Prakash, Amit 1993 'Ignoring strictures, Kama Sutra ads are back with a bang', in *The Pioneer*, May 16.

Quine, W. 1953 'Two dogmas of empiricism', in his *From a Logical Point of View: nine logico-philosophical essays*. Cambridge, Mass.: Harvard University Press.

—— 1960 *Word and Object*, Cambridge, Mass.: M.I.T. Press.

Redwood Research Service 1996 *An Index Survey of Cable TV in the Second Half of 1996*, Taipei: Redwood Research Service.

Reeves, Jimmie 1988 'Television stardom: a ritual of social typification and individuation', p.146–60 in J. W. Carey (ed.), *Media, Myth and Narrative* (Sage Annual Reviews of Communication Research 15), Newbury Park, CA: Sage.

Reid, T. R. 1995 'Japan quake in the eye of the beholder', *Guardian Weekly*, February 12 (originally printed in *The Washington Post*).

Ritzer, George 1993 *The McDonaldization of Society,* Thousand Oaks, CA: Pine Forge Press.

Robertson, Roland 1991 'Social theory, cultural relativity and the problem of globality', p.70–90 in A. King (ed.), *Culture, Globalization and World Systems*, London: Macmillan.

—— 1995 'Glocalisation: time-space and homogeneity-heterogeneity', p.25–44 in M. Featherstone et al. (eds.), *Global Modernities*, London: Sage.

Rohlen, Thomas 1973 '"Spiritual education" in a Japanese bank', *American Anthropologist* 75 (5): 1542–62.

Rorty, Richard 1980 *Philosophy and the Mirror of Nature*, Oxford: Blackwell.

Rosaldo, Renato 1994 'Whose cultural studies? Cultural studies and the disciplines', *American Anthropologist* 96 (3): 524–29.

Ruin, Påhl 1999a 'Priset på golfmedlemskap ett tecken på Japans kris', *Dagens Nyheter*, January 24.

—— 1999b 'Kuponger ska få fart på företagen', *Dagens Nyheter*, February 10.

—— 1999c 'Nationalsången och flaggan symboler för kriget', *Dagens Nyheter*, March 28.

—— 1999d 'Ensam om att vara pappaledig i Tokyo', *Dagens Nyheter*, June 29.

—— 1999e 'Fuchino, 84, bor hos sonen', *Dagens Nyheter*, June 23.

—— 1999f 'Unga japaner revolterar', *Dagens Nyheter*, March 31.

Sahlins, Marshall 1976 *Culture and Practical Reason*, Chicago: University of Chicago Press.

Said, Edward 1978 *Orientalism*, New York: Random House.

Saigon Times 1997 'The bustling market', p.13, April 12.

Salmond, Anne 1982 'Theoretical landscapes. On a cross-cultural conception of knowledge', in D. Parkin (ed.), *Semantic Anthropology*, London: Academic Press.

Schilling, Mark 1997 *The Encyclopedia of Japanese Pop Culture*, New York: Weatherhill.

Schmitt, Bernd and Alex Simonson 1997 *Marketing Aesthetics: the strategic management of brands, identity, and image*, New York: Free Press.

Schneppen, Anne 1999 'An der Schwelle des Neuen Jahrhunderts zeigt Japan bei der Identitätssuche Flagge', *Frankfurter Allgemeine,* July 23.

Schodt, Frederik 1996 *Dreamland Japan: writings on modern manga*, Berkeley: Stonebridge Press.

Schwartz, Adam 1996 'Get my censor sensor', *Far Eastern Economic Review*, p.61, June 6.

Schudson, Michael 1978 *Discovering the News: a social history of American newspapers*, New York: Basic Books.

—— 1984 (1993) *Advertising, the Uneasy Persuasion: its dubious impact on American society,* New York: Basic Books.

Second City, The 1998 'A brief history of the second city', internet: http://www.secondcity.com/histry.html, accessed on 8 March, 1998.

Sekiguchi, Susumu 1996 *Terebi Bunka: nihon no katachi* (Television Culture: the shape of Japan), Tōkyō: Gakumonsha.

Sengupta, Ranjana 1991 'Who's the boss, anyway?', in *Indian Express*, September 15.

Severino, Rudolfo 1998 'Asia policy lecture: What ASEAN stands for', a lecture given at The Research Institute for Asia and the Pacific, University of Sydney, Australia, October 22.

Shah, Amrita 1997 *Hype, Hypocrisy & Television in Urban India*, New Delhi: Vikas.

Shiraishi, Saya 1997 'Japan's soft power: Doraemon goes overseas', p.234–72 in P. Katzenstein and T. Shiraishi (eds.), *Network Power: Japan and Asia*, Ithaca: Cornell University Press.

Sigal, Leon V. 1986 'Sources make the news', p.9–37 in R. Manoff and M. Schudson (eds.), *Reading the News*, New York, Pantheon Books.

Silverstone, Roger 1994 *Television and Everyday Life*, London and New York: Routledge.

Simoes, Frank 1993 'A perfect pair of breasts', in Khushwant Singh and Shobha De (eds.), *Uncertain Liaisons: sex, strife and togetherness in urban India*, Delhi:Viking.

Sinclair, John et al. 1996 *New Patterns in Global Television: peripheral vision,* Oxford: Oxford University Press.

Skov, Lise and Brian Moeran (eds.) 1995 *Women, Media and Consumption in Japan*, London: Curzon.

Slack, J. 1996 'The theory and method of articulation in cultural studies', in D. Morley and K-H. Chen (eds.), *Stuart Hall: critical dialogues in cultural studies*, London: Routledge.

Smith, M. 1995 *Engaging Characters: fiction, emotion, and the cinema*, Oxford: Clarendon Press.

Smith, Richard 1993 'China's race to capitalism', *New Left Review* 199.

Sowell, Thomas 1994 *Race and Culture*, New York: Basic Books.

SPA 1998 'SMAP = Owarai baretei shinkanron' (The evolution of SMAP = comedy variety), February 25: 35–43.

Sreberny-Mohammadi, Annabelle 1991 'The global and the local in international communications', p.118–138 in J. Curran and M. Gurevitch (eds.), *Mass Media and Society*, New York: Edward Arnold.

Stam, Robert 1992 'Mobilizing fictions: the Gulf War, the media and the recruitment of the spectator', *Public Culture* 4 (2): 101–126.

Stefánsson, Halldór 1998 'Media stories of bliss and mixed blessings', p.155–66 in D. Martinez (ed.), *The World of Japanese Popular Culture: gender, shifting boundaries and global cultures*, Cambridge: Cambridge University Press.

Straubhaar, Joseph 1991 'Beyond media imperialism: asymmetrical interdependence and cultural proximity', *Critical Studies in Mass Communication* 8 (1): 39–59.

Stravens, Felix 1996 'Advertising in Singapore', p.273–91, in K. Frith (ed.), *Advertising in Asia: communication, culture and consumption*, Ames, Iowa: Iowa State University Press.

Strom, Stephanie 1999 'Solidly pacifist Japan rethinks its pacifism: Vulnerability and realpolitik fuel changes', *International Herald Tribune*, April 9.

Sugawara, Sandra 1998 'In Japan, a system that chokes reforms', *International Herald Tribune*, October 17–18.

Sullivan, Kevin 1999 'Economic decline pries open the playgrounds of the rich', *International Herald Tribune,* May 28.

—— and Mary Jordan 1999 'Japanese retirees head back to work', *International Herald Tribune*, July 14.

Tada, Michitarō 1988 'Osaka popular culture: a down-to-earth appraisal', p.33–53 in G. McCormack and Y. Sugimoto (eds.), *The Japanese Trajectory: modernization and beyond*, Cambridge: Cambridge University Press.

Tan Yew Soon and Soh Yew Peng 1994 *The Development of Singapore's Modern Media Industry*, Singapore: Times Academic Press.

Tansey, Richard et al. 1990 'Cultural themes in Brazilian and US auto ads: a cross-cultural comparison', *Journal of Advertising* 19: 30–39.

Telegraph 1988 'Padamsee: TV needs a creative chief', February 14.

Thakur, Sankarshan 1985 '1985: the year of the ad?', in *Sunday*, April 14–20.

Thapar, Raj 1991 *All These Years*, New Delhi: Penguin Books.

Thompson, John 1990 *Ideology and Modern Culture,* Cambridge: Polity Press.

—— 1995 *The Media and Modernity: a social theory of the media*, Cambridge: Polity.

Thompson, Kenneth (ed.) 1997 *Media and Cultural Regulation*, London: Sage.

Tomlinson, John 1991 *Cultural Imperialism: a critical introduction*, London: Pinter.

—— 1997 'Internationalism, globalization and cultural imperialism', p.117–162 in K. Thompson (ed.), *Media and Cultural Regulation*, London: Sage.

—— 1999 *Globalization and Culture,* Cambridge. Polity Press.

Traube, Elizabeth 1996 '"The popular" in American culture', *Annual Review of Anthropology* 25: 127–51.

Tsutsui, Sayo 1997 'Conversational joking on Japanese television in everyday life: fools and their foils pair off in the Kansai region', unpublished paper presented at the American Anthropological Association Annual Meeting, Washington, D.C., November.

Tuchman, Gaye 1978 *Making News: a study in the construction of reality*, New York: The Free Press.

Turner, Victor 1974 *Dramas, Fields, and Metaphors: symbolic action in human society*, Ithaca: Cornell University Press.

Usunier, Jean-Claude 2000 *Marketing Across Cultures* (3rd edition), Harlow: Prentice Hall.

Vakil, Ardarshir 1998 (1997) *Beach Boy: a novel*, New York: Charles Scribner.

Van Maanen, John 1988 *Tales of the Field: on writing ethnography*, Chicago: Chicago University Press.

Van Wolferen, Karel 1989 *The Enigma of Japanese Power*, New York: Knopf.

Veblen, Thorstein 1899 *The Theory of the Leisure Class: an economic study of institutions*, New York: Random House.

Vietnam Business News, 1996 'Competition in Vietnam's TV market is heating up', p.24, April/May.

Vogel, Ezra 1989 *One Step Ahead in China: Guangdong under reform*, Cambridge, Mass.: Harvard University Press.

Watson, James 1997 *Golden Arches East: McDonalds in east Asia*, Stanford: Stanford University Press.

Weber, Max 1946 (1918) 'Politics as a vocation', in H. Gerth and C. Wright Mills (eds.), *From Max Weber: essays in sociology*, Chicago: University of Chicago Press.

Wernick, Andrew 1991 *Promotional Culture: advertising, ideology, and symbolic expression*, London and Newbury Park: Sage Publications.

Westney, D. Eleanore 1996 'Mass media as business organizations: a U.S.-Japan comparison', p.47–88 in S. Pharr and E. Krauss (eds.), *Media and Politics in Japan*, Honolulu: University of Hawai'i Press.

White, Merry 1994 *The Material Child: coming of age in Japan and America*, Berkeley: University of California Press.

Wikan, U. 1990 *Managing Turbulent Hearts: a Balinese formula for living*, Chicago: Chicago University Press.

Wilk, Richard 1994 'Colonial time and TV time: television and temporality in Belize', *Visual Anthropology* 10 (1): 94–102.

—— 1995 'Learning to be local in Belize: global systems of common difference', p.110–133 in D. Miller (ed.), *Worlds Apart: modernity through the prism of the local*, London: Routledge.

Williams, Raymond 1976 *Communications*, Harmondsworth: Penguin Books.

—— 1977 *Marxism and Literature*, Oxford: Oxford University Press.

Williamson, Judith 1978 *Decoding Advertisements: ideology and meaning in advertising*, London: Maryon Boyar.

Willis, Paul 1990 *Common Culture: symbolic work at play in the everyday cultures of the young*, Buckingham: Open University Press.

Wilson, T. 1997 'Truth and dare: Chinese weekend paper rakes scandal and bucks', *Far Eastern Economic Review*, August 14.

Wolff, Janet 1999 'Sociology and border disciplines: opportunities and barriers to intellectual growth: cultural studies and the sociology of culture', *Contemporary Sociology* 28 (5): 499–507.

WuDunn, Sheryl 1996 'Japan may approve pill, but women may not', *New York Times*, November 27.

—— 1997 'What's love got to do with it? Koreans ask', *International Herald Tribune*, April 18.

—— 1999a 'Japan gives consumers free money', *International Herald Tribune,* March 15.

—— 1999b 'American "geisha": Culture shock in Japan', *International Herald Tribune,* January 8.

—— 1999c 'A Japanese manager commits hara-kiri over company downsizing', *International Herald Tribune*, March 24.

REFERENCES

—— 1999d 'Japan's tale of two pills: Different fates for Viagra and birth control', *International Herald Tribune*, May 3.

Xie W.X. 1997 'Zai hezuo zhong qiu gaige, qiu fazhan, qiu tigao' (Calling for reform, development and improvement in the midst of cooperation), *South China Television Journal* 3: 11–16.

Yamamoto Taketoshi 1984 *Kōkoku no Shakaishi* (*The Social History of Advertising*), Tōkyō: Hōsei Daigaku Shuppankyoku.

Yano, Christine 1998 'Letters from the heart: negotiating fan-star relationships in Japanese popular music', Paper presented to the Yale Council of Asian Studies Conference, 'Fanning the Flames: fandom and consumer culture in contemporary Japan'.

Yeo, George 1993 Speech given at The Third Annual Conference of ASEAN Ministers, Manila, Philippines, December 16.

Yoshimoto Kōgyō 1992 *Yoshimoto Hachijūnen no Ayumi* (*A Stroll Through Eighty Years of Yoshimoto*), Ōsaka: Yoshimoto Kōgyō, KK.

Zha, Jianying 1995 *China Pop*, New York: The New Press.

Zhao, Yuezhi 1998 *Media, Market, and Democracy in China*, Urbana and Chicago: University of Illinois Press.

Zipangu (ed.), 1998 *Japan Made in USA*, New York: Zipangu.

Zoetmulder, P. 1982 *Old Javanese-English dictionary* in two volumes, with the collaboration of S. Robson, The Hague: Nijhoff.

LIST OF CONTRIBUTORS

Katherine T. Frith is Associate Professor and past Chair of the Advertising Program in the College of Communications at the Pennsylvania State University. She is currently on leave teaching at Nanyang Technological University in Singapore. She has edited two books: *Advertising in Asia: Communication, Culture and Consumption* (1996) and *Undressing the Ad: Reading Culture in Advertising* (1998).

Ulf Hannerz is Professor of Social Anthropology, Stockholm University, Sweden. He has taught at several American, European and Australian universities and is a former Chair of the European Association of Social Anthropologists. His research has been especially in urban anthropology and transnational cultural processes, and his most recent books are *Cultural Complexity* (1992) and *Transnational Connections* (1996).

Mark Hobart is Senior Lecturer in Southeast Asian Anthropology at the School of Oriental and African Studies, University of London. He has worked in Bali since 1970 and has been researching Balinese theatre and television for over ten years. He is head of the Balinese Television Project, which has one of the biggest collections of recordings of non-Western television in the world.

Shuhei Hosokawa is Associate Professor, Humanities and Social Sciences, at the Tokyo Institute of Technology, Japan. His principal research fields include the cultural history of Japanese popular music since the mid 19th century and the Japanese-Brazilian community. He has published numerous articles in *Popular Music*, *Cultural Studies*, *Japanese Studies* and other international journals and has co-edited, with Toru Mitsu, *Karaoke Around the World: global technology, local singing* (Routledge, 1999).

Koichi Iwabuchi completed his Ph.D. in Media and Cultural Studies at the University of Western Sydney Nepean in 1999 and is now Assistant Professor at the International Christian University, Tokyo. He had published articles in English and Japanese on media, cultural globalization and national/cultural identities in Japanese and East Asian contexts. He is completing a book tentatively titled:

Returning to Asia: Japan in the cultural dynamics of globalization, localization and Asianization.

Kevin Latham is Lecturer in Social Anthropology at the School of Oriental and African Studies, University of London. He has conducted research into both traditional and mass media in contemporary Hong Kong and China. His interests cover journalism, television, cinema, consumption and popular culture. He is co-editor of *Consuming China: Approaches to Cultural Change in Contemporary China* forthcoming from Curzon Press.

James Lull is Professor of Communication Studies at San Jose State University, California, USA. He is author or editor of ten books, including *World Families Watch Television* (1988), *Inside Family Viewing* (1990), *China Turned On* (1991), *Popular Music and Communication* (1992), *Media Scandals* (1997), *Media, Communication, Culture: A Global Approach* (2000), and *Culture in the Communication Age* (2001). He holds an honorary doctorate in Social Sciences from the University of Helsinki, and a post as Adjunct Research Professor at the University of Colima, Mexico.

Elizabeth Naoko MacLachlan is an Assistant Professor in the Department of Japanese Studies at the National University of Singapore. Prior to receiving her Ph.D. in Anthropology from Columbia University, she worked as a reporter for the Japanese program 'New York-ing'. Her dissertation focuses on Japanese television journalism and the negotiated process of creating 'national' news broadcasts.

William Mazzarella is a Lecturer in the Committee for Degrees on Social Studies at Harvard University. He received his BA in Social Anthropology from Cambridge University in 1991, and his Ph.D. in Socio-Cultural Anthropology from the University of California at Berkeley in 2000. His dissertation examines the production of advertising and the cultural politics of globalization in contemporary India.

John McCreery is Vice-President and Managing Director of The Word Works and part-time Lecturer in the Graduate Program in Comparative Culture at Sophia University, Tokyo. By training an anthropologist, he has lived and worked in Japan since 1980. During much of this time he was employed as a copywriter and creative director for Hakuhodo Incorporated, Japan's second largest advertising agency. He has recently published *Japanese Consumer Behavior: from worker bees to wary shoppers* in the *ConsumAsiaN* series (2000).

Brian Moeran is Visiting Professor of Media, Communication and Japanese Culture at the Copenhagen Business School, Denmark, and has held chairs in Japanese Studies at the Universities of London and Hong Kong. By training a social anthropologist, he has spent almost twenty years living in Asia and his research has focussed on cultural production in Japan. He is the author of numerous books, including *Women, Media and Consumption in Japan* (edited with Lise Skov) (1995) and *A Japanese Advertising Agency: an anthropology of media and markets* (1996).

Carolyn Stevens is Senior Lecturer in Japanese Studies, Melbourne Institute of Asian Languages and Societies, at the University of Melbourne, Australia. She is trained as an anthropologist, but has also worked as a translator and artistic consultant for the long-running Japanese rock group, the Alfee. She is the author of *On the Margins of Japanese Society: volunteers and the welfare of the urban underclass* (1997), as well as of various journal articles on Japanese welfare, public health and popular music.

Joel F. Stocker is Foreign Research Fellow at the National Museum of Ethnology in Suita, Japan. He wrote his Ph.D. dissertation at the Department of Anthropology, University of Wisconsin, Madison, on the production, marketing, and consumption of comedy and 'Osakanness' in Japan. Currently he is researching Kansai-area media companies' development of entertainers, shows, and audiences, as well as audience engagement in those processes of cultural (re)production within Japanese media culture.

INDEX

advertising 5, 17, 18, 20, 21, 26–7, 28–9, 77–8, 151–219; endorsement 2; practices and processes 20–1, 156, 157–64, 171–97; presentations 157, 159, 160–1, 162, 164–7, 287; study of 151–2, 169–71, 198–201 *see also* globalization

advertising agency 23, 24, 25, 26–7, 29, 30, 79–81, 152–3, 154, 155–6, 157–64, 186, 190, 198, 205, 273–90

advertising campaign 2, 6, 10, 20, 28–9, 32, 151–3, 164–7, 171–90

advertising industry 20, 132, 184, 186, 189, 273, 287, 288 *see also* media industry

animation 3–4, 5, 13, 25, 27, 43–5, 55, 261, 280, 281, 289

anthropology 6, 7–10, 19–20, 34, 126–8, 146, 248 *see also* ethnography

articulation 57, 101, 200, 243

ASEAN 1, 76–7, 78, 85, 86

Asia: constitution of 1–2

Asian: culture(s) 13, 47; media 10–15, 34, 50, 136; values 11, 35 fn., 42, 69, 84, 86

audience 5, 6, 9, 12, 16, 18, 20, 21, 61–2, 90, 92–3, 98, 99–102, 182, 199, 224, 227, 229, 231, 232–3, 234, 237, 247–8, 254, 257, 273; and media production 21–2, 226, 227–8, 229–30, 257–9; and media reception 7, 9, 16, 18, 20, 29, 35, 54–74, 98, 109, 162, 198–217, 224–5, 248, 264–6

autorientalism 13, 193 fn.

Bali 5, 20, 21, 23, 58, 199–217

Baudrillard, Jean 169, 170, 201, 208–9, 272–3, 290 fn.

Beverley Hills 90210 66–70, 74 fn.

Bourdieu, Pierre 24, 26, 30, 34, 156–7, 241

brand *see* corporate identity

bricolage 215, 289

cable TV 4, 59–62

capital: cultural 23, 29–30, 31, 288; economic 23, 29, 30, 31

cartoon *see* animation

CCTV 4, 44, 94

celebrity *see* star

Channel [V] 2, 3, 5, 59

China (PRC) 2, 3, 4, 5, 17–18, 19, 39–40, 41, 42–5, 48–9, 50, 51, 89–107

civilization 15–16, 29, 41, 50–1, 57

class 14, 125, 176, 254

CNN 2, 12, 60, 61, 74 fn., 136

colonialism 1, 10, 11, 55, 61, 73, 74

comedy *see* manzai

comic *see* animation

commercialism 24, 31, 97, 191, 273, 289

commodity *see* product

condom 6, 32, 169, 172–4, 177–8, 180, 185, 190, 193–4 fn.

consecration: cycle of 32–4

consumer culture 71, 103

consumption 21, 23, 25, 169, 176, 184, 197, 206, 207, 212–3, 216–7, 218 fn., 231, 232, 241, 247, 248–9, 265, 267; production of 21–3, 32, 223–91

corporate identity 25, 252, 259, 260, 274–5, 277–8, 284, 287

correspondent *see* foreign correspondent

cosmetics 2, 4, 154, 240, 285, 287

creolization 15, 54

cultural event 25, 29, 32–3, 274, 281–5

cultural flow 41–3, 47–8, 52, 54–6, 71 *see also under* media flow